LETS GO United States of America!

Americans Need Not Apply!

I0119986

A perspective on illegal and legal immigration in America

If you are out hunting for a job, make sure you engage with much tolerance as more and more jobs are now filled with illegal foreign nationals

Jobs are hard to come by and you can blame the government for that. In over 50 chapters, each reading like a complete essay, we discuss jobs in America. We'll tell you where they have gone and how to bring those rascals back. And, folks, we plan to bring those jobs back alive.

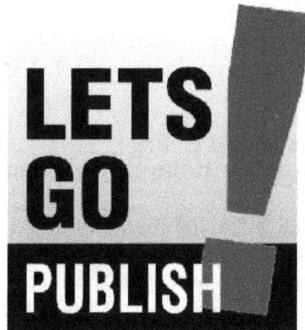

LETS GO PUBLISH

BRIAN W. KELLY

Copyright © 2011, 2016 Brian W. Kelly   Editor, Melissa L. Sabol
<u>Americans Need Not Apply!</u>   Author Brian W. Kelly
A perspective on illegal and legal immigration in America.

Disclaimer: Though judicious care was taken throughout the writing and the publication of this work that the information contained herein is accurate, there is no expressed or implied warranty that all information in this book is 100% correct. Therefore, neither LETS GO PUBLISH, nor the author accepts liability for any use of this work.

Trademarks: A number of products and names referenced in this book are trade names and trademarks of their respective companies.

Referenced Material *: The information in this book has been obtained through personal and third party observations, interviews, and copious research. Where unique information has been provided or extracted from other sources, those sources are acknowledged within the text of the book itself or at the end of the chapter in the Sources Section. Thus, there are no formal footnotes nor is there a bibliography section. Any picture that does not have a source was taken from various sites on the Internet with no credit attached. If resource owners would like credit in the next printing, please email publisher.*

Published by: .... LETS GO PUBLISH!
Publisher: ....Brian P. Kelly
....
Editor: ....Melissa L. Sabol
Mail Location: ....P.O. Box 834, Scranton, PA
Web site .... www.letsgopublish.com

Library of Congress Copyright Information Pending
Book Cover Design by Michele Thomas, Editing by Melissa L. Sabol

ISBN Information: The International Standard Book Number (ISBN) is a unique machine-readable identification number, which marks any book unmistakably. The ISBN is the clear standard in the book industry. 159 countries and territories are officially ISBN members. The Official ISBN For this book is on the outside cover: **978-0-9841418-5-2   0-9841418-5-5**

The price for this work is :   **$14.99**
USD
10   9   8   7   6   5   4   3   2   1

Release Date: April 2011 – September 2016

Dedication

I dedicate this book

To all of the wonderful Americans out there,
Struggling to get by at a time in our country's history;
Which is very uncertain.

I hope the job that you have, you can keep,
And that if you are temporarily unemployed, I hope that your next job
Is your best ever.

Please take nothing for granted and take nothing from the government
As it is just a small piece of what you put in.

I regret to say that our
Government may very well not be on your side in whatever
It is you choose to do next.

Be wary, be smart, and make sure that
Everybody you choose to trust in the coming years
Is trustworthy.

I wish you the best.

!

Acknowledgments

I would like to thank many people for helping me in this effort.

I appreciate all the help that I have received in putting this book together as well as all of my other 78 published books.

My printed acknowledgments had become so large that book readers "complained" about going through too many pages to get to page one of the text.

And, so to permit me more flexibility, I put my acknowledgment list online, and it continues to grow. Believe it or not, it once cost about a dollar more to print each book.

Thank you and God bless you all for your help.

Please check out www.letsgopublish.com to read the latest version of my heartfelt acknowledgments updated for this book. Click the bottom of the Main menu!

Thank you all!

Table of Contents

Preface:

This book is slightly modified in 2016 over its original printing in 2011. It is still very current other than the names of the politicians who are gone but not forgotten.

Most Americans are aware of the major battle that has been going on from day one of Obama times until Obamacare passed. It continues. When the Obama travesty passed the 111th Congress and became law, real Americans began to get enraged and engaged. For over a year, Healthcare, aka, Obamacare was the only order of business on the government's agenda, though the economy was in freefall and jobs were being lost as rapidly as snowflakes in a blizzard.

Americans are clamoring for jobs but all that has been given by the President and his coterie is lip service. Obama is a fine politician but any other compliment is stretching the truth. The President has stopped talking about Jobs again. He never tried to help Americans.

He has had a lot of rhetoric but no action. He has done nothing to relieve the major regulatory burden on business to help begin a jobs engine, and he will not even admit that foreign nationals are stealing American jobs. He simply does not care.

It can be argued that the single biggest private sector jobs killer that passed in the 111th Congress is Obamacare. Ironically, it passed during a period in which President, Barack Hussein Obama had just promised that he was done with his healthcare agenda and he was going to concentrate on Jobs! Jobs! Jobs! Whether he changed his mind or he simply lied, Obamacare won the day over American jobs.

Many good jobs are not coming back because of Obamacare. As true as this is and as welcome a day it will be for Jobs when Obamacare is ended, this is not the focus of this book. Along with freedom from business crippling regulations, It is however, one of the major realities behind why the unemployment rate is so high. It is not the only reason, however. The other reasons are indeed the big story in this book.

Besides the Obama impact, many more jobs are not coming back because corporations have (1) taken them overseas via offshoring, (2) brought in legal foreign nationals with visas to do the work, and (3) have committed felonies by hiring illegal foreign nationals to take American jobs via onshoring. As hard as it may be to believe, American corporation in defiance of US immigration law have brazenly offered jobs to illegal workers to complete their 1-2 punch for labor arbitrage.

The corporations could not have done this by themselves. They have a number of staunch allies in their battle for increased profits at the expense of American jobs. The most loyal of these allies has been the government and our friendly politicians. The President and Congress have done more to keep American jobs from Americans than all the stimulus dollars that have been wasted on pet pork projects and payback to campaign donors.

President Obama has made a lot of promises about illegal immigration and jobs but he has never linked the two. What about his promises? To be kind, we can say his promises are prevarications. Media critics from the past have said that W. C. Fields was so good at lying and kidding and joking that he made prevarication into an art form. The President clearly is an artist. He is the Prevaricator in chief.

Alan Caruba in his January 26, 2010 factsnotfantasy.com blogspot hits the nail on the head. He says:

"If Ronald Reagan was the Great Communicator, then Barack Hussein Obama will be known as the Great Prevaricator."

Why does the President offer no solution for jobs? Can it be that he has no solutions, and he hopes his distractions will permit the major topic of 2011—jobs, to go un-discussed? He has avoided bringing jobs to America and now it is 2016, and he is almost gone. Thank God Donald Trump will be our next president to avoid Hillary giving us four more Obama years.

The reason why you have not heard about jobs other than the weekly unemployment charts and an occasional clerk position available in Mumbai is that the illegal residents in the US now hold many of those jobs, and they are not interested in Americans making a comeback.

Robert Reich, former Labor Secretary under Clinton, now a Professor at UC Berkeley sees it this way:

"Since the start of the Great Recession in December 2007, the U.S. economy has shed 8.4 million jobs and failed to create another 2.7 million required by an ever-larger pool of potential workers .... The Great Recession has accelerated a structural shift in the economy that had been slowly building for years. Companies have used the downturn to aggressively trim payrolls, making cuts they've been reluctant to make before. Outsourcing abroad has increased dramatically. Companies have discovered that new software and computer technologies have made many workers in Asia and Latin America almost as productive as Americans, and that the Internet allows far more work to be efficiently moved to another country without loss of control."

In this book, we will discuss the notion of offshoring as well as a new notion that Brian Kelly calls onshoring, which is like offshoring in that the labor rate goes down, but the jobs stay in America. There is only one way to do that.

In this world in which both legal and illegal foreign nationals hold more and more of the jobs, and are getting 85% of the new jobs when the baby boomers retire, Americans need not apply. It does not matter what "nationality" you are or of which descent you may be. Don't bother applying. That means Irish Need not Apply! Syrians need not apply! Italians need not apply! Spanish need not apply! Polish need not apply! Americans simply need not apply, no matter what origin.

How many of our parents went through tough times when they arrived in the USA finding bigotry instead of work, when they sought employment? You've heard the stories at the evening dinner table. Eventually our parents all got jobs and America toned down its ethnic prejudices. Today, however, all American citizens are feeling a new kind of prejudice in the workplace. It's an economic prejudice carried out by greedy businesses. It cries out "Americans Need Not Apply!" You're wasting your time.

Brian Kelly is one of America's most outspoken and eloquent conservative spokesmen in the country. Kelly is a nationalist and a populist and he loves America. He is the author of Taxation Without Representation, Obama's Seven Deadly Sins, and 77 other popular books. Like many Americans, Kelly is fed up with a progressive liberal agenda in Washington that places foreign workers in front of Americans.

Endorsed by the Independence Hall Tea Party in 2010, Brian Kelly tried to do something about it. He ran for Congress against a 13-term Democrat and, in a three way race he spent just $4500 of his own money and, as a virtual unknown, he captured 17% of the vote. Kelly then supported Republican challenger Lou Barletta, a conservative leader on immigration policy, and helped him win a resounding victory in the general election. Mr. Kelly is now evaluating a potential run for the Senate in Pennsylvania against Bob Casey in 2012. We'll see!

Kelly wrote this book to help Americans know what we can do to force our government to retake control of our borders, ensure our national security, enforce our laws, protect American jobs, and keep all Americans from being overwhelmed by illegal immigration and millions of temporary visas that are together killing job opportunities for Americans.

Like you, Brian is especially frustrated with the devastation that illegal immigration inflicts on law-abiding Americans. He's read the intelligence reports, has researched and written about the topic for years, and he knows how intolerable illegal immigration can be within all of our neighborhoods and especially in the workplace. Kelly has heard all the bunk about how our country can't function without illegal aliens and has compelling answers to those who think Americans are wimps who need foreigners to pick up after us.

Today's economic story can be spelled out in three words, Jobs, Jobs, Jobs. American workers are losing their jobs and one of the biggest reasons today, besides the poor economy, is that illegal aliens are being given those jobs by US corporations. American businesses are no longer very patriotic. Their interests are to compete with the slave shops in Asia and hell holes across the world. In industries that reluctantly hire Americans, the pay, even in the US, is slave wage level. Illegal aliens have brought the wage scale down so substantially that there are few well paying jobs today in America. Moreover, we know that any desperate group of people, such as illegal foreign nationals, is not only happy to take American jobs, but by living here, they also commit many crimes. Unfortunately, our leaders think that is OK. Why do illegal alien murderers and rapists walk free along our streets. Why do our laws not permit them to even be questioned?

Americans Need Not Apply! is a book that needed to be written, but which no one had the guts to write it until Brian Kelly took up the task. For all Americans, who care about the USA, Kelly offers a compelling plan to keep us safe, and to get Americans back to work. Few books are a must-read but <u>Americans Need Not Apply!</u> is at the top of the list. It is in there!

I hope you enjoy this book. I hope that it inspires you to take action to do your part to help change the members of the government of the United States. Let's start by replacing all liberal progressives in the House and Senate. They have brought his devastation on all Americans, regardless of whether they are Democrat or Republican. There is only one way out of this conundrum, and this book has the facts to help us get the job done. Thank you for bringing it home with you.

I wish you the best

Brian P. Kelly (LGP Publisher!)

About the Author

Brian W. Kelly is Assistant Professor in the Business Information Technology (BIT) program at Marywood University, where he has also served as the IBM i and midrange systems technical advisor to the IT faculty. Kelly has designed, developed, and taught many college and professional courses. He is also a contributing technical editor to a number of IT industry magazines, including "The Four Hundred" and "Four Hundred Guru" published by IT Jungle.

Kelly is a former IBM Senior Systems Engineer. He has an active information technology consultancy. He is the author or of 44 books and numerous articles about current IT topics and generally conservative thought. Kelly is a frequent speaker at COMMON, IBM conferences, and other technical conferences and user group meetings across the United States.

Over the past five years, Brian Kelly has become one of America's most outspoken and eloquent conservative protagonists. He is the author of Taxation Without Representation, Obama's Seven Deadly Sins, Healthcare Accountability, and other conservative books. Endorsed by the Independence Hall Tea Party in 2010, Kelly ran for Congress against a 13-term Democrat and, took no campaign contributions, spent just $4500, and as a virtual unknown, he captured 17% of the vote—www.briankellyforcongress.com. Kelly then supported Republican challenger Lou Barletta, a conservative leader on immigration policy, and helped him win a resounding victory in the general election. Mr. Kelly is now running for the US Senate from PA against Bob Casey in 2018. We shall see!

Chapter 1   Is Illegal Immigration a Solution or a Problem?

Up to 50 million or more illegal foreign nationals

The United States is now occupied by 20 to 60 million more illegal foreign nationals than were not in the country for the Reagan amnesty in 1986. That is an awful lot of people. To put that number in perspective, the legal population of Canada is just 34 million. If all resident illegal foreign nationals were in a separate US state, it would be the most populous state in the nation.

Progressives, who lobby that illegal aliens should not be deported, complain regularly that Americans have become very comfortable referring to this "happening" as an invasion. They believe that labeling illegal aliens as invaders is inaccurate and insulting and they do not want to hurt their feelings. It is OK if Americans get their feelings hurt in this process, but we'll hold on that for now.

The definition of an invasion is simply "any entry into an area not previously occupied." That proves the term "invasion" is accurate. As for insulting, besides not being called invaders, they do not want the invaders called "illegal aliens" either. Yet, in US immigration law, that is the term used. So much for insulting! That means that they are illegal aliens plus invaders, as well as illegal foreign nationals. The latter is because they have allegiance to a foreign country, not America.

The real problem of course, is progressives want them to be treated as citizens the minute they escape from the border guards. So, it is not what Americans choose to call the invading illegal aliens, it is that the progressives had hoped we would ignore their presence in America. Just because they are in every city in the US, what difference should that make?

Fat chance they won't be noticed! There are massive numbers of illegal Hispanics and illegal Latinos in this country in all places, today. All have either entered illegally or overstayed their visas. Regardless of what the progressives think or want you to believe, their presence in this country is rightfully termed an "invasion." Were these millions invited or did they break in? We know the answer and that is the source of the collective angst of 90% of US citizens who feel discomfort because of their illegal presence.

There are very few Americans who are against a reasonable amount of legal immigration, with no preference for race, nationality or ethnicity. But, most Americans are against any amount of illegal immigration, regardless of race, nationality or ethnicity.

So, why are there so many illegal foreign nationals dwelling and working in this country if it is not something the American people desire? They were not invited by the American people. However, it can be argued persuasively that they were invited here by lax US government immigration policies and greedy business owners.

Over the last twenty years, the government of the US has been hijacked by progressive liberals and the existing state of affairs on immigration is something they very much desire. And, yes, George Bush is a progressive and a business owner, and his decisions regarding illegal foreign nationals clearly reflected that posture. Americans today are fighting both the progressives in Washington, and the businesses in Corporate America, to return the United States back to American citizens.

Unfortunately, the horses are clearly out of the barn and the Illegal aliens of today do not appear like they intend to go back any time soon.

One of the unmentioned facts about illegal aliens of today compared to those of yesteryear, is they don't even look for short-term permissions. They don't intend to go back. One could create an effective argument that postures that rather than retreat, they would prefer to amass more and more Hispanics and Latinos together in America. They are not interested in the melting pot or assimilation. In fact, they want the national language of the US to be Spanish. Unlike times past, these folks are more prepared to overtake Americans in America, rather than assimilate, judging by their sheer numbers and their anti-American demonstrations.

Before California Mexicans came the Chinese

California always had a large population of illegal migrant workers. Some of you who have been to Nevada County and Oroville California may be familiar with the Chinese Temple and other remnants of the bygone age of the Chinese Miners. The Temple was reopened in 1949 as a California State Park, more or less as a monument to days long past.

This particular site and others like it had been abandoned in the 1880's when the Chinese miners or railroad workers who lived there returned to China about the time that the railroad was completed. There is a parallel with today's Mexican invasion. The Chinese came to America in the 1800s because of a poor situation in their home country. Like the Mexicans, they sent money home regularly and did not assimilate into the American culture of the day. Their culture may have been even more isolated. The Chinese reaction to America was a big first dose of the value of borders, language and culture.

Unlike today's Mexicans, when their work was done, they went home. They did not want to change US culture into Chinese culture. For example, they had no desire for everyone to speak and act Chinese. There was no movement for example, to press 1 for English, 2 for Mandarine, or three for Cantonese, etc.

In their heyday, the Chinese had quite a thing going in California. Like the Mexicans, they provided a reliable source of inexpensive labor and they offered a wide range of services. They knew how to make a buck. For example, they offered laundries, garden fresh vegetables, firewood and of course domestic services.

Because they were miners and they worked on the railroads, they also bought tools, supplies and mining equipment from American manufacturers. Nevada County California reports they collected $103,250.00 in Foreign Miners Tax almost exclusively from the Chinese between 1850 and 1870. Unlike the Mexicans migrants, and this is a lesson for illegal aliens, they did not use any of the government infrastructure (schools, hospitals, etc.). And, so it was not costing Americans every day for the Chinese to live in the US.

When the Transcontinental Railroad was built in 1869, thousands of Chinese became unemployed along with a lot of Americans. California went into an economic depression, much like today, and many blamed the Chinese. When things did not improve, in 1882, Congress passed the Chinese Exclusion Act, which suspended the immigration of "laborers" and prohibited naturalization of the Chinese. There were no anchor babies as the Chinese women did not often come to America. The men worked hard and had simple pleasures in life, including brothels. The Chinese mostly stayed away from any potential conflict with Americans other than wanting their jobs when there were none, and when there were not enough jobs for both Chinese and Americans, the Chinese had to go.

The government, rightly or wrongly protected Americans above foreigners. During this period, many Chinese chose to return to China. There is another parallel of the Chinese with the Mexican migration to the US. After the Chinese Exclusion Act, Chinese who migrated to the US despite the ban were looked upon similarly as illegal aliens today and were subject to deportation.

On Dec. 13, 1943, during the War, President Roosevelt repealed the Chinese Exclusion Act because China was such an important ally of the United States against Japan. Clearly the act was unfair to Chinese immigrants as the small numbers that were in the country could have and should have been made citizens. They had built the transcontinental railroad for heaven sake and despite that, they were encouraged to go back to China. Yet, Americans were out of work. Today, we have millions of Americans out of work and as many as 50,000,000 illegal

Hispanics in the country and the government has decided that Americans need not apply. Things have clearly changed.

Illegals are just nice guys from other countries?

Do these poor souls from other countries now represent a threat of any kind to the well being of American citizens? Americans have been told numerous times by progressive government officials and by business and union leaders that illegal aliens do not commit any more crimes than anybody else and that they are simply hard working contributors to American society. Moreover, we have been told that when they work, they do only jobs that Americans won't do.

If you have just a modicum of objectivity, even if you are pro-amnesty, you can see the untruths in those statements. However bad the problem was twenty or ten or five years ago, or even just one year ago, the problem is far worse today. And, how do you solve a deteriorating problem? Our newest President thinks the best way is to ignore the problem or make it worse, and he has done both.

The principle of judicious neglect

President Obama reminds me of my first orthopedic surgeon when I herniated a disc years ago when I was in my twenties. The surgeon cautioned me that I would not see him in the hospital often because he used the principle of judicious neglect. I saw this man once upon entering the hospital through the ER and once upon discharge a week later. His bill, however showed no sign that there ever was neglect. So, I guess we can say that the President uses the principle of judicious neglect regarding the illegal alien situation, along with just a little extra nega-intervention, to help rapidly turn it into an unsolvable crisis.

As an aside, my disc problem soon became a crisis as I missed eight weeks of work and came back to IBM with a back brace at 29 years old. I wore the brace for another two months. In all my years at IBM, the total of all sick days taken, other than that nasty disc problem came nowhere close to 8 weeks. This was a crisis for me, indeed. I do understand neglect.

Perhaps if it were only neglect, we could forgive the President for his inaction. But he has taken action to assure inaction. I call it nega-intervention above. He has ordered the stoppage of regular enforcement for people who jump the border or overstay their visas and who now reside in the US. The current White House chooses not to enforce our immigration laws because, after all, illegal foreign nationals are not doing anything wrong.

They merely violate immigration law by crossing the border and then they live in America, which is also against the law. As you probably know from being an American, our President took a different oath than all other Presidents. His oath permitted him to enforce the rule of man rather than the rule of law. The Constitution for President Obama is a historical document, not the law of the country. Only he, not Washington or Lincoln, or even Clinton, has the right to pick and choose the laws he enforces and defends. Unfortunately, our

President Obama has decided that immigration law is one of the laws he does not like. He treats it like it is not worth the parchment it is printed on. Ask him!

President Obama, who is continually riding the permissive immigration slippery slope, would argue to the death that illegal border hoppers and illegal residents have committed no crimes. ON all other matters that would bring him the proverbial Jackie Gleason "humma humma," he pleads the silent fifth. He and Michele have a fifth of Scotch and then they are both silent for eighteen hours. OK, that may not be it. But, the president is not prepared to admit that to survive, of course, illegal foreign nationals must engage in at least petty identity theft and perhaps the absconding of a valid SS #.

Both of these activities are federal crimes but Obama does not see it that way. He asks: "have they really done anything wrong?" Any American committing identity theft would be in jail. Can we find a clue in that simple fact? Is President Obama merely a kinder, gentler soul than the rest of us? Surely, it can't be that he does not give a darn about real Americans.

The overarching theme of this book is the impact of foreign workers, especially illegal foreign workers on America and Americans. In addition to taking American jobs, illegal foreign nationals have a negative impact on the quality of life on much more than the job front for regular Americans. We discuss many of these notions in this book. The impact on American jobs is a very important part of this theme and it includes the rationale of American companies for hiring illegal workers instead of Americans.

President Obama is mentioned often in this book because as some would say, right now, "he is the man." He may not be the man we want, but, he is the man.

Are citizens of the world necessarily US citizens?

Like President Reagan in 1986, President Obama thinks all illegal foreign nationals should be US citizens and his idea of comprehensive immigration reform is to make them citizens immediately if not sooner. If the President were not involved in a ton of other controversial initiatives that are also against the will of the American people, he would be more believable on this issue, and he would surely have more energy for the illegal immigration debate. Because his opinion is so clearly anti-American, however, my friends and I are very pleased that he has little time for this matter. He does use Harry Reid as a fill-in, but thankfully Harry has yet to deliver.

You may recall the Reagan plan permitted any illegal foreign national who registered with the government in 1986 to gain citizenship and to bring in any relative for an unimpeded path to citizenship. It was part of the 1986 law. So, Reagan not only granted amnesty as Obama would like to do, he also sent an invitation for a lot of people from Mexico and elsewhere, who were not illegal residents in 1986 to *come on down*, sign up with Bob Barker, and join the new anchor citizenry corps.

The best thing I can say about President Obama in regard to his posture on the problems in the US caused by illegal immigration is that I think he has great compassion for the poor, though he does want to use your wallet and not his to help the poor. Watching his legislative initiatives, you can see the Obama way. However, the Obama way always ends up with somebody designated as poor by his regime, thereby becoming eligible to receive something from somebody else. The "somebody-else," of course, may also be poor but that is not the President's problem.

The President really does not like rich guys or businessmen, though he himself is a multi-millionaire, with a lot of multi-millionaire friends. One who would not be schooled in the art of verbal evasion might even call him, ahem, *rich.* The Obama family and friends and all progressives appear to be excluded from his line of thinking against the rich. It does not take too long to see that President Obama is no less disingenuous as his progressive friends regarding illegal immigration. Therefore, in this book, he is treated more as the problem, than as the solution.

Obama may be a good guy but it is hard to locate old friends of his to vouch for him. Nobody can be located to say: "Oh Barry, great guy, do not worry about him!" Nobody is doing handstands in the outfield or running up and down the bleachers screaming that they were his classmates and they too should be millionaires. They are just not out there to be found. Even MSNBC has not reported about them.

The FBI files

I am not going to get into a battle over his birth records. I'll spare you that. My friends see him in much the same way as a former key witness in a trial who is now part of witness protection. It is like he has had his past wiped out. Perhaps he has had a facial makeover so none of his college buddies recognize him. That would explain a lot. Has his past been created for him by an FBI playbook? The FBI has done a great job if this is the case. If we now have a witness protection person as President, it is more than likely a first for the USA.

The folks from his class at Columbia University, the exclusive University in New York, not Bogota, claim to have never met him as a classmate. Barack Hussein Obama is a mystery alumnus of Columbia. Like my friends suggest, the only rational explanation is that he is a graduate of the Witness Protection System and all governmental and media sources are doing a great job in keeping his real legacy a secret. Bravo to the media for keeping the secret! Please know that this brief overview of the President's possible background is intended as light humor, but it is probably as accurate as anybody else's guesses.

On the deathby1000papercuts.com blog, they like to poke a little fun at this mystery man. It is a bit crass but it makes a point. They cite the words of author, Mencius Moldbug to describe the Obama Columbia phenomenon:

> "What is the chance that a budding young politician of undeniable talent and promise spends his junior and senior years at Columbia, and no one remembers him? What is the chance that my right ass cheek, through spontaneous quantum vibration, suddenly transmutes into a hemisphere of polished gold? Don't you feel these probabilities are at least roughly comparable?"

Our President, right or wrong

Regardless of the truth of whom he is, Obama serves as President of the US of A and in that capacity, his thinking according to my thinking is a bit lopsided. At best, he is misguided on major issues. Unfortunately, the people of America are concerned about those issues and illegal foreign nationals being protected by the President is a big one of those issues. Along with many conservatives, Democrat and Republican, I find it difficult to believe that a man with Obama's extremely far left principles could ever have been elected by the strong God-fearing people of the United States. If Guinness is ever in charge of finding the eighth of the wonders of the world, the Obama election should get a strong nomination.

Obama does not intrinsically hate America but he sees its faults more regularly than he sees America's exceptionalism. This President is continually apologizing for America as if he is apparently ashamed to be American. His mission seems to be to correct America's faults as he defines them. It is hard to find any love for America in the President's heart as viewed through his rhetoric, and he seems that he would be happier if he were either the supreme ruler of the entire world or the President of Columbia University, whichever position wields the most power. Being President of the United States at the moment appears to be a mere, *inconvenient truth* for the family to endure. He appears handicapped as President of the US in ever achieving positive world leadership status and so the Columbia University position may have to be in his future in order to achieve self actualization.

Walk like an Egyptian

During the beginning of 2011, we all watched the President contemplate the best action for his regime to employ in Egypt and then Libya, This was a Rahm Emanuel crisis that could become a big campaign opportunity. It could not go by without the President gaining political capital. But how? The press was needed and they came through big-time. The press gave Obama credit for all the successes and with perfect timing; they blamed Mubarak and Ghaddaffi for all the failures. Obama stood back waiting for somebody to say something for which he could take credit. Robert Gibbs and Jay Carney working all night could not have served it up better, and the obsessed press gobbled it up as if it were the truth. But, the truth could never be so good.

It was as if I was watching the master, Peter Sellers, as Chauncey Gardner in "Being There." Obama solved the Egyptian crisis and for weeks uttered nothing about the Libyan crisis in the true spirit of Chauncey, the one-time gardener. He did this in the same way that Chauncey solved all of his problems—merely by being there and having the press make his divagations appear to be heroic. But, then again, this book is not about Obama, nor about Egypt, but it is a lot about the Chauncey Gardner philosophies of this government, including illegal migration being accepted as the given gospel by an eternally biased media.

I can tell you—"All things Obama" is not the treatise of this book but soon I will have to prove it. The fact is, however, the President can stop all the migration nonsense at any time, but he chooses not to do so. I have only the power of the pen. I can't stop anything—nor can you—until next election. The President can end the nonsense but he does not want it to end it. Meanwhile Americans want it to end. The President is the boss so he wins. That is why it is not ended and it will not end with this President in charge.

Like it or not, Obama is the most important player of all in the illegal foreign national, illegal worker world of 2011. That's why things are not about to change without some "Egyptian-style" clamor from all the people. Stay off the streets, please, but make sure you keep writing the President about how you feel about legal and illegal immigration and its impact on American jobs. Maybe, just maybe, he will eventually get it.

Newsmax interviewed renowned conservative commentator Dinesh DSouza in February, 2011 and gained a phenomenal perspective on who the President really is and how he feels about America. See if this doesn't match your opinion. Because a real democracy in Egypt may very well result in a government detrimental to both Israel and to US Foreign policy, DSouza says:

> This puts Obama in an interesting bind. It's not surprising that he's been pretty coy, saying almost nothing. I think he's trying to decide how to come out on this. In Obama's view, the United States is a neo-colonial power occupying Iraq and Afghanistan, DSouza says. He sees the Muslims fighting against America as freedom fighters. This gives him a somewhat romanticized view of Islamic radicals.

> As a result, Obama may not view the Muslim Brotherhood as a problem. In his eyes, they may be good guys trying to liberate Egypt from this horrible dictator Mubarak, supported by us, the rogue nation, So Obama might encourage the democracy movement, not because he's an idealist about democracy, but because he might approve of the overthrow of a pro-American dictator and a reduced footprint for America in that region.

Sometimes I ask myself which side the Chief Commander is really on. It is scary that I even think that way. I have never asked myself that question about any President ever before— ever.

As much as Obama has real compassion for the poor, as previously noted, the President has great disdain for the rich. Like most progressives, who like to distribute other people's wealth, President Obama has excluded himself from the domain from which he gets his statistics and he has also excluded his wife.

> If you are collecting money for the poor, don't plan to take any from Michelle and I, as we worked hard for ours. Take somebody else's.

OK, that is not a quote, but it is what I see in practice. Both Obama's are now filthy rich themselves and so without excluding himself and Michele, he risks the boomerang effect on his many potshots against those who have been able to amass a larger fortune than Obama himself. He can't let "the man" take his money. Take theirs. Ironically, he is now, "the man." As a community organizer, it is a puzzlement how he was able to make his first million in the first place—and then lots more.

The community organizer job, one would think does not pay very well. In Obama's words, people who make over $250,000 per year are to be considered rich for tax purposes. That would place Obama and family among the mega-rich. His huge income over the past few years seems to be mostly because of book sales and his popularity in being the President of the United States. A look at his tax returns and you can see that Obama's charity is a bit light, though admittedly not as light as Joe Biden's $369.00 per year average over the last decade. Regardless, most progressives are disingenuous regarding wealth. Theirs is theirs and yours is to be redistributed. Obama is one of many very wealthy progressives, who choose not to care about regular Americans and who choose to redistribute none of "theirs."

If Obama wanted to handle immigration in a fashion in which Americans would like, he would already be doing it. So, please do not count the President on our side in this battle between Americans and those foreign nationals, mostly illegal, who are taking American jobs every day.

President Obama sheds tears thinking that not all illegal aliens are citizens but some might argue the tears are because there are so many future Democrats and potential Obama worshippers waiting in the on-deck-circle—and so far they are not getting in. The President thinks it is only fair that these potential supporters get their chance to bat for the "D" team. So, why not bring them all in?

Obama may not know why this is a bad idea but most Americans do know. If we in the US agreed to do something as foolish as to grant another amnesty, life would never be the same. In addition to this meaning we could never uproot the 50 million illegal foreign national now here, there would be another 50 million, as illegal as the last 50 million illegal aliens, who would quickly follow. By declaring "relative" status, they would be here waiting to get the jobs of the former 50,000,000 illegals as soon as they are available. .

The bigger problem perhaps might be that Mexico, whose population now is estimated at just about 110,000, would have little to no population in short order if the US keeps calling "amnesty.". Maybe that would not be a problem at all. All things do find equilibrium. Perhaps the nice warm Mexican climate could attract out-of-work Americans for some reverse colonization.

Secure the borders now

There are few people other than progressive ideologues who are not demanding that our elected officials secure the borders immediately, with armed force if need be. Moreover, *We the People* are calling for the deportation of every last illegal alien as soon as possible. With this as the case, folks, *We the People* have clearly elected the wrong government.

The good news for the country is that every two, four, and six years, the people do get another chance to get it right The records of the current government and the last, and back to Reagan on the topic of illegal immigration, show all Presidents earning "F" grades. The song would say, "They done us wrong!" The record from Reagan on has been about as bad as it can get. So it is not just Obama, but he is our guy right now, and that is why things on the immigration front do not look so good.

The grades in the record for the current government are the worst they have ever been. This current executive branch has chosen openly not to enforce the borders and not to deport illegal residents. Despite the US Constitution ordering otherwise, the Obama administration steadfastly refuses to do its job. George Bush was terrible on illegal immigration but Obama is truly the worst ever.

Regarding the recent liberal rants (pro-gay marriage to anti-TEA party) from what seems to be all members of the Bush family—three generations worth, Barbara the mom, to George W., the son to Barbara the grandkid, it is fairly obvious that the Bush's are and have always been major league progressives. Secret note to Al Gore: "*We the People* caught on to the chicanery. You, Bush, Clinton, Bush, Bush, Bush, Bush, and Obama, are progressives on the same team. So, let's not ever hear about your buddy Jeb on the national conservative stage."

It's amazing what some people will do for a job. Yet, I see nobody from the mainstream media embracing any Bush even now that they have all outed themselves as progressives. Katie Couric still does not use any members of the Bush family to support her arguments even though the Bush's are as much against the TEA party conservatives as are the most brazen card carrying liberals. Hey don't forget that Barbara Bush Sr. has suggested that Palin "stay in Alaska."

Never being able to explain the Bush posture on illegal aliens properly, I am finally glad to know he is simply not one of us, and he has never really been one of us. They are all progressives and therefore they are for open borders. They may be for their America, but they are not for ours. Worse than that, they seem to care nothing about their fellow Americans—those of us who do not live on big ranches or behind walls and gated communities. They have their substitute players from south of the border warming up; ready to go after what was once a dream for Americans.

This refusal of elected officials to abide by US law is a big reason why the TEA party has taken firm root. Unresponsive government created the TEA party. People are riled up. November, 2010 was the first of a number of critical elections to test the resolve of the American people. The results of 2010 are in and it seems that only the states with a preponderance of illegal aliens voted to keep their progressive representation. I'll bet you an Acorn on the results of 2012.

There are a few good Americans in Congress.

President Obama shows disregard for the Constitution in many of the acts he has perpetrated in his several years in office. A growing number of conservatives see his most egregious and contumelious betrayal of our Constitution as his statement to Senator Jon Kyl, conservative Arizona Republican. Obama unabashedly informed the Senator that the administration was not going to enforce security on our southern border for political reasons.

He felt that if he did his job on immigration then the Republicans would get too content and would have no reason to compromise on an amnesty bill. When the President of the United States makes a decision that by any reasonable standard constitutes an impeachable offense against the Constitution, what should be the result? Consequently more and more conservatives are calling for his impeachment. Progressive liberals may suggest this is just sour grapes but when the President says he is not going to do his job because of future elections, what is the proper response?

Americans are made to look stupid and to look like the bad guys by the press regarding their desire to stop illegal immigration. The press slaps around regular Americans favoring the illegal foreign nationals in news article after news article. The progressive press is on the side of the foreigners. Ironically, the subscriptions of the most progressive papers are heading downward because regular people can no longer trust what they say. Consequently, many conservatives and independents have already begun to get their news from more reliable sources such as Fox News and the Internet.

Maybe the New York Times and other liberal progressive outlets will be able to sell lots of papers in Mexico or maybe they will just have to stop publishing rubbish because the people aren't buying it, and the people are not buying their papers. Or, maybe as Glenn Beck might predict, George Soros, the inimitable spooky dude, might buy all the papers and create a natural eco-newspaper-compost-pile.

Who is responsible for the illegal immigration crisis?

Americans are incensed that they are being blamed for the illegal alien crisis. One after another, progressives and un-American businessmen present their cases that illegal workers are necessary for the good of the US economy. Can the US do without Mexican labor? Have US workers gotten as lazy as the progressives suggest from government handouts, that we now need Mexicans to come in to do our work for us? I don't think so! Look no further than the progressives that have ruled our country for far too long and you will see a team of non-patriots pumping out misinformation and pure propaganda just so you will like them. Don't like them. They are scoundrels.

To answer those who argue that the US cannot do without illegal workers because illegal Mexicans and others do all the menial work in this country, I performed copious research for the one true answer. There are a few chapters in the book dealing with this topic. For now, on the way to that one true answer, I found a number of good Americans, including Congressman Steven King from Iowa and a writer named Frosty Wooldridge, who have taken a shot at helping us all know what it might be like if there were a day, in which there were no illegal immigration. After a few more paragraphs, I will outline some of the things that we would miss.

By the way, these points are in no particular order of importance because it would take forever to group them in a meaningful way. If we had no illegal immigration, what would it be like -- even if it were just one day? The coming list precedes an article by Congressman King that I copied from his web site. It is very well done. Mexicans and others who have crashed the border are getting pretty cocky about their servitude here in the US and they have decided to slam Americans on numerous occasions. One of their latest onslaughts is what they call a "No Gringos" day.

No Wetbacks Day?

If Americans had a "No Wetbacks" day, we would be racists but that doesn't help make my point so I will get back on point.

In case you are wondering what a gringos is; it is you. Look no further. Though this list is from way back in 2006, it does catch the right slant on the attitudes of our helpful Mexican friends toiling on our behalf in the US of A.

So, again here are the things we would not have in a given day if there were no illegal workers to do our bidding: {feel free to scroll or page}

- ✓ Easy conduit for terrorists entering the USA
- ✓ Escalation in crime
- ✓ Additional illegal foreign national prisoners to support for years
- ✓ More traffic accidents
- ✓ Less illegal anchor babies born
- ✓ K-12 education costs for illegal immigrants.
- ✓ Overcrowded emergency rooms
- ✓ Paying for emergency room service (taxpayers)
- ✓ Hospital closings / service cut backs
- ✓ Third world diseases
- ✓ A day of welfare costs
- ✓ Massive costs to society – over and above contributions
- ✓ No one to smuggle heroin across our southern border
- ✓ No one to smuggle cocaine across our southern border
- ✓ No one to smuggle methamphetamines across our southern border
- ✓ No one to smuggle marijuana across our southern border
- ✓ One day supply of methamphetamines (80%)
- ✓ 12 U.S. citizens who would have been killed would be saved. Otherwise they would die a violent death at the hands of murderous illegal aliens.
- ✓ 13 Americans would survive who would have been killed by uninsured drunk driving illegal foreign nationals.
- ✓ Hospital emergency rooms would not be flooded with gunshot wounds
- ✓ Hospital emergency rooms would not be flooded with anchor babies
- ✓ US Citizens would not be standing in line behind illegal foreign nationals for vital services
- ✓ Eight American children would not suffer horror as a victim of a sex crime.
- ✓ Citizens paying for the criminal activities of illegal foreign nationals
- ✓ Drivers without licenses
- ✓ Drivers without insurance
- ✓ Workers who work off the books
- ✓ Workers who do not pay taxes
- ✓ Communes living 20 to a trailer

- ✓ Communes with three families to a house
- ✓ Five cars parked on the front lawn
- ✓ Nobody expecting more free medical care
- ✓ Nobody expecting more free schooling for their children
- ✓ Nobody expecting free out-of-state tuition in our colleges
- ✓ Nobody expecting free delivery of their anchor babies
- ✓ Nobody expecting chain migration of their relatives
- ✓ Spanish not spoken for one day
- ✓ 1600 cars not stolen in Phoenix
- ✓ Depressed Wages -- meatpacking from $19.00 per hour to $9.00
- ✓ Yes, of course there is more.

Frosty Woolridge suggests that this list accelerates daily. He wrote these comments about the situation as he sees it. It is compelling:

> "In Denver last week, (2006) I.C.E. arrested 122 illegal aliens on a government contracting job. One hundred and twenty-two Americans should have been working those jobs. By mid week, one illegal alien had hung a hangman's noose around a woman and dragged her two miles down the street with his truck until there was nothing left of her to identify her body. That wouldn't have happened if Bush did his job. Not a day later, an illegal alien walked up and shot a man as he pulled his work materials out of his car trunk to start a job. Again, it wouldn't have happened if Congress did its job. I could write another 1,000 incidences each week that occur because illegal aliens run lawlessly around our country with impunity."
> http://www.newswithviews.com/Wooldridge/frosty191.htm

In Hazleton PA, we have our own Lou Barletta, who I respect as an American hero and patriot on the major issue of the illegal occupation of American soil by foreign nationals. Progressives have Barletta pegged as a bad guy because they know he is right. They cite that he has lost Hazleton's case twice against the ACLU in court. They recommend that the former Mayor retreat and let the illegal foreign nationals have their way in Hazleton.

Hazleton's new Mayor, Joseph Yannuzzi is now completing Barletta's term since the former Mayor was rewarded by constituents in five counties of Pennsylvania for his strong stance on immigration. Former Hazleton Mayor Lou Barletta is now Congressman Lou Barletta from the 11th District of PA, having replaced thirteen-term Democrat Paul Kanjorski. Mayor Yannuzzi is just as committed to solve the illegal alien problem in Hazleton and he is confident that he will ultimately win Hazleton's case in the Supreme Court. I praise his efforts.

Representative Steven King, though an incumbent in 2010, was elected again to Congress and should have been. Among other great things, he works for the people of America. He wrote the letter immediately below. Not many have the courage of Mr. King to write such a letter. He has emblazoned this on his government Web site for all to see. Here it is. You'll like it even though it is about five years old. Some things are eternal in their wisdom.

From the Desk Of

Representative Steve King
5th Congressional District of Iowa

Biting the Hand That Feeds You

May 5, 2006

On May 1st, the activists who brought you thousands of Mexican flags flying in marches down the streets of our cities are now bringing you "Nothing Gringo Day". With help from the Mexican government, Mexican unions, Mexican political groups, and through the Spanish language radio and newspapers, the call has gone out to make America experience a total boycott, both here and in Mexico. Talk about biting the hand that feeds you.

Just the word "boycott" sparks the image of noble dissent in the face of economic or social oppression. I think of American colonials bucking British economic interests in retaliation to the Stamp Act. Or perhaps the ostracizing of Irish landlord Charles Boycott, the namesake of the verb for all tyrannized people. If not tyrannized, at least disgruntled. If not disgruntled, maybe just bored.
Yet, isn't the key to a successful boycott an economic or social upper-hand? The cost must be felt if the offending party be forced to reform. For example, how does boycotting a movie you had no intention of going to affect the box office? More people probably see a boycotted movie due to the attention than if it had simply been ignored.

President Carter thought he was on to something when he kept American athletes out of the 1980 Moscow Olympics. That showed 'em. That particular boycott neither got the USSR out of Afghanistan nor brought down the Berlin Wall. It just caused our own athletes to suffer.

The May 1st anti-Gringo-fest is also being billed as "A Day Without Immigrants" which is a misnomer on a couple of counts. First, the threatened boycott fails to conjure the image of a Norwegian refusing to buy his May 1 lutefisk at the corner Fareway. Second, the pro-amnesty groups are insistent on confusing legal and illegal immigration. Let's not start mixing our apples and oranges. The issue before Congress is illegal immigration. Perhaps the May 1st boycott should give America a glimpse into "A Day Without ILLEGAL Immigration."

What would that May 1st look like without illegal immigration? There would be no one to smuggle across our southern border the heroin, marijuana, cocaine, and methamphetamines that plague the United States, reducing the U.S. supply of meth that day by 80%. The lives of 12 U.S. citizens would be saved who otherwise die a violent death at the hands of murderous illegal aliens each day. Another 13 Americans would survive who are otherwise killed each day by uninsured drunk driving illegals. Our hospital emergency rooms would not be flooded with everything from gunshot wounds, to anchor babies, to imported diseases to hangnails, giving American citizens the day off from standing in line behind illegals. Eight American children would not suffer the horror as a victim of a sex crime.

On the negative side, the price of a pound of tomatoes might go up from $0.79 to $0.80. That is unless you have a garden. But I'm guessing that the Mexican drug lords are not taking May 1st off. Neither will the 11,000 illegal invaders that pour over our border every other day of the year. It is a safe bet that the U.S. Border Patrol will have a very busy "Nothing Gringo Day."

Since September 11th, it remains true that OBL is the greatest threat to America. I will leave it to the reader to decide if the greatest threat is Osama Bin Laden or the Open Borders

Lobby. The emerging cheap labor "ruling class" in America is the strongest supporter of amnesty for illegals. Their anti-American "new servant class" has chosen to boycott them; the very definition of irony. On May 1st, Primero de Mayo, Americans will observe, as illegal immigrants celebrate, "Bite the Hand That Feeds You Day."

*** End of King Letter

http://www.newswithviews.com/Wooldridge/frosty191.htm

Chapter 2   Illegal Immigration Is Not a Victimless Crime

The perpetrators: corporations, small businesses, unions, government (progressives)

The popular count for the number of illegal aliens in the US is about 12 million. Mysteriously, however, this reported number has remained constant over the years, as if it was not increasing. The only explanation I can give for that is that the progressives have been in charge for a long time, and they do all the counting. Many experts estimate that anywhere from a million to three million migrants come to the US illegally each year. You can bet those 1 to 3 million people do not go back home each year. So, it is illogical to suggest that there are just 10 or 12 million illegal foreign nationals residing in the US.

Is the government lying or do they just not know? Let's see if we can figure it out. Suppose use a middle figure between 1 and 3 million. Let's say 2 million illegal aliens per year jump the border and find a place to live in any of the 50 states. If we go back to 1986, twenty-five years ago, during Reagan's amnesty, this would mean that an additional 50 million illegal aliens, now illegally reside in the US.

Even with the Internet, admittedly there is no accurate way to track down and report the true number of illegal aliens in the country. Nor can we track down the participation level of the tons of illegal aliens involved in real crime. Just like there is no accurate census of illegal aliens, there is no means of keeping track of all the crimes, especially the ones in which nobody is caught.

We have an unfettered immigration policy; we have porous borders; we have sanctuary cities, and with Obama at the helm, we have an intentional lack of enforcement. So, what does that get us? It gets us illegal residents. Many of these in recent years thumb their nose at regular Americans as their numbers are increasing.

One could say we asked for what we got but that would be incorrect. However, if we say (1) corporations, (2) small businesses, (3) unions, and (4) progressive liberals in government have asked for this, we would be 100% correct. You are reading this book, because you are on the other side of the mess. You want Americans to have the jobs before any visitor to this country, legal or illegal is hired. So do I. But the four constituencies noted in the beginning of this paragraph do not care about regular Americans. In fact, they are rooting for the team that right now is playing against the Americans. Greed and power are powerful forces.

They've grown accustomed to crime

Because illegal foreign nationals live in crime infested territory in their native countries, they are more apt to commit a crime to defend their small, beginning share of the American dream in this country. In fact, their response to small provocations would understandably be in much larger measure than the affront. Let's look at some more facts to make this case.

District Attorney John M. Morganelli is an ardent defender of American rights, He is from Northampton County, Pennsylvania, 1992-present. In recent testimony before the House Subcommittee on Immigration, Border, Security and Claims, Morganelli, a US Patriot and an expert on the crimes of illegal aliens, stated:

> "Unfortunately, the majority of illegal aliens who are here are engaged in criminal activity. Identity theft, use of fraudulent social security numbers and green cards, tax evasion, driving without licenses represent some of the crimes that are engaged in by the majority of illegal aliens on a daily basis merely to maintain and hide their illegal status.
>
> In addition, violent crime and drug distribution and possession is also prevalent among illegal aliens. Over 25% of today's federal prison population are illegal aliens. In some areas of the country, 12% of felonies, 25% of burglaries and 34% of thefts are committed by illegal aliens."

Ignoring the "minor crime" such as ID theft and property crimes being committed by illegal aliens, here is a summary on some of the collateral damage reaped in crimes as a result of tolerating illegal aliens in the USA. The following bulleted statistics are part of the Morganelli quote:"

- In Los Angeles, 95% of some 1,500 outstanding warrants for homicides are for illegal aliens. About 67% of the 17,000 outstanding fugitive felony warrants are for illegal aliens.

- There are currently over 400,000 unaccounted for illegal alien criminals with outstanding deportation orders. At least one fourth of these are hard core criminals.

- 80,000 to 100,000 illegal aliens who have been convicted of serious crimes are walking the streets. Based on studies they will commit an average of 13 serious crimes per perpetrator.

- Illegal aliens are involved in criminal activities at a rate that is 2-5 times their representative proportion of the population.

- In 1980, our Federal and state facilities held fewer than 9,000 criminal aliens but at the end of 2003, approximately 267,000 illegal aliens were incarcerated in U.S. correctional facilities at a cost of about $6.8 billion per year.

- At least 4.5 million pounds of cocaine with a street value of at least $72 billion is smuggled across the southern border every year. ..

- 56% of illegal aliens charged with a reentry offense had previously been convicted on at least 5 prior occasions.

- Illegal aliens charged with unlawful reentry had the most extensive criminal histories. 90% had been previously arrested. Of those with a prior arrest, 50% had been arrested for violent or drug-related felonies.

- Illegal aliens commit between 700,000 to 1,289,000 or more crimes per year.

- Illegal aliens commit at least 2,158 murders each year – a number that represents three times greater participation than their proportion of the population.

- Illegal alien sexual predators commit an estimated 130,909 sexual crimes each year.

- There may be as many as 240,000 illegal alien sex offenders circulating throughout America. Based on studies, they will commit an average of 8 sex crimes per perpetrator before being caught.

- Nearly 63% of illegal alien sex offenders had been **deported** on another offense prior to committing the sex crime.

- Only 2% of the illegal alien sex offenders in one study had no history of criminal behavior, beyond crossing the border illegally.

- In Operation Predator, ICE arrested and deported 6,085 illegal alien pedophiles. Some studies suggest each pedophile molests average of 148 children. If so, that could be as many as 900,580 victims.

- Nobody knows how big the Sex Slave problem is but it is enormous.

- The very brutal MS-13 gang has over 15,000 members and associates in at least 115 different cliques in 33 states.

- The overall financial impact of illegal alien crimes is estimated at between $14.4 and $81 billion or more per year. Factor in the crime as a result of the cocaine and other drugs being smuggled in and the number may reach $150 billion per year. "

If nothing else, this list above dispels the notion that illegal immigration is a "victimless crime" and it dispels the myth that Americans need not control our borders. Another startling statistic to throw back at progressive liberals, who want an open borders policy, is that 60% of the crimes being committed by illegal foreign nationals are by those who were previously deported.

A source for these compelling facts is:
http://www.usillegalaliens.com/impacts_of_illegal_immigration_crime_summary.html

Allowing our borders to be disregarded, coupled with little national commitment about doing anything about it, has resulted in growing mayhem by illegal alien criminals. Illegal immigration is not a victimless crime!

The lawyers argue that once a little bit of something is permitted; it creates a slippery slope making the next and the next and the next event even easier than the first. Immigration crime occurs as soon as the illegal foreign national crosses the border. To survive underground in the US neighborhoods, the crimes multiply. Illegal aliens have thus grown accustomed to committing crimes. From their perspective, law enforcement in the US does not seem to care.

Growing up south of the border is tough for illegal foreign nationals

When in their home countries, the illegal immigrant becomes accustomed to unenforced laws and they learn how to deal with the corruption in their own countries. When they come here, they expect things to be better but they are suspicious. They bring these negative attitudes with them, expecting that law enforcement in the US will also be passive and uncaring.

There is a story on the Internet about how these attitudes affect the ability of illegal workers to blend in with the multiple customs of payment in the US. Within the past few years, there is the story of an illegal foreign national working on a job site. He became very angry because he was not paid by the end of the work day. Prior to the current job, he had been accustomed to work as a "day laborer." In this capacity, he was always paid when the work day was done.

More reputable contractors operate on a pay period basis. He did not know this. So, when a more reputable contractor put him to work and at the end of the day informed him that payroll would cut him a check at the end of the pay period, the illegal became enraged because he thought he was being cheated. So, as might have been the solution in his home country, he killed the contractor.

Another story shows how an illegal killed a young woman because she was driving a car that had the same look as the vehicle of a rival gang member. Knowing he had made a mistake, the illegal alien escaped back to Mexico and was not sent back for trial because Mexican authorities feared that he would be executed for his crimes.

In another story, an illegal alien was the driver of a vehicle with stolen plates. He was driving without a license or insurance, which is the norm, when he hit and killed a young bride. So, based on the theory of fight or flight, the illegal alien took off and attempted to run, knowing that if he could remove himself from the scene of the accident, he would never be found. He was successful.

US laws favor illegal aliens so much more than American citizens that our hospitals and medical clinics have become overrun by people who come to this country without insurance or any means of paying for medical treatment. Yet, our Congress has passed laws that they may show up at an emergency room for one reason or another, and they must be treated and nobody can demand payment or discuss their immigration status. The impact of course is that hospitals in the southwest have been forced to go out of business and / or insurance rates go up. Nothing is free. Hospitals have to charge more next time you or a member of your family must go in for assistance, if you can get through the huge line of illegals first.

Line jumpers and jobs Americans won't do

There is also this annoyingly wrongheaded notion that illegal workers only take the jobs that "Americans" don't want. It is time to put this to rest. The reality is they're taking the jobs that our teens and elderly and even unskilled adults would take if they only had a chance to get them. Wherever you go, from McDonalds to the hotels in your town, illegal foreign nationals are taking all of the entry level jobs that would be training our young people what it is like to work. This would ultimately give them the ability to earn some money for themselves to get a start in life. Illegal foreign workers have mostly put an end to these opportunities for Americans.

Meanwhile Africans, Asians, Europeans and other ethnic groups who try to get into the US legally are often thwarted because the US is over-filled with illegal aliens. These groups attempt to go through the proper channels. The deck is stacked against them since the illegals do get preferential treatment. Why is this so? The answer is simply that they are willing to run through the desert or swim across the Rio Grande. Many ask why the Hispanics and Latinos from south of the border are allowed here without restriction but other ethnic groups are excluded or severely limited? The fact is it pays to come to the US illegally and that is because of practices that work against the American people and all people. It is unfair and we have our leaders to blame.

The United States should even the playing field and should not discriminate against or for any group of people because of their ethnicity. Moreover, extra credit should not be given to those who have broken US immigration laws. In fact, the law-breakers should go to the back of the line or be kicked out of the line permanently.

Many of the serious crimes in this country are committed by illegal immigrants. The progressive liberals try to convince wide-awake Americans that the facts are not so and that what we see is not so. These illegal alien and amnesty supporters suggest that the American citizens who complain about illegal immigration are racists. They see you and I as the problem. The invaders from the south are OK. They expect that those who have yet to form an opinion on the matter, if there are any such people left in the US, will believe there are a lot of racists like you and I in America. They use the press to forward their bias that anybody who suggests there are very real problems associated with illegal immigration is a liar. It is the press and the government, in cahoots, that consistently lie, and many corrupt businesses support their every move.

Effects of illegal immigration & specific issues

There is a tremendous body or thought written about illegal immigration. The facts, opinions, and ideas of a ton of people from government officials to business executives to ordinary people are well recorded on the Internet. Many focus groups have been assembled to identify the areas of US life affected by illegal aliens. The long list below was compiled from a focus group of citizen activists who have been engaged in the struggle to have America's borders secured and existing immigration laws enforced. As you will see by scanning this huge, but not exhaustive list, they tell us many different reasons why Americans are alarmed about illegal immigration. Most of the big issues are included in this list. Here it is in alphabetical sequence:

- ✓ Anchor Babies: Birthright Citizenship Exploited
- ✓ Anti-American Attitudes
- ✓ Anti-Semitic Attitudes
- ✓ Attacks on Border Patrol and Law Enforcement agents
- ✓ Attacks on Free Speech in America
- ✓ Animal Abuse Increases
- ✓ Census Numbers: Negative Impact on Congressional Representation
- ✓ Civil rights: Devalued by comparison to illegal actions
- ✓ Child Endangerment
- ✓ Child Molestation
- ✓ Closed and Overcrowded Hospitals and Emergency Rooms
- ✓ Cost of Translators
- ✓ Consulates issuing Matricular Cards (ID Mexico won't even accept)
- ✓ Day Laborers loitering and creating public hazards
- ✓ Depreciated Wages for Americans and Legal Immigrants
- ✓ Deterioration of Common American Culture
- ✓ Desecration of the American Flag: Foreign Flags used aggressively
- ✓ Disrespect for American Laws
- ✓ Document Fraud
- ✓ Drunk driving injuries and deaths: Hit and Runs
- ✓ Ethnic Cleansing and Race Riots
- ✓ Farm animals with in city limits
- ✓ Food Poisoning
- ✓ Foreign Influence on US Politics
- ✓ Gangs, Graffiti, Drugs, Cartels, Smugglers, and Violence
- ✓ Gang Rape and unreported rapes
- ✓ High Birth Rates and Overpopulation
- ✓ Human Sex Slavery
- ✓ Identity Theft
- ✓ Increased Crime
- ✓ Increased Taxes for Americans
- ✓ Increased pressures on infrastructure (roads, traffic, water, sewer)
- ✓ Infectious Diseases
- ✓ Lost American Jobs
- ✓ Lost American Sovereignty
- ✓ Lost Self Governance of American citizens Vs. Globalism and Elitism
- ✓ Male Chauvinism: Gender inequality
- ✓ Not Speaking English, loss of common language, Press 1 for English
- ✓ Overcrowded Schools and Negative Impact on American Education
- ✓ Overcrowded single family homes
- ✓ Overcrowded Jails and Prisons
- ✓ Public Sanitation Loss: Trash and human waste in towns
- ✓ Racist Groups and Race Based Politics
- ✓ Remittances: Billions of dollars sent out of the US Economy

- ✓   Rule of Law: Fundamental principles of America sacrificed.
- ✓   Separatist Movements: Demands for autonomy
- ✓   Smear Campaigns and Lies: Dirty Politics
- ✓   Stolen American Taxpayer Resources: Tuition, Welfare, Licenses
- ✓   Taking limited seats in colleges at taxpayer expense
- ✓   Tax payer funds going to special interest groups (example) "LaRaza"
- ✓   Terrorism Threats and Loss of national security
- ✓   Trash and Negative Impact on Environment at border
- ✓   Unfair to Legal Immigrants
- ✓   Unfair Business Competition for law abiding companies
- ✓   Unlicensed and Uninsured Motorists
- ✓   Untaxed Wages
- ✓   Voter Fraud

It may not be easy being an illegal foreign national in the United States. It is not easy being an American living with the effects of illegal migration. Americans have been very patient with their government regarding the effects on the home life as a result of illegal foreign nationals ruining America because their allegiances are with other countries. Guests do not behave as illegal foreign nationals behave when residing in the US. It would be fair indeed to lift the guest status from these invaders once and for all and eliminate the threats of the large list of infractions above and the many problems that will come if this major invasion is not stopped immediately.

Chapter 3   Increasing Border Violence: Spillover from Mexico?

The FBI Does a Great Job for Americans

Border crimes are increasing rapidly though US officials, especially Homeland Security chief Janet Napolitano, are prone to downplay the notion. I am not talking about mere border crossings, which surely are a crime, but instead a wave of the most serious crimes you can think of, just miles below the border and sometimes even in the USA. We're looking at drugs, murders, kidnappings, rape, beheadings and the most gruesome crimes imaginable. Just in mid February, 2011, for example, two ICE Agents were attacked by the Cartel, with one being shot dead.

The FBI noted a recent increase in the level of drug trafficking-related violence within and between the drug trafficking organizations in Mexico. The question many are asking, "Has any of this violence spilled over into the United States?" Ask any of the sheriffs down south what they think. However, as one would expect in a country more absorbed with politically correct perfection than solving real problems for the people, U.S. federal officials deny that the recent increase in drug trafficking-related violence in Mexico has resulted in any spillover into the United States. The best the feds will say is that they acknowledge that the prospect of such a spillover is a serious concern. In other words, they are glad things are still OK. Many on the Southwestern border do not see it as being so tractable.

Demand for drugs

Buried in many of the reports generated from all of the activity at the border, is the notion that the problems are driven partly by U.S. citizens demand for drugs. Perhaps this is part of the overall problem but it is not an excuse that the US is doing so poorly in its "War on Drugs." The implication is that all the Mexicans are doing is fulfilling US demand. Though the drug trade is in the mucho $Billions, the violence occurs because this is not a perfect world and the traffickers do not share their loot equally. They do not play nice at all. They compete seriously for business and they use all means at their disposal to, among other things, control the smuggling routes into the United States. Violence, unfortunately for all, including innocent bystanders in Mexico and in the US has become the primary means for settling disputes.

Statistics on violence

Congress continues to press for information about what they see as spillover violence but Homeland Security, just as vigorously defends that it is not an issue. Sometimes things are just a matter of semantics. The interagency community, for example defines spillover violence as violence targeted primarily at civilians and government entities—excluding trafficker-on-trafficker violence. Those outside of the government think this is a way for the government to look better than their record. Such experts and scholars see the idea of trafficker-on-trafficker violence as central to spillover. So, like most information from our government today, it is speckled with propaganda that favors the report writers.

Admittedly, there is no single source of reliable, comprehensive, publicly available data to definitively answer the spillover question. But, when you see bullets sprayed into the US and innocent deaths, and farmers fearing for their lives, you know this is not because one or two illegal aliens happened to stroll by their farms on their way to a meatpacking or construction job.

Much of the information in this chapter comes from work the FBI has done and a huge government report commissioned by Congress. All of this stuff is available on the Web for those who want to pursue this angle more thoroughly. Despite what appears to be some pressure to purify the government reports so nobody looks bad, the data is about as frank as one might expect, and there is good information to be gleaned.

For an Aug 24 2010 official government report on spillover violence, I would recommend taking a run out to http://www.fas.org/sgp/crs/homesec/R41075.pdf. It is titled, "Southwest Border Violence: Issues in Identifying and Measuring Spillover Violence." Another great source is the FBI reports that are best found by typing the following into your web browser search engine: www.fbi.gov/news/stories/2010/august/southwest-border -- this is not a URL.

Sheriff Paul Babeu says Napolitano is a propagandist

Though Janet Napolitano in her January 2011 state of Homeland Security speech said everything was fine and better than in the Bush days, Arizona's Pinal County Sheriff Paul Babeu, who was named Sheriff of the Year in January 2011 by the National Sheriff's Association is not buying it. Unlike Napolitano who talks the talk, Babeu must walk the walk, and it is a very dangerous walk.

The Sheriff's perspective is that Napolitano's self-praise did not reflect conditions on the ground in Arizona. He cited that in 2009, and 2010, the amount of illegal drugs entering the state that has been confiscated by local authorities has doubled. Moreover, the number of pursuits of criminal illegal aliens has tripled. Babeu is puzzled why the person in charge of safety in the US is more concerned about establishing a fictitious record than solving problems.

In his own words in an interview with CNSNews.com, Babeu asked, "Why isn't the secretary of Homeland Security speaking to these threats? Why does she keep trying to convince us through argument that everything is just fine to the point that she's trying to hypnotize us into believing this crap." One could conclude that the newest US weapon used by

Homeland Security on the war against drugs and the war against illegal aliens is "propaganda." But, who is that going to help?

Yet, very few conservatives find much truth in Homeland Security Secretary Janet Napolitano's ramblings. For example, on February2, 2011, The Secretary was honored for the "lie of the Day," on the Laura Ingraham Web site. Try this on: **It is inaccurate to state, as too many have, that the border is overrun with violence and out of control.**

Al Queda and the Simpsons

The fact is that right next door to the US, in Mexico over 30,000 people have been killed in drug-related violence since 2006. The Miami Herald recently suggested that the Mexican Drug Lords make Al Queda as relevant as the "Simpsons." Even major tourist destinations such as Acapulco are reported to have their morgues with an overflow of bodies in what they can only call "grisly" shape. According to the Miami Herald, Acapulco's morgues have bodies with multiple mutilations and a number of dismemberment is not uncommon. And, some of the brutalized victims are minors.

Reporters talk about beheadings and murders from Cancun to Acapulco right to the U.S. Border to Guadalupe - with no end in sight. Those, who despite the carnage can still find some humor in describing it, suggest that with the increased body count, one might want to travel to someplace less dangerous than Mexico -- like perhaps Iraq or Afghanistan.

Last June in El Paso, stray bullets from a drug-related gunfight hit City Hall. In August a stray bullet struck a University of Texas at El Paso building. And, as most Americans know, American Tourist David Hartley who was jet skiing on Falcon Lake, which sits right on the border near Laredo Texas, was shot by a Mexican gunman in October. There have been others.

On January 14, 2011, a Mexican gunman took a shot at four highway workers with a high-powered rifle across the border in an isolated ghost town east of Fort Hancock, Hudspeth County.

Kidnappings by the cartels and the gangs who work for them have become a serious problem in several U.S. cities on the Southwest border. In the past, kidnap victims were usually rivals in the drug trade. Sometimes victims were kidnapped for revenge, sometimes to intimidate. Paying a ransom was no guarantee the victim would be released. However, when the gangs realized how easy—and profitable—kidnapping could be, they started abducting anyone who looked wealthy enough to command a hefty ransom, and that included Americans on either side of the border. Is that spillover?

In the Texas border town of McAllen, for example, the rate of kidnapping has nearly quadrupled. Between October 2008 and September 2009, 42 people were kidnapped in the McAllen area, compared with 11 the previous year. And many kidnappings go unreported because the victims themselves may be involved in illegal activity and don't want to contact authorities. Is this spillover?

The fact that Mexican nationals feel perfectly comfortable shooting at U.S. highway workers within the boundary of the U.S.A. tells us loudly that it is time to do something logical instead of just for show to stop this madness. Let's put up a real fence that cannot be climbed over or under, put a little jolt on the fence, get enough military to the border, and close insanity down for good. Do we really think that throwing money at the Mexican Government for the supposed "War on Drugs" is really working? Some suggest that the overall effect is like giving the pharmacy keys to a junkie.

Shut down the border

When the US finally has the will to shut down that border, using real troops with live ammo, with fences that burn the skin, and no restrictions on those protecting US citizens, then and only then, will traveling to Mexico no longer be suicidal. Until, then, stay away and stay far enough away that your fate is not to be broadcast on the evening news, returning home in a body bag or in the opposite lane so you don't get shot again.

Why would anybody think it was not safe down there when entire police departments have resigned in Mexico and left whole towns unprotected to be controlled by those who use violence to get what they want? Why have some wealthy and upper-middle-class Mexicans recently begun to buy second or third homes in the US? Can it be that they are concerned about the state of violence in their own country?

It is not a new phenomenon for the US government to be at least concerned about what is going on. The U.S. Department of Defense, for example has been very concerned on many fronts. In fact, just a few years ago, the DOD issued a report that listed Mexico and Pakistan as countries whose governments face a threat of rapid collapse.

A lot of miles to cover

Protecting the southern border is a big job for anybody, even the USA. The border extends nearly 2,000 miles, from San Diego, California to Brownsville, Texas. At many points along the way, criminals carry on their trade with surprising ease and deadly results. The Drug cartels seemingly operate unrestricted, transporting kilos of cocaine, marijuana, and meth, and they use local gangs who think nothing of kidnapping and murder. They traffic not only drugs but also smuggle human cargo with the help of ever-available corrupt public officials. The pockets of the politicians are lined with riches from looking the other way.

The FBI sees all of these offenses as a major challenge to law enforcement. They suggest that all together, there is a threat not only to the safety of our border communities, but to the security of the entire country.

Even in the Northern US, we know that the U.S. government has built fences in a lot of places across the border but there are just as many places where there are no fences. Even when there are barriers, the US adversaries continually try to defeat them, and in many cases they are able to defeat them. They are resilient. They do not quit. They tunnel under, fly over, or they just cut through the multitude of defenses and fences the US puts up. The US attempts to keep them out. Unfortunately, the end result is that Americans are like the mole in whack 'o mole but it is the bad guys who hold the big mallet?

Why do the bad guys go to so much trouble?

The answer is quite simple. Money! The cartels make billion-dollar profits trafficking drugs. Their gaining and controlling border access is critical to their operations. It is serious business. They use any means to maintain their control. Bribery, extortion, intimidation, and extreme violence are common tools. The FBI compares some areas on the Mexican side of the border as being so violent, it is reminiscent of Al Capone and the gangster era of Chicago in the 1930s or the heyday of the Mafia's Five Families in New York. As bad as you can think their "work" may be, the stories show it can always get worse.

For example, In Tijuana, there was a man who became known as "The Strew Maker"—El Pozolero—working for one of the cartels. He dissolved hundreds of murder victims in acid to dispose of the evidence. In Juarez, decapitated heads of murdered cartel members have been displayed on fence posts to intimidate rivals. That is why so many Americans will not give up their guns and it is why we choose to have a strong defense, even if Janet Napolitano doesn't completely get it.

One of the things that contribute to the flow of drugs and illegals into the US, according to the FBI, is the corruption right at the border. There are more and more US border guards who turn to corruption. These officials have great power as they have the authority to wave vehicles through checkpoints. These vehicles may carry illegal human cargo, or various types of narcotics. Worse than that—they may also carry pieces of the next dirty bomb—to be brought in by terrorists. The FBI and the DEA are working very hard to make sure the worst that can happen never happens. We need to admire these brave agents, while we work to assure that they are always permitted to do their jobs and are never victimized by the politically correct in our government.

On their Web site, the FBI shows the documentation they are producing about the types of issues that they have been encountering on the border. You can tell in the tone of their writing that they must be disgusted at what they are finding, especially when it is one of us. They cannot stomach the occasional US Border patrol agent who is also employed by the other side. Just a few extra waves of the hand, a few extra cars making it through, and in one day, such a border agent can earn the equivalent of another year's salary. The temptation is great, indeed. Here is the FBI's own story of Michael Gilliland, an agent gone bad.

> "In the surveillance footage taken hours before his arrest, U.S. Customs and Border Protection Officer Michael Gilliland can be seen nonchalantly waving a car through his lane at the Otay Mesa Port of Entry in San Diego. He was knowingly allowing illegal aliens across the border, and he would do this several more times throughout the evening. His actions that night would earn him nearly the equivalent of his annual salary—and eventually a five-year prison term.
>
> Gilliland, a former U.S. Marine and veteran Customs and Border Protection (CBP) officer with 16 years of experience, has been in jail since 2007. But his case continues to illustrate the pervasive problem of corruption along the Southwest border and the damage that can occur when officials betray the public's trust.

Although the vast majority of U.S. government employees working on the border are not corrupt, as one senior agent who investigates such crimes noted, "Even one bad apple is too many."

Of our 700 agents assigned to public corruption investigations nationwide, approximately 120 of them are located in the Southwest region. We work closely with many federal agencies, including CBP and the Drug Enforcement Administration. The result has been more than 400 public corruption cases originating from the Southwest region—and in the past fiscal year more than 100 arrests and about 130 state and federal cases prosecuted.

We have 12 border corruption task forces in the Southwest, which consist of many state and local law enforcement agencies as well as our federal partners. Recently, we established a National Border Corruption Task Force at FBI Headquarters to coordinate the activities of all regional operations.

At our Border Corruption Task Force office in San Diego, Special Agent Terry Reed—who headed the Michael Gilliland investigation—points out the "Wall of Shame." Displayed are pictures of a dozen former officials convicted of public corruption offenses in the San Diego area. They are a diverse group of men and women from a variety of state and federal government agencies. They were all in it for the money, sex, or both—a fact not lost on the drug cartels.

"The cartels have developed into very sophisticated businesses," said El Paso Special Agent Tim Gutierrez. "Despite their brutality and violence, they use sophisticated tactics."

The cartels actively engage in corrupting public officials. They recruit by exploiting weaknesses, sometimes gaining intelligence through surveillance methods usually employed by law enforcement. Cartel members have been known to observe inspectors at ports of entry using binoculars from the Mexican side of the border. Maybe an inspector has a drinking or gambling problem. Maybe he flirts with women and could be tempted to cheat on his wife. Maybe an employee is simply burned out on the job.

"If you're an inspector and you are legitimately waving through 97 out of 100 cars anyway," Gutierrez said, "and you realize you can make as much as your annual salary by letting the 98th car go by, it can be easy to rationalize that."

"The cartels are always looking for the next Michael Gilliland," Agent Reed said. "But using our combined investigative and intelligence gathering skills, the task force has been very successful in rooting out corrupt public officials at the border."

Thanks to the big money from drugs, the cartels have enormous power. Money is power. As noted in this chapter, they have no problem using their $Billions to bribe, intimidate, and murder to get what they want from police and government officials. From Tijuana to all points east, the cartels offer what is called the choice of "the silver or the lead." The silver is the money and the lead is the bullets. Many well-intentioned public servants who had been able to resist outright bribes have been compelled to look the other way when their lives—or the lives of their families—have been threatened. The fact is: these are not hollow threats. The evidence is out there. They will kill you.

While the billion dollar trafficking operations of the cartels bring major crime and violence to both sides of the Southwest border, it is the street gangs that carry out the cartels' especially dirty work. They do the smuggling, extortion, and murder. The FBI, DEA and others work hard to understand the gangs and the full scenario. Knowing their structure, culture, and tactics helps in a variety of ways. Knowing the membership helps sometimes even more.

Figure 3-1 Vanload of drugs confiscated near border. Photo courtesy of DEA

Figure 3-2 Methamphetamine confiscated near the border. Photo courtesy of DEA

Figure 3-3 Twelve lbs heroin from Project Deliverance. Photo courtesy of DEA

Figure 3-4 A Barrio Azteca gang member's tattoos. Photo courtesy of DEA

The agents get tips from police officers on the street, and they recruit sources from the ranks of disgruntled gang members. They also make contact with recently arrested gang members who may be looking for better treatment in exchange for their cooperation. This information often leads to more arrests, and more drug seizures, as well as the prevention of serious crimes such as kidnapping or murder. It is a tough job and there are many brave men and women on our side doing this job every day. We thank them.

A lot of good stuff happens at the El Paso Intelligence Center. It is led by the U.S. Drug Enforcement Administration. The site shown in Figure 3-5 provides tactical intelligence to law enforcement around the world through watch operations, analytical support, and access to a variety of state and federal databases.

Figure 3-5 El Paso Intelligence Center

The true meaning of "spillover"

Janet Napolitano and her well trained U.S. federal officials categorically deny that the recent increase in drug trafficking-related violence in Mexico has resulted in a spillover into the United States. So, does all this mean there is a spillover or there is not? It would be comical if it were not so serious that Homeland Security holds special meaning for the word "spillover."

As shown in this chapter, there certainly is anecdotal evidence and even publicly available information that the FBI is involved in a large and increasing number of cross-border heinous crimes including kidnapping cases? Is this spillover? There is evidence that hundreds of people in the southwest border-states---mostly affiliated with drug trafficking organizations, have in some way been kidnapped for ransom or retribution.

Who do you believe on the issue of the spillover? Does all this criminal activity that seems obviously related to the Mexican drug trade add up to spillover? Who really cares whether "spillover" is the operative word? It is quite obvious from all the mayhem that the US is under attack. It is past the time to act swiftly to stop it before it spreads, but it is clearly time to stop it once and for all.

Chapter 4   Is the War on Drugs Working?

Should drugs be legal?

We do have it good in the US. Most Americans have good food to eat and have some level of Medical care and the police keep us all safe. Instead of trying to make it bad for us, all other countries should make it good for themselves. There is no question, however, that it is much easier to live on the US side of the border with Mexico than on the Mexican side—in many ways. Right now, for example, it can be argued that Mexico is drowning in drug-related bloodshed. The statistics say that in 2010, the country suffered just about 12,000 murders. Why is that?

In the Northeastern states, we see the problems with illegal immigration in a different light than in the Southwestern States. In the Southwest, people are dying because of the US war on drugs. They are not dying because a few million illegals want to get meatpacking wages. There appears to be minimal benefit overall to the big War on Drugs because like most US wars, we do not play to win. Yet, a lot of people die. People are dying on both sides of the border. So, the real question is, "does this war have any prospects for success and if it does, what must be done to help success be the default rather than what we now seem to be experiencing?

I think that unless we take a few Divisions of our Finest from Iraq or Afghanistan and send them in to wipe out the enemy just below our border, they may never be wiped out. We play too nice. They won't be wiped out in the war on drugs under today's circumstances as all of the official agents who are charged with fighting them, are under-armed and under-resourced, and under-missioned. We purposely (probably because of budgeting) do not provide an overwhelming force that would assure victory. We have never been staged to win. And, so we do not win and nobody expects us to win.

The raw facts, readable by an idiot, show that the war on drugs simply isn't working. Politicians on both sides of the border, unaccustomed to telling the truth, have decided to keep their opinions in this regard to themselves. Yet, once released from the shackles of possibly getting shellacked (nice term eh!) in the next run, a.k.a. the shackles of potential reelection—even politicians can and do feel obliged to tell the truth. The whole world was surprised recently, for example, when former Mexican President Vicente Fox began to lead the band and the chorus while still toting his cowboy-boots and still wearing leather. At 68, he is truly free at last, and thinking less of legacy than of the truth.

We know that Fox, a Clark Gable—like, handsome and dapper individual, who ruled Mexico from 2000 to 2006, had once declared that the elimination of the drug kingpins was the "mother of all battles." Though he engaged ferociously, Fox lost the battle and turned the losing war over to Felipe Calderon.

In my humble opinion, the reason for the lack of success is that it is a matter of government v private industry. Government cannot win v the private sector unless the war is a real war. The only real thing that governments do well is amass armies and wage big wars. As much as it pains me to legitimatize the drug trade, the fact is there is no government corruption and largesse that has pre-ordained the outcome. Government cannot defeat private industry if it is free. The Drug war is not viewed as a real war and soldiers are not fighting it as if they are at war. Thus, for those on the cartel side, it has meant easy times in the drug industry.

How many people need to die to know that something is not working? Moreover, in the war on drugs, who, in the US is it that we are protecting? Will they ever be satiated with the contraband coming from the Southwest? Is it our children, our parents, our friends, or whoever that we wish to protect? Americans unfortunately, love drugs and they / we have the money to pay for them and so we do.

Free drugs at last

Why are American lives and Mexican lives being lost in the "War on Drugs?" I mean, are those who choose to engage in bad behavior any more important than the 12,000 Mexicans who died violent deaths in the drug war last year? What about the untold American deaths on the streets? Why are American lives (the users) in a voluntary vice more important than the 15,000 innocent souls, who because of their behavior, are destined to die this year?

Vicente Fox, under no pressure to run for office again in Mexico, though perhaps, he would be a contender in the US if he were v Obama, says his views have indeed moved toward the other end of the spectrum. He now favors full-on legalization of the production, transit and sale of prohibited drugs. Fox is most explicit about marijuana but says the principle applies to all illegal drugs. Drugs are bad news for everybody, but 12,000 people dying on the Mexican side this year and who knows how many violent deaths on the US side in the future makes this war intolerable. Is the war winnable? I don't think so without a huge big bang type sacrifice. If there is no big bang for political reasons or otherwise, then what is the best alternative? Can we really regulate behavior? If the kids stop eating Big Macs and Kids Meals because of Michele, will the adults give up drugs? Even the Russians eventually gave Vodka back to the people.

V. Fox is a real fox. He said, for example, in his best attempt to describe why the war cannot work, "Prohibition didn't work in the Garden of Eden. Adam ate the apple." Prohibition did not work in the 1920's and even with strong opposition it had to be repealed as the deaths and the violence were worse than the stink of gin and the shakiness of the population. We cannot regulate people's behavior and perhaps we should not, unless their behavior is a clear and present danger to society. Some would suggest that the regulation of behavior creates far more danger.

Fox thinks that the production chain needs to be taken from the hands of criminals and placed into the hands of producers. He sees farmers that produce marijuana and manufacturers that process it and distributors that distribute it and shops that sell it. Fox argues that he does not see that drugs are good but the war against drugs, he sees as unwinnable. His argument is compelling though we would like it to be otherwise. Perhaps more people will be better off without all of the blood battles?

Pat Buchanan, a conservative with his own ideas about everything, like most of us, cannot stand to see the trauma caused by drugs in the US on regular people, but especially our children. Yet, he offers that it is all but impossible that the US can win a drug war when millions of Americans, who use recreational drugs, are the reason the cartels have the cash to bribe, murder, and behead whoever it takes to win the war. This permits the self-indulgent Americans who are hooked and want it no other way, to be supplied with their drugs?

Milton, Mao, or Buchanan?

Buchanan opines that there are just two sure ways to stop the drug war post haste. He notes there is Milton's way and Mao's way. Mao Zedongs and his communists said no to drugs in a way that nobody in Western Civilization could handle. Yet, it solved the problem. Mao killed users and suppliers alike. He saw them as social parasites. In the end, there were a lot of dead, but nobody was clamoring to get high. It worked but there were a lot of dead souls. We are heading in that direction if we insist on defeating the evil of the drug trade.

Milton Friedman's way, according to Buchanan was always to decriminalize drugs and call off the war on drugs. Friedman never liked the war from the first moment he sniffed its malodorous badness. Buchanan's is very much the same approach that Vicente Fox is suggesting. Richard Nixon, in 1972, before he had his own war of survival, declared a War on Drugs. At the same time Friedman, writing for Newsweek at the time as Buchanan recollects, objected on ethical grounds. He stated:

> "On ethical grounds, do we have the right to use the machinery of government to prevent an individual from becoming an alcoholic or a drug addict? For children, almost everyone would answer at least a qualified yes. But for responsible adults, I, for one, would answer no. Reason with the potential addict, yes. Tell him the consequences, yes. Pray for and with him, yes. But I believe that we have no right to use force, directly or indirectly, to prevent a fellow man from committing suicide, let alone from drinking alcohol or taking drugs."

Buchanan continued "Am I my brothers keeper?" asked Milton, answering, "No."

> "Americans are never going to adopt the Maoist solution. Look around. The users of drugs are all too often classmates, colleagues, friends, even family. Indeed, our last three presidents did not deny using drugs.

> Once, a Christian America outlawed and punished homosexuality, abortion, alcohol, loan-sharking and gambling, all as criminal vice. Now, homosexuality and abortion are constitutional rights. Gambling and booze are a rich source of government revenue. And loan-sharking is done by credit-card companies, and not just the Corleones.

Will we raise the white flag in the drug war, as well?

Which is the greater evil? Legalized narcotics for Americas young or a failed state of 110,000 million on our southern border?

Some choice. Some country we've become."

Ladies and Gentlemen, this is not necessarily a pretty world in which we live. The beauty of America is there in this overwhelming sense of freedom given to everybody, just because they / we are here. For those of us who do not smoke, for example, it is the freedom to breathe clean air that we enjoy. For those of us that do smoke, it is the ability to smoke unimpeded by the intolerance of a few bastards who choose to take the smoker's freedom away.

Personally, I hate smoke and smokers who blow smoke in my face but this drug thing is worse than my disdain for smoke. I hate seeing real people higher than a kite on marijuana or whatever it is that makes the cartels smile. They will be high anyway. They would blow smoke in my face anyway. I can handle all that compared with having any of my freedoms repressed. Maybe we can keep the cartels smiling with no violence if we (the government) all put our guns down on this one and say again that prohibition has not worked.

We did not win the war, but maybe we can win back a life without these asinine, senseless everyday battles?

Chapter 5   Southwestern Border: A Gateway for Terrorists

Who Comes Across the Border?

There are just a few states that can rightfully be called the Southwestern States. Americans in the Northern states have a great amount of empathy for the plight suffered by those Americans in the Southwestern states. In the Northeast, the problem is illegal workers taking American jobs, whereas in the Southwest, the big problem is imported violence.

When you research what is going on in the Southwest, the results do not come back simply as a bunch of future roofers or future grape vine harvesters or future factory workers or future meatpackers, who came over the border today, who simply are looking for immediate success. Who are they, then?

There is lots written about who comes across the border. The source for much of the facts presented in this chapter, come from this URL: http://www.abc15.com/dpp/news/region_central_southern_az/other/terrorists-crossing-az-border-into-u.s.%3F

Arizona gets a lot of claptrap from the rest of the US for the positions it must take against illegal foreign nationals to help protect its citizenry from danger. What a shame that is. Pennsylvanians have it tough enough fighting for jobs every day against the illegal workers who migrate north from south of the border. For Pennsylvanians it is a simple fight to win out in a "fair" marketplace. We are not yet getting shot and so the situation for Arizonans and all those along the Southwestern border is clearly more severe.

Pinal County Arizona is a hotbed for activity, and I am glad it is not Lackawanna County, PA. We in PA appreciate the brave folks in AZ taking this fight to the border and we think we need to do what must be done at the ballot box for Americans all over the country to prevail. In this way, Arizona and Pennsylvania win. It is OK that some bureaucrat counting stats for Janet Napolitano do not do as well.

For now, let's go back to Arizona because that is where the battle is being fought. Let's dig down a little into a special cell block deep inside the Pinal County Jail. In here, there are about 400 inmates awaiting trial or extradition. Do you think that all they tried to do was cross the Arizona border from Mexico? As you evaluate the facts, you would see that just about half of them are actually from Mexico. This particular cell block is a "way station" for the immigration process. Inmates are held here after being detained and later their disposition is settled.

Why should anybody be concerned about such an innocuous place?

Well, maybe it is that the origin point of the inmates gives cause for concern for some critics and even honest lawmakers.

The day that the sampling of criminals' origins in this chapter was taken, for example, according to official records, this Homeland Security "way station," was holding inmates from Iran, Iraq, Afghanistan, Pakistan, Egypt, Lebanon, and the Sudan. How did they get there? Keep reading.

Just say it is ok!

Senator John Kyl from Arizona, a man for whom the progressive liberals, who want open borders, have no warmth in their hearts, sees the problem as a lot more than simple border jumping. Kyle notes that "They're coming from all over, and one wonders whether some of them are coming in here to commit acts of terror."

For those of us in Pennsylvania, John Kyl is the real Arizona Senator, not in the spirit of John McCain, who can't seem to make up his mind on the immigration issue. Kyl has been championing the cause of conservatives regarding illegal immigration since 2002. He sees it like it is. He sees it like you see it. He knows that many of the "undocumented's" from south of the border have not crossed over in order to compete for best the "meatpacker of the year" award. They are not expected to sign up for the bake-off, any time soon. They have better ideas.

For example, Agents on the border have recovered military-style patches on clothing near the border. These were shed to keep the country of origin and the purpose of the visit hidden from officials who might come in contact with the illegal foreign nationals who trek these routes to "freedom." Among the recovered patches include those that contain the word "martyr" in Arabic. There are patches that show a plane appearing to fly into sky scrapers. There are a number of these items that have been recovered. Check out the patches below. You can clearly see a patch with an Arab insignia on the left which reads "martyr," "way to eternal life" or "way to immortality." The badge on the right is the illustration of an airplane about to collide with a tower. Who do you think these folks are?

These photos are from the 2006 congressional report. What do you think they mean? Would this be the typical outfit for an illegal planning to join the United Farm Workers union?

Figure 5-1 Martyr and Jihad Emplems from captured "uniforms"

Perhaps this evidence of terrorists crossing into the US just as other illegal foreign nationals do—is merely anecdotal but, then again, perhaps it is supported by facts that the US government chooses not to release. I have not observed willingness, for example of HS Chief Napolitano to release anything that would make her department look like border security needed more work, even if it did. Can any of us conclude that we can trust the government?

Yet, according to Homeland Security documents obtained by undercover personalities from various TV stations, ICE officials detained 45,279 undocumented immigrants classified as OTM (other than Mexican). While the vast majority were from other Central American countries like El Salvador, Honduras and Guatemala, officials also arrested 10 undocumented immigrants from Iran, 10 from Iraq, six from Lebanon and 19 from Pakistan. Are we kidding ourselves? How many terrorists were involved with 9/11?

To show how easy it is to cross the border into the Southwestern states, look at this border spot in New Mexico (picture below – Figure 5-2). There is just a small strand of barbed wire separating the two countries. This photo is from the 2006 congressional report. Are we really trying to dissuade people from coming?

Figure 5-2 US Budget Problems on Barbed Wire???

The Freedom train surely does pass through Mexico and 'Special-interest countries' and smart Mexicans and others from within Mexico know how to get the opportunity for a ride to the US border. It looks like this train, as shown in Figure 5-3 is very popular. Illegal aliens from Central America ride atop this freight train leaving Arriaga, Mexico, en route to the U.S. (The photo is courtesy of Hogar de la Misericordia, a.k.a. Home of Mercy.

Figure 5-3 The Part of the Love Train Where There is Love

Several times in this chapter we have referenced the 2006 congressional report on border threats. It has been a great source of information on terrorism on the border. Though prepared back in 2006, this report on border threats is by **The House Committee on Homeland Security Subcommittee on Investigations.** It is titled, "A Line in the Sand: Confronting the Threat at the Southwest Border". This report noted that 1.2 million illegal aliens were apprehended in 2005 alone, and 165,000 of those were from countries other than Mexico (OTM). Of the 165,000 OTM illegal aliens, just about 650 were from what are deemed "special interest countries." Is that not a lot of potential terrorists?

There are other reports in which the "special interests" were substantially higher. Special interest to the Border Patrol means, "Designated by the intelligence community as countries that could export individuals that could bring harm to our country in the way of terrorism."

TV Stations from Florida and Atlanta often do expose's on the border situation. In a recent broadcast, Atlanta's WSB-TV2 aired broadcasts that discussed the inmate population in both a Phoenix detention center, and also in a Florence AZ detention center. These centers had illegal alien residents that included detainees from as far away as Afghanistan, Armenia,

Bosnia, Egypt, Ghana, Iraq, Iran, Jordan, Kenya, Morocco, Pakistan, Sudan, Uzbekistan, Yemen, Botswana, Turkey and many other countries. None of these detainees were looking for construction or meatpacking jobs. What were they looking for?

In the 2008 Yearbook for Homeland Security on Immigration Studies, 5,506 of the detainees were from 14 "special-interest countries." It is tough to get the right numbers on these special statistics, but I relate the numbers that I have anyway because anything more than zero potential terrorists is cause for alarm.

J D Hayworth or John McCain?

Former Representative J.D. Hayworth, who for some reason, which I cannot figure out, lost to Senator John McCain in Arizona in the last election, is very vocal about the problems that US government negligence on border issues have caused in Arizona and the country at large. Hayworth was interviewed by WSB-TV2 and he had a lot to say such as:

> "We have left the back door to the United States open; we have to understand that there are definitely people who mean to do us harm who have crossed that border."

Islamic radical groups that support Hamas, Hezbollah and Islamiya Al Gamat are all active in Latin America, according to the 2006 congressional report. "These groups generate funds through money laundering, drug trafficking and arms deals, making millions of dollars every year via their multiple illicit activities. These cells reach back to the Middle East and extend to this hemisphere the sophisticates' global support structure of international terrorism."

Going back to May 2001, just a few months before the Sept. 11 terrorist attacks, a former Mexican national security adviser and one time U.N. ambassador, Adolfo Aguilar Zinser, warned those paying attention that "Spanish and Islamic terrorist groups are using Mexico as a refuge."

The 2006 government report was just 39-pages, yet it demonstrated that our enemies live among us. For example it notes that in March 2005, Mahmoud Youssef Kourani, an illegal, made it across the Southern border with a little help from his friends. Kourani first bribed a Mexican consular official in Beirut to get a visa. He eventually pleaded guilty to providing material support to Hezbollah. It just happens that this guy, Kourani, was the brother of the Hezbollah chief of military operations in southern Lebanon. Still illegal, he lived comfortably in Dearborn, Michigan, while he solicited funds for Hezbollah terrorists.

In 2007 World Net Daily reported that President Bush's top intelligence aide confirmed that Iraqi terrorists were captured coming into the United States from Mexico.

In 2009 the Society for Risk Analysis conducted a study, which they titled: "Analyzing the Homeland Security of the U.S.-Mexico Border." The study used a mathematical model that predicted the likelihood of terrorist infiltration across the border with Mexico. The Stanford and George Mason researchers concluded that chances of OTM terrorists reaching the US from the southern border were as high as 97 percent. In the 2005 Congressional Research Service report for Congress the report warns that "Terrorists and terrorist organizations could leverage these illicit networks to smuggle a person or weapon of mass destruction into the United States, while the large number of aliens attempting to enter the country illegally, could potentially provide needed cover for the terrorists."

http://www.kfoxtv.com/news/25800422/detail.html   In November, 2010, KFOX in El Paso, Texas reported news about terrorism on the border. The report acknowledged that Homeland Security in June 2010 had clarified once and for all the terrorism situation on the border. The HS conclusion was that there was no credible evidence of any terrorist groups operating along the Southwest border. One continually must ask whether anybody is in charge of this important agency. KFOX took issue with the Napolitano report and noted that their evidence proves terrorists have crossed the border and some have even been captured in the US.

Retired INS agent Michael Cutler sums it up by saying that the terrorist border threat has been covered up by the US government. ""Incredibly the government is attempting to keep the citizens like a bunch of mushrooms ... keep us in the dark and feed us a bunch of manure," Cutler said.

Do you remember the 300 Somalis that were being trained in the Southwest? Representative Michael McCaul of Texas sums it up: "To this day we do not know where those 300 Somalis are. We do know they are in the United States." There are many people being apprehended, but there are also many people slipping through the cracks on our southern flank that are very dangerous.

The progressive liberals would like you to ignore this threat. ICE has documented that aliens from the Middle East are regularly smuggled to staging areas in Central and South America, awaiting transport to the US border. Members of Hezbollah have already entered the United States across the Southwest border. And if the threat from afar is not enough, military and intelligence officials have identified Venezuela as a major potential hub of terrorism in our hemisphere.

Venezuela consistently works against the US in whatever ways they can to hurt us. For example, they routinely issue identity documents to "migrants" that could easily be used to obtain a visa and enter the country. With as many as 50 million illegal foreign nationals in the US today, we can all bet that many are here as terrorists, just waiting their opportunity.

Though this book is mostly dedicated to the jobs issues caused by illegal aliens, illegal foreign nationals taking American jobs is very innocuous compared to terrorists entering the US for their intended murderous purposes. Both, however, are part of the same problem caused by the negligence of the US government in protecting the borders and rounding up the bad guys once they sneak in. You can bet that on their way to committing terrorist acts, the OTM, illegal alien from a special interest country is able to get a job and sustain himself, while preparing for his future imbroglio. The fact is that with loose borders, and minimal post-facto enforcement, there is an ever-present threat of terrorist infiltration over the Southwest border that needs to be addressed definitively and immediately.

Just a few years ago happenings

On Wednesday, Feb 23, 2011 FBI agents arrested Khalid Ali-M Aldawsari. This young man had trained a good part of his "grown-up life," to be a terrorist. Universities and the government have a special outreach program for Muslim students from Saudi Arabia, land of 911, hoping when the students go back, they will like Americans. Alawsari was in the U.S. on a student visa (F visa) and his arrest was for attempted use of a weapon of mass destruction. He had already obtained most of the supplies such as nitric and sulfuric acids, a hazmat suit, wiring, a smoldering iron kit, making phenol the last key component of the plot.

Chapter 6   Does Illegal Mean Illegal?

Immigrants? Migrants? Pirates? or Thieves?

The illegal immigration problem in this country is out of control and has been out of control for far too long. It is long past the time that our representatives in Congress should have solved this problem once and for all. If it can't be done today, tomorrow sounds a lot better than next week. These people who have come from other lands and crossed the border illegally are criminals for coming uninvited into our sovereign country. Those who have overstayed their legal invitation are in the same boat. They are illegal foreign nationals, a.k.a. illegal aliens.

The preponderance of illegal aliens are from south of the border and they should have no more right to be here than an illegal African, Irishman, Korean, Italian, or Swede. They broke our laws coming into the country and they continue to break them in order to survive and then ultimately, they break them again as they come out of the woodwork when they need help. Their children get free scholarships to our public schools. When they need healthcare, they crowd our ERs, and in some cases have forced hospitals to go out of business under the weight of unreimbursed expenses.

Hard as it is to believe, being in an illegal status does not preclude anybody from gaining Emergency Room benefits paid for by citizens through higher insurance premiums. I am not suggesting they do not get care, but once they cost the country money, especially after breaking our immigration laws, it is time overdue to send them back, not release them to the community. Once here, illegal aliens forget about their illegal status and so do our representatives. The illegal foreign nationals soon figure out how to take from our abundance (taxpayers) and in thanksgiving, they take our jobs and they tell others to come.

They are not illegal immigrants. They are not even immigrants. They are aliens and/or foreign nationals. If there is no green card, the person is an "illegal alien" or as noted in popular-speak, an "illegal." A green card holder is not even an immigrant. He or she is officially a "resident alien." No green card holder argues with this title.

Illegal aliens are not immigrants

Immigration refers to the legal movement of people between one country and another. **So,** at the bottom of this big mess, the illegal aliens are breaking the law, and they are already criminals from the moment they step foot in this country without the proper documentation, and without benefit of a proper customs screening, green card, visa, passport, etc. And, by the way, they may also be terrorists.

Under the current law, most illegal migrants face a misdemeanor charge for violating provisions against crossing the border without authorization documents or not crossing at a border station. There are felony provisions in current law but they are applied only to those who are committing other crimes such as smuggling or drug dealing. However, if it is your second time caught, the crime is upgraded to a felony. This may change in that there has been a movement afoot in Congress within the last several years by the Republicans to make just one illegal entry a felony. This was once part of the big amnesty bill. It was one of the good features, which, overall, thankfully did not pass. .

In addition to those who cross the border without authorization, other foreign nationals who may enter legally may become illegal because they violate the terms of their visa or work arrangement. Both types of illegal immigrants are deportable under Immigration and Nationality Act Section 237 (a)(1)(B) which says: *"Any alien who is present in the United States in violation of this Act or any other law of the United States is deportable."* This law has been on the books for a long time. The government chooses in most cases not to enforce it. Our government, elected by the people, is the source of our problem. The Constitution does not give the government the "option" of enforcing laws. The government is duty bound to enforce the law.

The government now works for special interests and not Americans. Americans are losing many jobs because of government's lax enforcement of current laws. Groups like the TEA Party are fighting to establish a Congress and a new President who will represent Americans and not foreigners and special interests.

The borders of the U.S. are infinitely porous, with holes and tunnels and hiding places. The southern border is the big issue since it leaks like a broken faucet and the government makes very few plumbers available. Most Americans are in favor of a big wall or fence to keep those who don't belong on American soil from ever reaching this country. Just like your home, people must knock to enter. If they show up without knocking in your living room, you would be both afraid and enraged. The border is the entrance to all the homes of Americans and must be protected from unauthorized entry.

Though Mexico, Central America, and parts of South America may very well be hell holes with corrupt governments and lousy economies, the U.S. cannot continue to absorb so many oppressed masses of poor people at once. Check out this video at your next opportunity and ask yourself why Congress does not understand the extent of the problem?

Immigration_by_the_Numbers.mov - Google Video
http://video.google.com/videoplay?docid=4094926727128068265&q=roy+beck&hl=en
http://www.numbersusa.com/index

The real deal and the inconvenient truth

There are lots of arguments that the May Day demonstrators put forth about how essential illegal aliens are to America. That was lost on most American citizens who had a tough time digesting that an illegal alien had the right to make demands on American citizens. Americans reject categorically the notion that illegal immigrants are essential to the U.S. economy and they reject the George Bush oft-repeated notion that illegal aliens perform jobs Americans will not do. Barack Obama seems to have an even stronger position on illegals than Bush. He sees no problem. In fact, if he has his way, all border violators will be citizens much sooner than later. That is why we highlight the President in Chapter 1. .

An inconvenient truth is that most foreign nationals do not want to work in agriculture, picking berries, or whatever. They quickly move into the more lucrative services industry, or construction, or warehousing, or their apparent favorite, the meat-packing industry. There are plenty of Americans who could and would fill those jobs, but they are no longer available for Americans. The illegal does not mind lowering the average wage in construction or meatpacking or whatever, since the agricultural wage is so low, any wage is greater and there is always the fear that being illegal may cause deportation or incarceration. .

The big corporations and even the small contractors know a better deal when they see one and they find it far more profitable to employ easily exploitable illegal aliens who have little recourse but to accept the long hours and low wages, and no benefits. There is a high cost to US taxpayers for illegal workers and American businesses pay none of that load. Most Americans handily reject the current thought that illegal aliens give back to the U.S. more than they take—in income taxes and social security and in their labor.

Studies show that somebody working with falsified documents, committing identity theft is probably not paying income taxes. However, even if they are, they have committed a felony by falsifying their ID in order to pay those taxes. You and I would be in the Big House if it were us. Why there is a lax standard for foreigners and a tight standard for Americans is another source of public angst about illegal foreign nationals living in America.

Most Americans do not think that illegal immigrants should be permitted to get drivers licenses, or get free healthcare, or other public services including education. It is actually a joke that our government admits they have committed a crime and yet when they show up for a handout they are not immediately deported after receiving their needed services. Only those who abide by the law and play by the rules should be allowed access to services for which American tax dollars pay.

When you ask yourself how can this be solved, you are on your way to solving this scourge on America. Americans will only get their jobs back and have living wages and safer neighborhoods, when we replace Congress with living beings who are Americans first. We need to send the Congressional relics and any progressive President, such as George Bush and Barack Obama; back home to never serve again as they have served us poorly.

Chapter 7   A Riddle to Solve Who's Who in Illegal Immigration?

Be all that you can be---legally!

Desperation often breeds creativity. Though illegal aliens have the option of picking an ID packet up at a flea market in many cities for just upwards of $100.00, they have figured out an even better deal. Extended family or friends or just plain old profiteering legal foreign nationals can make their stay in America even nicer.

When and if an employer takes the fake ID and sends in the tax with their 941A employee report to SSA, the Social Security Administration knows that something is wrong because there is not a match. They do not contact INS or suggest the business be raided because they too have become capitalistic. If the product is selling, let the proceeds continue. Their product, "no identification provided" continues to give them the proceeds from those illegals, which have been forced to pretend that they are legal. So, the SSA just keeps the money... as if they don't work for us. I am not suggesting they give it back. But, maybe they can help us in the identification of bad companies and the deportation of those here illegally.

Borrow a friend's ID card!

Getting off the SSA for now, if you are illegal and you can borrow the card of a legal resident, you can get a better deal all around. Look for a family member or a green card holder who maybe goes back to Mexico for the winter or somebody who can't work anymore but needs to show earnings to stay in the country. The illegal becomes that person at work. It's magic. This is identity theft for sure but the person from whom it is stolen is complicit. They too benefit from the charade. Only the American worker and taxpayer suffer.

Since legal American residents can lose their green cards if they stay outside the country too long, for those who have returned to Mexico, it is very useful to have somebody working under their identity north of the border, adding to their social security contributions. Those who go back to Mexico also get the benefit of a few thousand dollars in legal US unemployment benefits while back in Mexico. Americans are so nice to accommodate such chicanery! It's like it isn't theft at all. But, if you or I did that, you know we would be in the hoosegow!

The benefits of undetectable theft

There is no greater motivator in life than survival. Consider a factory worker who immigrated as a child and is now an American citizen. The fake ID business is so good that she occasionally uses somebody else's identity to work. When the crop is poor and work is scarce, she chooses to work under somebody else's SSN. This way she can get U.S. unemployment benefits under her own name and number and add that to her take-home wages. There are other factories and canneries in which some folks work their own SSN and then also lend their number to somebody else working the fields or the packing plant. This might be called the "double-good-deal."

To the SSA, it looks like the person is working two jobs. This pads their earnings so they get a bigger income tax return and they get a bigger social security benefit. And the illegal alien they are assisting has a more solid ID than the one they could get from the flea market. This whole illegal alien problem is a web of intrigue, deceit, and small time corruption. Organized crime could not organize this any more efficiently.

But, it is not a good thing for US citizens or US workers. US workers are not privy to how to pull off these extra deals using ID cards. The illegal foreign nationals are the perpetrators who make this all happen for their benefit while our very own "honorable" representatives are fiddling and dithering.

Chapter 8   Many Come Across—Few Go Back

They like the jobs!

Mexico, for sure, is not the only country exporting people of Hispanic origin to the United States. However, Mexico is the largest country doing so. A combination of poor conditions in Mexico and a search for the American citizens' dream brings millions across the border every year. The path to the U.S. is thread bear with no vegetation while the return path to Mexico is lush, pure, and of proof set quality.

Estimates are that more than ten percent of Mexico's population already lives in the United States. I would suggest it is more like 35% as Mexico's population is barely over 110 million. A substantial portion of those here are illegal.

Popular reports suggest that there are about 12 to 20 million illegal aliens living in the U.S. but there are other estimates that bring this closer to 50 million. Considering that the agreed on number of foreign nationals coming into the US to live is 1 million to 3 million per year, it's a good thing that most of the visitors choose to be nice. In the 24 years since Ronald Reagan's unsuccessful amnesty program, the number of people is more like 36 million to 72 million on top of those that were made legal in 1986.

That's an awful lot of immigration for any one country to swallow and digest. But nobody's really noticed all the new people because the U.S. is so big. OK, I am kidding. You may recall that former El Presidente Jorge Arbusto (George Bush in Spanish) informed all American citizens that it is OK that illegals take the potential jobs of Americans since these foreign nationals do only the jobs that American's will not do. Barack Obama shares Bush's sentiments but he had been waiting until all the other controversies clear his desk before he takes a real stand and grants all illegals full amnesty. Now that there is a split Congress, Americans hope he does not get his way.

Jobs in America

Somehow those meat packing jobs and construction jobs must not be good enough for Americans. The fact is that nobody, foreign national or American citizen wants to be paid less than subsistence wages for picking grapes, berries, cherries, apples, or any other fruit or vegetable. That is admittedly hard work. On the other hand, if the foreign nationals were not there to do the work, perhaps the pay rate would be appropriate for the work level. To live and to live well, an American or a foreign national will do whatever work it takes. Think about the huge logging machines that clean out forests. Technology could be used to pick harvests with the same sensitivity that it could be used to change a baby's diaper. But those machines would cost more than illegal labor... at least initially. What is fair is always fair.

Chapter 9   The Illegal Road from Mexico –

A tough trip

When foreign nationals arrive illegally into the U.S. they are heroes by anybody's standards. Looking for what's best for them, they first cough up about $2500 in cash, which is a far better deal than the Chinese foreign nationals at $60,000 per person. Then they endure a hot day in the back alley slums called "stash houses," along with maybe 5,000 others waiting in similar plight 'til nightfall. In the pitch of dark, they submit to an adventure through the hills and the desert with their "coyote" (profiteers who help smuggle aliens into the US. And life may not be good, but they hope soon it may be better.

When they finally get to climb the fences and through some stroke of fate, they are on US soil, they feel like thousands of law enforcement agents, knowing they are coming, are waiting for them across a 2,000 + - mile frontier. There are not enough agents to keep them all out. About 1/3 are captured but 2/3 of the daily traffic across the whole border, which some estimate at about 20,000 or more, make it to safety in the U.S. away from the border guards and the poverty of native Mexico or South America.

Safety is not immediately available on the US side. The next 50 or 60 miles into Texas or Arizona or California are also tough because that's where all the American immigration police look for illegal foreign nationals and when they find them, they are supposed to be processed and deported. The next time caught, it is a felony but that doesn't seem to matter anyway. Lots of what illegal aliens do are felonies. US citizens would be locked up for the type of everyday crimes (ID-theft, etc.) but the U.S. government does not seem to care. The first order of business for the illegal foreign national, upon finding some sanctuary, is to get an American job.

America on the cheap

If you talk to some Mexican illegal foreign nationals, they will tell you that you do not have to pay $2,500 in all cases. You can do it on the cheap. It is just more dangerous. In all cases, however, you need a "coyote." Others say you get what you pay for. Some guys are cheaper because they don't pay off the police—not the American police but the Mexican police. The Mexican police have a number of different sources of income. Besides being paid by the Mexican government, they engage in dishonest activity both directly and indirectly. They are "independent contractors,' in that they take a nice cut of the coyotes' business in order to let them proceed unmolested.

The coyotes who give payoffs sometimes tip off these police about those that do not "give." The police get upset because they do not want to lose this underground "business," so they take those that they apprehend back to headquarters, and they beat them as a matter of procedure. This happens to everybody according to those who have been caught. Then, as an additional source of revenue that otherwise would have been lost, they steal whatever money the poor migrant might have before they are eventually released. And, they have not even made it to the US yet. So, as much as it is improper for these folks to take over the US and its jobs, nobody can deny that the successful illegal migrant is a brave caballero.

We made it!

To themselves and their friends, once they make it, they are indeed heroes. To the American citizen, they are illegal foreign nationals who ultimately have a negative impact on the lives of US Citizen's. They take US citizens' jobs and thus they help make wages lower and lower and lower. Yet, nobody, even Americans, blames them for trying. And because US Representatives are ambivalent, nobody sends them back. Unfortunately for Americans wanting decent paying jobs, this encourages more to come, and the job market for Americans shrinks further.

Those who are caught close to the border are finger-printed, photographed, and summarily deported after being held for a few hours. Their hearts are broken but they come back over another day. The strong hearted eventually make it. It is much easier for the illegal foreign national once well beyond the border, since they are free to move about the country. Unless they are criminals and even then, sometimes those that are caught in mainstream U.S. cities are released. As we learn as time goes by, even repeat criminals are released and not deported. No problemo.

There is a big exception. If the illegal foreign nationals are captured by Sheriff Joseph Arpaio, Maricopa County in Arizona, things are never as good. Sheriff Joe runs the largest prison in the southwest and he has no problem locking up anybody who breaks the law.

http://www.mcso.org/index.php?a=GetModule&mn=Sheriff_Bio

They Come from All Places South

Some in the U.S. may assume that these foreign nationals all come from Mexico within fifty miles or so of the border. This is not the whole truth. Many have caravanned thousands of miles. Many of them are from Mexico's drought stricken interior while others have fled the uninviting extremes of Central and South America. This latter group had already crossed into Mexico illegally and their journey is far more perilous than the native Mexicans.

The fact is that illegal aliens will do just about anything to have a job when they first arrive but later, they find they can do better and they too go for the American dream while in illegal status. That is why American jobs for low-skilled Americans are in such short supply. Sometimes, they show up on your worksite and sometimes they take your job. But most of the time they get a job someplace else so that when you lose your job, the job they did get, could have been available for you—but it is no longer available to any American.

It is not my intention to be cruel or insulting to the "permanent visitors" from other countries that have crossed our borders without our permission. SO, let me again define the term illegal alien. This term refers to foreign nationals who voluntarily violate U.S. Immigration and Nationality law and who settle in the United States. Though nobody in government (the people charged with caring) seems to care, it is a violation of the Immigration and Nationality Act, which is something we all should read.

Thus, according to American law, illegal foreign nationals are subject to deportation after a hearing with an immigration judge. It just doesn't happen anymore. That is because of President George Bush, and now Barack Obama and the Executive Branch of government fail to enforce the laws. Worse than that, they go out of their way to make it more difficult for Customs Officials and Immigration Officials to do their jobs effectively. Now in 2011, there is still no movement to better respect our laws. Like George Bush before him, for his own agenda, President Obama has opted to ignore the laws.

Thus, the hard work that an illegal alien expends on their journey to the US becomes payday for the illegal since the US government chooses to let them stay once they are here. Thus Americans lose and Foreigners win.

Chapter 10   Operation Wetback

One time consequences of illegal migration

Kelly Lytle Hernandez, writing in the Western Historical Quarterly, Winter, 2006 - "The Crimes and Consequences of Illegal Immigration: A Cross-Border Examination of Operation Wetback, 1943 to 1954" dug way back in history to enlighten us that the government was not always so lax as that run by the current set of "honorables."

The Operation Wetback campaign officially started in 1954 but the crackdown on mostly Mexican nationals started more than ten years before this. Nonetheless, during this campaign, at a time when the US was serious about its immigration policy (In other words it did not merely consist of a wink and a game of peek-a-boo), the border agents applied U.S. immigration law as intended. This particular campaign against Wetbacks resulted in the deportation of over one million persons, mostly Mexican nationals. The term "Wetbacks" now has politically incorrect connotations but back then it referred to those individuals crossing the Rio Grande in inner tubes—thus they came to the U.S. with a "wet back."

As the story goes, U. S. Attorney General Herbert Brownell ordered that in the summer of 1954, Operation Wetback would commence. It was to be an intensive and innovative law enforcement campaign designed to meet head-on the ever increasing number of illegal aliens crossing into the United States from Mexico.

To get this serious problem under control a team of 800 Border Patrol officers conducted raids through a number of southwestern states. Along with roadblocks, mass deportations, and a general no-bull strategy by the beginning of 1955, it paid off by having over one million persons, almost all Mexican nationals apprehended and deported.

The border patrol, was placed into action in the 1920's. They had been doing a fine job even before 1954. Year after year, the border patrol worked hard to detect and deport illegal aliens, which in these politically correct times are often referred to as undocumented workers. During the first half of the 20th century, the border patrol was able to forge good relations with Mexican officials and both countries worked in close collaboration to solve what was perceived to be a mutual problem. Together, U.S. and Mexican immigration officers came up with collaborative strategies that prevented and then punished the crime of illegal migration. Today, of course it is a game of US v them. But, even worse than that, the average citizen does not have the President or Congress on their side.

The US Border Patrol involved in migration control along the US - Mexico border were the primary force in the operation but as noted, the cross-border history of Operation Wetback reveals that Mexican officials actively participated in the planning and implementation of policing unsanctioned migration along the border. With substantially less people than is apparently needed today, they were able to do their jobs because both governments encouraged their efforts. Today's US border patrol seems to have both governments working against them.

What happened? If there was another ounce of cooperation today between Mexican and U.S. Officials, on illegal migration it would certainly be lonesome. There is cooperation on the "War on Drugs," but many of us see this war as long lost. At least stopping illegal migration has a chance.

Choose elected officials carefully

Don't blame it on the boss-a-nova. This is one of those times that if you "blame" George for it before 2009, you'd be 100% right. You would have to look no further. But George is now gone. Barack Obama has been in office long enough to take on the blame. We have met the enemy in this battle and unfortunately for us all, it is the US President and the Congress. Whatever new Congress we get in 2012, and whatever new President, it is critical that it is not pro open borders or things will get much worse.

There is little we can do until we can get rid of the progressive liberal Senators and the most far left President in American History. We did get a new House in 2010 and in 2012 let's also get a new President. We must do the same in the Senate. Watch your congressional candidates in 2012 as well as the Presidential candidates in 2012. If they look anything like Bush or Obama on the border, look someplace else. Please do not bring them to the White House.

The last believable thing that President George Bush said was right after 911 when he appeared to be much more genuine than he showed to be in practice. When he euphemistically referred to how he was going to capture and punish terrorists who operate against the US, you may recall one of his infamous lines was "we're going to smoke 'em out." I loved it. Americans loved it.

But Bush's real life was being a progressive disguised in conservative skin. He was disingenuous and very progressive on immigration. He and his whole family still are progressives so I hope there are no other Bush's in line for the Presidency. Though they may be conservative on a few issues, the Bush family, Jeb included, do not reflect the everyday American stance on illegal migration and border enforcement.

The Bushes now describe the rest of us as isolationists and nativists because we do not have the enlightened view of the "W." Laura Ingraham and many other real conservatives, look at Bush and his condescending view of regular Americans as progressive elitism at its finest. The reason the conservative agenda was forgotten for W. Bush's eight years is because he was a progressive.

This is our country, thankfully and we can get rid of all those who think their progressive agendas should dominate the thinking of the American public. Americans are no longer snookered. The sleeping giant is well awake and the days of illegals trumping citizens rights are just about over.

Ole "smoke em out" resonated well with the people and George Bush appeared to be an honest man. I am not exactly sure that smoking them out has worked or if it were even tried but, watching his posture on the border, it is very clear that he was never working for us.

The current administration appears to be following the Bush lead on illegal aliens. The problem will not be solved until the problem with the Presidency is solved. Keep John McCain out of the mix because he would be worse than Bush and Obama. He can't even tell himself the truth. American jobs for American workers and safe borders and no illegal migration are not platitudes. They are the absolute minimum for any national candidate to accept before they should have a chance for our votes.

Though most of us can admire the tenacity of a Wetback making it to safety, 50,000,000 Wetbacks is nothing short of an invasion, no matter how nice we would like to be. It is high time for another "Operation Wetback."

Chapter 11   Anchor Babies

The Children of Illegal Aliens

Have you ever heard the story of an Iowa corn farmer, played by Kevin Costner, who heard voices and with the help of James Earl Jones, Burt Lancaster, Amy Madigan, he interpreted the voices as a command to build a baseball diamond in his corn fields. The theme for the ball field was, "if you build it, they will come," referring to the defamed Chicago Black Sox of yesteryear. They did come and it was a great movie called *Field of Dreams*. Though movies are not real life, often they help us tune into the emotions that make people, in this case angels, do what they do.

Let's try these on: "If we invite them, they will come." "If we seem like we are inviting them, they will come." "If we have not closed our doors, they will come." If they know what is good for them, they will come." Since our leaders have a hard time doing what is good for its citizens, they will permit them to come and pay them for coming.

The biggest attraction, which can be thought of as the biggest invitation for an illegal foreign national is the opportunity to have your child born a US citizen. This is also one of the stickiest points on the illegal migration fight. The argument is that the fourteenth amendment implicitly permits hundreds of thousands of illegal aliens to become citizens of the United States automatically at birth. Those on the other side of the argument point out that the amendment relies on a well-known fraudulent Supreme Court interpretation

Section 1 of the amendment, whose liberal interpretation permits American-born children of drive-bys, passer-bys, drop-ins, fly-ins, as well as lost mothers, to be made citizens of the US by default is as follows:

The Fourteenth Amendment

Section 1. *All persons born or naturalized in the United States, and subject to the jurisdiction thereof, are citizens of the United States and of the State wherein they reside. No State shall make or enforce any law which shall abridge the privileges or immunities of citizens of the United States; nor shall any State deprive any person of life, liberty, or property, without due process of law; nor deny to any person within its jurisdiction the equal protection of the laws.*

Don't get depressed. Nothing is ever completely as it seems. Lawyers on both sides of the 14th amendment issue think they are right and though the illegal alien side has clearly been winning, there is good reason to believe US citizens will be able to have this lure for illegal aliens shut down soon through legislation or through the court system.

For Blacks only

Those against the broad liberal interpretation cite the history of the 14th Amendment and have put forward that its purpose was not to include a path to citizenry for Mexicans or Guatemalans but in fact was to finally cure a leftover problem of slavery for native born black Americans, and former slaves.

The intent of the 14th Amendment never applied in any way to illegal aliens. During Reconstruction, it was to undo the wrongs that had been perpetrated against black people for many years prior to the Civil War.

Together the Thirteenth, Fourteenth, and Fifteenth amendments to the United States Constitution, passed between 1865 and 1870, the five years immediately following the Civil War have been called the "Reconstruction Amendments." This was a big change to the Constitution sometimes referred to as the Civil War Amendments. They were intended to restructure the United States from a country that was (in Abraham Lincoln's words) "half slave and half free" to one in which the notion of liberty and freedom would be explicitly extended to the entire populace, including the former slaves and their descendants.

Quite frankly, it was also a time that women's suffrage was a hot topic, but the leaders did not want to take anything away from the purpose of uniting the country after slavery had been eradicated so they put off the notion of suffrage for later years. Anchor babies would never have made it to the list. The suffragettes were in line long before there were any anchor babies.

One major objective of the 14th Amendment was to reverse the Dred Scott Decision and provide that the freedom of black Americans and former slaves would never again be questioned by a less-friendly Congress. Thus, American-born children of American black citizens were to be citizens of the United States. Additionally, Section 2 of the Amendment was written in many ways to further the cause of black suffrage. This was never intended as a Hispanic or illegal alien moment in history. So, as slaves were made citizens, so also their children. There were no illegal foreign nationals included or intended.

14th Amendment solved a Black issue

It was a great moment of achievement for those people who had been quite literally, in bondage. Thus it was a black issue. As hard as the women suffragettes tried to include women's suffrage in the 15th Amendment, because this was for blacks and to make right the wrongs of slavery, women had to wait their turn and the black population had top priority for the framers of the amendment. Blacks and blacks alone were on the minds of the legislative leaders to make up as much as possible for the sin of slavery. Prior to that point, the white American majority would not provide to its black citizens the type of egalitarian way of life that they themselves had been denied only a few generations prior to the passage of this amendment.

To repeat, this was for blacks and only blacks or former slaves as a reading of all of the documentation dictates that one conclude. It was so blacks and former slaves no longer had to have an unequal citizenship. There was no intention for this amendment to apply to illegal foreign nationals or any invaders from other countries. It was about Americans—black Americans. For records purposes, we can safely say that there are no illegal foreign nationals today who were slaves or descendents of American slaves. If any such person exists, I would be the first to suggest they have earned their citizenship.

It thus follows that this was not intended for children born in the U.S. of two non-citizens having no right to citizenship since there was no intention in the 14th Amendment to make legal citizens of the American-born children of illegal parents. The intention in different words was so that states that prior to the 14th Amendment had the authority to grant or deny state citizenship, which automatically brought U.S. citizenship, no longer, would be able to deny blacks from being citizens of their states.

Instead of state citizenship providing U.S. Citizenship, the 14th Amendment revised the notion so that U.S. citizenship provided citizenship in all states. It helps to remember the context in which this Amendment, the 13th and the 15th were cast. It was right after the Dred Scott Decision and the Civil War and America was preparing the heart of its laws to assure that former slaves had the same rights as other Americans.

Naturalization and Citizenship

There are accounts of the intention of the court and the history of the Amendment that do more than just indicate that the Supreme Court majority in 1898 got it wrong intentionally. They ruled in favor of a Chinese person, in the case: United States v. Wong Kim Ark. At this time, the Chinese Exclusion Acts (Like slavery, not one of America's proud moments) denied citizenship to Chinese immigrants just for being Chinese. Moreover, by treaty, no Chinese subject in the United States could become a naturalized citizen.

Wong Kim Ark was born in San Francisco. At age 21, he returned to China to visit his parents who had previously resided in the United States for 20 years. When he returned to the United States, Wong was denied entry on the grounds that he was not a citizen.

The question before the court was "Could the government deny naturalization to persons born in the United States in violation of the Fourteenth Amendment?" The Conclusion of the court was "No." The government could not deny naturalization to anyone born in the United States. To reach this conclusion, many legal scholars believed that Justice Gray's tedious majority opinion were off base but not because he did not understand the law but because he did not personally like the law and chose not to follow it.

Over 100 years later Justice John Paul Stevens, the most senior Associate Justice of the current Supreme Court of the United States at the time, took issue with this inept attempt by the majority to rewrite the Constitution: "A refusal to consider reliable evidence of original intent in the Constitution is no more excusable than a judge's refusal to consider legislative intent." Stevens was an Associate Justice from December 19, 1975 until his retirement on June 29, 2010. To this, I might suggest that a case be brought to the court as soon a possible as we already have a clue as to its sentiments.

There is a phrase in the amendment under which those against anchor baby citizenship base their claim. Most scholars believe that this five word phrase, "subject to the jurisdiction thereof," in Section 1 was intended by the writers to exclude automatic citizenship from those American-born persons whose allegiance to the United States was not complete.

Since foreign born nationals owe allegiance to their native countries, their main jurisdiction is their home country. This is clearly the case of illegal aliens who are temporarily or unlawfully in the United States, solely because their native country has a claim of allegiance on the child. Thus, the completeness of the allegiance to the United States is prejudiced and logically rules out automatic citizenship.

I pledge allegiance

Immigration law says that any person wanting citizenship must renounce allegiance to any other country permanently and pledge allegiance to the US and then wait two years for any action on citizenship. Again, this rules out the idea of a pregnant woman in her eighth month coming across for the purpose of giving her child the greatest gift.

History also has noted that Aaron Sargent, a Representative from California during the 1870 period in which the Naturalization Act of 1870 was instituted, contended that the citizenship clause was not a de-facto right for aliens to obtain citizenship. The logic surrounding this claim was that no one came forward at the time to dispute his conclusion because it was clearly not the intent of the Amendment to grant a legal status to the offspring of those who had broken US law.

In summary, the premise behind the 14th Amendment, America's first and only constitutional birthright declaration, which occurred in the year 1866, was simply that all children born to parents who owed no foreign allegiance [such as citizenship in another country] was to be citizens of the United States. There was more written at that time such as Sec. 1992 of U.S. Revised Statutes which notes that the same Congress adopted as national law in the year 1866: "All persons born in the United States and not subject to any foreign power, excluding Indians not taxed, are declared to be citizens of the United States."

The law includes the phrase, "excluding Indians," but the 14th Amendment does not. However, since Indians on reservations at the time owed allegiance to their tribes, and they were permitted to do so by nature of their treaties, the framers believed that it was implicit that American Indians were not citizens per se because of such divided allegiance.

When the 14th Amendment was put forth and approved, it was not unanimous. But, the notion of illegal aliens having citizenship was not the prevailing question. Even the dissenting minority affirmed that the result of the citizenship clause was designed to ensure that all persons born within the United States were both citizens of the United States and the state in which they resided, provided they were not at the time subjects of any foreign power.

Sen. Lyman Trumbull at the time Congress was debating the National Birthright Law (same period in history as the 14th Amendment was constructed) re-stated during the drafting that it was the goal to "make citizens of everybody born in the United States "who owe allegiance to the United States." All of this debate puts substantially more meaning into sometimes mindless recitation of the pledge of allegiance. These are just not idle words and allegiance is critical to US citizenship in all respects.

Despite many considering the 14th amendment as "not settled law," Congress has not seen fit to make the situation better since the 1898 Supreme Court Decision. It will be up to the voting class to be sure that its Congress gets enough pressure to make sure that this becomes settled law and that it is settled for the common good of the United States, not for the good of those in Mexico or those who merely wish they were of the Unites States.

With the right of Initiative as an amendment to the U.S. Constitution, citizens would not have to wait for their representatives to do the right thing. Initiative, however, Is not the subject matter of this chapter. But, if Initiative were in the Constitution as an Amendment, the law could be written and submitted by a citizen or citizens. But, the right of Initiative is probably further away than the proper clarification of the rights of "anchor babies."

Citizenship Reform Act of 2005

There have been recent attempts to get this correct over time but they go no place and then disappear if not acted upon by the Congress in that session. A bill brought forth in 2005, for example, would have denied U.S. citizenship to children born to illegal immigrants.

Supporters said the bill, Citizenship Reform Act of 2005, which ultimately died from inaction, was intended to control the number of hopefuls who think they have an innate right to claim citizenship—and thus claim the rights and benefits that come with it. Liberal opponents said the measure was "extreme" and would be likely to face constitutional challenges. It will come again and this time it needs the same support as the full border fence which, though promised, has yet to arrive.

Some Citizen Opinions

There is substantial emotion about the idea of anchor babies being automatic citizens. For example, here are a few harsh posts from upset citizens. This post is crass indeed but it shows the emotion that exudes from the issue.

> ... birthright citizenship is a powerful impetus for so many of these illegals. Once they get their hands in the entitlement system, they keep breeding to ensure their spot is safe. They use this to supplement whatever salary they may have or they just lay around doing nothing. They ignore the very children who were created in order to have the opportunity to work the system. To remove this from amendment 14, would also cause their breeding frenzy to cease. They don't want to have to support their children; they want the taxpayer to do that.

Another post

> The United States Constitution was/is written for the Citizens of the United States and does NOT apply to Foreign National ILLEGAL aliens. The United States Constitution is NOT the World Constitution nor the Western Hemisphere Constitution nor the Americas Constitution and therefore does NOT apply to any other Foreign Nations or Foreign Nationals.

Here is an academic viewpoint:

> "The present guarantee under American law of automatic birthright citizenship to the children of illegal aliens can operate...as one more incentive to illegal migration and violation by nonimmigrant aliens already here. When this attraction is combined with the powerful lure of the expanded entitlements conferred upon citizen children and their families by the modern welfare state, the total incentive effect of birthright citizenship may well become significant."

Profs. Peter Schuck and Rogers Smith, "Consensual Citizenship," Chronicles, July 1992

Other Thoughts of American Citizens

Most U.S. citizens believe that the automatic citizen benefit for anchor babies, as they are called, is really not intended by our Constitution and they cannot understand why it is even being debated. If the parents are illegal so is the child. It's a matter of getting the correct interpretation of the 14th Amendment through the Congress or through the courts.

Meanwhile, each year, some estimates suggest as many as 400,000 women enter the United States illegally to give birth, knowing that their child will thus have U.S. citizenship. Their American-born children immediately qualify for a slew of federal, state, and local benefit programs. In addition, when the children turn 21, they can sponsor the immigration of other relatives, becoming the "anchor babies" for citizenship for an entire clan.

One might ask if there is any precedent to offering citizenship to illegal residents in a state. Back in colonial days, the English made citizens of all newborns born in England and the colonies and thus subjects of the Crown. Great Britain and Australia repealed such rights to anyone born on its soil in the 1980's after documenting abuses similar to those facing the United States today.

In June 2004, the Irish had the opportunity to vote on this matter in a national referendum and they opted to end automatic citizenship for any child born in Ireland regardless of the parents' residence status. Ireland thus was the last European Union member to permit pregnant foreigners to gain residence and welfare benefits as a result of birth in the country. It's high time for the U.S. to make this a priority.

What is the Meaning of Automatic Citizenship?

1. Higher Taxes: Undeniably at huge amounts to taxpayers

2. Disrespect for the rule of law: Congress rewards law-breakers and punishes those who get in line for legal citizenship

3. It means Congress must interpret the 14th amendment so as not to include the offspring of illegal aliens. According to the amendment itself, this is within Congress's prerogative.

Again, where are our lawmakers and our best lawyers on this issue? If an astute and highly competent American trial lawyer were to take a case to the Supreme Court, this dark period of American History would be over soon and there would be no illegitimately legal way for automatic citizenship. Short of that happening, the legislature must act swiftly.

Chapter 12   Build It or Not, They Will Come!

How can we get them to leave?

Intentional or not, there is trauma caused by illegal aliens to America's citizens. Illegal foreign nationals have affected many aspects of life in the United States of America. Though the citizens of the US do not agree 100% on the matter, better than 90% think that the problem should be solved without a Reagan style amnesty program. The illegal invaders clearly must be stopped at the borders and there is much support for shutting down the employers in the U.S. to solve the drain on taxpayers. This would create a natural attrition back to Mexico without the need for mass deportation. And, as a side benefit, Americans would again have a shot at low-level and entry-level jobs.

The right-wing radio talk show hosts have made a big deal about the illegality of illegal migration to the US. Nobody sees it as being good for US citizens or for illegal aliens. US Senators and Congressmen, however, appear impervious to the drain on the lives of American citizens. These elitist representatives are not caught in the cramped housing and the poor living conditions that have become part of everyday neighborhoods.

US laws do not apply to illegal aliens

For those of us not living in gated communities, we see that somehow the dwellings of illegal foreign nationals are not subject to the same building codes as ours are. The maximums for fire and health reasons, for example, which apply to the rest of the citizenry, do not apply to the foreign nationals. The double standard today has one standard of law enforcement for Americans and another standard of law enforcement for illegals. Yet, the laws are the same.

In Mexico, Americans do not get the benefit of the doubt. In America, Americans do not get the benefit of the doubt. For some reason, US laws do not apply if you are illegal, but if you are a citizen, you may go to jail if you do not comply. This double standard exacerbates an already tenuous situation.

It simply is not fair to Americans

With more children in school from people who do not contribute to the system and more people using social services, and of course healthcare services, the citizens are getting whacked with an ever increasing local tax burden so much so that many cannot endure the expense themselves. If you live in gated communities as most, if not all Senators and House members, you don't ever see it. You can be as munificent and benevolent as you like doling out taxpayer money for a "good cause." Dear Representative: "Put your own money up if you are so committed!"

If like most of US, you, the reader, live in the open neighborhoods of America, it does matter and it matters an awful lot. Additionally, if you are a laborer or a tradesperson - construction, plastering, roofing, it matters also because as the supply of illegal labor increases, you either cannot get work or you no longer can get a decent wage rate for your labor. In many industries, average wages continue to decrease and as your coworkers retire, they are most often replaced, or shall we say displaced by illegal foreign nationals. It is a big problem for Americans, which our representatives in their closed neighborhoods, do not face. When they convene in Washington, they forget who elected them and they take the other side.

When somebody crosses the U.S. border without invitation or prior approval, it's the same as if they came to your house for supper and you have no clue who they are or why they are there? Most may very well be good people but they committed a crime when they entered our country. All illegal immigrants are illegal aliens but not all illegal aliens are illegal immigrants. Nothing about their personhood is illegal. The illegal tag comes because they have broken the law of America by their mere presence in our country just like somebody breaks the law when they come into your house uninvited and they demand dinner.

Chapter 13   The Mexican Government Exports Its Poor

Government helps Mexicans make the border run

The preponderance of illegal aliens comes from Mexico and they are citizens of Mexico. Others come through Mexico to get to the US from the southern Americas. The Mexican Government assists its citizens on their trips to the US In fact, they create and print pamphlets for their citizens which encourage Mexican nationals to make the run for the border. The pamphlet makes sure that the soon-to-be illegal alien knows their rights once they arrive in America. The "Guide for the Mexican Migrant," (Figure 13-1) shows illegal aliens crossing the Rio Grande, traipsing through Arizona, and avoiding border patrol agents. Then, it instructs them on how to hide in American society so they are not caught.

Mexico does not have a neutral position in this issue. And the US takes no action against Mexico for this obvious abuse of our borders. The whole pamphlet is available for downloading at diggersrealm at the following URL: http://www.diggersrealm.com/mt/illegal_alien_comic_book/GuiaDelMigranteMexicano.pdf

Figure 13-1 Guide for the Mexican Migrant

On the Diggersrealm site, the pamphlet once could be gained through a link directly to the Mexican Government site but for apparent reasons, this is no longer a valid URL. The little book helps the illegal alien once in the U.S. in that it covers the rights they have if caught including the right to not disclose their immigration status. That is our law? Why is that our law? Who does it help? Regardless of your opinion, the illegal invader is not required by our laws to tell us their immigration status.

It is really outrageous that rather than actually trying to discourage illegal aliens from making the trip and therefore reducing the death toll in the desert, the Mexican government would rather create this colorful cartoon-like manual (sorry about the b/w look) that encourages and gives a sense of hope to those that may be contemplating the border hopping.

In case you were wondering, the U.S. has no such pamphlet for Americans. The U.S. has the same instructions for all Americans who wish to travel abroad at http://travel.state.gov/passport/passport_1738.html.

This site instructs US Citizens. It says that they must get a passport to visit a foreign country - even Canada and Mexico. The U.S. government does not tell its citizens, "Bon Voyage," go wherever you want; break whatever border laws you want; and don't worry, we'll help you get around the host country's laws with this pamphlet.

What are the rights of US Citizens who travel down into the southern hemisphere without documentation? How many ways can you say, "None?" If we were to evaluate the guidance in the pamphlets to Mexican migrants as an indicator of how nice we would be treated in Mexico, we could logically conclude that Mexico is a sweet, benign democratic country that is very interested in the desires of its citizens. But, their pamphlets don't govern their behavior towards us.

They put the pamphlets together to document our laws and ways of behaving here, so that their citizens know their rights. The fact is that the Mexican Government and Mexico in general does not treat illegal foreigners anywhere close to how they expect their citizens to be treated in the US. You would be at your own peril traveling to Mexico and there would be no welfare net or medical net to catch you if you happened to take a fall.

Mexico needs to pay for its own poor

There are many opinions brought forth on this issue by progressives in the American mainstream press, who always seem to have a better way to spend your money than you would choose yourself. Many opine that full and immediate legalization is the only fair, just, and humane thing for the US to do. After all, since our economy is dependent on the hard work of Mexicans and others who come north to make a better life for their families, undocumented workers must be allowed to come out of the shadows, etc. etc. We hear this ad nauseam.

President Reagan tried to be as kind as he could be when he advocated amnesty as the solution in 1986. Unfortunately, the documented result of his benevolent legislation shows that benevolence is not always the winning hand. Americans now know that Reagan amnesty, which was the greatest and the fairest, did not work and cannot work. The government of Mexico did not want it to work. They treat the US as fools. Otherwise, they would not choose to continually export their poor northward. They never send any billionaires or billions along with the poor?

Mexico plays the U.S. for a sucker and we are suckers for sure because the best men in America choose not to run for public office. So, the bottom of the US barrel, get elected, and then they get suckered by every two-bit country that ever looked for a handout. The handout of course was earned in the marketplace by the amazing American capitalists, not the US government that enjoys confiscating the good earnings of others.

W. C. Fields used to say, "Never give a sucker an even break and never smarten up a chump!" Mexico does neither and they have the United States right where they want us. A good US government would try to figure out how to legally collect some payback from Mexico for all of the costs we have borne.

The American government needs to make an accounts receivable call on the Mexican government and the rich citizens of Mexico, who choose not to take care of their own poor. These well-to-do Mexicans are very culpable and the U.S. needs to hold them accountable for a large proportion of the financial burden that the taxpayers of America have endured. The Americans making the sales call should be from the General Accounting Office and they should have a tractor trailer with them that contains the printed itemized bills of services rendered for Mexican citizens from providers all across the US. And they should stay until they collect the debt.

Rich Mexicans do not get taxed to help their own poor. They export their poor to America instead, where they expect U.S. taxpayers to pick up the tab. The best accountants in the US, working with the GAO need to calculate and present these bills for services to Mexico and our government should then work to collect them through the world court and whatever means it takes. Mexico is a rich country and they have a lot of resources including lots of oil. Only the less fortunate people in Mexico are poor. It's time for our southern neighbor to pay its due. If it took care of its own people, there would be no need for migration.

Mexico is a rich country

Mexico is by far the richest nation in Latin America when measured by GDP, and by a large margin. For years, the country has had the highest GDP in Latin America, far more than runner-up Brazil. Even on a per-capita basis, Mexico is second only to Argentina. Besides its fabulous shorelines, the country is rich in petroleum, silver, copper, gold, lead, zinc, natural gas, timber, etc. etc.

Reports show that half of all of Latin America's billionaires, 11 of 22, call Mexico their home. Recent statistics suggest that the country's tax revenues from the rich are about 14% of income v 28% for the US. Can this be why the Mexican government and the Mexican elites send their poor to the US? In this way, it is our high tax rates and our tax dollars that are spent to help the people from Mexico. It is a fact that the wealthy class in Mexico just do not want to pay taxes, so our government chooses to pay for them.

The United States of Mexico is a large country fashioned in many ways after the United States of America. It consists of thirty-one states and a federal district, its capital, Mexico City. It has a very lively economy, the 12th largest in the world by gross domestic product (GDP). Financially, it is on a par with countries like Canada and Spain, though admittedly income inequality is still very high. With such wonderful land and so much seacoast, Mexico has a lot to share and it needs to start sharing with its citizens rather than taking from the United States of America.

The prosperous in Mexico are perhaps even more clever in keeping their wealth than our own rich. For years, they figuratively present a bill to the US for their lack of support of their own people, and, as you know the US pays this bill. This must end and the money must be returned to US taxpayers.

Chapter 14   The Bush Border Legacy

Democrat and Republican elitists keep status quo

For his own reasons, George Bush defended, justified and facilitated an influx of illegal aliens into America and he steadfastly opted not to uphold the Constitution of the United States as executive officer of the country. How is that for a legacy? President Obama has followed his lead. Both immigration teams were instructed not to enforce the laws, not to close the borders, not to shut down the businesses that hire these people, and not to mess with the people living illegally in America.

Yet, the Mexican citizens in Mexico liked George Bush as much as Katie Couric and company liked him and then and like Sarah Palin now. The Mexicans showed ole Jorge that they hated him, though he still defends them. Maybe they were reading American Newspapers and watching MSNBC? When Bush visited Mexico, unlike the respect Fox and Calderon receive here, the Mexicans showed a deep animus for the American President.

They actually hated him and showed it. They protested his visit to Mexico quite vehemently burning U.S. flags and telling the President to "Go to hell!" There were a number of liberal Americans saying the same thing so the Mexican outrage was unnoticed. There was no sympathetic press coverage. The American press did not defend their American President because it was "Bush." That says something about the honesty of the press doesn't it? The irony is that Bush was fighting for the Mexicans and their plight in America, not for the American Citizens. He and the whole Bush family still are.

This was ironic in so many ways since Mr. Bush had done absolutely nothing to stop the Mexican invasion of the United States. The Mexicans undoubtedly had read the New York Times. It is also ironic that when Bush visited Mexico, the Mexicans could all come together to protest his visit and they can hold protests in the United States every May. However, these same people refuse to come together to protest their own corrupt government. What's that all about?

George Bush could have made it real tough on these folks and that is what Americans actually expected their President to do. Bush simply chose not to enforce the law. Thanks to George Bush, in fact, Mexicans already had most of the notions for which they continued to protest. He never took any real action to control our border. He certainly had the authority for eight years to clean up the mess. He simply chose not to take the side of the illegal foreigner nationals and he fooled a lot of us along the way.

Nobody can say the President failed in his attempts to clean up the border in those eight years. He did not fail at it. He just did not do it. In fact, during the Bush years, the number of raids on businesses hiring illegal foreign nationals and deportations went down substantially compared with even the Clinton years. The numbers are again less with Obama at the helm. If Obama and Bush were co-presidents, things would be the same, and neither man would be displeased.

If George Bush had taken a stance on illegal immigration and its impact on American life, his overall legacy could have been more positive and perhaps the Republicans would have been assured a President in 2008. Maybe not! But, by deploying a pro-Mexican strategy on the border, Bush won no real American points and no American hearts.

And those politicians in the great six-year majority enjoyed by Republicans, who did not criticize Bush's perverse stance, in which Mexicans had more rights than U.S. Citizens, will be remembered for a long time to come in the history books and in future elections. In fact, in 2006, the Democrats took care of most of the Republicans. Disgusted Americans gave the Democrats a majority in both Houses. Only now are Republicans recovering somewhat.

"No more George Bush type pandering to illegal aliens" is one of the clear messages from the Republican loss. Even with a pro-Mexican strategy, the irony is that Mr. Bush still was not loved south of the border, nor was he a favorite of the northern press. And, it does not look like that will change now that he's been back in Crawford for awhile and he speaks more openly as a progressive. The W's winning days are over. Let's just put a big X over that W and hope the Bush days are long gone.

Chapter 15   The Corporate Tab for Illegal Workers

Put together a tab for the expense of illegals

Who or what is responsible for the increase in crimes and gangs, the terrorizing and downgrading of once respectable neighborhoods? Where did all this "hell" come from? The biggest perpetrators in illegal immigration are business owners who take advantage of this sorry lot of impoverished masses for their own gain. The excessive number of poor illegal aliens takes its toll on the alien community as well as American society in general.

The progressives in government help businesses by not enforcing the laws. They live, protected in their gated communities and are unaffected by the trauma they help create or they would know from their own pain, the causatum of their poor leadership. There are big money damages for all that has been taken from the treasuries at all levels of government in the US to assist the needy illegal aliens. US citizens pay a lot of taxes for to give illegal foreign nationals their free rides. The people deserve to have this expense reimbursed to the treasury. The payee should be the corporate elites and the businesses who have gained by pocketing their illegal profits.

One of many solutions to the problem

What should the illegal alien get from these oppressive corporations and other businesses who have exploited them for increased profits? There are a few charitable options. At a minimum, they should get an all expenses paid safe trip home from their corporate sponsors and a small stipend for food. The full cost of this should be paid from the profiteering U.S. corporations and to the extent it can be collected, from the Mexican Government. The toll is large and once the toll is on the Tab, it then needs to be paid.

Add it up and collect it

It all needs to be added to the totals calculated by the accountants and presented for payment. The Citizens of the United States deserve better from our representative government than permission to fire Americans and hire illegals. It is the business owners and corporations in the US who helped sections of America become third-world nations. These companies enticed illegal aliens to work for peanuts to fatten their bulging wallets. The drain on America needs to be tabulated and presented to the perpetrators of this chicanery. It is their expense, not mine, not yours, not my children's, and not your children's.

I would also suggest fines to these corporations over and above the sum of (1) cost to the taxpayer for services rendered in social services for the illegal alien employee and his family - past and future 'til problem resolution, the (2) cost for job displacement that can be claimed by a displaced American job holder, (3) the administrative cost of the full program and (4) the sponsorship cost, safe return money, and the small stipend for each alien to be able to go back to Mexico to start over the right way. There should be no free ride for the profiteering corporations and even small businesses who thumbed their nose at Americans to make a better buck.

The GAO accountants or the CBO Accountants, whoever is deemed more honest by a collection of citizens, maybe the TEA party accountants, need to put a price per head based on estimated numbers of illegal aliens and children of illegal aliens born in this country. This price would include all four cost components as well as some penalty of varying appropriate sizes that would be assessed based on how forthright the corporation is in providing the information on its current and past illegal alien population. If the corporations passed the illegal wealth on to the stockholders, then the accountants can figure how much needs to be returned by the stockholders for the malfeasance of the corporations they own.

Once such an equity law is passed or even before, within a specified short period, businesses that have employed illegal aliens would be required to send a registered letter to the immigration department outlining their violations in terms of the number of past and present illegal aliens in their workforce. Following this, businesses would have another longer period (perhaps six months or a year) to provide the specific names and sums paid (over the table and under the table) for the services of potentially illegal aliens. A business tax should also be added to the tab for the taxes that would have been paid if the wages were to have gone to Americans. This too needs to be collected.

Again, the sooner and the more forthright the disclosure, the lower the fine should be. Moreover, during this period of reconciliation, the corporation and its officers may get amnesty from prosecution for all *under the table* payments that it made for the past twenty or thirty years. Any business not providing full disclosure before the specified final date should pay a huge fine and the company would be subject to a fine-tooth audit by the U.S. government. If we don't trust government entities to perform the audit then let our representatives commission the TEA party or a faith based organization or any certifiably honest organization to do the audit.

These businesses that have profited by using illegal labor instead of American employees should pay the full expense of that audit. Additionally, without full-disclosure, its officers would not automatically receive amnesty from prosecution.

More than likely, under all circumstances, we will need to vote in all fresh faces in Congress to get this done. The 112th Congress has yet to prove its worth but the new members seem to be doing well for the people. The 111th Congress did not even know how corrupt it was or it would not have shown its face in public. No kudos, just shame on the 111th US Congress, the worst in American history.

So that companies would not go out of business from the burden of this law, auditors could assess the ability to pay and make payment terms accordingly. No fines or fees would come from operating income so the firm would be able to operate unencumbered by a cash shortage. The payment would come from after-tax undistributed profits. The current shareholders would not receive their normal dividends -- as much as 75% of such proceeds would go to the government (only if the government were trusted) to pay the TAB. The government itself, untrustworthy as it is now known, must be enjoined from spending this on anything other than unemployment compensation or debt reduction. No redistributive programs for new found poor should be permitted by the citizenry.

I would also suggest that companies and shareholders be liable for up to twenty years for past already distributed profits since these profits came directly from the backs of illegal aliens. For twenty or more years the progressive owners of commerce dumped the expense of social care for their labor arbitrage onto the American taxpayer, thinking it was free. This plan places the burden of repayment on the very people in the corporation, the progressive ownership who feigned compassion for illegal aliens while their goals were to exploit them to the point of slavery and indentured servitude.

Too many progressives, who regularly hire cheap and illegal labor, benefit from the toil of illegal aliens for us to honestly believe they are for the rights of the little guy. These progressives in essence benefitted from slave labor. Yet, they would have you believe that it was not them but some other wealthy class in the US doing the dirt. At a minimum, these progressives should be receiving far fewer dividends. To exclude small time IRAs from the mix, special considerations can be made so that it is not the almost poor who are paying this TAB back to themselves. Administrative costs plus enforcement costs should be paid on an ongoing basis by the corporations and their dividend elite—the many progressive rich that benefited from the government largesse.

Additionally if we could find a few legislators, since they surely are involved in this chicanery, who's net worth increased more than their congressional salaries, there would be another source of repayment to the American people.

Payback is a bitch!

Chapter 16   Illegal Labor—Spiritual / Humanitarian Side

Desperate and Destitute people arriving daily

There are spiritual / humanitarian as well as economic reasons why the progressives in America feel that anybody who wishes to enjoy the American Dream should be enabled and empowered to do so - on us. On the spiritual side, even if they hop the border, swim across, or overstay on an expired visa, progressive Americans think that these poor souls, mostly from south of the border, must have their burdens lightened by the promise of amnesty with no threat of deportation. It's good for their spirits.

It would appear that their concern for these mostly desperate and destitute people, who travelled through dangerous byways to the ultimate freedom, has no limitations as long as somebody else pays the bill. Progressives call for the continual nurturing of these unwanted foreign visitors even if they may present a burden on the rest of Americans. For progressives, the borders are always open and if an illegal foreign national makes it here, they believe the illegal alien should immediately reap the benefits of the American Dream. For progressives, it is perfectly OK that these many benefits doled out to the illegal foreign nationals be paid for by taxpaying Americans. Thus, in a world order designed by progressives, the rights of the illegal foreign nationals trump those of average American citizens.

Those of us who are against unrestricted illegal immigration know that the foreign national who illegally enters this country is trying to better him or herself. We know they are poor and needy but that does not give them the right to anything in America. Yes, we'd like them to feel better but we'd like them to get that good feeling in their own homes in their own countries.

Both the left and the right in America should agree that there is no "right" to migrate if it means trespassing on someone else's property. The open borders crowds, who mostly are lefties, unfortunately don't get it. They imply that anybody who does not think exactly like them is a racist, a xenophobe, a bigot, or some other uncomplimentary labeled term. Moreover, those who do not agree cannot possibly be humanitarians, who actually care about the poor souls who are now in our midst.

Just because many Americans are for restrictions on illegal immigration does not mean that such proponents feel no compassion and want to close the borders and completely end all forms of immigration. Americans do have compassion for the poor in Mexico and other poor countries south of the border but we also have a right also to be concerned about the lack of assimilation, the gangs, the dope dealers, and the cost of education, social services and health for illegal foreign nationals. There are poor in all countries and this does not motivate Americans to agree to remake America into Ireland, Ethiopia, Sicily, Darfur, Bangladesh, Norway, or any other country. The same applies equally to Mexico.

Speaking of averages, the average Mexican wage is about $4.50 a day, payable in Pesos. That's a little less than 60 Pesos a day. Those in the agricultural industry in Mexico make even less. Even China does better at about 40 RMB per day = $5.50. But both are low compared to American standards. So, for any progressive that wants to be a humanitarian, the best way is to help these people where they live, not force them into a life of poverty. Progressives should feel free to take out their own wallets and help whoever they wish, but they have no right to wish the souls of 50 million people on their fellow Americans.

US wages are top flight compared to $4.50 per day. These compare with $7.25 per hour in the US. In 2010 Mexico raised the minimum wage by 4.85 percent, which resulted in the fourth year of salary increases being outstripped by Mexican inflation. With the minimum wage in the US being about twelve times that of Mexico, it is no wonder the US is a magnet for migrations and it is no wonder why the incoming illegal worker does not complain. It is also no wonder why more and more Chinese also make the expensive escape trip to America, but perhaps the Chinese are really seeking freedom. At least for now, the US has lots of that.

On the Spiritual Side, Who Cares?

Greedy, profit hungry American employers are more than happy to take advantage of the situation, offering the long-suffering Mexican a better opportunity than in Mexico but a deficient wage nonetheless. Nobody really cares about what this does to the victim.

A byproduct of the greed of American employers is that the Americans who once received a living wage from such companies can no longer even get those jobs. Many economists have formally studied the matter. The results are conclusive. And, so, the director of labor market studies at Northeastern University in Boston argues confidently that the large supply of illegal aliens has displaced low-skilled U.S.-born workers, particularly the young and the poor, from what have been reasonable jobs. So, a lot of Americans have been affected economically as well as spiritually by the spread of illegal labor.

A virtually unlimited supply of cheap labor

With the supply of illegal immigrants so large, businesses have unprecedented access to the illegal workforce and they love it. It is much easier for companies to have indentured servants, a form of slave labor, who complain about nothing, than to hire Americans and be forced to comply with US labor laws. The US unemployment rate is currently 9.6%. Most good manufacturing and service jobs have gone offshore, and others are quickly following. High tech jobs are being taken by legal aliens with H-1B visas, who either become citizens or go on to become illegal laborers. They rarely return to their countries of origin. Meanwhile low tech jobs are being done by illegal aliens at a rate of 6 to 1. Yet, still the Democrats wonder what happened to them in the last election. Jobs! Jobs! Jobs!

While an individual may be able to survive on such meager wages ($4.50 per day) in Mexico, it becomes more difficult for those with families to have a life. With such low wages, about 40% of the Mexican population is below the poverty line. Though unemployment is about 4% in Mexico, it is estimated that more than one quarter of those working are underemployed.

The pot at the end of the rainbow

Most illegals, which enter the US, either travel through Mexico or are in fact from Mexico. It is a harrowing experience, both dangerous and frightening. To reach America is a great accomplishment for an illegal alien. Progressives want these new "immigrants" to think of their arrival as having reached the pot at the end of the rainbow. The spirits of the exploited should be thrilled that they have arrived.

Progressives see no problem with government forcing Americans to share their "limitless" bounty with those new arrivals, illegal though they may be, to help these intruders enjoy the American dream. They may very well have good intentions but the virtual "Welcome Signs" they erect do not please the vast majority of Americans who think Mexico, not the US, is the right place for Mexicans to live. Mexico, a rich nation by most modern standards, should take care of its own.

In 2004, quite a few years ago, on CNN, the Lou Dobbs show shined a big light on Mexican wealth. With a twelve percent average tax rate compared to the US at 26%, the Mexican rich simply like to keep their money rather than take care of their own poor. The low tax rates and the push of the poor onto American taxpayers enable them to do just that.

In the 2004 show, Professor Grayson, of William and Mary College noted the following about Mexico:

> "There is a small economic elite who live like maharajas, and there's a political elite that protects them. Our border provides an escape valve which really lets the Mexican political and economic elite off the hook in terms of providing opportunities for their own people."

In the current recession, the whole world is aware that the pot of gold in the US is depleted. We're using other country's gold to pay our bills. For the time being at least, besides the gold, even the rainbow and the pot are gone as the US economy is now burdened by almost $5 trillion in new Obamadebt, from the last two plus years alone. Some economists suggest that the once mighty United States is approaching bankruptcy. What is to blame for the US decline? Some on the left would scoff if I suggested that illegal immigration is a major contributor. Can progressive policies, such as unrestricted illegal immigration and government redistributive give-aways, bailouts, and the stimulus du jour be a big part of the reason? How about an underground economy in which illegal foreign nationals pay no income taxes? How about a new breed of Americans making half of the inflation-adjusted income their forefathers earned?

Regular Americans see this as a time to tighten their belts, not to be welcoming new house guests. Progressive Democrats and progressive Republicans, however remain undaunted. They see no reason why beleaguered Americans should not tighten even further to continue to be able to afford the everyday influx of illegal foreign nationals into American society.

Progressives as a rule want to help everybody who is down. Downtrodden Mexicans and others here illegally are just one more cause in the bag of progressive causes. Though this is admirable, a closer look would show it is not altruistic. Progressives, which I have researched, from President Barack Obama to Vice President Joseph Biden do not match their propensity to help the poor with the kind of real charity that begins at home. In other words, their charitable contributions as a percentage of disposable income do not indicate a strong desire to share their personal bounty. It is in fact, quite the opposite. The charitable contributions of hard-line progressives such as the two noted above are paltry at best.

Therefore, their means of helping illegal aliens and helping their other causes is to use other people's money. That means yours or mine, but not theirs. Since the progressives have more or less controlled the government for the last twenty years, it has been very convenient for them to use their power of taxation to aid their causes. Many an illegal alien has benefitted from their largesse.

So, progressives use a general redistributive Robin Hood scheme to take from the rich and give to the poor. However, in the case of illegal foreign nationals, in many ways, they are taking from the American poor and giving to the illegal poor. One would think that with such motives as helping others through the god of government, the progressives would be the leaders in paying taxes for the good of their policies. Not hardly! Instead, they limit their personal giving by using the finest accountants to tune their tax returns to avoid paying even their fair share. So, their redistributive schemes to help illegal Mexicans and others are built on the government's ability to tax regular people, not on the joy they receive from giving themselves.

As a rule, illegal foreign nationals in America come here poor and they stay at a major disadvantage all their working lives. Their abject refusal to learn English assures a life of poverty and that is another reason why progressives do not insist they learn the language. For their own selfish business interests, while anticipating the societal revolution, progressives need a lower, lower-class than simply poor Americans, to further their own financial and societal gain.

Despite the burden on the American people, there is an innate sense of spiritual goodness in just about all Americans. Americans wish the plight of the illegals was less onerous. Therefore, when the American pot appeared to be full and swelling over, most Americans did not begrudge just a few illegal foreign nationals getting some help from our government. Now that illegal immigration is out-of-control, with as many as 50 million illegal foreign nationals lurking in the shadows, Americans are re-thinking the wisdom of doing anything that looks like an invitation to anybody to illegally resettle in America.

Unfortunately, nothing seems enough for the progressives in the US. By not enforcing security at our borders, the progressive leaders in our government welcome more and more illegal foreign nationals into the country without so much as asking for an ounce of documentation or allegiance in return. Consequently, there are many pockets of ethnicity in this country that are fully devoid of patriotism for the US. Their allegiance is with their home countries and they would have no problem being the majority "race" and language in the US.

Figure 16-1 The desire to be the majority

Even in these tough times, progressives still think it is good that US citizens give up their small stake in America and in many cases their jobs to help foreign born illegal nationals. Many progressives, though they are American citizens themselves, see little honor in America and they are not very proud to be American. They do not care very much about America's own citizens. They find little redeeming value in the notion of patriotism and love of country. So, they do not differentiate illegal and legal immigrants from American citizens.

Their overarching goal is for those who live in America illegally to become full citizens of the US without ever having to swear allegiance to the US or even learn its language. This is not the legacy of Ellis Island immigrants and so there is much resistance from regular Americans to this notion called amnesty. In essence, today's progressives have taken the wrong side in the battle of whether the limited American dream is to be lived by its citizens or the illegal foreign nationals living within the US borders.

When our grandparents came to this country they had to have a complete medical screening, and many immigrants at the time were held in quarantine on Ellis Island. It was also mandatory that every immigrant have a working use of the English language. Eventually all immigrants had to swear an oath to become citizens. Nowadays, these huge groups of illegal foreign nationals secretly residing in our country with a sworn allegiance to another country do not serve America or Americans very well. And, the progressives, who still do not like America, are fine with that.

Many ordinary citizens use the term invasion to describe the mass migration to the US from Mexico and thus the people in the invasion are dubbed as invaders or illegal invaders. A lot of good things happened when the potential European immigrant of the past several centuries stopped at the gates to be checked out. This is sorely missing regarding illegal immigration today. These "invaders" come unannounced and are subject to no screening. Additionally, they have no deep desire to become American.

If the rite of citizenship is what they need for free passage to the American dream, that is OK and for such a "gift," they will go through the motions for sure. But by and large, the people coming here to work are not interested in becoming United States citizens. In fact, their working here is often temporary by design so that they can afford things back home such as financing the completion of their villas in Mexico.

There is no question that it is much easier to be poor in the US, with active social services than poor in Mexico with no such help. No matter what you have been told, illegal foreign nationals make ample use of our welfare, food stamps, medical systems, and free education systems. Of course, with incentives like this, the American dream is realized very quickly by the illegal class. But their dream creates chaos for others, and overall it raises nobody's spirits.

English, Please!

A very big problem among other big problems is that there is too much diversity among Americans already and Mexicans and other invaders of the last 50 years or so do not seem to assimilate well. Thus each new group of illegal aliens creates more diversity. So, we get another set of different cultures pouring across our porous borders and people mostly unwilling to learn simple English.

Meanwhile the American people as taxpayers foot the bill so that our progressive government can cater to a non-English speaking class of people. This is not good for America. It is important that our country as any sovereign nation have a common language and culture in order to be cohesive. We call this assimilation and for years it has worked quite well until the progressives began to tout difference instead of sameness. After permission, assimilation work has always been done in the US "melting pot" with the product being ready for citizenship in several years after arrival. Those were the days.

The net effect then of this new group of illegal workers into the American mainstream is that nobody is really happy at the bottom. The illegal is at the bottom and the newly unemployed Americans are at the bottom. A broke, but seemingly benevolent US government cannot take care of anybody at the spiritual level, though all basic needs for all illegal aliens are paid by those Americans fortunate enough to still be employed.

Chapter 17 Illegal Workers: The Economic Side

A boost with reduced opportunities for Americans

Economically, small and even larger business owners continue to sweat over Congressional debates on illegal immigration because they have a big stake in the outcome. They fear a future without "guest workers." To serve their ends, businesses as well as their progressive allies in the government propagate the big lie that there are jobs that Americans "just won't do." This George W. Bush era phrase turns the stomachs of most able-bodied citizens as today's Americans are no longer easily fooled by their agenda-laden, propaganda-filled progressive-dominated government. By having posited the notion that Americans won't work, these businesses benefit handily from the lie. It gives them the right excuse to raise their profits by firing native-born American workers and hiring illegal workers for substantially less pay.

Economists love this influx of cheap labor since it is "good for the economy." They admit that for the last decade about 85.5 of every 100 new workers were "new immigrants" and most of these were and continue to be illegal. The new immigrants most often displace young workers, American citizens, and prevent American teenagers from ever becoming employed. They stand in the way of Americans getting entry-level jobs in most industries. Americans are not shut out from trying. They can try to get an entry level job even if they are not Hispanic and illegal or Latino and illegal, but chances of success are slim to none.

On the positive side, this does help the illegal immigrant meet their financial needs in an otherwise mostly unfriendly world of American citizens, many of whom now see them as invaders. The progressives, however, say that they are not invaders. They say they are just good people looking for a good life. Unlike Ellis Island "immigrants," who looked to become Americans while going after the American dream, average illegal foreign nationals today voluntarily segregate themselves from everyday Americans. They seem to prefer to live together with other illegals forming a mini-Mexico wherever they go.

In this light, the illegals, as a rule, do not want anything American, other than American money. As a rule, as noted in previous chapters, they have no plan to learn English or to participate in anything else American. Despite this, the progressives see no problem with illegal foreign nationals taking the American dream from native-born Americans and making it their own.

Economists will tell us that we cannot do without the illegal aliens who now hold many American jobs. Many Americans however, would like to give it a shot. Economists note that without these illegal workers, America would have a decline in its labor force of 3 to 4 percent and that would hurt the country. I see it differently. A decline of 3 or 4 percentage points would get the unemployment rate down to about 6%, which is far better than 9.6%.

Rather than acknowledge the dot com bubble, economists still prefer to credit the influx of illegal aliens as one of the prime reasons that the country grew as much as it did in the '90s. To rub it in to American workers, they suggest that this great economic boon came directly from the hard work of illegal immigrants.

Some economists take this notion further and they say that if illegal workers were not available in the US, many jobs would not be done at all. They insist that native-born American workers, wanting higher wages for the same work done cheaply by illegal labor, would rather sit on their duffs than help American businesses add to their success. I think that is stretching it a bit but it is true that Americans do demand a living wage. If illegal Mexicans demanded a living wage, perhaps there would not be as many jobs held by illegal foreign nationals, and perhaps more Americans would be employed.

For now, however, let's continue discussing the bright side of illegal immigration. It certainly does enrich the businesses that cheat their fellow Americans by hiring illegal workers. The rub to Americans of course is that the economists want you to imagine a world without fruits or vegetables as if lazy American workers would stand idly by and let the crops rot on the vine. Though not true, this type of progressive propaganda helps justify that businesses hire illegal workers over Americans.

Progressives still like to cite a 2004 story that makes American workers look like slugs compared to hard-working Mexicans. This is the story of the lettuce shortage of 2004. The Bush Administration instituted a crackdown on illegal immigration in 2004 that sent a lot of illegals packing for south of the border. Knowing George Bush's record on illegal workers, this must have been accidental or perhaps it was a mistake.

Since there was still lettuce to be picked in the fields, the economists blame the shortage of illegal workers as the reason why the lettuce crop in the Western United States was left unpicked. The reported loss for this bad stroke of luck for companies depending on illegal aliens was about $1 billion. Many growers complained that they had to leave their fields un-harvested, and ultimately, to rot.

The farm capitalists still argue that to hire Americans to do this work would have been too costly as wages would have needed to be raised substantially for it to be worth it for US native-born workers to do the work. So, the broad-minded business farmers decided that it would be less of a loss over time if they left their lettuce crops to rot. Rather than risk higher wages, the farmers let the crops rot. It was not the American worker who brought this shortage on the country. It was the greedy corporatist seeking to suppress wages. Once they raised the rates for Americans to pick the crops, they felt that the wages would have to remain high. So, for the farmers, destroying the crops by letting them rot was their best long-term economic choice.

The economists blame the workers for this so you see there is a major disconnect between fact and fiction. Why not just pay a living wage?

Is Illegal immigration a solution for something?

Is illegal immigration a solution for a problem or is it a problem itself? Few economists will argue with the concept that the economy is stronger because of the presence of this ready-made low-cost labor force. For example, the Bureau of Labor Statistics estimates that 22 percent of all construction workers are foreign born. Though many think that illegal workers are picking beans and fruits all day, they in fact now do the work Americans love to do. Construction workers have always been paid well. Not so anymore. There are 2.4 million illegal immigrants working in the construction sector in the US today. Beans and apples and berries have lost out to framing, drywall, and roofing, Construction is the largest source of jobs for illegal labor. So, yes, illegal immigration is a solution and a godsend for companies who want to pay cheap labor rates. But, it is a problem for the rest of us.

It would be impossible for any American to disagree with the fact that the US owes its standard of living to some of the unfair and sometimes illegal practices of many employers. The price of fruits, vegetables and berries, even chicken, ham, hot dogs, and steaks, etc. is reasonably low in the US because many in the farming and meatpacking business use illegal workers. Exactly how much of the savings is passed on, however, is not clear.

Business has gotten good at the proverbial "ripoff"

Some farm workers have permits of sorts, both active and expired, but almost always unverified. Some have no work permits at all but are favored by what I heard the other day called agriculture's own, "don't ask don't tell" program. Even progressives are not messing with this program. It is these workers who help harvest American crops and who help their employers make larger and larger profits. These profits so far at least have not been passed on to the consumer in any considerable way. If they were, homes would be substantially cheaper, not just a few thousand dollars less, and the impact on the cost of produce would be a lot more than just a few cents a pound.

The bottom line is that the big winners in the illegal worker game are the employers. Absent from the winners' circle is the American worker who loses his job to an illegal worker. Absent also is the illegal worker who gets the job. Finally, there is no room in the winners' circle for the American consumer who still pays top dollar for products made by illegal, poorly-compensated workers. To borrow a term from the 1960's, the whole charade is a big "ripoff." Bernie Madoff would have fit in well with those who perpetrate this scheme on the livelihood of American workers and on the backs of illegal workers.

The many defenders of illegal immigration continue to press that the jobs noted above must be performed by "undocumented workers," simply because "no one else will do them." Since Americans had been doing this work for centuries before the illegal alien arrived on the scene in recent years, you know this argument is faulty. There is a partial truth however to the statement but the whole idea amounts to a big lie. The full truth is that there are many native-born Americans and other citizens who will do the same job for similar pay. More and more American employers simply prefer to hire illegal workers rather than Americans because it is more convenient. Why is this?

The "new" best worker cannot read or write or "complain."

Those employers who use undocumented workers have what might be called "ideal workers," and are in no hurry to get rid of them. In essence they have indentured servants who are under their full control. What employer in his right mind would get rid of someone who works hard, needs no health coverage, takes any pay amount and smiles, never to complain to any government agency about anything -- including unsafe work conditions?

Illegal workers can be used and misused by employers. Nobody knows and nobody cares-- even those loveable progressives that we have been discussing. Perhaps the progressives who suggest there are spiritual and humanitarian reasons for supporting amnesty really have an economic agenda? The bottom line is that employers can bend, spindle, and mutilate illegal foreign nationals with impunity. They still work after abuse. They come without all the hassle of those pesky labor laws and minimum wage issues associated with real Americans. The deal is so tempting that otherwise good men and women are more than willing to break the law to hire them.

If all the workers in America, in all industries were paid at least the minimum wage, were provided health care and were permitted to disclose unfair work practices, employers argue that costs borne by these industries would sky rocket and their precious profit margins would fall. This may or may not be true -- just like Americans won't do certain kinds of work is not true. There is always more to the story.

Regardless, as we discussed in Chapter 15, if the apportioned social cost of the benefits that illegal workers enjoy in the US were added to the employers' total tax bill, the proposition would not look so favorable to risk getting thrown in the slammer. Keep in mind please that hiring an illegal worker is illegal. In the US, illegal means against the law, but that does not seem to matter when there is no enforcement.

If all American workers existed merely to help employers become billionaires, clearly this would be the time for many regular American workers to step down from their jobs so that companies could make huge profits and so that their owners could live high on the hog. In America, however, we have another pesky notion called "God," and this one God, most believe, created all people as equals.

Yes, Virginia, that means that illegal workers, native born American workers, and employers are all equal in the Lord's eye. In America, under the watchful eye of the Constitution of the United States of America, "citizen" is the top rank. The Constitution was framed to honor God. Neither employer nor employee is considered differently under the laws of America. Finally, it helps to remember that in America, illegal aliens have no legal standing whatsoever.

Overall, this notion of God and the Constitution means that neither corporations nor other greedy employers have a God-given right to pick and choose the laws they obey. The Constitution does not care if employer compliance to US laws impairs their ability to reach billionaire status. American workers, who are equal citizens under the law, are covered under the same protective umbrella of the Constitution as are American employers who also are citizens. In other words, under the Constitution both are equal.

As previously noted, citizens are the highest ranking people who reside in the US. Thus, when employers choose to employ illegal non-citizens, they are taking from citizens who have a Constitutional right to compete for employment with all other citizens. All citizens have a Constitutional right to be protected from having to compete with illegal workers and other outlaws for employment.

Missing from the picture here is a government that should be working for the people (citizens) and who should be closing down businesses that fire Americans and hire illegal foreign nationals.

Make sure your vote counts in every election from now on to assure that a just and honest representative government is elected -- a government that puts American citizens first—right where we belong.

Chapter 18   What is wrong with Illegal Immigration?

A quick snapshot -- Are benefits worth the costs!

Now that we know that illegal immigration and the thought of amnesty appeals to the progressive's sense of justice in a humanitarian, and spiritual way, and we know that illegal immigration really does help American employers economically to rapidly and massively increase profits, can we agree that these two major benefits are enough to call off the dogs? Should Americans say "Well, it is good for the progressives in the government and it is good for the employers who stop using American workers, so why not just go along to get along?" I don't think so! *We the People* come first.

The spiritual (humanitarian) and economic benefits of illegal migration can be measured with a thimble compared with the trauma caused to America. The true spiritual and economic costs are way too high to not address the immigration problem as a real national crisis in need of a real national solution. The fact is, as we have been preaching, there is a great deal wrong with illegal immigration, regardless of what you hear from progressives and progressive economists.

US social services consumed by illegal aliens

If it were not for the devastating effect on the US unemployment rate with illegals gaining 85% of all new jobs, the biggest problem caused by illegal foreign residents would be the depleting effect these undocumented migrants have on social services. In addition to halting job opportunities for entry level positions and others, illegal workers have had a devastating effect on the pay, which all American workers receive in industries, in which illegal aliens are the norm, rather than the exception.

Study after study shows that the word, *Jobs, Jobs, Jobs* can be repeated as many times as you like without materializing one new job. Worse than that, if a job appears on the scene, chances are better than 6 to 1 that it will be claimed by an illegal foreign national. American companies know that there is no border enforcement, no risk of deportation, and no risk of incarceration for hiring illegals. So, why not follow the money? And, they do!

Just like US citizens, illegal foreign workers need social services to sustain their very existence. Their effect on social services in the communities in which they live has been very costly and harmful in a number of documented ways. In law enforcement for example, the US spends multiple billions of dollars attempting to secure its borders. Though many of us see our side being undermanned, border security does apprehend some illegal immigrants; it does jail some of them, and it does deport some of them. Unfortunately, it does this in a hapless and helpless "what's the use" fashion. Many Americans think those in charge of the border patrol would prefer giving new drivers licenses and a huge "welcome" gift box to every detained illegal alien rather than sending them back to their home countries.

Besides the fact that merely being in America without a passport is a crime for a non-citizen, the US government chooses to baby those who commit immigration crimes. And, so, without the benefit of even an interview with US authorities, once caught, illegal foreign nationals are more often than not, let loose in America to do as they please. In recent years they have been arrested at alarming rates, not because they are merely in the US but because their plight causes them to commit other crimes against American citizens—from identity theft to murder. More and more of those arrests, including hit and run and other crimes, as I have observed first hand, result in Immigrations and Customs Enforcement (ICE) releasing the perpetrators back into the community. Though most are not bad people, if they were not here, their crimes would not be committed and US citizens, along the border especially, would not have to live in fear.

Many Americans have a difficult time believing that our lawmakers have taken from the public treasury at the federal, state, and municipal levels to accommodate the needs of those who violate our borders. Rather than use our funds to eliminate this scourge on American life in general, our legislators use the US Treasury to provide aid and comfort to those who perpetrate crimes against the citizens of the United States. The influence of progressives in recent years has been so dominant that laws have been passed granting people, whose mere presence in the country is a criminal act, almost limitless access to US social services from education to health care.

Public Education

Let's look at public schooling, which, because it is wasted on non-citizens, is a major social drain and economic drain. It is not free. Americans pay for it. Some say many and some say most "undocumented workers" do not pay taxes. Taxes at multiple levels help pay for schools, and due to their criminal status, the illegal foreign national is basically exempt from taxes. Yet, by law, their children are allowed to get a free education on the back of Joe the plumber and Harry the taxpayer.

Knowing how important children are for parents, the many levels of government in the US could not have given the potential illegal border crosser a better reason to come over illegally. If I were a foreign Mexican or a Latino, I too would see this as an opportunity that I could not deny my children. And, so they come, with their children. Then, their children get an education in our taxpayer funded schools on US soil paid by US taxpayers.

Because the extremely rich in Mexico choose to keep their money for themselves, there are no major grants or funding sources or even occasional "thank you's" that come in from Mexico on a regular basis for the social services we provide. Thus, US school districts are hurting while trying to educate American children along with a multitude of other children, whose parents are illegal foreign nationals from many different countries, but mostly Mexico.

As a logical person would expect, with extra students, but little to zero extra funding, many schools in the U.S. face severe overpopulation issues. This, of course rolls over into a superabundance of other societal issues.

Free health care for illegal aliens

In this short list of pressures, the final social service negatively affected by the influx of illegal foreign nationals of all ages is health care. Obamacare was not needed to give illegal aliens health care. They had it already. Emergency rooms run under a law called the Emergency Medical Treatment and Active Labor Act are obliged to treat all patients the same, without regard to ability to pay. This is the same care many poor Americans receive and it is a good and humanitarian thing. However, it is not without substantial cost. ER personnel from across the US know this law simply as EMTALA, pronounced "emtalla."

This law says that anyone, legal or illegal is entitled to medical treatment in any emergency room facility that accepts federal government funding. After one receives treatment, the law says they are to be presented with the bill for the services. The bill cannot be presented even one minute before the service is complete or the hospitals would be in contempt of the law. It is rarely paid.

EMTALA is the anti-patient dumping law enacted because hospitals without such constraints were dumping critical patients either back to their premises or on the doorsteps of other hospitals, once they knew they could not pay. This was horrible. So, EMTALA is not bad but how it is implemented is not in the full American spirit. Moreover, since illegals do not have to confess their illegality, they are emboldened at the point of service and demand perhaps even more than perhaps they should with no humility or thankfulness, and no intention to ever pay. No deportations ever occur even after substantial services are taken. Who do you think pays? The American taxpayer. No bill is ever sent to Mexico. BTW, Mexico has no such EMTALA law for Americans in Mexico.

The problem is that in the migration manual "Go to America and Enjoy the American Dream," (just kidding about the manual), the potential illegal foreign national is counseled that they do not have to pay the ER bill. About this part, I am not kidding.

As often as they are treated, illegal foreign nationals and their families rarely pay their hospital bills. And so, the amount they collectively do not pay by design has often resulted in hospitals closing their doors. When the hospital remains open via creative accounting, it always follows that patients, who are American citizens pay higher health care costs to make up for the shortfall. As you would expect in a broke, but still giving country such as the US, the average taxpayer ends up footing the bill when the day is done.

Employers shortchange their illegal workers

Adding to the social burden, the many illegal foreign nationals working in agriculture, construction, housekeeping, and other industries have an even more direct negative effect on the social umbrella. Clearly a company bold enough to engage in labor arbitrage using an illegal workforce has no desire to offer its employees health care. In fact, the workers are lucky if they receive adequate pay to support their needs without having to steal. Stealing, of course is another social cost. The fact that employers shortchange their illegal employees adds to the public social cost. They have to get their care from someplace and if the only person who benefits, the employer, is absent from the mix, then who is it? It's Joe the plumber and Joe the taxpayer.

Labor arbitrage – the final anguish

The new Robber Barons, engaged in the seduction and abuse of illegal workers use labor arbitrage as their final weapon to assure the absolute minimum labor cost. Thus, wages in many fields have dropped significantly for legal workers, mostly because illegal workers take those jobs for less pay. Prior to the time that legitimate companies were emboldened to hire the continuous stream of illegal workers into the U.S., blue collar workers in key industries were capable of making middle class wages. With the downward pressure on wages, and the sucking up of the unions to the illegal foreign nationals, blue collar work in just about all industries has come to mean poverty level wages and poor to zero health care coverage. Why the unions serve up their own workers still is puzzlement. Why the workers still support such unions, perhaps is an even greater conundrum.

US immigration line: unfair to citizens of the world

At one time, the US had a nice, orderly immigration strategy. Huge influxes of people from any one nation or collective of nations were not permitted because it is not good for the complexion of the US melting pot. Moreover, the US is a worldwide magnet and those in other countries seeking citizenship, going through hoops to achieve it, are annoyed, to put it mildly, that the US honors the place of rowdy line-jumpers before those who have legitimately applied. Moreover, the people who want legal admittance really want to be Americans, and they are patiently waiting for the call.

Think how frustrating it is to hear of people sneaking into the U.S. and working toward an American dream without waiting. Then imagine the frustration of those who wait and finally get into the U.S. legally only to find that the work that once was available is now taken by those who jumped the line ahead of them, who still are not legal. Moreover, because the illegal population has demonstrated on the streets of America under Mexican, Guatemalan and other Southern Hemisphere flags, many US citizens are turned off by their arrogance. The citizenry is sick about the masses of illegals who think they have rights in our country, but they are especially upset about any line jumper who does not really want to be American being permitted to live in America.

Americans often suggest that "learning the language" is a great first step in being accepted but even this is too much for many of our unwelcome visitors, and of course the progressives are against anything that helps America.

We have a full chapter in this book on whether illegal immigration is good in other ways for America. So, as we ask quickly right now as we begin this reading adventure: "is illegal immigration good for America?" We intrinsically know the answer. "No, it is not good!" America, like all sovereign nations, including Mexico should be able to pick and choose the potential citizens who come into its country legally. Illegal immigration may be good for the American employer's wallet in the short run. They make millions in profit annually by exploiting cheap labor. However, in the long run illegal immigration has already proven to be a scourge on America and American citizens.

Conclusion: A problem worth solving?

As noted elsewhere in these many early chapters, the progressives who have had control of the US government since Ronald Reagan, Democrats and Republicans alike, believe that illegal immigration is good for America. They are wrong. Yet, that's why this government, a government, which knows how to shoot a Tomahawk missile from a submarine in the Atlantic Ocean to intercept a spitball before it hits the ground in Ohio, has yet to find a solution to end illegal immigration. Surely a government that can build a Tomahawk missile can solve any problem if it were committed to doing so. The only logical conclusion is that our government, Republicans and Democrats alike do not want to solve the problem of illegal immigration.

The progressives, who run the government of the US today, believe that it is your job and my job to support poor and uneducated foreign nationals as residents of our country, regardless of the path they choose to get here. They want to convince us there is no problem to solve. Americans definitely don't hate immigrants, but we do hate line jumpers and those who feel entitled to our good will without having to work for it. Moreover, we are quite tired of having to support dead weight. Our immigration authority has the right to not accept unskilled labor if we choose. But, with border hoppers, this sovereign nation does not even get to inspect those who the progressives suggest are entitled to stay merely because they have arrived.

From a practical standpoint, we Americans do not need any more uneducated citizens. It is not our responsibility to provide line jumpers a better job. It surely is the duty of their home countries, Mexico or otherwise. Now that the people are taking an active role in government, there is a good chance that after a few more years of public scrutiny and wariness, the progressives will go underground for another fifty years and we can solve many of our country's big problems, including illegal immigration.

Chapter 19   Why Do Mexicans Come to America?

Anybody looking for a winning lottery ticket?

On the spiritual / humanitarian side of the immigration issue, as discussed in Chapter 16, most Americans are well tuned in to the fact that things are lots better in America than in Mexico and other nations with so many poor. Progressives of course think this means that Americans should give up their own dreams so the incoming Mexicans and others can have theirs. Win - lose propositions rarely succeed however in any aspect of life. Most Americans would be happy with a win - win approach to illegal immigration by improving conditions in the home country of the illegal foreign national, which in most cases is Mexico.

A permanent solution for Americans could be realized if first we understood exactly why Mexicans want to come to America. Making these reasons go away would go a long way in solving the spiritual / humanitarian side of the rationale for open borders immigration to the US. An objective then would be to fix the issues that make Mexicans want to come to America.

Poverty is an unfulfilled dream

Since Mexico is the largest exporter of its people to the US, let's look at Mexico as the example country for this analysis. One of the biggest reasons why Mexicans come to America is the lack of good jobs in Mexico. Additionally, there is the folklore of making plenty of money in America so it can be sent back for family members in Mexico to live more comfortably. Additionally, life in Mexico is fraught with many dangers and oppression. On top of it all, the biggest draw for Mexicans to America is the opportunity to leave it all behind to become permanent legal residents and to then live the proverbial American dream.

Expanding on the mindset of those who come to America illegally, statistics show that the majority of the Mexican people live in unimaginable poverty compared to American citizens. There are few good jobs in Mexico that are open to the lower class of Mexico's population, and there are few services available as the rich in Mexico assure that their taxes are kept low. Thus, the Mexican people work for almost nothing in Mexico if they can work at all. I can recall my first visit to Tijuana where I came face to face with young children selling sticks of gum to Americans, hoping to find a few generous Americans to make their day.

The Mexican government does very little to persuade Mexican business to improve their wages and working conditions. Yet, much to the ire of ordinary American citizens, the same government does intervene in US affairs to make it easier for their poor people to be exported to the US. As you will see in this book, Mexico itself is not a poor country per se. It is a country blessed with an abundance of natural resources from agriculture to crude oil to precious metals and minerals. So, the Mexican people should have a shot at a Mexican dream. For its own reasons the Mexican government appears to prefer to keep its poor, poor and its rich, rich. Surely the culture as it exists does not encourage the poor to move up the food chain.

Rather than accept Mexico's castaways, many argue that it would be far better for the American government to put pressure on Mexico's leadership to help its own people. Without a compelling reason to change the status quo, Mexicans will continue crossing our border illegally to find good jobs that will actually allow them to live in a far better manner than in the squalor and the abject poverty to which they are accustomed. However, their lives will be far short of a dream and the more they come to America, the more they are helping to make our country into a penniless, almost-broke, third world nation..

The Mexican government does benefit by exporting its poverty as the US bears much of its social costs. Additionally, Mexico benefits as the illegal foreign nationals reportedly send over $20 billion per year to their relatives back in Mexico thus aiding the Mexican economy. So, to say the Mexican government is an advocate of amnesty for illegals would be an understatement. The Mexican government depends on sending illegals to America for its own prosperity. So, a solution would have to offset the natural advantages for the government and for the rich in Mexico. The US would be better off sending Mexico $20 Billion a year to stop the flow.

The long term solution to the squalor in Mexico and the hardships endured by everyday Americans in dealing with what rightfully can be termed an invasion is to end the incredible inequities between the rich and poor in Mexico and to help Mexicans have a better life in their own country. By letting Mexico continue its Ostrich policies means a continual outflow of billions of dollars to Mexico each year from the tepid US economy, and the taking advantage of countless illegal immigrants who are literally driven to America for relief.

Unless you happen to reside in a US border town or in the inner cities where gangs rule, the US is a pretty peaceful place to live. Mexico on the other hand is becoming more and more dangerous as a place to live or even to visit. There have always been fewer freedoms granted by the Mexican government than in America. But, recently, the drug cartels operating in Mexico have made life a living hell for Mexicans just south of the border and beyond.

For example the cartels have begun kidnapping Mexican citizens for ransom. Additionally, they engage in open gunfights with Mexican police and military forces. People are being killed every day. Many are brutalized and beheaded. Since there is no right to a speedy trial in Mexico, innocent prisoners may sit in a Mexican jail for years simply awaiting trial. The deck is even more stacked against lower class Mexicans to ever make it out of the lower class.

The US government, active in so many different countries trying to achieve order and justice for people across the world, seems to have forgotten that Mexico too needs our help—in Mexico. In fact, Mexico should be the country that we help the most as it is our closest southern neighbor. No wonder Mexicans want to come here—legally and illegally. In many ways, it is like escaping prison or worse yet, escaping hell. Things have to change in Mexico. Unlike countries half-way around the world, the US is affected negatively by Mexico's inability to solve the problems that cause its citizens to desperately want o-u-t.

The drug war must end with the government being victorious, or just ending the war, and a government has to come to power, preferably by election as a revolution is not in the offing. This new government, or at least a government with a different mindset on exporting poverty, with the assistance of the United States, can actually give Mexicans the freedoms that they deserve.

Of all the illegal aliens who migrate to the US, most are in the category just explained. They are escaping a country that has become a prison. Yet, there are people who come from Mexico who more than anything want the opportunity to be American citizens. They see the magnificence of our country and they want to be a part of it, not wanting to live as exiled Mexicans within the US borders. They want the real opportunities of America and they want to learn English to be a contributor to the American dream. Like the Irish, the Poles, the Italians, and Germans, they want their children to be Americans while still maintaining some of their original culture. They want to be rid of the inequity that Mexico has caused for so long. These are the people that America should welcome with open arms. However, under the circumstances that exist today, this is not about to happen.

So, now we know a few more reasons why Mexican immigrants come to America. Ideally, with the help of the American government, international agencies, and the American people there can be a day that Mexicans who want to remain in Mexico as Mexicans will be able to flourish in safety in Mexico. The immigration issue can thus be solved and no longer be such a divisive issue in America. And, while we are at it, let's set the goal that Mexico, with its miles and miles of beautiful seacoasts, and its warm climate, can become a magnet for migration of people of all nationalities from America and across the world to share in Mexico's new-found bounty.

Chapter 20   Immigration Policy -- the Mexican Way

The Plumber Also Writes!

Joe "the plumber" Wurzelbacher, the real plumber who met then candidate Obama at a rally and took him on, one on one, on the income redistribution theme, has been making the rounds since his great sparring match with the to-be-elected President. "The plumber" minces no words as he slams Mexico for its tough immigration policy but as you will see, he slams it harder because it is implemented by a cadre of corrupt gendarme. He wrote a column for biggovernment.com in 2010 after Congress saluted the President of Mexico with a standing ovation for bashing Arizona's tough immigration law.

> "I guess Mexico 's President Calderon forgot to mention what happens to illegal immigrants on his southern border when he came to Congress to scold us for "discriminatory" treatment in Arizona.
>
> They are summarily raped or killed and commonly stripped of every meager possession they carry by soldiers and policemen. Arizona 's new law is downright humane compared to Mexico 's brutal treatment of illegal immigrants and his false indignation was the height of hypocrisy."

Joe is my kind of plumber!

Mexico has a breakthrough idea for the United States. Unlike our policy, which depends upon the progressive administration du jour choosing the parts of immigration law to enforce, this one is solid with no wiggle room. It is in fact a rational immigration policy that most real Americans would implicitly love if it were ours.

However, Mexican officials would prefer that the US ignore their fine policy and instead keep the hodge-podge we have or better yet, change it to grant all illegal Mexicans amnesty and green card or citizenship status. Mexico's effective immigration policy is not something they highlight to Americans, because for its own reasons, Mexico wants its citizens to live in the US. But, since it is codified in written law, the Mexican immigration policy is available for all nations to see. Why Mexico wants to lose all its citizens to America is a puzzle that we do not attempt to fully solve in this book.

The Mexican plan, if implemented in the USA, would save the US many billions of dollars per year. Gaining the most would be California but like most good ideas, California's voters would more than likely reject it. The plan is so simple that it can probably be copied onto a cocktail napkin, or on the back of a two-dollar bill. Perhaps somebody in one of the 40+ Mexican Consulates in the US can email or fax a copy to any of us, so even the napkin would not be required.

The Mexican plan is well proven and it works first time, every time, big time. Nobody questions the effectiveness of the Mexican immigration plan. That should be proof positive of the worthiness of looking south of the border for an immigration policy that works. Washington will never come up with its own. Mexico's effective policy is used mostly to stop its southern neighbors from passing through Mexico on their way to illegal status in the US, but it is just as effective for those whose final stop is Mexico. Another strong proof of how well the Mexican policy is working for them can be seen by the direction of the traffic. It is all coming from Mexico. When was the last time you saw anybody from the US or Canada fighting to get into Mexico? I rest my case.

Yes, though the children of many of its citizens do attend public schools in the US on our taxpayers' dimes, Mexico, which annually deports more illegal aliens than the United States does, has much to teach us about how to handle the "immigration issue." My father-in-law, Smokey Piotroski, often used this one line saying, which I picked up from him, to describe situations like this. It is as simple and to the point as Mexican Immigration Law. "Treat people the way they treat you."

Under Mexican law, it is a felony to be an illegal alien in Mexico. Despite its technical accuracy, the term "illegal alien" is politically incorrect in the US. However, it is very correct in Mexico. An illegal alien in Mexico is not a Mexican. He or she may very well be a US citizen or a Canadian or someone from another part of the world. They may be in Mexico simply going for a joyride or perhaps they are there to do some business or have some other fun. We won't mention jet-skiing as we have seen that has become very dangerous and deadly. Regardless of their purpose, undocumented foreign nationals are plain and simple not welcome in Mexico by the Mexican authorities or the drug cartels. One would think a similar policy can be just as effective for the US.

You and I both know that certain justices on the US Supreme Court, other US courts, and many of our "bought and paid for" federal politicians have been openly seeking to bring American law in line with foreign legal norms to suit their own egalitarian philosophies. Despite this trend, it is noteworthy that nobody has argued the case that the US should begin to look at Mexican law for a solution to immigration. Should we not study how Mexico deals with illegal foreign nationals in its own country? There is a real lesson there and it would be good to know what it might teach us about how best we can solve our problem with invading foreign nationals.

We have a problem today that Mexico does not have because we have not learned our lessons from Mexico well enough. We have not studied Mexican laws well enough. It is time to do so. Mexico has a single, streamlined immigration law that ensures the following about foreign visitors and immigrants: To be in Mexico, you must:

1. Be in the country legally.
2. Have the means to sustain yourself economically.
3. Not be destined to be a burden on society.
4. Be of economic and social benefit to Mexican society.
5. Be of good character and have no criminal record.
6. Be a contributor to the general well-being of the nation.

Can't we get that small amount of prose on the back of a US $1 or $2 bill so we do not forget it? Mexico in this case is a fine teacher but the US and our officials are second-rate students. The Mexican law also ensures that their government personnel, who are in charge of immigration, perform or assure the following:

A. Keep a record of each foreign visitor
B. Assure foreign visitors do not violate their visa status
C. Assure foreign visitors are banned from interfering in the country's internal politics
D. Assure foreign visitors, who enter under false pretenses, are imprisoned or deported
E. Assure foreign visitors violating the terms of their entry are imprisoned or deported
F. Assure that those who aid in illegal immigration are sent to prison.

By the way, no records get lost in Mexico.

Who could disagree with such a law? It makes perfect sense for any sovereign nation that wishes to protect its sovereignty and its people. The Mexicans are smart on immigration and the US officials in Washington are plain dumb, or perhaps like all politicians, they are dumb like foxes.

Mexico has this thing called a "Constitution," modeled after our own, which strictly defines the rights of its citizens. And, here is the good part. Their Constitution also delineates the denial of many fundamental rights to non-citizens, legal and illegal, documented and undocumented.

Whoops, I misspoke. Undocumented aliens get arrested in Mexico. They have no rights. Visitors are not permitted to exist within Mexico without passports. Therefore, the undocumented in Mexico have no rights. Is there a double standard here? Is Mexico not the country that lectured Arizona on its harsh law that demands documentation? Yet Mexico is a country that tolerates little to nothing before sending even passersbys to prison.

The Mexican Constitution Spells It Out

Under the Mexican Constitution, for example, something called the "Ley General de Poblacion, or General Law on Population," spells out specifically the country's immigration policy. Again I repeat my father-in-law's prescription for how to live: "treat people the way they treat you." We can learn a lot about how to treat our own illegal alien population from such good teachers as those who write the laws and enforce the laws in Mexico.

The Mexican law is immigration law as it should be written and more importantly, the Mexican government enforces it to the letter, albeit arguably they enforce it perhaps even too harshly. Have you heard about the illegal foreign national problem in Mexico? There is none. Have you heard about undocumented US citizens in Mexico? There are none. Violations do not happen in Mexico. Besides the stats, Mexican weather is a heck of a lot better than the Northeastern states.

So, knowing how strict Mexican immigration law is naturally brings up some logical questions for those of us concerned about the de-facto Mexican invasion of the US. Why would Mexicans, who want to come to the US and want to stay here, become upset regarding any of our watered down, bad-mouthed, and un-enforced laws. If somebody painted a logo to represent our American de-facto immigration policy with its lax enforcement, would it not be a "WELCOME" sign?

Regarding Mexican outrage at us, you may recall the summer of 2010, for example, as the Arizona Law was all over the news. Immediately on passing SB 1070, the Mexican Embassy released a statement expressing concern that the law would lead to racial profiling and that it would damage cross-border relations. It had a lot to do with the perception that stopping people who look Mexican and who also look suspicious was unfair to legal immigrants who might be caught in the web, unnecessarily.

The statistics show that most invaders from Mexico are in fact Mexicans who mostly look like Mexicans. However, in the US, if you say somebody looks like a Mexican, it might be an unacceptable term, though the Mexicans I have noted in my travels seem to like the reference to the homeland. They are not interested in being labeled, Irish, for example.

The Arizona statute has come under fire across the globe because the progressives in the US do not like it because it gave Arizona a chance to actually be effective in dealing with a big problem. So, the progressives all over the world have fanned the flames of discontent. The law requires lawmen to ask any suspicious looking person, who may also be Mexican or Hispanic or Irish, for proof of identity. Most US citizens have a driver's license and all foreign visitors and visa holders must carry passports according to federal law, so why would this be such a burden?

The key part of the Arizona law that the ruling class progressives do not like is not the Mexican or Irish heritage part. It is that the person stopped must appear suspicious for some other reason than "race." Not speaking English is not permitted to be factored in. Most Irish learn English to survive and most Mexicans speak their own language to survive. I would bet, however, that Mexican law permits their police to listen to the various dialects of Hispanic speech and anything other than pure Mexican would involve a stop. South Americans in Mexico are often abused by the police. How do the Mexican police know the difference without dialect profiling?

In Mexico, Irish would be stopped without having to utter a word because they do not look Mexican. People happen to be very identifiable by nationality characteristics. Irish for example are typically very white--so white that our skin is actually pink. People are not stick men, all drawn with just a few lines, all basically the same. People can be identified by how they look, and they can be slotted into general groupings by those characteristics. Irish look Irish. Hispanic and Latino are two groupings that would typically be applied to a grouping that would include illegal foreign nationals from south of the border. It's just the way it is. Occasionally the person making the ID may be wrong. So what! What is the big problem with that?

Is it fair with the Mexican reaction to Arizona's law and other US laws to ask if Mexicans officials ever stop people in Mexico who do not look Mexican? I do not recall any time, at least in the last 50 years that the US government has tried to interfere with Mexican law, which is much harsher in its intentions and in its enforcement than US law.

Do you ever feel that it is time to take our politically correct US world and get back to reality? Sometimes we find ourselves using politically correct language even with our friends and relatives because the government corporate media complex has trained us with subtle propaganda that it is not good to win. It is not good to be exceptional. It is not good to own a nice home or drive a nice car. It is not nice to call something what it is. In America, it is actually not good to be like those who suggest those things.

We can't even tell each other the truth because in this upside down, politically correct world, the simple notion of frankness and the truth do not fit in. Sometimes the truth hurts and we wouldn't want to do that—even if it is the truth itself that hurts. Yes, the truth does hurt sometimes and we are being hurt every day by the truthful reality of 30 to 50 million Mexicans and others living in our land. Yet, the progressives tell us we are supposed to pretend it is not happening.

In this chapter as you have seen, we try to egg-on the progressive ruling class to decide to adopt the Mexican immigration laws so that native-born Americans can gain back control of our borders, language, and culture. The US has always been a melting pot of all kinds of ethnic backgrounds. As nice as Mexico is and as nice as Mexicans may be, the solution is to let Mexico stay as the United States of Mexico and let the US to continue as the melting pot while staying as the United States of America. There is no reason to vacate Mexico so that the US becomes Mexico by accepting all of its citizens as US citizens and Mexico becomes an empty wilderness.

The bottom line is that the US needs to protect its own sovereignty and its borders by adopting and enforcing Mexican-like statutes. There may be uproar in Mexico, but there are things one country must do for itself, even if it does not please another.

With its own tough immigration laws, Mexico has had a "do as I say, not as I do" modus operandi regarding immigration. They would like the US to be snookered into submission by accepting flapdoodle piled on more flapdoodle. However, that is not fair to US citizens, especially considering that the well-to-do in Mexico pay very little in taxes compared to their US counterparts.

Yes, Mexico has a lot of poor because their tax structure favors those who have rather than those who have not. Mexico has found it expedient for its own reasons to offload its poverty to the US rather than address it at home. In that regard, they would probably denounce any law put together to protect US borders and they would more than likely again call it a manifestation of American racism and bigotry. So what; we know what is best for our country.

Our own US based media unfortunately has picked the wrong side in this battle for American rights v foreigner's rights. The media, because of its progressive bent, does not fight for regular Americans. We should turn them off for all the help they have given us. MSNBC, ABC, and CBS and other un-American forces would agree with Mexico's condemnation of you and me, and would try to bring the guilt-trip of the progressive ruling class to the American general class.

Felipe Calderon would probably address Congress again if the US takes bold action to protect its borders and deport illegal aliens. The wimps in Congress and the President would more than likely apologize, and try to reverse any laws made to help US. You see, unlike Mexico, our leaders want the foreign invasion to continue because it makes them feel good. American citizens, however, must hold firm that this is our country and Americans come first. The progressive ruling class, which we have been talking about, well, they can all just go home and stay out of sight for the next 50 years, after the next election.

When you have the opportunity, take a look at the Mexican Immigration Law. Also, look at this great piece at http://www.usatoday.com/news/world/2010-05-25-mexico-migrants_N.htm as it puts our issues in perspective.

"Treat people the way they treat you."

Chapter 21   US Immigration Policy - The Ellis Island Days

Give me your tired, your poor—Your huddled masses yearning to breathe free

U.S. Immigration really has not changed in about two centuries other than the U.S. government's new exceptional tolerance for lawless invaders from foreign countries. Illegal foreign nationals, with allegiance sworn to another country, is probably not the Founders' idea of how to grow the U.S. population the right way if it must be grown at all. That's not to say immigration per se is anathema to the Founders' view of America. On the contrary, it's quite integral. Hence there is the existence of *legal* avenues for obtaining American citizenship.

Americans have a right to choose who comes into our country just as we have the right to say who comes into our homes. We have the same right to determine who is to be kept out. Proponents of open borders suggest that immigration is a long standing American tradition, and it can be a benefit to our society and our economy. However, even an untrained eye can tell that unregulated lawless immigration is not immigration; it is an invasion.

Figure 21-1

Ellis Island

Statue of Liberty seen from the S.S. Coamo leaving New York.
1941.

"Give me your tired, your poor. Your huddled masses, yearning to breathe free.
The wretched refuse of your teeming shore. Send these, the homeless,
tempest-tossed, to me; I lift my lamp beside the golden door"

Figure 21-2

Immigrants with their belongings pictured outside the Main Building at Ellis Island.

Many of our ancestors passed through Ellis Island to enter this country. Estimates show that at least half of American Citizens had at least one relative pass through the welcoming island. I'll bet most of them were tired and poor. The island was not just a spot on the shores of the U.S. where people got their name changed. No, Ellis Island was in many ways the equivalent of a passport center at a time when there were no such things. It was just far enough away that immigrants thought they were already in America, yet, they were not on the mainland. Immigrants got their "passport" to enter the country by being scrutinized at the gate. Ellis Island was thus an immigrant screening center. It officially opened as an immigration station on January 1, 1892. Most of us were not alive at that time so eye witness accounts have been scarce.

During World War I, when there was no immigration due to the war, the island was temporarily used by the military to detain suspected enemy aliens and after that it was used as a way station for returning servicemen who were sick or wounded. It is a real treat cruising down the Hudson heading for the Caribbean, as I have had the pleasure of doing several times, seeing Mother Liberty on her island keeping watch on America. Ellis Island opened up again in 1921 with 560,000 new eager immigrants being processed.

A quarter of the way into the 20th century, just like now, there was concern about immigration. The Congress was concerned about the numbers of immigrants and so the Immigration Act of 1924 was passed to restrict immigration to more appropriate levels and this event marked the end of mass immigration to the United States. Ironically, though in 1924 Congress thought 560,000 was too many. Over one million to three million Mexicans and others from south of the border are reportedly scheduled to invade this country in 2011 and 2012 . Each and every year we beat our million man quota, whether we want it or not.

With the outbreak of World War II, Ellis Island saw use again as a detention center for alien enemies during the war. Ever concerned about security from our enemies, the Congress passed the Internal Security Act of 1950. This act banned immigrants who had been members of Communist and Fascist organizations from entering the US. This had to be tough. Today's precautions are designed to keep people with wisdom teeth pain out so their screaming does not wake up the ICE people preparing to give US protection. That is a joke but it is indicative of the lack of real enforcement from which we suffer.

After the passing of the Immigration and Naturalization Act of 1952, Ellis Island saw less and less immigrants. Many of our grandparents had already made the run. Finally, in November 1954, Ellis Island closed its doors as an immigration processing station.

Figure 21-3

Immigrants from "Prinzess Irene" going to **Ellis** Island 1911.

IMMIGRANTS FROM "PRINZESS IRENE" GOING TO ELLIS ISLAND

Figure 21-4

A 46-star American flag dates this photo of the Great Hall between 1907-1912.

photo courtesy of the National Park Service

As an important point of note, after 1924, Ellis Island became used as the "center of the assembly, detention, and deportation of aliens who had entered the U.S. illegally or had violated the terms of admittance." Why is this in quotes? This was written about Ellis Island and displayed at the memorial by *The Statue of Liberty-Ellis Island Foundation*. Those words ring hollow today as the current US administration, despite the ease with which terrorists can enter our country through the southern border, and through the airways, chooses not to enforce US immigration law. Without the public's approval, they have chosen not to deport aliens in mass though they all have "violated the terms of admittance." One might ask "what did the Statue of Liberty Island Foundation know that the current U.S. government does not know."

Despite the Bush, Clinton, Bush and Obama administrations' intentional failure to protect the U.S. from an invasion of illegal foreign nationals, this country continues to have the right to screen entrants. All countries have the right to weed out the wheat from the chaff to assure that only good people become part of our citizenry. Additionally, the "bad" people, potential enemies, who might be harmful to the nation, have always been deported until recently. Deportation was always part of the country's protection from undesirables. However, today's politicians per their self-interest in reelection have decided to wink and nod from behind their gated communities rather than face the music and do their jobs for the American people.

Open borders and an uncontrolled entrance policy, especially in the wake of 9/11, is ludicrous. There is no inherent cruelty to be inferred from a nation protecting its own borders in the name of security. There is no racism. All sovereign countries have that right. Even Mexico exercises that right quite regularly. It is basic. Unfortunately, the sovereignty of United States has been compromised by corrupt politicians and greedy businesses, and it no longer has the most fundamental power of all -- the power to defend its own borders.

And, so, this invites what we have already received and that which threatens us continually-- lawlessness, disorder, and potential disaster. Our government is smug in thinking that we have beaten off all potential attacks since 9/11. Only a buffoon, a dunderhead, or a politician, or worse yet---a person who is all three, would conclude that all is well after September 11, 2001. After such a calamity no sane leader would permit the gates to the country to be wide open. An impartial observer, watching US border actions from afar would use just three words to characterize them: *dumb, dumb, dumb*. The people believe in a sound immigration policy that must be enforced. However, multiple administrations have chosen to not deliver the will of the people.

Figure 21-5

Immigrants aboard a ship heading for the Port of New York, circa 1892.

Chapter 22   Reagan Amnesty Was Not Immigration Reform

Illegal aliens are in all states

A lot has changed since the immigration study conducted in 1990. The study was by the U.S. Commission on Immigration Reform and is available for download at http://www.utexas.edu/lbj/uscir/exesum94.html. I read the report and found it very comprehensive and unlike most of what comes from Washington today, it is very fair for Americans. It is my-kind-of fair to illegal foreign nationals. In the document, illegal foreign nationals or, as they're more colloquially known, illegal aliens, are clearly identified as a problem, not euphemized simply as US residents with inalienable rights to the hard work of others nor as a mythical solution to worker shortages or the need for more people in the 48 attached states.

Though one would think that Alaska and Hawaii would not have an illegal immigration issue, even they are affected. Yes, as hard as it is to believe, illegal workers do find their way into Alaska and they have become a drain on the state's economy. More difficult to believe is that they are not from Russia or Canada. They are part of the same invasion of illegal foreign nationals from south of the border. Though it costs money to get to Hawaii, it also cost money to hire a *coyote* for safe Rio Grande ingress. There are many creative ways to get to Hawaii. Since it is a state, all you need is a valid driver's license (no passport) to fly via commercial airlines. It is a beautiful state and the underground economy for illegal foreign nationals has recently begun to flourish.

Illegal aliens can get to Hawaii because they own valid driver's licenses, even if they are derived from identity theft. They can fly around the continental US and to the non-continental states and territories. One way tickets would be dead giveaways if US Immigration and Customs Enforcement (I.C.E.) actually cared about enforcing the borders.

Democrats, businesses, & unions are on the other team

 Which of the illegal foreign nationals, whom you know, if once given amnesty, would be inclined to either vote for the Democratic Party or immediately want to join a union? The answer is of course is that they all would have an undeniable incentive for Democratic loyalty and union membership. Businesses of course use illegal workers to increase corporate profits. Unions hope to use illegal workers when they are given legal residency to increase the total paying union dues.

Businesses are not very interested in making illegal workers citizens. They actually like having them as serfs with very little rights so that they make few demands in the workplace. If they were to become citizens, they would be Americans like you and me. Americans want fair wages for their work. Thus, after any amnesty that might ensue from our inept Congress, without securing the borders first, businesses would continue to seek and to employ new crops of illegal aliens since it is good for business. Unions would like illegal workers to be citizens so that they pay union dues like everybody else.

Most of us know that "Comprehensive Immigration Reform" is a euphemistic term that includes the big item, "*amnesty for illegal foreign nationals.*" Between 1990, when the commission produced the immigration report cited above, and today, when the government, against the will of the people, has decided that enforcing our borders is not a priority, and that illegal foreign nationals do not need to be deported, we citizens have lost control of our government.

Citizens across the country, of Irish, Polish, German, Mexican, French, English, Spanish, South American, Chinese, Cuban or Russian pedigree and in fact citizens of all national origins, are clamoring at levels as high as 70% and greater to have the US government defend our borders and remove illegal residents. The reason for the clamor is that the national government has decided this is not important and in fact has begun to impede the state governments from taking action on their own. States such as Arizona have been demonized by the powerful amnesty block for trying to preserve America's borders while the federal government takes no meaningful action to stop the flow.

Everybody thinks the border jumpers are a big problem. The guilt-ridden elite grown-up hippies in the open borders amnesty block think the problem is that folks can't just pop in from south of the border and elsewhere and immediately claim citizenship. Yet, they do not leave their wallets in the I.C.E. office in case somebody needs a helping hand. U.S. citizens pay the medical tab as well as the K-12 education tab for illegal foreign nationals. The gap between conservatives and progressives is huge on this issue. Conservatives think deportation is an acceptable option. Progressives, on the other side of the issue believe that U.S. citizens should be providing the full complement of welfare services to our guests from the south, and deportation must be off the table. And, if it would not be too much trouble, a nice social security check would go a long way to rid the progressive of his or her guilt. But, please do not ask them again to leave their own wallets at the gate.

Reagan did not get it right

Other U.S. citizens who make up the guilt-free majority are not interested in giving up America to up to fifty million or more foreign nationals who have invaded the country with relative impunity. The intense debate has been going on for quite some time. On March 4, 2007 in a speech to the Lincoln Club Annual Dinner, former Senator Fred Thompson offered these comments about immigration solutions:

> "The government could start by securing our nation's borders. A sovereign nation that can't do that is not a sovereign nation. This is secondarily an immigration issue. It's primarily a national security issue. We were told twenty years ago if we produced

a comprehensive solution, we'd solve the illegal immigration problem. Twelve million illegals later, we're being told that same thing again."

Thompson is referring to the last great amnesty that occurred in 1986 under the Reagan Administration--the good old days. Since Reagan's amnesty, at a rate of 1 million to 3 million illegal foreign nationals or more jumping the border each year, one could conclude that the number is more likely 24 million or more. If the estimate is 3 million a year, as some suggest, then we already have over 50 million in the US.

Illegal foreign nationals occupy every state in the continental United States and they are creating issues in Alaska and Hawaii also. President Reagan supported the 1986 amnesty program as a humanitarian idea. He was not interested in changing the geography of Mexico. He was a good man trying to do a good thing. Humanitarian efforts do not work with people who think they have an entitlement to the assistance of the US government. And besides, as my great friend, Professor Dennis Grimes often tells me, "no good deed goes unpunished."

Those who come illegally to America are not only willing to invade our country but they lie and cheat and use fraud out of necessity to achieve their ends. If you and I lied and cheated and used fraud to achieve our ends, we would be behind bars. Besides compromising its security, today America looks like a fool to its citizens and the world as its policies are confusing and its enforcement is lax. Every sovereign nation in the world protects its borders except one, the United States. Even Mexico has a tough policy on illegal foreign nationals -- even if they come from the United States.

Some countries will sentence violators to ten years of hard labor and the prisoners do the full time unless either Bill Clinton or Jimmy Carter makes a personal, impassioned visit. Some countries put a bullet hole through the invader's forehead, and ask questions later. If the wounded survive, perhaps they get free medical attention. Why does the US, after being attacked by illegal foreign nationals on 9/11 take this threat so nonchalantly? The answer is simple: Bad leaders beget bad leadership.

Come On Down!

Historians know that the 1986 Amnesty was not intended to be the first of many amnesties. It was not intended to tell would-be illegal border crossers to "come on down." Somehow, however, that is the message that went across the Rio Grande.

Figure 21-1 Bob Barker: "Come On Down!"

Reagan's amnesty was supposed to be an experimental plug in the flow of human beings from a supposedly poor country to a supposedly rich one. It was for real and it was supposed to last. Unfortunately, it was implemented by big government and we both know that big government doesn't work. Reagan saw his amnesty as a onetime thing and in his eyes; the problem was to be fixed as the legislation was passed. Reagan intended his humanitarian gift to illegal foreign nationals to be the "last amnesty." Those who implemented the program had their own ideas.

Yes, he was pushed by liberals in Congress like Ted Kennedy to enact the legislation originally, but he did it, and maybe at the time, with "just" 2.7 million illegal foreign nationals to absorb -- maybe it was justified. Reagan believed sincerely that this would settle the issue by legalizing just about all illegal foreign nationals already in the United States once and for all so such a condition would never exist again. Additionally, the Reagan idea was also to control future immigration. It was to be **the** solution. America learned a lot in the process. Among other things we citizens learned a reinforcement of the notion that no good deed goes unpunished. And, we have been punished ever since.

From 2.7 million to 50 to 60 million in 25 years

At the time, there were a reported 2.7 million illegal foreign nationals, mostly from Mexico but there were people who had crossed many borders with impunity to get to the US from South America. They had settled in America and, after going through some major Reagan hoops to help assure they would be good citizens (such as the requirement in the law to learn English), they were granted their coveted citizenship. If the borders were closed, as promised, that would have been a good thing. But, they were not and the illegal influx increased and the number of businesses in the US willing to risk imprisonment to make big profits also increased.

Family reunification – the killer poison pill

Before the ink was dry on the amnesty legislation, the citizens of the U.S. began the process of being manipulated by both our government and the new American citizens. As soon as the first foreign nationals were made legal, a plan in the legislation called "family reunification" made the act a sham. Not only did the U.S. immediately get 2.7 million more citizens but under "family reunification" provisions, each of the 2.7 million were able to immediately sponsor almost any number of relatives, who also would, as immediately as their sponsors, become citizens of our great country.

There are reports from this period of some new citizens abusing this privilege by bringing in 80 or 90 additional persons and sponsoring them as citizens. I have never seen a count on the exact number but surely it was far larger than a second 2.7 million, and the fact that all of these people, through luck or through fraud were in our country, the magnet was turned up 100 fold.

Oh, and that notion that once all the new citizens came to town, the problem would be over. That did not happen either. The government of Ronald Reagan and future presidents forgot about the enforcement aspects of the law. They were never put into practice. Thus, the 1986 amnesty left the gate open to still more massive numbers.

So, when real Americans complain about illegal foreign nationals appearing any place they choose in America and taking over town after town, with no action from the feds, this is real. It is a situation that continues to be caused by an inept and uncaring government that has chosen not to listen to its citizens.

Do as I say, not as I do

There is a profound disconnect between the lofty ideals of the "humanitarian" elite and its members' daily lives which generally consist of zero personal contact with illegal aliens. The very people they aim to "help" are among the missing in the gated neighborhoods of the progressives. Relieving the progressives of self and social guilt comes with robbery, rape, and homicide. But, being removed from it all, these are things that one reads about at Starbucks, down the street from the gated communities whose gleaming McMansions eulogize the psychotropic lifestyles and delusions of harmony that birthed such guilt in the first place.

Even the left-wing household language shows this disconnect in clarion terms: "undocumented workers" and "foreign nationals" cover the reality of illegal immigration like something that we wouldn't want to touch with a ten-foot pole or even talk about in palpable terms. You won't find an undocumented Mexican at a dinner party here. But you will find a self-styled nobility of justice whose only connection to illegal immigration is the ignorant viewpoint that everyone else can adapt to rampant crime and unemployment by... opening their minds. How quaint. There is little concern for solving a resource conflict here, but as the last in line to be tangibly affected by what's going on in America, why not pass the time with a self-congratulatory belief in "equality?" It's all about feeling good. Sound familiar? Some things never change.

Because there is no leadership in the federal government and they will fight to the death to keep their power over immigration, citizens who remember that amnesty does not and cannot work are fighting hard to get the borders secure. And that "family unification" thing, if the bleeding heart anti-American hippies now running the government are able to pull off a Reagan style amnesty again, this time without the English language requirement of course, the only opportunities for employment for Americans will be as guest workers on Mexican farms. One more amnesty and Mexico will have no population left so getting hired may be an issue. All of Mexico will be here.

Americans can solve any problem that we wish to solve

Before I turn you over so you can read the 1990 plan, the reference of which is at the beginning and end of this work, I would like to ask you the question, "Who says Illegal Aliens are too big of a problem to solve?" Whoever they are, they are ruining America in many, many ways, and many other writers have spoken about those many ways.

No, I am not racist though that has been redefined as "anybody who has any issue with a progressive." I just see things the way they are. if Mexico is so great, why is most of Mexico trying to leave the country.

Please take the below link for the full report. For something commissioned by the government, it is actually very good and very telling. You will be surprised.

http://www.utexas.edu/lbj/uscir/exesum94.html.

Chapter 23   US Wars with Mexico -- The Seeds of Discontent

A quick look at migration terms and immigration law

This book is about illegal immigration. This is a phenomenon, in which people without legal permission, cross a country's border, and then proceed to dwell there. Technically, because the individuals who cross the border owe their allegiance to a foreign power, the people are rightfully called "illegal foreign nationals." To define the phenomenon a little differently, illegal immigration is the act of migrating to a country without having the legal right to do so. A docile term for a person who migrates to a country without the legal right to do so is thus, an illegal alien. The term illegal alien is the proper term for a person that is alien to the United States, who is in the country illegally. The term merely dwells on the foreign aspect of the intruder whereas the term "foreign national" implies that the person's allegiance is not with the new country, but with a foreign power. To get the full sense of the criminality of being an illegal alien, here is the US code:

Under Title 8 Section 1325 of the U.S. Code, "Improper Entry by Alien," any citizen of any country other than the United States who:
…Enters or attempts to enter the United States at any time or place other than as designated by immigration officers; or
…Eludes examination or inspection by immigration officers; or
…Attempts to enter or obtains entry to the United States by a willfully false or misleading representation or the willful concealment of a material fact;
…Has committed a federal crime.

Violations are punishable by criminal fines and imprisonment for up to six months. Repeat offenses can bring up to two years in prison. Additional civil fines may be imposed at the discretion of immigration judges, but civil fines do not negate the criminal sanctions or nature of the offense.

One would think the current administration has never read this law.

The quiet "War" with Mexico

Most of the illegal foreign nationals who have invaded the US are from Mexico, though there are substantial numbers of people of other national origins. Because of the vast numbers of Mexicans in the US who are here illegally, many have suggested it is a continuation of the conflicts from the 1800s between the US and Mexico and that the invasion in essence gives Mexico a means of retaking the territory it lost to the US in those wars.

One can describe the beginning of the conflicts between the US and Mexico after Mexico gained independence from Spain, in very gentle terms, like as if these "neighbors" had known each other and were buddies for a long time. In fact the neighbors hardly knew each other at all, and resented each other as strangers. So you can relate to other accounts about the US and Mexico, I merely use the neighbors reference to introduce the conflict.

As you will see as we get into the nits and grits, which bring out many of the bloody details, it was between 1846 and 1848 that two otherwise openly friendly neighbors, the United States and Mexico, went to war. It was a defining event for both nations, but it was not the first war, though it would be the last. It transformed the continent of North America and it helped solidify the identity for both sets of peoples.

The beef that Mexicans have with the US and the reason many see the massive migration to the US as an invasion, more than just a few people looking for jobs, is clarified by looking at what Mexico lost at the close of the war with the US. Think of it. By the war's end, Mexico lost nearly half of its territory, the geography of what today is the American Southwest. It extends from Texas to California, and it includes all the border states as well as pieces of other states such as Colorado and Nevada.

Even before the Mexican American War began, the two neighbors did not always see eye to eye. What started off as settlers occupying almost free land turned into a major conflict and the ultimate results of the conflict have determined the present borders of the United States of Mexico and the United States of America. One of the most famous conflicts in American / Mexican war history is the battle of the Alamo.

Figure 23-1 The Alamo, before being a fortress, as Drawn in 1854

The battle of the Alamo

There are very few Americans who are not familiar with the battle of the Alamo, which occurred in American History from February 23rd to March 6, 1836. The Alamo itself was created in 1718 as a Spanish mission. Its purpose was to Christianize the Indians, who were indigenous to the area. In fact, the original name of the Alamo was Mission "San Antonio de Valero."

By 1793 the facility closed as a mission as most of the Indians had died of disease and / or pestilence during the interim. By 1803, the Alamo had begun to be used by the Spanish Army in Mexico to house troops. A Spanish cavalry unit from Alamo de Parras, Mexico settled in the place and that is where it got its name, *the Alamo*. As an aside, the word "alamo" in Spanish means cottonwood as there were many cottonwood trees in that area of what was to become a big attraction in San Antonio.

At this time, however, Spain still occupied Mexico until about 1821 when Mexico won its independence from Spain. Mexico had some admiration for the government of the United States and the work of the founding fathers and so after gaining independence, in 1824, they fashioned their Constitution as a free country using the US Constitution as a basis.

Texas at this time was part of Mexico. Soon after Mexican independence, the Mexican government opened up Texas for colonization. They offered land very cheaply to new settlers. One after another settlers came in droves from other parts of the United States as well as directly from Europe. They moved to Texas and were afforded much opportunity and a fresh start.

Santa Anna knew things were not going well

Santa Anna, who many recall as a major figure in the *Battle of the Alamo* was a Mexican General, whose full name was Antonio Lopez de Santa Anna. In 1833, he was elected President of Mexico, and though his country was founded to be free, Santa Anna, with his huge presidential power and military experience soon turned Mexico into a dictatorship. He raised taxes and governed harshly and passed many unreasonable laws to further subjugate his people as well as those from many other countries who had settled in Texas. The settlers soon became very unhappy with their new home and it did not take long that the winds of revolt were in the air.

In 1835, concerned about the possibility of a Texas revolt, Santa Anna sent his brother in law, General Martin de Cos, to bolster the Alamo as a Mexican stronghold in Texas. Cos arrived and quartered himself and his troops in the Alamo, in San Antonio and it was he who converted the former mission into a fortress. He brought heavy armaments. He placed approximately 20 cannons around the walls and it was an ominous site for the Texans. He was preparing for a siege and battle.

Cos tries to keep control

To keep better control of the settlers, Cos declared martial law and began to jail settlers for no apparent reason. As an aside, American settlers in Texas were called Texians. The Texians were talking openly about a revolt. Cos's tight-fisted actions brought the threat of revolution to a reality. Within two months, by December 1835, 400 settlers, led by a settler named Ben Milam had conquered the Alamo. Cos raised a white flag and surrendered. It was April 21, 1836. Compared to how Americans would ultimately be treated by Santa Anna, Milam was a true gentleman.

Cos took off as soon as he could and fled to Mexico, leaving everything, including his vaunted cannons behind. Cos promised not to return. However, he was not greeted too well when he returned to Mexico. 1000 Mexican soldiers had been defeated by 400 determined settlers. Santa Anna was very angry and for him, it became a matter of honor to avenge this defeat. Santa Anna planned from that moment to teach the Texians a lesson. He raised an army, which he personally led to San Antonio to take on those Texians who held the Alamo.

The Alamo was being decommissioned by the US

Just about 100 Texians were stationed at the Alamo after Cos's defeat. Alamo forces grew slightly over the next several months. Eventually Alamo co-commanders, James Bowie, and William B. Travis arrived to help bolster the troops.

It did not take Santa Anna long to begin his March. On February 23, 1836 he arrived in San Antonio de Béxar with about 4000 Mexican troops. On this day, he was just about ready to begin his war to re-take Texas. He asked Travis to surrender the Fort. Travis answered the Mexican General's surrender ultimatum with a cannon shot.

At first, for about 12 days or so, there were small skirmishes with few casualties. Travis was well aware that the 4000 Mexicans would eventually overrun the Alamo as the fort was not capable of withstanding such a pounding. He wrote letters pleading for more men and supplies, but less than 100 additional soldiers arrived. After 12 days, the defenders had surprisingly withstood the onslaught of this huge Mexican army.

Ironically, as the story goes, soon after Cos's retreat, James Bowie had been sent by Sam Houston to tell the unit to abandon the fort as its location made it virtually unsustainable. When Bowie got to the Fort, however, he had a change of heart. He could not bring himself to destroy the old mission. Moreover, the word had broken that Santa Anna was already on his way to the Alamo. Bowie and others became even more determined to save the Alamo

Once the fighting began, Travis was well aware that defending the garrison was a death mission. All who stayed, who by this time included a number of settlers along with Davy Crockett and the Tennessee boys, who had no real skin in the game, but who had come just to help, were told clearly by Travis that they were almost certainly going to die if they chose to stay. Travis drew a line in the sand and all the men but one crossed the line knowing death would soon be calling.

James Bowie had pneumonia. He was the only one not to cross the line, and as the story goes, he requested to be carried across the line on his cot. There were 189 patriots in all whose fate had been sealed by that line in the sand. Meanwhile, during the 12 days of skirmishes, the rest of Texas had some news for Mexico. On March 2, 1836, Texas declared its Independence from Mexico. Unfortunately, this did not help those struggling to defend the Alamo.

The defeat of the Alamo forces

San Antonio typically enjoys fine weather and just as Mexico proper, it gets mighty hot down there. On March 6, 1836, the morning was chilly. In the pre-dawn darkness the Mexicans attacked with their bugles blowing "Deguello" (no quarter to the defenders -- death by beheading or slit throat). Mexican soldiers attacked from all directions. The defenders were just about out of ammunition at the time but they repulsed the attackers twice with some musket fire and cannon shot. The third time, the Mexicans made it through the well-battered north wall.

Travis was felled with a single shot through his forehead. He laid cross his cannon. The Mexicans swarmed through and they were everywhere, just as in the movie. They were ruthless to the defenders, putting to death just about all of them with grapeshot, musket fire and bayonets. Without ammunition, Crocket was killed while using his rifle as a club. Bowie, when found, after fighting from his cot, was riddled with gunshot. His pistols were emptied and his "Bowie Knife" was bloodied.

Crockett, using his rifle as a club, fell as the attackers, now joined by reinforcements, which stormed the south wall, turned to the chapel. The Texians inside soon suffered the fate of their comrades. Bowie, his pistols emptied, his famous knife bloodied, and his body riddled, died severely on his cot.

These Mexicans would live to regret their cruelty

This Alamo massacre was a pivotal event in the Texas Revolution. Santa Anna's cruelty during the battle motivated many Texians—both settlers and adventurers from the United States—to join the Texian Army. Their mission was revenge and they had their day. After a major setback in the Goliad Massacre, in which James Fannin and about 400 Texans were executed by order of Santa Anna, the patriots were further motivated and enraged. There was a lot of fire in the hearts of the Texians.

On April 21, 1836, Sam Houston defeated the Mexican Army at the Battle of San Jacinto, thereby ending the revolution. By October, Sam Houston was elected President of the free and independent Republic of Texas. On March 1, 1837, the United States recognized Texas's independence. Despite the Texas victory, a bigger war with Mexico was about to re-draw the borders of both countries for a final time.

The Big War between Mexico and the United States

From 1836 to 1845, there were occasional skirmishes between the Texians and the Mexicans. On December 29, 1845, the United States of America formally annexed the Republic of Texas as the 28th state of the Union. This was done of course after all of the necessary sign-offs and agreements were completed by the governments of the Republic of Texas and the US.

The War between Mexico and the United States began on April 26, 1846; just four months after Texas became a state. The Mexican government started the war by attacking American troops along the border of Texas and Mexico. Some historians suggest Mexico was provoked into starting the war by the US so it could grab territory. This book's short look back at the history of that time does not try to settle this question. However, it is part of the basis for some Mexicans and radicals today believing that the US should give the Southwestern States back to Mexico.

The war was fought on various fronts. By sea, there was a naval blockade off the Mexican coast in the Gulf. Additionally, by land, American forces invaded and conquered New Mexico, California, and various parts of northern Mexico. The war lasted just a bit over a year and was ended when U.S. Gen. Winfield Scott penetrated most of Mexico and occupied Mexico City on Sept. 14, 1847. This was a point in which the war was really won, yet it continued. Considering that is about a 450 mile trip from the US border on foot and horseback, Scott's Army performed brilliantly. Part of their journey was also by sea.

US & Mexico peace terms

Shortly after the occupation of Mexico City, on February 2, 1848 at Guadalupe Hidalgo, Mexico gave up and signed a treaty with the US. The Mexicans were outnumbered militarily and with many of its large cities occupied, Mexico could no longer defend itself. It had little choice but to make peace on any terms. Clearly the peace terms were advantageous to the victor, the United States of America.

Mexico gave up a lot in this war. In addition to Texas, Mexico also ceded California and New Mexico. This brought all of the present-day states of the Southwest into the United States. This was known as the Mexican Cession and included present-day California, Nevada, Utah, parts of Oklahoma, Arizona and New Mexico. Arizona was originally administered as part of the Territory of New Mexico until it was organized into a separate territory on February 24, 1863. Additionally, Mexico relinquished all claims to Texas, which had already become a US state before the beginning of the war, and it recognized the Rio Grande as its southern boundary with the United States.

Despite the formality of Mexico admitting that it no longer had any claim to any part of the Southwestern States, there are a number of radicals today who still think that this territory is theirs. So much for treaties!

Chapter 24   Reconquering the Southwestern States by Mexico?

Will squatters' rights again prevail?

For the last ten years, as the unofficial population of illegal immigrants may very well be approaching 40 to 50 million illegal residents, there are certain Hispanic groups, which are part of a movement that sees the current occupation by Mexico's illegal foreign nationals as a lot more than harmless. Certain Mexicans have been dreaming about this for years. Now, with an approaching majority of Mexicans and other Hispanics in the US Southwest, certain Mexican radicals see an ultimate de-facto Mexican re-conquering of the U.S. Southwest as an event coming in the not-too-distant future. And, they are quite happy about it.

Though the bean counters suggest that only 56% of the illegal foreign national population are Mexican citizens, there are few Americans who buy off on such a low percentage as most of the workers we all come in contact with are of Mexican descent. The long-known and often reported Hispanic movement's dream of retaking California, New Mexico, Arizona, New Mexico and a few more states to some observers is already almost a de-facto reality. If Mexican and U.S. policies, according to some immigration watchers were intended to prevent such an occupation and takeover, they have clearly achieved the opposite effect.

Americans see a massive influx of illegal immigrants and an importation of abject poverty, along with a growing ethnic population with a far greater loyalty to Mexico than the US. From back in 2002 when articles about Mexico conquering the Southwest using nothing more than squatters' rights were in the headlines, this has been a front burner issue. In fact, many of those commenting at the time, believed that if the issue was not addressed and solved then (2002) or within a few years it would probably be irreversible. In other words, perhaps some time in 2004, the southwest was conquered and we are still waiting for Mexico to physically claim its new territories and announce its gains.

Create an In-tact Mexico

In a 2004 interview with World Net Daily, prominent Chicano activist and University of California at Riverside professor Armando Navarro offered that a breakaway from the other states of the union is a distinct possibility if the Hispanic segment of the states' population reaches even greater proportions. Of course the way he said it, was by using some code words, such as "if demographic and social trends continue, secession is inevitable."

I can recall Lincoln started a war over actions like secession way back in the 1860's. Perhaps secession is now politically correct as long as it is not conservatives in Arizona working the idea. Giving a few states back to Mexico with a deep apology may be a modern progressive's dream, but most Americans are not too keen on the idea.

The one thing about this notion, silly as it may seem to those just learning about it, is that illegal immigration is clearly fueling the aims and the dreams of Hispanic radicals. No, they are not like Palestinian radicals but who knows when Palestinian radicals became like Palestinian radicals. The known problems with illegal foreign nationals taking American jobs may become the least of our issues.

In 1995 for example, Navarro said that the influx of Mexicans into the United States was leading to "a transfer of power" to the ethnic Mexican community -- at least in the Southwest. Navarro predicted that in the next 20 to 30 years that Hispanics, legal and illegal, would make up more than 50 percent of the population of California. Having better than 50% of the population of anything gives a majority and majorities rule. Navarra saw the radical idea of an Aztlan, as a definite possibility.

Reconquering the Aztlan

Citizens of America, feel free to put the word Aztlan into your favorite search engine to read more about it. But, for now, let's just say that it is the mythical birthplace of the Aztecs. In Chicano folklore, the Aztlan is an area that includes California, Arizona, Nevada, New Mexico and parts of Colorado and Texas. The Aztlan dream is to create a sovereign state, which would be called "Republica del Norte," the Republic of the North, as we would say it in English. But, this state would speak Spanish as its only language, just as Mexico speaks only the Spanish language as its official language. As a first run, this idea combines the American Southwest with the northern Mexican states and the long term dream is an eventual merge or reunification with Mexico.

The proponents of the notion of an Aztlan, both citizens and illegal foreign nationals, see themselves as figuratively trapped in the Southwestern US without a real homeland. They think of themselves as "America's Palestinians." No, I am not kidding. You can check this out further on their website, the "Voice of Aztlan" at http://www.aztlan.net/.

The many Mexicans who dream of Aztlan see themselves as part of a transnational ethnic group known as "La Raza," which translates to "the race." A 2004 editorial in the *Alta California,* had this to say about the Palestinian connection: "both La Raza and the Palestinians have been displaced by invaders that have utilized military means to conquer and occupy our territories."

So, now you got it. By prevailing in the final war against Mexico in 1848, the US, for more than 150 years has occupied important portions of Mexico. Do you buy that?

Give California to Mexico??

Whether the guilt-ridden, dope-affected progressive hippies, who are the ruling class in the US as of 2011 are radical enough to sign up to give a few states back to Mexico as a nice apology, is a matter to be decided by the non-hippie young leader, President Barack Hussein

Obama. Shall the US appease these "Aztlan" radicals while concurrently giving amnesty to those illegal foreign nationals presently occupancy of a goodly portion of what would be the remaining United States? Perhaps by soliciting a few states from Canada, the US can keep our number at 50 states--as long as the new, former Canadian states are little guys.

With the guilt-ridden hippie loons as the ruling class in America, unfortunately, I cannot honestly say that they won't give up anything to anybody, as long the receiver is non-American. Americans are bad and so they need not apply. The Administration loves the notion of redistribution. A nice move like handing over about six states to Mexico could be viewed as just the ticket to save the Obama Administration. This would be known as the grand redistribution on this side of the border or *redistribución de la gran* on the southern side. So, it is anybody's guess whether this will come to pass. But, with all of the absurd legislation that was passed in the 111th Congress, this is not beyond the point of valid speculation.

In earlier parts of this chapter, we explored the wars of the early to mid 1800s which pitted various Republics such as Texas as well as the United States of America itself against the United States of Mexico. Remember that this is not a fable. Many Mexicans continue to hope for a "reconquista," which is a reconquest of territory the country lost when Mexico was defeated by the US. It helps to know that Mexico signed the 1848 Treaty of Guadalupe-Hidalgo to end the Mexican-American War, while American Generals waited impatiently in Mexico City. Some say to the victors belong the spoils while others, such as the progressives in America, who see everything in 3-D without glasses, don't see it so plainly.

The concern for regular Americans who are intensely tuned into the issue is that there are a number of history writers who have cast the US as the bad guy in those prior battles. They suggest that the US provoked Mexico into the war so that Hollywood would be part of the US, rather than part of Mexico. OK, the Hollywood part is not exact but Hollywood is included in the California part of the post 1848 US.

It is true that Mexico did lose the war in 1848, but those that believe that this was all about territory see the introduction of illegal foreign nationals into the US as the continuation of the war of 1848. This time, there are no bullets flying or muskets blaring, but the Aztlan supporters see Mexico on schedule to win this newest war of the 21st century. In terms of the sheer numbers of people Mexico sends to occupy the U.S. illegally, the worst that happens to their soldiers is that they get jobs in the US. Radical Mexicans see US inaction of their occupation as very promising. A 50 million person invasionary force is about as big as it can possibly get.

If the US chooses to act decisively against a perceived eventual takeover, it will not happen. But, the US that I have been writing about could care less about losing territory as long as most people got some ice cream. Only continual TEA Party victories as in 2010, can assure that the result of the treaty of 1848 will hold true. Navarro is no dummy and just like his Palestinian counterparts, he knows as he told WorldNetDaily. "that is not a reality based on what Mexico does, it's based on what this country does."

Let's talk a bit more about the possibility that Southwestern US can be conquered by Mexico without firing a shot.

'America's Palestinians'

On its website, a group called "La Voz de Aztlan," the Voice of Aztlan, as introduced earlier, identifies Mexicans in the U.S. as "America's Palestinians." But the threat of secession is not merely from groups that might be considered on the fringe, the noted anti-Mexican vigilante Glenn Spencer insists, citing the declarations of Mexican leaders, up to the highest elected office.

For example, former Mexican President Ernesto Zedillo appealed to La Raza in a 1997 speech in Chicago. He said that he "proudly affirmed that the Mexican nation extends beyond the territory enclosed by its borders and that Mexican migrants are an important – a very important – part of this."

Why would the Mexican President at a time during the Clinton Administration boldly make these statements? The objective of the radicals then was to enable Mexicans to hold dual citizenship with the US so they could always pose as US citizens in the best interests of Mexico.

With a sleepy American public that does not think anything bad will ever happen as long as BOH is in charge, along with a politically correct Congress, the invasion and full colonization of America by a foreign country may already be proceeding quietly, on schedule. Things may be moving along one state at a time while you are reading this book. I'd prefer not to ever say "I told you so." I sure hope that nothing like this can ever be.

California would be the first. Of course this would happen, only if there was a real plan. It would be seen in retrospect as methodical and perverse. Mexican consulates already seem to dictate US policy in many parts of our country. Mexico's President Calderon visited Washington in 2010 and made huge demands. The people are coming over our borders come quickly much like water over a broken dam. The best our 111th Congress can do for Calderon is apologize. Do we have some other matter in the 112th Congress?

The Mexican Invasion: Help me or else

It is not the intention of this book to dwell on the financial issues that illegal foreign nationals create at the local, state, and national level, though these are covered lightly in other chapters. American taxpayers pay dearly to give a gift of kindness to many and in return, Americans get many more illegal residents. One could readily conclude that it is part of a reconstitution plan but that is hard to prove other than through the anecdotal evidence in this chapter and the many pieces written about the Mexican invasion on the Internet. One thing few deny is that American workers lose approximately $800 billion in wages per year due to illegal aliens taking over American jobs. One thing out of all this is true for sure. Soon, it will be a $trillion.

So, here we are in this chapter, and we are suggesting indeed that the wars between America and Mexico are quietly back on. Yet, there are no bullets, and at least that is good. Mexico sends people rather than bullets and the occupancy of the people is far more important than violence.

Ironically, there are those in the US that do not like the California or the Hollywood way of life and how they let their state get taken over by Mexico and others. . Thus, some Americans would be happy to say, "Hosta la vista, California," rather than put up anything from their treasuries to help stop the invasion and they might not mind a re-conquest.

The states affected, other than Arizona and Texas seem like they are not putting up a fight. So for some Southwestern states maybe a re-conquering by Mexico would be OK if Hollywood were located in "Mexico # 2" instead of the US.

Maybe Californians would like that better for all I know. They don't think like we do back East. So, ask yourself, especially if your state is not part of the six states that would be affected. Would it be bad for America to be split up? Would it be OK if Texas became a state of Mexico? Should California become part of the Aztlan dream? If we choose not to protect our borders, is this not what we will get? Rather than have part of Mexico in each of the 50 states, should Obama simply redistribute a few border states to Mexico so that those of us that do not think like them can all live in peace and harmony?

Most real Americans have an answer to all this baloney. It is time to get tough! Lincoln knew when he had to get tough. It was actually time for the US to get tough a long time ago. When the tommy guns and the bazookas are blasting so close to the border that Obama sends down signs suggesting not to travel close to the border, as the first line of defense, we know we are in trouble.

Is Obama the problem? Was Bush the problem? Is Congress the problem? Yes! Yes!, and Yes! again. America needs to watch its southern border more closely than the border of any Mideast country. While La Raza thinks that Mexicans in the US are like Palestinians, it is time to take action before we are as hapless as Israel in dealing with the Palestinians. How about this simple precept to keep good Americans knowing we can solve our border issues: "America first and always!" Then, we will intrinsically know what to do.

Chapter 25   Are Progressive Liberals Anti American on Immigration?

They choose illegal migrants above regular Americans

The one word answer to what is wrong with America in the second decade of the 21st century is "Progressives." We've checked them out earlier in this book, but now that we know more about illegal aliens, we have a lot more to cover. A look at history and you can see we had the same problem in the second and third decades of the 20th century. Have you ever heard of Woodrow Wilson?

Glenn Beck is Woodrow Wilson scholar of our ages. More importantly, he is the consummate professor. Those of us who teach in academia because we have professional credentials, and not the requisite academic credentials (PhD.) know how hard it is for a great teaching talent like Glenn Beck to ever gain any position in academia as a ranking professor. My highest degree is an MBA.

When I got my position at Marywood University as *Instructor*, I was told by the person interviewing me that with all the books I had on my resume, from reputable publishers, that I should be able to be an Assistant Professor. Though she was a Ph.D., she wasn't kidding. I serve at this moment as Assistant Professor in Business Information Technology in an academic world in which typically only Ph.D's survive. This is my seventh year. You may know that in America, PhD's don't even have to speak understandable English to be able to teach our children. So, It gives me great pleasure to have fought the odds and to be able to teach at Marywood University, simply because I know my subject matter better than anybody else. .

Glenn Beck, like myself is not a born PhD. However, Liberty University recently conferred upon Glenn Beck an honorary doctorate. He is the best professor I never had for a class. I try to do my best and I am paid to do so but Glenn Beck is the best. Having a Ph.D and being able to teach are two different things. I know about Woodrow Wilson, because of Glenn Beck. I may just get one side from Beck, but I was never interested in any sides until Beck made it important. I hope many from now on provide the good Doctor with the letters equal to his fine teaching talents. In my opinion, as a thirty year College professor, nobody can teach as well as Glenn Beck. Even if you do not like the subject, you can learn from Glenn Beck.

Whether the subject is income redistribution or illegal immigration, the root cause of the problem associated with these notions is the style of government that quietly has overtaken the US over the last twenty plus years. Progressives embarrassed themselves and the country so bad in the 1920's that they went underground and it took fifty or sixty more years for them to have popped their heads out of the ground. Well, "they're baaaaaack" and just like last time, when they arrived they were somewhat invisible. Emboldened by having gotten a pure-bred progressive president elected in 2008, the progressive agenda is huge, radical, and it is basically insatiable.

Today's progressives mostly consist of liberals and confused former liberals who got sick of defending the "L" word. Some argue that the pickup of the term "progressive" is a reaction to how conservatives reduced the "L-word" to a pejorative back in the 1980s. Under this new code word, liberals have been able to cloak themselves while they are again able to engage in the good fight--without having to defend liberalism. The word, progressive technically does not mean liberal but in practice for many of the old "L" squad, it serves them just as well. Conservatives, Libertarians, the Religious right, and others were very successful in associating liberalism with immoral activity and anti-capitalism. Most regular people have little real understanding of the word progressive so the old liberals have been able to make a huge comeback fighting under this new "progressive" flag.

In reality, progressives are further left than liberals and they espouse a philosophy that government is good and individualism and freedom is bad. The individual should subsume himself to the great god of government. Government is all knowing and all good, and of course liberalism is so color blind that it has no problem labeling whites as racist, just because they are white, unless, of course, they are avowed progressives. Feel free to learn more about progressives at:
`http://agonist.org/20090325/so_what_is_a_progressive`

In essence, these folks are the same nasty liberals as in the 1980's but with more of a Marxist slant. To avoid confusion, and to assure that the regular people can get the right feeling about this new term for an old brood, Rush Limbaugh refers to them as *progressive liberals*.

Michael Savage minces no words in identifying what he sees as a real scourge against the American way. Savage, another leading conservative radio voice like Limbaugh sees both liberals and progressives as "degenerates . . . on an express train to hell." From President Bush I to President Obama, the new progressives have had control of the government for a long time. They are the reason things are not good.

And, yes, I know that the Bush's were Republicans. The reason little good happened regarding immigration in the Bush years is because he governed as a progressive Republican. Conservatives would do well to drop the word "Republican" when describing any of the bushes, sorry, Bushes. The Bushes are progressives. See them that way and we will all be better off. I can only speculate but I would think the *bushes,* green though they may be, are conservative. .

One thing is for sure. Call them liberals or call them progressives. They surely have not helped America in a number of serious issues. In fact, they are unabashedly on the other side. To help you identify the spirit of today's progressive, I like to use a few other terms that describe them well. They are the vintage 1960's hippies. They are the elites who have slowly taken over the government with their guilt-ridden ideology. They are trying to make up for being born rich, without having to give their money away. And, whether you have a spare buck or not, so they don't have to spend theirs, they want you to grant them easy access to your wallets.

Until the past year or so, these overgrown hippies hid their ideologies. However, from the time of Obama, the prince of the progressives, they have been living openly among us. They think it is OK. They think they have the power to ignore immigration laws as well as the Constitution to achieve their goal of amnesty for all illegals. When Arizona passed its law, which is no stricter than US immigration law in that it assures the protection of American citizens, progressives appeared all over the US to help strike it down.

To refresh our memories on the Arizona bill, you may recall that Arizona Governor Jan Brewer signed SB 1070 into law on April 23, 2010. Fairus.org notes that the legislative intent of the bill, set forth in Section 1, states that there is a compelling interest in the cooperative enforcement of federal immigration laws throughout all of Arizona, and declares that the intent of the law is to make attrition through enforcement the public policy of all state and local government agencies in Arizona. The provisions of the law are intended to work together to discourage and deter "the unlawful entry and presence of illegal aliens and economic activity by illegal aliens in the United States."

Arizonans live in fear from the constant flow of criminal elements through the state. People are dying in Arizona because of inaction on illegal immigration; yet, the progressives still had a hissy fit about the new law, even though overall it was no more stringent than existing federal law.

The Arizona law, for example declares attrition through enforcement as the official state policy so the goal is for the illegals to vacate the state. It is set up to mirror existing federal laws so it is no better or worse, but since the feds are not doing their job, it gives Arizona the opportunity to handle its own problem. Police are instructed under the law to check the status of those they reasonably suspect to be illegal aliens but they may not use racial profiling. Finally, it prohibits the use of sanctuary city type laws by Arizona localities.

Arizona saw itself between a rock and a hard place. The FBI crime index shows that though the crime rate in Arizona has dropped a bit, it is still near the top of all U.S. states. Arizonans see a major correlation between crime and the illegal population. Arizona was the #1 state in the Union from 2000 to 2006 in per capita crimes. In 2008 it had dropped to #4. But even now, with a major crackdown on crime unmatched in most other states, Arizona's crime rate is still 29% higher than the national average. Yet, the progressives in our government want Arizona to merely grin and bear it, so that the progressive plan for open borders and amnesty can be accomplished.

US Congress bows to Mexico

Either the Democrats in Congress are all progressives or they were coerced to stand when the Mexican President recently derided America and the Arizona law. You may recall that the Arizona law riled Felipe Calderon so much that he literally made a House call on our government to tell us how bad we are. The President of Mexico came to our US Congress, and he expressed his disgust as he decried the US for this Arizona law and for any other state to have the gall to pass such unfriendly acts towards their friendly southern neighbor. It's like Calderon wanted the Congress to believe that Mexico's dumping of two to three million people over the border per year should be looked at in the same innocuous way as a pilot expelling 300 gallons of unneeded fuel into thin air. The problem of course is that the fuel evaporates. The people stay.

I wish I did not have to apologize for my President's apologies. The US President has becomes the world's foremost expert in apologies, and so having another man in Washington with the title President (Calderon) was just too much for the Obama regime to dismiss. Our apologetic President and the Congress did the only thing they could, when beseeched by Calderon to damn Arizona.

They apologized for all of the many mean Americans who live in our country. Clearly bad Americans forced Arizona to pass its law. BHO and our inept US Congress made the Mexican president feel good about his exportation of humans across the border. Congress apparently did not want him to go back home thinking that in some small way, Mexico was in the wrong. What a bunch of wimps we have in charge of our government. They are what you may feel free to call *progressives*.

The shock for asleep Americans is that Congress did not defend the United States even when the President of Mexico called them out. These aging hippie buffoons of the 111th Congress agreed with the Mexican visitor who came to read US the riot act. Most real, pay-attention Americans, expected nothing more from the 111th Congress, the worst in American History; we got what we all expected.

But even that was not what really riled all Americans. It is nice to treat a guest, a foreign dignitary with honor. After taking his insults about America, the Congress, dunderheads and morons as they have surely become, chose to throw both America and Arizona under the bus.

Rather than defend Arizona, one of the 50 US states, or the US, where we all live, they gave the President of Mexico a standing ovation for deriding the US and a US state. Calderon comes in and damns the US for the Arizona law. The US is a sovereign nation. Yet, the Congress bows to Felipe Calderon. The federal government has no power but for the people, and the states are the ministers of the people.

The feds do not get it correct on much nowadays and on the Calderon visit, they were all wrong. In November, 2010, Americans showed what they thought of this sick Congress as we sent home a goodly number of these, our boneheaded dimwits, along with their Mexican friends. They do not care about you or I or any Americans. Each election we must do more until we expel them all. It's all about saving America.

Please do not forget, however, that you and I and the rest of the regular people--- we still run the country. The representatives we select are here to serve US. The fact that they do not serve US is not reason to send them back to Congress in any election. It is reason to send them home. And, as upset as you are because they do not listen and as bitter as you are because they unabashedly place their needs ahead of the people do not get disgusted and say you will not vote. When we choose that course, they win, always, and forever. Please make a difference by voting each chance you get.

With such an interesting and complete immigration law of their own, why is our otherwise US-friendly southern neighbor pushing US to water down our immigration laws and policies? Clearly Mexico's laws offer the toughest restrictions on the continent!

You see, since a felony in Mexico is a crime punishable by more than one year in prison, Mexican law says that any wandering US citizen has committed a felony merely by being an illegal alien in Mexico. Yet, our own US Government does not find it offensive to discover an illegal worker from Mexico on our streets, and so the US will not arrest him or her "unless they are known to have first committed a more serious crime." And they don't really do even that because they would rather forgive the transgressions of non-Americans.

Is ID theft a crime?

For its own reasons, the US government does not consider ID theft a crime for any illegal foreign national. Yes, it is a crime for Americans---sorry! In Northeastern Pennsylvania, my home, the US government does not even consider hit and run a crime. A few months ago, five illegals were caught and brought downtown and processed after a hit and run on the Market Street bridge in Kingston, PA. When the requisite phone call was placed to Immigration and Customs Enforcement (ICE,) the illegals were released to continue to do their thing. Residents in Wilkes-Barre, where the illegals call home, saw them coming back home free to roam.

Wilkes-Barre is about 1500 miles from Mexico. If illegals are not deported for crimes in Wilkes-Barre, you can bet they are not deported in New Mexico or California. How did they get all the way to Wilkes-Barre PA?

ICE considers certain things crimes only for Americans. The crimes of illegal aliens are simply a means to an end. Without crimes, illegal foreign nationals cannot exist in the US and so, since the progressives, who run the government, want illegals to live with impunity in the US, the selective enforcement of the laws gives them an entitlement to commit certain crimes, even though they are real crimes. American citizens, I repeat, have no entitlement to commit crimes, nor should foreign nationals.

Non-citizens are given more rights than citizens. How else could the illegal survive other than by taking Uncle Charley's identity? In some cases, they may also need to take Uncle Charley's wealth?

Therefore, to enable them to live in the US, ID theft and pure theft and even hit and run by an illegal alien are not on the list of our serious crimes. A sober executive of another country would readily conclude that no intelligent life lives in the US.

But, what if it was your iPod or your cell phone or you laptop or your car that was appropriated by the new visitor, who just happened to sneak in from Mexico? Would that be OK? If an illegal alien has to steal from Americans merely to survive, the Obama gang says our Constitution should just recognize their need and let them get away with it. That is what your progressive friends in Congress believe also. The Mexican Constitution gives Mexicans all rights in their country but in the US, the Mexicans still have the rights because our lawmakers choose to ignore our Constitution.

Our Constitution was written so progressives, the ruling class governing the US today, could not give up all of the people's rights, the rights of regular Americans to the government or to anybody else for any reason. Our Constitution does not permit our government to give our rights to an illegal foreign national. Like the late George Carlin once said years ago in one of his shticks, if all your stuff were stolen by an illegal, who needed to do that to survive, "would it then be a sin, then, hah Father?" Should we not forgive their transgressions? Ladies and Gentlemen of America--so what if your car is not there in the morning? Is it not better that someone in need has a smile on their face? Of course not, that is just silly. But don't expect to ever receive a sane answer for that question from a progressive.

Hyannis Port wine is best

Now, what is fair is fair. So, let's say you made a burglary raid on one of the big properties owned by the ruling class. Let's say you went to the Kennedy compound in Hyannis Port or some other spot, and you weaseled your way in and you got to hawk a bottle of Dom Perignon or Cristal Champagne, both of which are known to set the average bloke back a few pence. If you were discovered, would the master forgive you, or would she press charges simply because you were not an illegal alien?

Would the "master" press charges if it were her last bottle of the precious bubbly and they were getting ready to pop the cork for a fun experience? Would it matter if you stole from them and you were an illegal alien? Would you be doing time, independent of your immigration status? I don't know the answer to that so we would have to ask the progressive master of the wine. However, I would expect the master to be quite upset.

Working class v elite?

The bottom line is that regular people do not see the illegal alien / worker issue through the eyes of the elite. The elite are unaffected by the filth and squalor and the smells of the crowded conditions in the cities where illegals dominate and survive. The elite progressives are loaded with money and can survive everything but a bloody revolution. Regular people are affected big time. A crime is a crime, regardless of if it is breaking into a country or stealing ID or not paying taxes while working. These are crimes for which regular Americans do jail time in similar circumstances in the US or any other country. As we have shown from page 1 of this book, that also includes Mexico.

So, what is the problem with the idea of common sense and fairness being applied to this big immigration crisis in America? Illegal foreign nationals belong in their home country, period. Moreover, while they are on illegal visitation here in the good ole US, they cannot simply abuse any of our other laws and be forgiven just because they already committed a crime by jumping the border. That would be a second law broken and that too is an offense for which they should do jail time -- just as Americans would do time in Mexico. Because they do not do jail time, that is part of the magnetic draw and it encourages to commit more crime. There is minimal risk for invaders to jump the border and come to the US and become a criminal or any other occupation they may choose. For some reason, all work, including being a criminal is easier to get in the US for illegal workers, and the jobs are more easily kept than any in Mexico.

Indocumentados ningún crimen/undocumented no crime

Nobody denies that the most frequent perpetrators of even the most "innocent crimes," such as ID theft are illegal foreign nationals. Those who have the unfortunate circumstance of being regular Americans, who happen to be ID thieves, executing such "innocent crimes," would be hard pressed to find a sympathetic jury or a sympathetic judge. US citizens would be found guilty of innocent crimes against US laws and would be doing hard time and for a long time.

Yet, ID theft by an illegal foreign national, a prerequisite for sustenance in the US is unapologetically forgiven by our progressive government. Can it be that the US officials making these decisions are mostly overdosed on legal prescription drugs at any time of the day (OK; that is just a supposition)? Americans know there is not a level playing field and they, by default, are looked upon less favorably by our own government than foreign invaders who come illegally and pillage as much as possible for the purposes of "survival." Getting caught means nothing in America like it means in Mexico.

Don't you think the Mexicans have it right? Being here illegally is a crime against US laws and it is time we enforce the laws. If the current President will not enforce American laws then there is this word that nobody wants to use to describe the proper process for US to execute. That word is "impeachment."

Is Mexico a lot smarter than the US? One thing is for sure, smart or not, they are not saddled as we are with these guilt-ridden 1960 vintage hippie types who now comprise the progressive ruling class in the USA. Most of these have sprung from wealth or from the political class--some local, some state, and some national. They all have some degree of money that is much larger than regular Americans and small businessmen. Corporate executives long to be part of this semi secret group and as their wealth increases, they sometimes get to take the secret membership rite and they get to recite the progressive credo.

I am assuming all this, of course, because I have not been invited. But, you will find these progressive elites in the Council on Foreign Relations, the Trilateral commission, the Skull and Bones Society, the Bilderberg Club, and other secret world societies that may be part of "the new world order." These are the people who rule the world. Yes they even rule the USA, or so it seems when nothing makes sense.

What I see is a bunch of over-drugged hippies from the 60s, who are in major leadership positions right now across the world. They are the most disingenuous, hypocritical, sophist charlatans of all time. They do suffer from major guilt, perhaps because of their status or their wealth, I do not know for sure. They are for helping the poor, yet they want it to occur by some other means than their having to chip in.

You see, they want you and I to support the poor so they can take credit for inducing us. They want to redistribute our measly wealth, which in almost all cases is not as much as their annual earnings. They want to redistribute our jobs to illegal foreign nationals, and they want to redistribute your healthcare to those who choose not to work. In order to accomplish all that, these progressives as they do not mind being called today, want to raise taxes to redistribute your meagerness to people in more meager circumstances than you and I.

Unfortunately for America, our progressive leaders are so powerful that they most always get their way, regardless of who is in office. They want to take the bounty of America (not theirs, however as their retention of power is so important) and distribute it to the poor of the world, such as illegal foreign nationals in America. They want to take American jobs and give them to illegal workers simply because they are such nice people. This is the ruling class's continual slap in the face to all hard working Americans and it has really hurt the prosperity of just about all citizens. The elitist progressives in the ruling class will continue to be OK since their rules and tax laws somehow do not apply to themselves.

Only through elections and the purging of our own home-grown progressives will regular Americans have a fighting chance to prevail as the ante increases in the illegal immigrant game.

Chapter 26   The Takeover of the US by Progressive Liberals

De facto amnesty is in force right now

The President and Congress have stopped paying attention to the US Constitution. They are above it. The American people, however want the Constitution as the framework for all laws, and we want all laws enforced. Americans have been paying close attention and the days when lawmakers could get away with anything are coming to an end.

It was not too long ago on November 2, 2010 that Americans were so upset with Congress that we chased out the majority of progressives in the House, who had been running the country with impunity and we reduced the margin by six in the Senate. During the several months prior to the election, the mighty Obama and his minions in the administration, began a process of changing the effective status of all illegal foreign nationals to US citizens. I kid you not.

Not caring about the wishes and dreams of *We the People,* in September 2010, the Obama cabal decided it had the power to do as it pleased. This clever group of czars and former nobodies, who once claimed high positions in academic institutions but still hold on tightly to their 1960 hippy philosophies, began to realize that they might be able to accomplish even the outlandish without needing the Congress. Their plan was to get it done by wielding their almost limitless government power using executive fiat and regulations.

They acted quietly because the people were watching the Congress like hawks. Congress had been ignoring our will and had begun to legislate a huge expansion of government. Their new laws included the wholesale takeover of healthcare in the US, which is now dubbed, Obamacare. Even without the Congress's involvement, the executive branch of the US government, acting without constitutionally authorized power, began to take steps to make it easier for illegal aliens to find comfort in America.

The steps they took for example reduced the risk of deportation for tons of illegal foreign nationals. Scholars have referred to this new strategy as de-facto amnesty. This policy of helping illegal foreign nationals avoids the consequences of US immigration laws. It is against the laws of the United States and it is an affront to all American Citizens. It is actually more than that; it is an impeachable offense by the Executive Branch to avoid separation of powers. Now with at least one side of Congress back to the people's business, Americans are hoping to take some action to stop this illegal act by our government.

Who will it be to enforce the law against this power-hungry President and his minions and czars? The answer is a new and brave Congress. Thus it shall serve the citizens of the US well in each election to rid ourselves of all those who permit such travesties to occur. In

2010, the movement was to remove all incumbents in both the House and Senate. In 2012, it will be to remove all incumbents who have cheated us of honest representation.

How far do the progressives really want this redistribution of wealth, healthcare, etc. to go? The ultimate goal of progressivism is for the government to own everything and give to the masses just what is needed to live. On the way to achieving the ultimate government god in the progressive movement, some very unnatural things would very well occur. One of the last steps would be full government ownership. If that sounds like communism, it is because the basic underpinnings of progressivism are Marxism.

Right now, we are in the redistribution phase and taxes are an easy means of achieving that. That is why the government wants to whack the rich. They argue about tax cuts for the rich knowing that no economy can ever break out of a recession when the proceeds of the rich go to government rather than to expand their businesses and hire new workers. Progressives believe the rich are bad simply because they are rich and they need to be punished simply for being rich. Ironically progressives are rich but they do not count themselves.

Progressives at the top of our government are rich also but they make sure their legislation protects their hordes of cash so that they are enabled to fund all of the work they do "for the people." In other words, progressives want you and I to pay but not them. Progressives as you are learning have an insatiable appetite for the asinine.

When the rich are looking for crumbs from the tables of the middle class, the progressives will still not be satisfied. It will not be until all crumbs are owned by the government. On the way to full dependency on government, you might very well see rewards to those who accept dependency as inevitable and punishment from government to those who don't. Too far out you may think?

For example, can you not hear an argument out there somewhere that people with nice homes have those homes simply because the poor must live in squalor. That is why the middle class and the rich have such nice accommodations. You may or may not know that the very idea of a middle class as a notion is anathema to progressives because the middle class typically does not need the government. Progressives want just poor and rich and they only need the rich until they can make them poor and completely dependent on the god of government.

Once the rich are reduced in status, (those rich who are not part of the ruling elite of course), you might see a fully functional progressive regime begin to reward the patient poor by giving them the homes of the formerly rich as well as well as those of the middle class, since the middle class will be gone in this brave new world. Perhaps the progressives would be charitable in this work and perhaps not because, they too are only human.

Would a 10% random drawing per year work well for this country? Say it were structured as the national draft lottery in the 1970's. Is this all that would be needed to redistribute the homes of the rich and the middle class to the very poor first and then to the poor, trickling the rewards of progressivism upward in the food chain? In 10 years, perhaps the middle class and the rich would be resettled into the housing projects and the poor would be able to enjoy their lives in the homes of the rich and the former middle class. This would be a progressive Utopia! Now, you know what progressives are all about—as long as they are excluded from the heartache, of course.

The power of government would be well known then and nobody would think of speaking against a government so powerful that it could take your living quarters and give it away. Poof! All can be done without firing a shot. As the ten years go by slowly, there would be some dissidents but the ruling elites will know how to handle that situation. There are a lot of models out there that do not permit dissidents to interfere with the good work of the government.

While the redistribution of homes may be the penultimate, along the way of course the healthcare scenario would be solved easily. Once the people recognize that the power is not of the people but of the government, they would necessarily fall in line quickly, even if it were with faux allegiance. Then, while the single payer system is instituted by your friendly progressive government, your health insurance can temporarily be redistributed along with housing until after the ten years there is no need for health insurance as the all-powerful progressive government will handle it all. Elections, which will have been outlawed by the government by then, will no longer get in the way of good government. All goods will have been redistributed from the haves to the have-nots.

Soon, all living beings in the US would be dependent on the good will of a fair and caring government for healthcare and all other facets of life. Life savings is another unnecessary item. Why should only some people have life savings? Life savings would easily be confiscated by the government simply because it is a manifestation of the greed of certain people to have more while others have less. A good and caring government can solve that by giving this accumulated wealth, gained from the backs of the poor back to the poor where it really belongs.

Yes, this may be taking the argument ad absurdum but this is the natural way for achieving Marxist principles as espoused by progressives without having a blood bath, or a coup, as typically happens in such revolutions. Check out those of Mao in China and Stalin in Russia and you can see the blood that can be avoided. Perhaps ad absurdum is where we are heading. Perhaps not. The statistics do point to the former. The good news is that there would be no illegal aliens in this idyllic scenario when this occurs as all people in the US will be citizens, and the poorest among us will be taken care of first.

The Dependency Index

You may be aware that the dependency rate in the US, like the unemployment rate is actually measured. The Heritage Foundation created an instrument which they call the index of dependency on government. This conservative think tank has some bad news for those thinking that government is not making itself more pervasive in our lives. You'd never guess that in the first full year of Obama, 2009, the Americans dependence on government grew by 13.6%. That is more startling than the unemployment rate and it is the biggest increase since 1976. This is super good news for progressives since such a large percentage of the goal could be accomplished and nobody is even talking about it. It makes the rest of the progressive goal even more achievable.

Remember the ultimate goal of progressives is dependence through redistribution. Obama's far left policies and the fact that the 111th Congress has been either AWOL or sipping Nancy Pelosi's wine, helped aid the movement to full dependency at a fast forward clip towards its ultimate goal.

Since illegal foreign nationals are among the poor when they arrive in the US, the federal government's progressive administration would not be happy until they could include these "immigrants" in the redistribution scheme for housing and all other benefits. When they become citizens they can vote and the first two things that will happen will be registration as Democrats, and joining a union. For those already in the country, it's probably time for some squalor redistribution to the middle class and formerly rich. Robin Hood, played by the government is coming and all Americans, including what will be called the former middle class, are being targeted as if we are all rich.

The illuminati know that Americans have lived high on the hog for many years and they resent it. The ruling class elites will not be asked to chip in to help the illegal foreign nationals be assimilated in the US once they are free from the danger of deportation. That's not how the scheme works. Those such as you and I, the regular people, will be asked to pay the full price. Whether it comes from housing redistribution, health redistribution, pension redistribution, or life savings redistribution, or from plain old taxes, Americans will be paying the bill. The penultimate treat for an illegal foreign national would be to be sitting in your favorite bar stool drinking your favorite beer at your favorite tavern paid by ATM withdrawals from your favorite life savings account.

Of course I am kidding to make my point but plan on this costing you and me big time, one way or another, sometime soon.

Overall, this chapter is very scary as it is about how the clever progressive anti-constitutionalists in the administration have been able to mutate US immigration enforcement strategy in ways that minimize the possibility that the 40 or 50 million illegals living in America will ever be deported. Additionally, their actions are destined to mute the impact of any state or local laws designed to deport vast numbers of these foreign invaders.

Perhaps discussing this anymore is meaningless blather as we are at a point in which it may really be all over. Many in the American Southwest believe the US has finally lost its war with Mexico without a shot being fired, and those of us at the top of the country know the real border is creeping up through the states. If Mexico were to declare victory and simply march on the Southwestern States, would there be any resistance?

With our real army fighting winless wars in Iraq and now Afghanistan, the Mexican Army might just as well go right on to Washington and claim it all for Mexico. After a few bows to the new world leaders, Obama would surrender. Wouldn't that be something unusual? While we are fighting foreign wars, Felipe Calderon, Daniel Ortega, Hugo Chavez, Mahmoud Ahmadinejad and their cohorts can cross the border unimpeded (hey nobody's looking anyway) and they can carve out a route from Arizona on the way to take over Washington in a bloodless attack. There are reports that the Iran's Republican Guard is in Venezuela already. If the takeover were to happen, Mexico and its allies would be the foremost power in North America.

I regret that I seem to have been on a silly path from which this chapter could not escape. However, keep in mind that Obama sued Arizona for protecting itself. Now, that the Prevaricator in Chief has given illegal aliens a free pass in the US, and Harry Reid is still bringing the D.R.E.A.M. Act up once a month, it has become more and more difficult to tell real silliness from reality.

Chapter 27   Illegal Aliens, Progressivism, and Public Dependency

Who pays when government spends?

I would like to start this chapter with a few guiding words from a few of the masters. Though long gone, their words continue to guide us. First, along the notion of progressivism, a form of socialism in which wealth gets redistributed; former Prime Minister of England, Margaret Thatcher is the one to rely on for the best advice:

"The problem with socialism is that eventually you run out of someone else's money" - Margaret Thatcher

With all of the magnificent thoughts and eloquent oratory put forth by our progressive liberal friends, including our President Barack Obama, the Orator in Chief, we often think they must be right because the rhetoric sounds so good. But, then we do some more thinking and we know it isn't so. The great communicator, President Ronald Reagan always knew the right words to fully describe such a paradoxical situation:

"Well, the trouble with our liberal friends is not that they are ignorant, but that they know so much that isn't so." - Ronald Reagan

"Socialism only works in two places: Heaven where they don't need it and hell where they already have it." – Ronald Reagan

"The most terrifying words in the English language are: I'm from the government and I'm here to help.' " – Ronald Reagan

" The taxpayer: That's someone who works for the federal government but doesn't have to take the civil service examination." – Ronald Reagan

" Government is like a baby: An alimentary canal with a big appetite at one end and no sense of responsibility at the other" – Ronald Reagan

This chapter is about public dependency and how the progressive liberal socialists desire to make everybody dependent on the government simply because the government is all good and all knowing and in many ways is "a great replacement for any god." No god is necessary in a progressive world, including God, Himself. . This notion of *no place for any god* is not mine. It is how progressives represent themselves. They cheer so hard for the ultimate reign of government that one would think the government was some type of team and as players on that team, they are willing to dedicate their all for its success. Team government, however, has very few redeeming qualities.

To get a better picture of the notion of government dependency and the progressives, I went back to a TV interview from February 5th, 1976 for Thames TV in Great Britain. On the "This Week" program Prime Minister Thatcher was interviewed by journalist Llew Gardner. This is not the whole interview but it gives the essence of the thinking held by Prime Minister Thatcher. As good a communicator as Ronald Reagan was, Margaret Thatcher was every bit his match. They were friends.

For those looking for the reasons why progressivism cannot work and why illegal aliens must play by the rules, this interview is a great perspective. The whole interview can be found at http://www.margaretthatcher.org/document/102953
Margaret Thatcher. Here are some questions from Llew and Mrs. Thatcher's responses:

Llew Gardner
Well, I don't want to stay with the differences between you and the past administration too long. But, would it be fair to say, that you … under your leadership the Party is more dedicated to the principles of greater opportunity for the individual, and less interference by Government than it was in the past?

Mrs Margaret Thatcher
It would certainly be true to say that as the Labour Government's gone on, State interference has got greater and greater into the ordinary lives of people, and therefore it's become much, much clearer that we would have far less of that, leave much more choice with the ordinary people about how they lead their own lives, about how they spend their pay packet in their pockets, and I think you're quite right in saying that there has been much more emphasis on that.

Llew Gardner
… Yes, I'm having this difficulty. Is this because you really don't have any strong views about where the Party should be heading, or, is it that you see solely your task as bringing all the strings together?

Mrs Margaret Thatcher
Oh no, no. You know, we have difficulty with political commentators too. Er, I would have thought I'd given very clear leads in some of my speeches, er, there was the Conference speech, there was the speech which I did in America, which in fact, drew together a number of themes which I've been speaking about here. Perhaps I can summarise it best by saying this—Nations that have pursued equality, like the Iron Curtain countries, I think have finished up with neither equality, nor liberty. Nations, which like us, in the past have pursued liberty, as a fundamental objective, extending it to all, have finished up with liberty, human dignity, and far fewer inequalities than other people. Now, that was hailed as quite a distinctive lead at the time, since then …

Llew Gardner

... held a sort of Right Wing lead, in some way ...   .

Mrs Margaret Thatcher

... . Oh no, liberty is fundamental. Liberty, human dignity, a higher standard of living is fundamental. And, steadily, I think, people are beginning to realise that you don't have those things unless you have a pretty large private enterprise sector. Any Iron Curtain country has neither liberty, nor a very high standard of living. The two things go, economic and political freedom, go together. I've been right in the forefront of saying that, here, in the States, and it's very interesting to me now, to see a number of articles from people who are taking up the same theme. They are disturbed that Socialism is reducing liberty and freedom for ordinary people, and that's really what matters.

Llew Gardner

Do you believe in consensus politics, er, within the Conservative Party, do you believe that really we talked about the middle ground; the middle ground is the place you have to be?

Mrs Margaret Thatcher

I'm never quite sure what you mean be consensus politics. I believe that what most people want in their lives is what the Conservative Party wants to have for them. I believe that our policies are fundamentally common sense policies. Just let's take taxation for an example. Wherever I go I hear enormous resentment about the amount which people are paying out of their own pay packet in tax. And, this goes right across the income ranges. Socialism started by saying it was going to tax the rich; very rapidly it was taxing the middle income groups. Now, it's taxing people quite highly with incomes way below average and pensioners with incomes way below average. You look at the figure on the beginning of a pay slip, sometimes it can look quite high, look along the slip to the other end, and see how many deductions you've had off, those deductions have increased enormously under Socialism ...   .

... because they've put it ... can-can I just finish, because it's an important point? Public expenditure, which they always boast about, is financed out of the pay packet in our pockets. People are saying that they really think too much is being taken out of the pay packet for someone to spend on their behalf, and they'd rather be left with more, and it's now well-known that Socialist Governments put up taxes and Conservative Governments take them down. It's part of our fundamental belief giving the people more choice to spend their own money in their own way.

Llew Gardner

There are those nasty critics, of course, who suggest that you don't really want to bring them down at the moment. Life is a bit too difficult in the country, and that ... leave them to sort the mess out and then come in with the attack later ... say next year.[.

Mrs. Margaret Thatcher

I would much prefer to bring them down as soon as possible. I think they've made the biggest financial mess that any government's ever made in this country for a very long time, and Socialist governments traditionally do make a financial mess. They always run out of other people's money. It's quite a characteristic of them. They then start to nationalise everything, and people just do not like more and more nationalisation, and they're now trying to control everything by other means. They're progressively reducing the choice available to ordinary people. Look at the trouble now we're having with choice of schools. Of course parents want a say in the kind of education their children have. Look at the William Tyndall School—an example where the parents finally rebelled. Of course they did. These schools are financed by taxpayers' money, but the choice to parents is being reduced.

Look at the large numbers of people who live on council estates. Many of them would like to buy their own homes. Oh, but that's not approved of by a Socialist government … . oh no! But that's absurd. Why shouldn't they? Well over thirty per cent of our houses are council houses. Why shouldn't those people purchase their own homes if they can?

*** End of Thatcher interview.

In essence, more government means the government takes your money and chooses for you. Less government means more freedom and more money in your wallet. Do you want freedom of choice or do you think government workers are all smarter than you and they know better than you how to spend your money? With regard to the problem at hand, illegal aliens and illegal immigration, government has decided that helping Americans is not enough and now, since government is progressive and almost all-powerful today, your pay is to be used to help the illegal foreign nationals who have invaded our country. Yes, you can blame all of your disposable income shortfall on the d-gooder progressives, the throwback hippies from the 1960's whose objective is to make all people dependent on the US government.

Check your email

You never know what gems you will find when you check your In-basket. The notion of dependency and brother's keeper and all the good words come out in the little story about the ant and the grasshopper. Recently I received this in my email. It offers a modern, progressive version of the story in addition to the original. Let's start with the original:

The Ant and the Grasshopper—old version

The ant works hard in the withering heat all summer long, building his house and laying up supplies for the winter. The grasshopper thinks the ant is a fool and laughs and dances and plays the summer away. Come winter, the ant is warm and well fed. The grasshopper has no food or shelter, so he dies out in the cold.

The ant is a conservative and the grasshopper is a liberal progressive.

The moral of the old story is simple " Be responsible for yourself!"

The Ant and the Gasshopper—modern version

The ant works hard in the withering heat and the rain all summer long, building his house and laying up supplies for the winter. The grasshopper thinks the ant is a fool and laughs and dances and plays the summer away.

Come winter, the shivering grasshopper calls a press conference and demands to know why the ant should be allowed to be warm and well fed while he is cold and starving.

CBS, NBC, PBS, CNN, and ABC show up to provide pictures of the shivering grasshopper next to a video of the ant in his comfortable home with a table filled with food. America is stunned by the sharp contrast. How can this be, that in a country of such wealth, this poor grasshopper is allowed to suffer so?

 Kermit the Frog appears on Oprah with the grasshopper and everybody cries when they sing, 'It's Not Easy Being Green ...' ACORN stages a demonstration in front of the ant's house where the news stations film the group singing, "We shall overcome."

Then Rev. Jeremiah Wright has the group kneel down to pray for the grasshopper's sake. President Obama condemns the ant and blames President Bush, President Reagan, Christopher Columbus, and the Pope for the grasshopper's plight.

Nancy Pelosi & Harry Reid exclaim in an interview with Larry King that the ant has gotten rich off the back of the grasshopper, and both call for an immediate tax hike on the ant to make him pay his fair share.

Finally, the EEOC drafts the Economic Equity & Anti-Grasshopper Act retroactive to the beginning of the summer. The ant is fined for failing to hire a proportionate number of green bugs and, having nothing left to pay his retroactive taxes, his home is confiscated by the Government Green Czar and given to the grasshopper.

The story ends as we see the grasshopper and his free-loading friends finishing up the last bits of the ant's food while the government house he is in, which, as you recall, just happens to be the ant's old house, crumbles around them 'cause the grasshopper doesn't maintain it.

The ant has disappeared in the snow, never to be seen again. The grasshopper is found dead in a drug related incident, and the house, now abandoned, is taken over by a gang of spiders who terrorize the ramshackle, once prosperous and peaceful, neighborhood.

The entire Nation collapses bringing the rest of the free world with it.

The moral of the new story is "Be careful how you vote in 2010, 2012, 2014, etc."

 I've sent this to you because I believe that you are an ant - not a grasshopper! Make sure that you pass this on to other ants. Don't bother sending it on to any grasshoppers because they wouldn't understand it, anyway!

-- end of email --

Redistribution begins with you

The progressives, in the form of the great god, el governmente, have not been able to implement their full agenda because right when their guy got elected to the White House, the country decided to have some TEA. Citizens have had enough. The same bad feeling for the elite ruling class of progressives and their ideas and plans that was prevalent at the turn of the century is back. The good news for regular Americans is that *We the People* have given the notion of progressivism so much blowback that if we are lucky they will crawl back in their holes for another 80 years.

You know that the greatest tool of the progressive and the lure for those who feel disenfranchised is the notion of redistribution. Progressives want to redistribute all of your possessions to the needy but that is where their goodness stops. You see altruism ends at the door of the progressive, who wants your possessions redistributed, but never theirs. They need the mechanism of government to redistribute your possessions and that is why the progressives have become the ruling class in America. Even though they can easily redistribute their own wealth, they know that being penniless would not work out so well for them so they choose not to redistribute their dollars, but rather your pennies. You see, your pennies are fair game.

If they could convince you to feel as guilty about those less fortunate as the guilt they claim, they might be able to get you to give up a lot more. As discussed in other areas of this book, some of the items on their wish lists that they would love to get their hands on for redistribution include your pension, your life savings, and, of course your family home. You might be able to keep your home's contents and one of your cars. After all, you'll need a place to live.

Right now, the perspective of the progressive is that any upstanding lawbreaking illegal foreign national is more worthy to have your possessions than you. After all, you are probably a long-standing ugly American who has had it good all of his or her life. And, so, your average neighborhood illegal would be the proper recipient for your "stuff."

Who knows when such a bold move would be able to get past the electorate? You know if President Obama, despite his recent reelection "move to the center," could get this done, he would do so in a heartbeat. You do not count. Maybe this could never get by a newly vigilant electorate. Nonetheless, it helps to remember that the progressive dream is for everybody, who today is underserved can gain the benefits of those who, according to the progressives are over-served. In other words, if you work for a living, get ready to pony up your stuff for the people who are not as fortunate – especially illegal foreign nationals. As noted previously, since the progressives are the only ones who can mastermind this exchange properly, they would neither be on the giving end or the receiving end--well, unless some of your stuff looks good.

The notions of dependency and redistribution play a major role in progressive thinking in the 21st century. Since progressives have had control of the government for some time in one way or another, some of the game is not new. However, President Obama has ratcheted up the game to unprecedented levels. His redistribution implementations, since he has the power, are often programs requiring hundreds of billions of dollars each and they total trillions. Somebody is paying for this and so far the answer is our grandchildren.

There is no better dependent person than somebody who is frightened to begin with, who must be kept safe or the establishment will ship them back to where they belong. Illegal foreign nationals fit the bill perfectly. Progressives do not have to train these poor souls to pay homage to the good god of government as they will pay homage to anybody who will help them survive.

Progressives are more than willing to confiscate your property to help these new illegal arrivals to America. They do not want the poor to advance. Instead, they want them to remain dependent on government while the progressives make the rest of us dependent. You, on the other hand, would never need government if it were not for the progressives.

The taking of some or all of your property by the government makes you dependent just like the illegal foreign nationals. Dependency is a big goal and this is a two-for. Redistribution makes you poor and elevates the poor to be ever thankful to the government. Both therefore become dependent on the good will of Uncle Sam. And that is the goal of the progressives, and with Obama, they are getting us there a lot sooner than anybody might have thought.

Rugged individualism, survival of the fittest, and individual freedom are terms that make progressives shudder. It is a sad life depending on somebody or something else for all of your needs. Yet, if a liberal progressive government can gain control of your life, it is a big win for them. Amnesty, scholarships for illegal aliens paid by you and all of the giveaways that are given by progressives to the poor that come out of your pocket contribute to the ultimate victory of the progressives, when the government they control, controls it all.

There is no such thing as a free lunch.

Chapter 28   The Invasion of the Body Snatchers

If you fall asleep, you may become a progressive?

I have been accused that when I write and even engage in simple conversations, I talk in circles. It is probably true. It's part of me. I am all about analogies and I have to remind myself at times to talk directly. Even the very first girl for whom I was smitten had to endure what she called "talking in circles." There is nothing like the innocence and just plain cuteness of those early encounters. Mine lasted four years. I was so afraid of the opposite sex that I did my best to speak indirectly so as to never get pinned down in an embarrassing situation. I have grown up since then and I speak my piece but I still like using those little analogies that perhaps make my speech unique to me.

A lot of times as I was maturing, I felt like Jackie Gleason uttering his famous lines "humma, humma, humma." But, eventually, after a lot of circles, I did tell this particular young lady about my strong affections and she too confessed to me. Oh, yes, those were the days.

So, here I am in a chapter that carries over from the last several but in a more whimsical way. In this chapter, for awhile at least, I will be talking in circles. There are some nuances on immigration strategy to gain if you choose to read this whole chapter. Instead of continuing the heavy path, this chapter takes a very light look at one of the few ways that progressives could spread their message if we were all able to slip into the alternate universe of a horror film, at least temporarily. I hope you grant me the full poetic license in my writing. If I see you at the end of this chapter, that's great, but if I don't it is OK. There is much truth said in jest.

As we continue in this installment of dependency and the progressive mind, this chapter takes on the essence of an old-time horror movie. Having the leaders of America espouse the progressive philosophy (religion) for me, and have it become a reality would surely be more like the full horror of a midnight spook film than a Saturday afternoon matinee.

As nightmarish as it would be for you and me, for the progressives it would be an enticing dream.

Remember "Invasion of the Body Snatchers," that 1956 blockbuster hit? The premise is that the invaders place pods next to you while you sleep and the pod becomes you and you then no longer exist. Wikipedia has a few sentences that well describe this phenomenon:

"... the townspeople are in fact being replaced by perfect physical duplicates, simulacrums grown from giant plant-like pods. The Pod People are indistinguishable from normal people, except for their utter lack of emotion. The Pod People work together to secretly spread more pods — which grew from 'seeds drifting through space for years' — in order to replace the entire human race."

In the progressive's version of this movie, when you wake up, if they have managed to sneak a pod next to you, you will be converted to a hapless American with no future -- just like so many others who depend on the government. With this mind and an attitude change, you would then believe the government is your god and savior and there shall be no strange gods before the government.

The real test to see if the pod has worked would be to check your wallet. If you were to find a glow-in-the-dark card with your name on it-- all lit up with the word, "progressive" on the front, you would know that you have become one of them. You will have become a card carrying progressive all because you fell asleep and were subsumed by an errant pod. Once the pod becomes your imposter, you would never consider doing anything that formerly was on your "must do list." In the future, if you were ever able to recover from such a pod attack, you would resist falling asleep at all costs until the last of the pods were destroyed.

If you were to be subverted by a progressive's pod, it would mean that you would see the government as helpful in many ways. Nothing in reality would have changed, however, other than your new pod perspective. You would just feel better about the Obama regime, Pelosi and Reid, parsley, sage, rosemary, and thyme. When you looked again at our government choosing not to address its responsibilities, such as securing the border, rounding up illegal invaders, shutting down traffickers of illegal foreign nationals, or closing down the employers that literally feed the problem, you would find yourself defending these government actions as if they were OK. The pod would be the "about face" version of your conservative self.

In the illegal foreign national crisis, along with the illegal criminal crisis, you would find yourself on the side of the illegals. You would not be able to explain your change to progressive thinking to your conservative spouse or your conservative friends and you would begin to seek more liberal & progressive thinking people for your circle of friends.

You would not understand how your spouse could feel differently from the new you. He or she will have witnessed the terrifying sweat dreams and the nightmares during the evening of the pod transformation, but, as soon as you start singing, *Sweet Home Alabama*, more than likely, he or she would just give up on you unless they can find an effective antidote. If your spouse is a staunch conservative, you may have a chance. If not, he or she may be convinced by your rhetoric to join you as a pod-less progressive. Of course, you could always place a pod next to her/him and assure the change.

If they are conservative, you may be de-subsumed. Your spouse will know to pipe in with the antidote song verse written by Sarah Palin for the occasion. The song sounds a lot like the old Santana original from the 60s, "You've got to change your hopey changey ways, baby." If this high powered musical antidote is applied quickly enough, there would be a high probability of recovery and you could literally shed your pod like a rattler sheds its skin. But, none of this should really be necessary because, as Jimmy Clanton would say, it's "just a dream."

There could be good news buried in the bad regarding the pods, even if it were not a dream. With all the recent government spending, there is surely no stimulus money available for the progressives to buy the pods. Additionally, it is the economy stupid. So, more than likely, the pod manufacturers would have been suffering through the recession as are all Americans businesses.

These are surely tough economic times with business threats like cap and trade, Obamacare, the huge debt, expanding regulations, impending tax increases and with illegal foreign nationals taking American jobs. More than likely, the pod company, with progressive management, would not have made it this far into the recession. And, if the progressives have no more stimuli to spend, then pod sales would surely suffer.

Like many small businesses, the pod company would then be forced to close shop and that means that nothing, not even super-charged podcasts would be able to sell and distribute pods. It's this simple: no pods, no podcasts. A few jobs would be lost in the pod factories but the fight to get American jobs back from illegal foreign nationals would be able to continue without the threat of the progressive mind snatching pods.

Though some of those who have analyzed "The Invasion of the Body Snatchers" may see no inner meanings, there are many who make a link similar to the notion described so far in this chapter in which socialism, communism, and / or progressivism is the undercurrent. Wikipedia has an uncited section that explains this almost perfectly:

"The film is widely viewed as a covert indictment of McCarthyism, with the turning of people into their characterless doubles when they fall asleep representing the dangers faced of America turning a blind eye to McCarthyism. Others, though, have viewed it as a metaphor of alienation in modern mass civilization, or an allegory for the loss of personal autonomy in the [former] Soviet Union, or of bland conformity in postwar Eisenhower-era America. It is sometimes argued to be an indictment of the damage to the human personality caused by reductionist modern ideologies of Right and Left."

The Progressive analogy fits very nicely. It makes me want to go see the original or the 1978 Donald Southerland remake some time very soon.

Back to Reality

So now, back to reality, without even dreaming, one morning you may wake up and find that the progressive elite hippies from the '60s who are now running the country are having a flag burning celebration. They would be partying hard because they just learned that the very last batch of illegal foreign nationals have limbo-ed under the border line and are now legal US residents.

In this nightmare-like brave new progressive world, one of these new citizens would have the title to your house, would be enjoying your pension and life savings, your social security, your healthcare, and perhaps worse than that, your favorite barstool at the American Legion.

Because progressives are such fine people, you know your personal misery would not have been caused by force. No, your property and possessions will have been lost quite legally in a new government game of chance called the Progressive Fairness Lottery. After the switch, if you decide to drive by your old home sweet home, if that is how you would choose to use your weekly gas ration, you would see a newly minted citizen by your front lawn in your driveway, drinking your beer. If you are one of *We the People*, who have lived through Obamatimes, would that surprise you?

Read more on the topic here:
http://www.poder360.com/article_detail.php?id_article=4725#ixzz0zcBVfP8E

Watch out for the pods!

Chapter 29   Mr. Reid's Wild Ride

A wild, amnesty ride

For the second half of 2010 the President was faking right and going left on matters involving illegal foreign nationals. His new methodology is to make subtle regulation changes that more or less give de-facto amnesty to as many illegals as he possibly can. How can he do this? He is the President and the American people overwhelmingly elected him. One might say that we get the government we deserve.

During this same period until the Lame Duck time, other than Dingy Harry Reid, the 111th Congress had been hiding, hoping to trick the voters into thinking they were not the same tyrants who had passed some of the worst legislation ever. The Obama executive plan continued during this period and afterwards, to use two tried and true Obama gimmicks, trickery and unconstitutional tactics, to provide a sort of amnesty to illegals without requesting anything from them in return. The Obama team does not even ask for English or American allegiance in return. That would be too much of a burden on any illegal alien searching for the American dream.

Meanwhile Obama's favorite soft-spoken minion, Harry Reid of Nevada got the Obama message loud and clear so he got on the Obama plan very quickly. Mr. Reid and Mr. Obama are very like-minded on national issues. Knowing that he was heading for a big defeat, Reid took all of the Obama help he could in the general election and the people of Nevada came through for him. Reid's plan was to discredit Sharron Angle and it worked. Nasty and dirty Harry attacked the newcomer from the moment she won the primary. Near the end of the campaign he made Angle look like a racist to the Hispanic voters who represented 12% of Nevada's population.

Reid's reelection plan was structured so that he would look like the last hope for illegal aliens in Nevada. Reid whipped up this clever plan to help both himself and Obama. This plan made the amnesty slope real slippery. Not only would illegals be able to slide onto "Harry Reid's Wild Ride" to get into America, but it would help Mr. Reid finish a wild ride into a reelection. The plan was to convince illegal aliens (in case they somehow got to vote, ahem) and the Hispanic voting community that Harry Reid was the best friend this voting bloc had ever seen.

Mr. Reid became the champion of the illegal aliens while Sharron Angle took on the illegal immigration issue head-on for the good of all Americans. Reid forgot about America while Angle took a pro-American posture on non-citizens. Reid won the election hands-down after losing going in. Who knows if it was fair and above board? Harry Reid has a lot of power in Nevada and he used it well. .

The Hispanic / Latino community rewarded Reid with a Senate victory and punished Sharron Angle for rooting for Americans over illegals in Nevada. Using actual vote results from the state of Nevada, Harry Reid is estimated to have won 94% of the Latino vote. What Harry promised was nothing less than a dream. Somehow with only 12% of the Nevadans being Hispanic / Latino, Reid was able to overcome a 3% polling deficit and raise the ante by 5%. His actual election totals were more than 8% greater than his pre-election polling numbers. That's magic! Some say it was a little more than magic as Harry got a little help from his friends, but they stop short of suggesting chicanery was involved.

Latinodecisions.wordpress.com believes it was Latinos and the immigration issue that won the day for Harry Reid. "On the issue of immigration, Angle drew a line in the sand. While Harry Reid was on the side of immigrants," Unexplained in all of this is how Nevadans could thank Harry Reid, the leader in the Senate for delivering the highest unemployment rate in the nation to Nevada. With only 12% Latinos, who clearly voted on a single issue basis, other Nevadans must really like Harry Reid, or they did not vote, or perhaps elections in Nevada are a game of chance, and Harry Reid plays the best. The unions were also very helpful in the get out the vote effort for Mr. Reid.

Harry Reid's new monthly amnesty plan involves the often debated D.R.E.A.M. Act. I know that it was defeated in the Lame Duck session but Harry Reid still lives and breathes so we will see it again. The act would give young illegal foreign nationals a path to citizenship if they complete two years of college or two years in the military. To qualify, they also must have come to the country before the age of 16 and have been in the United States longer than five years. There are lots of benefits in this bill for illegals and all of it is paid for by US taxpayers.

It is enough to cause all Latino's with children up to and including thirty-five years of age to give big thank-yous and lots of love to Harry Reid forever if this ever passes. I wish the Irish had such a deal. Just kidding! It is a dream for non-citizens and their relatives. But again, there was more to Reid's victory than can be explained by any amount of dreaming. .

Dingy Harry as he is known to Rush Limbaugh, announced his plan in mid-September 2010 and some think this disingenuous plot was what won him back his Senate seat in Nevada. There is little evidence to contradict this notion, though it does not make sense since it affected only 12% of the population and may very well have worked the opposite for the other 88%. Yet, Reid won.

Mr. Reid and Mr. Toad - taking the people for a ride.

Everything Harry Reid does is political and it is typically bad for the people. For years, politicians let the most important bills, such as defense policy items; go by without trying to add questionable legislation to them as riders. When Harry became boss of the Senate, those days ended, much to the chagrin of a nation looking for leadership and not politics. Just like Mr. Toad has been having a great and wild ride in Disney World for years, Mr. Reid took the voters of Nevada on a wild ride in November. Nevada voters won't be able to undo the results of the big ride for at least six more years. For America, it means six more years of a crafty self-serving politician in a critically important national office. That's the bad side of elections.

Reid tries multiple times for the D.R.E.A.M. Act

In mid-September 2010, good ole Harry was at it again trying to do, under the cover of a defense bill, what would never fly by itself. Reid believes that the Constitution be damned if he can get one more inch of his progressive agenda accomplished. Here's what he did.

He attached an amendment to a defense policy bill that would help young illegal foreign nationals, who reside in the US and attend our schools (for some reason for free) to become legal U.S. residents. He defined a teen as somebody under 36 years of age. From Harry Reid's big toolkit, the benefits just keep pouring forth for US border jumpers. And, they get to ride the kiddie rides until they are 36.

Some think immigration became the issue in Nevada because President Barack Hussein Obama was under fire in the immigrant and Hispanic communities because he had yet to make illegal foreign nationals all legal. Harry let a lot of people down and the American people are happy that ole Harry did not get his way on the defense bill's D.R.E.A.M. rider. It failed. Harry and Congress so far thankfully have lost their bid to move this immigration reform bill through the Senate despite candidate Obama's promise to make it happen in his first year in the Oval Office. Oh, yes, even the President knows this is his second year-- though for most of the first year George Bush was getting the credit. Or was that blame?

One might call this a bailout with Harry taking one on the chin for the Big Gipper, BOH. What Obama cannot get through the front door, where the people are watching, Harry thought he could sneak it in through the back door? The midterm election was coming none too soon. For the people, there were no Obama and / or Reid epiphanies expected so their only chance was November 2, 2010, for this bad dream to end and hopefully for good. Mr. Toad's magic prevailed and Harry Reid emerged, full of bluster for his big win over Sharron Angle. From his actions since the election, Reid learned no lessons from his near-defeat, and he is ready for more of the same. And, that is bad for America.

Just a D.R.E.A.M.

After missing in the pre-election Congress, Reid pushed for the D.R.E.A.M. Act again in the Lame Duck session. The bill itself has been around for quite awhile and has always gone down with its sponsors. Yet, people like Harry Reid and Barack Obama have such tenacity that they keep bringing up this bad penny over and over, as if it is a shiny new dime, hoping to sneak it through in periods of weakness and darkness.

At best it is a controversial immigration measure. At worst it is the first wave of amnesty measures coming from an unresponsive and sneaky Congress. The replacement players for Congress were already lined up and were being trained so Harry will not be as big as he once was as 2011 rolls along. The D.R.E.A.M. act is a way to turn the spigot on just a little so that more and more illegal foreign nationals will find the trip to the US worthwhile and those thinking about leaving because of the economy may hang on a little longer to get their own amnesty. As the flow increases other acts like the D.R.E.A.M will open the spigot even further so that amnesty can be achieved through the back door. Progressive legislators like Harry Reid take wild rides quite often because their agenda is not a pro-American agenda.

So, America's "friend," Harry Reid began the dream by tacking on legislation to a defense policy bill, which the Senate took up a few weeks later and killed. In addition to the D.R.E.A.M. act, Harry also slipped in the entrails of the military's "don't ask, don't tell" policy to please some other constituents and politicize the defense bill even more. Rush Limbaugh's moniker for the Senator, Dingy Harry sure fits the bill.

Reid is convinced that Mexicans and other illegal foreign nationals are more important than Americans as he called the D.R.E.A.M. Act "really important" so it could give a path to citizenship for young illegal immigrants who go to college or serve in the military. D.R.E.A.M. is an acronym for Development, Relief and Education of Alien Minors Act. It is reported that it pays for college for illegal foreign nationals while Americans citizens get to pay off student loans for 30 years. A cynic would suggest the act was designed so that your kids would have a nice, even tempered, former foreign national as their boss when they scrounge enough to finally graduate from college -- if they can get a job.

Harry Reid told his people "I know we can't do comprehensive immigration reform." So, an incremental approach will have to do. Again Harry used some of his political bones to add the D.R.E.A.M. Act so that it would soothe the anger of the Mexican and otherwise Hispanic community in America, whose votes he sorely needed and whose votes Obama will need in 2012. It's them against US.

Some suggest that because the administration, Reid, Pelosi, Obama, et al, are not interested at all in doing what is necessary to create jobs -- other than rhetoric, making the D.R.E.A.M. act a priority could have moved immigration to the top of the agenda right before the election. This was intended to bring in a number of voters whose agenda has one item -- amnesty. And, if they get amnesty, they already have jobs and so the jobs picture immediately improves. Are politicians tricky or what?

Obama, in full candidate regalia offered his own words to describe how much he supports the D.R.E.A.M. act, which regular Americans would call the American Nightmare act. The Commander said: "I just don't want anybody to think that if we somehow just do the D.R.E.A.M. Act, that that solves the problem. We've got a bigger problem than that we have to solve. We still need comprehensive immigration reform. The D.R.E.A.M. Act can be an important part of that, and, as I said, I'm a big supporter of that. But I also want to make sure that we don't somehow give up on the bigger strategy."

The bigger strategy of course is that our President wants to give full amnesty to the world so that he can overwhelm his detractors by bringing in a new batch of citizens who immediately will like him, and who will vote for him forever until he dies. If Obama could replace you and me with these citizens he would, but if he could just get them in, it would do an awful lot to dilute our say in the matters at hand.

Obama therefore fully supports the D.R.E.A.M. act and neither he nor Harry Reid has stopped D.R.E.A.M.ing that it shall pass soon in the future. Even in the Lame Duck session Reid persisted in his attempts to get the bill passed. The American people however, affected every day by such impeachable practices, are not impressed by Obama's dreams, the "Dreams of his Father," Or Mr. Reid's wild rides.

Lame Duck D.R.E.A.M. provision defeated

Cooler heads prevailed on the D.R.E.A.M. Act rider to the defense appropriations bill, and, as noted previously, the Senate defeated the bill. However, never missing an opportunity to suck up to a constituent at election time, both Senators Harry Reid and Dick Durbin brought the bill up again in the Lame Duck session. Again, it failed. But we can expect it again in the 112th Congress.

The Dream in the D.R.E.A.M. -- an act

To sum up the D.R.E.A.M. Act, it is amnesty on a smaller scale on the slippery slope. It is simply another anti-American worker, anti-American student, anti-legal immigrant, pro-illegal alien bill that would put millions of Americans out jobs and reward millions of illegal aliens for breaking the law. I would expect that all Americans would oppose this legislation and write their Senators to vote No if it comes up again in the 112th Congress.

The D.R.E.A.M. Act is a real dream for the pro-amnesty crowd and is a clever attempt to dupe the public and start the slippery slope. It is not a small amnesty for a select group of individuals. In fact, it allows illegal "teens" (i.e., anyone under 36) to petition for their parents to become citizens. This leads eventually to their aunts, uncles, grandparents, and cousins coming to the United States and grandfathering into full citizenship -- all because of a 35-year old teen.

You see the law permits that as soon as D.R.E.A.M. amnesty citizens turn 21, or they are already over 21, they can bring in their parents. Of course their parents **more than likely are already in the US and they broke the law to get jobs and to get their kids into the country in the first place. This legalizes the people who have held American jobs illegally for many years. The chief criminals will be rewarded after all. And due to what we know of as "chain migration," the amnestied "teens"** will not come alone. Many more will get permanent U.S. residency as well. Many bloggers caught on to a post when the news of the D.R.E.A.M. Act was made public. All over the Internet you can see the words, **"In a nutshell - our Government has declared War on us."**

D.R.E.A.M. is an American job killer

At least 22 million Americans right now cannot find a job, while a significant portion of the 40 to 50 million illegal foreign nationals are already employed in the US. This "D.R.E.A.M." amnesty would put millions of Americans, not just the 22 million, as well as large numbers of legal immigrants, permanently out of a job. It will also increase the obstacles facing the children of our most disadvantaged and vulnerable citizens and legal residents to find and gain entry level positions.

Both Reid and Durbin seem to be very happy giving the rights and the wealth of Americans to illegal foreign nationals. You can bet neither of these guys will say "NO" to this or any amnesty bill but hopefully wiser men exist in the Senate. Soon, but not soon enough perhaps, both will get their day again in front of the people of the US. The D.R.E.A.M. act is not a dream. It is a bad law for Americans. It may be a good law for Harry Reid (2010 victory) and Dick Durbin (2014-- defended ACORN on the Senate floor) but hopefully you and I will end Reid's term as soon as possible (2016), and Durbin's in 2014 when he is up again. Yes we can! Never say never!

If this D.R.E.A.M. ever comes up again; all cool heads in the Senate and the House must say "no" again. Say "no" to the D.R.E.A.M. Act amnesty!

The latest amnesty news

Though President Obama has seemed to gain a comfort factor with the word, "shellacking," he has yet to grasp its full meaning in a political context. At the beginning of February, 2011, long after the shellac should have dried, our President and the infamous Senate Majority Leader Harry Reid again stated publicly that they both favor a massive amnesty for the 12-50 million illegal aliens currently within the U.S. Reid plans to help his friend Obama with the Hispanic vote by attempting to push amnesty legislation through Congress in 2011.

Unfortunately, Harry Reid has no shellac on him, just a close call from November, 2010. So, the failures of the most recent amnesty proposals have not convinced him that a majority of Americans stand against amnesty. For those of you reading this book, it is very disappointing, but do not be disheartened. Both President Obama and Senator Reid are very resilient and we should expect them to fall down and get back again on just about all issues, including amnesty.

Obama has proven himself to be the Energizer Bunny who can come back to life after being in the grave for months. He was able to give more speeches last year than the number of days in the year. Sarah Palin killed Obama with her 2008 convention speech but Obama was back on top just two weeks later. He and Reid are both very dangerous men. Now, again, they are calling for a comprehensive amnesty in 2011. I would not worry about it but it shows their brass. The bill will be soaked by a lot of scalding TEA and not go very far. But, like you, I wonder how many times do we have to see this thing? How many wild rides does Mr. Reid have in him and are the President's lives limited to nine?

You know from reading this book that more than 22 million Americans are still unable to find a full-time job, but millions of illegal aliens have non-agricultural jobs (and another few million still work on the farms, orchards, vineyards, etc.). I know that you know this is very unjust and that like me, it bothers you immensely. While American and legal immigrant families are struggling to make ends meet, perhaps as many as 30 million illegal alien families have no such struggle? They have jobs. This may not seem unjust to Harry Reid or Barack Obama but then again, we'd have to look pretty far to find their sense of decency.

With so many Americans unemployed, and many more underemployed, we simply cannot afford to give illegal aliens a free ride. Sorry Harry!

Chapter 30   Hazleton PA Defends the US Constitution

Unexpected population rise w/o increase in birth rate

Getting a little personal, I live in Pennsylvania, not too far from Hazleton, PA. Hazleton is a little town in Northeastern PA that was originally incorporated as a borough in two separate acts, with the second act being the beginning of 1856. For those living in Pennsylvania, you may know that was the year before the Stegmaier Brewing Company of Wilkes-Barre opened its doors, brewing its trademarked Gold Medal Beer.

The winning answer in your next trivia game is to the question, "Why is Hazleton spelled Hazleton instead of Hazelton?" The answer is that the name was unintentionally misspelled by a clerk during its incorporation as a legal entity. When Hazleton actually became a city back in 1891 its population was about 14,000.

In 1940, when coal was king in Northeastern PA, the population of Hazleton peaked at 38,000 and in the following years the decline of the anthracite coal industry saw a similar downturn in the population of Hazleton to less than 20,000 by 1990. Then, somehow, the population downtrend stopped and the population began to explode. Could the reason for the uptick in population have been the water? What else could explain the significant population growth?

Most of us around these parts know that it surely was not because the old farts in Hazleton decided to have more babies. In just a few years, by 2000, this city, which for decades had either no growth or declining growth found its population burgeoning by 20% to about 24,000. There is a lot more in this chapter than news about Hazleton's population count but, but please note that is a big increase for such a small town with no definable reasons. In other words, oil and gas were not discovered in Hazleton in 1990. City officials estimate the population has soared even since then.

In fact, there are published reports from 2006 that show Hazleton's population up by another 10,000 to approximately 34,000. At this time, the town's Mayor Lou Barletta decided to do something about it as the reason for the growth became more apparent. The Mayor found that there was a change in the physical characteristics of a preponderance of the citizens and his crime statistics took a huge jump while more and more illegal foreign nationals were being arrested.

As you might expect, it is hard to get an accurate count of the illegal foreign nationals, no matter where they live. Illegal foreign nationals do not stand in one spot long enough to be in any official population counts. The people of Hazleton were alarmed at what was happening and they asked their Mayor, Lou Barletta, what was going on!

Where did all these new people come from? Mayor Barletta of Hazleton may have originally asked the same question but he now knows the answer all too well. They are illegal foreign nationals, mostly from Mexico. Hazleton, some 2500 miles from California has a similar "invasion" issue as the state of California with illegal foreign nationals and it has been creating big hardships for all the people in Hazleton, including the illegals.

The only other explanations for the unofficial population increase were ruled out. There were no miracles causing a jump in the birth rate. Even the water cure could not turn Hazleton around so quickly. Fifty, sixty, and seventy year olds had not drunk the special coal mine water to reactivate their body parts for the big population expansion. The birth rate has not tripled or more in recent years or the hospital stats would show that. Procreation in Hazleton may not be doing badly at all but no city could grow this fast through normal means. The logical conclusion is that the City's statistics have been bolstered by an influx of illegal foreign nationals.

Because of the increased crime rate that comes along with a major increase in the illegal population and the decrease in the quality of life for citizens of Hazleton, Mayor Lou Barletta and City Council took action. The intent of the action was to have the illegal population, mostly new residents from Mexico, to self-deport. Their action was copied by a number of smaller municipalities bordering Hazleton and over 80 different municipalities nationally. Mayor Barletta became well known nationally as a defender of Hazleton and America. His popularity in the area is immense and he now is the Congressman from the 11th District of PA. He took his oath of office this past January 5, 2011.

The Hazleton ordinance is simple and to the point. It requires anyone attempting to rent, to first make a visit to City Hall to pick up a residency permit. At City Hall, the individual is subject to a background check to prove citizenship. If the background check does not confirm citizenship, they are not be granted a permit to live in Hazleton.

Landlords were expected to cooperate. Those who ignored the act would be fined. Somehow, the supporters of the illegals and the open borders, pro-amnesty contingent in the US did not like the notion that the little town of Hazleton would choose to act against illegal foreign nationals. If they did not shut down this truly American response, with more cities taking on the challenge, their goal of amnesty might not come to fruition.

Additionally, the ordinance required employers who hired illegal foreign nationals, who had not confirmed citizenship, to lose their Hazleton business licenses for five years. This act was less restrictive than Arizona for sure, as it did not require that people carry documentation at all times. Besides these two stipulations, the ordinance in Hazleton mandated English as the official language of the City. This part of the act was to save the City money by not saddling citizen taxpayers with wasteful spending by having to print city information in multiple languages. English is in, in Hazleton.

As expected, the illegal population across Pennsylvania and across America was up in arms as their objective is full US freedom for illegals. You see, they think that illegal foreign nationals have rights above and beyond those of citizens, so much so that they do not have to obey US laws and the laws of US municipalities. It is up to all Americans to lobby their representatives to enforce or replace the immigration laws so that it is obvious to all that illegals do not have the rights of citizens, and more importantly, do not have more rights than American citizens.

Of course, as long as they have committed no other crime, it would probably be OK to grant them the right to go home unimpeded—but just once. When Congress is back home for reelections in 2012, another way to have the will of the people affect the government is to again "throw all the bums out." The 112th Congress is nowhere close to finished, and already the bums are lining up to be noticed. Let's take their names and remember them appropriately.

Devvy Kidd, writing in a little piece she called "Why the Mayor of Hazleton Is Right!" on September 14, 2006 in NewsWithViews.com backed Lou Barletta and Hazleton 100%. She hammered the ACLU who came to the defense of the illegal foreign nationals residing in Hazleton and its surrounds. I have included some of Devvy's piece below so you can see how passionate people are, even those who do not even live in Northeastern PA, about the topic of illegal immigration in Hazleton. She writes:

"The American Communist Lawyers Union (ACLU) has once again taken the side of lawlessness by attacking the mayor of Hazelton, Pennsylvania for his stand on the illegals' invasion. Mayor Louis Barletta understands what the word illegal means and crafted new laws to do what Congress has refused to do: uphold Art. 4, Section IV of the U.S. Constitution which reads:

> "The United States shall guarantee to every state in this union a republican form of government, and shall protect each of them against invasion; and on application of the legislature, or of the executive (when the legislature cannot be convened) against domestic violence.

> "The ACLU howled [that] this last part of the ordinance was racist. This anti-American organization seems to forget, along with 35 of the counterfeit US Senate that America is and always has been an English speaking country. It is imperative that a nation have a common language. Diversity is a sickness that has divided America and promoted a clash between those who believe in a unified nation and those who seek to break it into a million pieces. Frosty Wooldridge has been chronicling this issue for years. I have also written on this -- what the controlled dominant media - including cable - deliberately ignore: illegals who are violent sexual predators, the increase of gang rapes by illegals on America's daughters and the slaughter of Americans by drunk illegals.
> …
> "True to form, the sue happy ACLU has filed yet another lawsuit claiming Hazelton is unconstitutionally seeking to enforce immigration laws. Only someone who is completely absent from reality can't fully recognize the destruction to this republic from the massive invasion of illegals that's been underway since 1986 when Reagan irresponsibly signed yet another failed "immigration reform" bill into law. Every Congress and president since then is guilty of shirking their constitutional duty to stop this invasion which has now reached critical mass. Not to be left out of the limelight, the Puerto Rican Legal Defense and Education Fund has joined in the fray

which is rather ridiculous since residents of Puerto Rico are American citizens. But, hey, any chance to use the race card keeps the donation coffers full. Braying ass, counterfeit U.S. Senator Harry Reid, also used the bully pulpit to chant racism as the basis for Mayor Barletta's stand."

Thank you, Devvy. Thank you for the facts, the perspective, and the emotion.

When Mayor Lou Barletta first learned of the lawsuit, he said, "We'll fight this to the highest court, I needed to do something to save this city. Illegal immigrants are ruining the quality of life, which is the best thing a small town has to offer."

Barletta of Hazleton runs for Congress

Mayor Barletta decided in 2010 for the third time to run for Congress. Many in Northeastern PA, Democrats and Republicans alike were hoping that three times would be the charm. Barletta faced the same nemesis, Paul Kanjorski a thirteen term incumbent whose 13th year has been his worst. Some say Nancy Pelosi did all of his thinking for him.

The people did the right thing. Lou Barletta, former Mayor of Hazleton emerged victorious in the 2010 General Election. He is now the US Congressional Representative for the 11th Congressional District in the State of Pennsylvania. Barletta has always been on the side of Americans. He is a brave man.

Un-American ACLU does not like Lou Barletta

"Those with brown skin and thick accents are coming under suspicion, even if they're citizens." Who would say such a thing? Ponder no longer. It was Vic Walcza from the ACLU as he gave his perspective on the Barletta law in Hazleton.

Suggesting that enforcement should specifically look for people who do not sound like or who do not look like the bulk of the people for whom you are looking defies common sense. I like to use the below analogy to demonstrate how ridiculous statements like Walcza's really are when examined with logic. See if this fits the situation.

Suppose only the giraffes are here illegally. They look like giraffes and they make nice little giraffe noises to communicate. There is no question they are giraffes and they are bad guys. If this is the case, why would we check out the elephants? It doesn't make any sense to check the elephants. We know the elephants are not suspects, so why check them out? It would be a waste of time and it would cost lots more to check the elephants so we can find the giraffes. It would simply be busywork. Law enforcement, paid by all the people cannot be engaged in busywork when there are real problems to solve.

If some giraffes that are caught in this web are actually OK, they deserve a big apology. Perhaps they should get a night on the town if they are inconvenienced. But, still, even if we get a few innocent giraffes, when the preponderance of the population of bad guys is in the giraffe species, it makes little sense to not acknowledge this. For the few mistakes we make, we can save a lot of anguish, money and time by not checking the elephants.

It would more than pay for the cost of the nights on the town and any inconvenience caused to the legal giraffes and it would make it easier to protect everybody. Isn't protecting everybody the real goal? Don't the misapprehended giraffes also benefit from that protection? Don't the obviously not suspect elephants gain by our not pretending that they look like suspects? How does it benefit the elephants to pull them over for a strip search when we know they are not suspects?

Only somebody wanting illegal residents to be treated as legal would offer the "brown skin" excuse, which Walcza raises. Should we be looking for blacks or whites if it is the browns who are illegal? Why is it that the AMERICAN "CLU" never seems to do anything for real Americans and it hardly ever gets anything right?

In a Hazleton Post-Gazette article back in 2006, Eugene Cannon, whose brother and I (unless I am mistaken) studied at King's College in the same major field of endeavor a long time ago, showed his support for the mayor and the law and he thinks the ACLU is way off base. Cannon says:

"The federal government has not been doing enough to stop illegal immigration. When Mayor Barletta advanced his initiative, it brought him national attention. I hope that will force the federal government to take some more direct action."

Amen!"

Chapter 31   Terrified Arizonans Pass Their Own Law

Progressives think Arizonans should turn other cheek

As previously noted, U.S. federal law is a lot tougher than the Arizona law SB1070 but the pro-amnesty pundits, and the over-aged hippie ruling class from the 1960's would prefer that you not know it. From the early chapters in this book, you now know that the feds in many instances choose not to enforce US immigration laws.

Since federal immigration law is not enforced, it does not really matter how tough it is. Over the past twenty years, the feds have come to think of the laws as optional. For each of the past twenty years, there has been less enforcement and in the last year of Obama, the laws have been almost completely ignored.

Arizona has had some people show up dead recently and so they are rightfully concerned about protecting their citizens. Without the helping hand of illegal immigrants, these one-time Arizona residents would still be alive today. So, Arizonans are ready for action to solve their own problem as *federal help* has become an oxymoron.

Dead rancher—killed by Mexicans—is this OK?

Robert Krentz, an Arizona rancher, for example, was gunned down early Saturday morning March 28, 2010 by an illegal immigrant while tending to fences on the family's 34,000-acre cattle ranch. According to neighbors, Krentz was a good man, who would help anybody, including hard pressed illegal aliens, no matter who they were.

Krentz had previously been burglarized, yet his charity prevailed right until the end. He often said that he would help any "illegal immigrant" that he could, and he did. In the end it cost him his life. If they came and asked for water, even after the burglary, Krentz affirmed he would give them whatever they needed to survive.

At 11 p.m. on March 28, a state police helicopter found Krentz in his ATV, slumped with the engine and lights still on. His dog had also been critically wounded by a bullet. The dog had to be put down but Krentz was dead when found. Neither made it through this encounter. Police tracker dogs followed the tracks of the killer back into Mexico, some 15 miles south of where Krentz was found. This was not deemed to be a coincidence. No progressives came to memorialize Krentz as a friend of the downtrodden. The media downplayed this event because it helped their cause of "open borders."

Progressives: illegals do not come to murder. They come to work.

Even good Samaritans are killed in the frightening battles going on in America's Southwest. Speculation is that Krentz may have been killed by a drug cartel scout, who was clearing the way for a shipment of drugs when Krentz probably surprised him with an offer of help.

Despite the death, the progressive advocates for illegal immigration argue that the killing was an aberration and that most illegal immigrants come to work, not to commit crime. Their message is to let it be. Yet, Robert Krentz is dead and will not be coming back. Most ranchers in Cochise County expect the progressives will have their way and they will receive little more than lip service from Washington and Krentz will soon be forgotten until the next death in Arizona.

So, Arizona, whose citizens have frequently been murdered and more frequently brutalized by Mexicans simply seeking the American dream, chose to create its own law to defend its people. But Obama said "no" and Eric Holder, the US Attorney General agreed and so the feds sued Arizona instead of fighting the border wars with Mexico. I suspect for those with a sense of adventure, it is a nice diversion. But, for those living along the Arizona border, it is a death sentence. With Washington thousands of miles away at least the President will not be harmed by his own decision.

All countries, including the US, require passports

The US law requires certain aliens to register with the U.S. government, and to have registration documents in their possession at all times. When you choose to travel to a foreign country, you cannot get out of the US without a valid passport so it is not cruel and unusual punishment to expect the same for those who visit our country. When you reach your destination, you must have your passport with you at all times.

If you visit the US legally, you must carry that passport with you at all times as your proof of identity. It is the way the law works in all countries. "Let me see your papers, please," is not a joke. In our country it is US federal law. And the federal law happens to be a superset of Arizona law. Arizona's law is nowhere as comprehensive as federal law. Yet, nobody complains about federal law because the progressives do not permit it to be enforced.

After Robert Krentz was killed by an illegal alien, Arizona recognized that it had to help itself. The progressives did not like this. They think Arizonans should simply lie down so the unfortunate foreign nationals can prosper, regardless of the harm they do in Arizona.

Progressives argue that carrying documentation is too much work for illegal foreign nationals to deal with. They seem to forget that all Americans in foreign lands must also carry such documentation. As noted, most often this documentation is in the form of a passport. Riding the trains of Europe as the train goes from one country to the next, border agents always come on the train. I can recall getting awakened a number of times to show my passport. The agents asked questions. Then they checked the passports and when all was

OK, they stamped all passports. Nobody gets by even while the train is moving. Border security is a trivial matter in no country but the US.

The Arizona Act takes the same covenant of the US law and makes it a state misdemeanor level crime for an alien to be in Arizona without carrying the required documents. What would Felipe Calderon recommend if he thinks this is too harsh? Looking at Mexican law, we see Calderon has already spoken. Mexico's law is substantially more restrictive.

The Arizona Law does have a few other provisions to help its citizens. Since certain cities such as Phoenix prefer no enforcement at all, the law is intended to get all Arizonans and all Arizona municipalities, including Phoenix, on board or they will be penalized for aiding and abetting illegal foreign nationals. It bars state or local officials or agencies from restricting the enforcement of the federal immigration laws and it has penalties for those sheltering, hiring and transporting illegal aliens. Ya gotta love it!

The idea according to the law is that illegal foreign nationals will leave Arizona rather than be caught in its proactive web. It seems like a good plan to me and it is a good plan for most people who do not want instant amnesty for Mexicans and other SOBs (from south of the border). It is a good plan for those that are not interested in returning to the old west style of justice when men sported six shooters in holsters and rifles attached to their saddlebags for their personal protection.

Soon, some worry, with no enforcement at the border and no ability to stop a perpetrator once identified, there may be so many Mexicans and other illegals in the US, that they will be running the US government. Though the argument is ad absurdum, it would place today's American as a person who would be unwelcome in both the United States of America as well as the United States of Mexico.

Nobody of whom I am aware has a problem with Mexicans running the Mexican government. Nobody has a problem with Mexicans residing safely in Mexico. As long as your neighbor chooses to live in their own home, rather than your home, chances are you will be able to get along.

The Critique of the Arizona law

Critics of the Arizona legislation, the progressives in our government, the ruling class, and other Mexicans wanting to make the great escape, are against anything that helps real Americans deal with the problems caused by illegal aliens and illegal criminals. Yet, the progressives in the ruling class do not want to be asked to unlock the roads through their gated communities to make themselves more accessible to the visitors from the south.

President Obama says that the Arizona law encourages racial profiling. That is drivel. If you, as an American want to keep the bad guys out of the country and they all look like X, can you see any reason why you should stop people who look like Y? Obama says that Arizona is not permitted to stop X's (the bad guys) alone. They must stop everybody or nobody. Isn't that plain stupid, and it shows why our problem with illegal aliens is so severe.

A sane country with a problem with X's would be working on the X problem and not on non-problems with Y's. That is why most Americans believe this notion of racial profiling regarding people who are X's, the most probable bad guys in this instance, should be deliberate but not because of racial aspects. Progressives know that by putting up a stink about anything, even silliness, is an easy way to shut down enforcement. The fact is that progressives do not want the laws enforced. All the talk is simply an Obama tactic of faking right and going left. "Just call them racists and we will have our way."

I am going to use an Irish analogy again to make my point. I have done this in several areas of this book, and I will again, because I am Irish. Using Irish as an example, I cannot hurt anybody or be accused of racism. If the Irish are invading, wouldn't most Americans have a problem with them simply because they were invading? If inexplicably overnight, wherever you looked, there was a guy or gal with red hair and freckles with a heavy brogue and perhaps the slight scent of John Jameson Whiskey on their breath, would that not be eerie. Would the non-Irish be comfortable with that? Wouldn't good Americans demand that blue or green eyed white people, with red hair and freckles, with perhaps just a slight hint of alcohol on their breath be stopped?

Sane people would argue, perhaps humorously that these are all characteristics of those under suspicion. Yes, that would make the Irish the suspects. And, if the Irish were invading at alarming rates, I would expect that not many Latinos would be checked or be OK with being checked? That, ladies and gentlemen, makes sense. To ignore the facts is nonsense.

To keep the critics at bay in Arizona, anticipating that asininity and its code term, racial profiling, would be the modus operandi of the opponents, so the Arizona legislature actually modified its bill with another Arizona House Bill # 2162 within a week of its passing SB 1070. The intent of the second bill was to address all of the concerns of the critics. But, even with this additional precaution, it was not good enough. How much is good enough for any group, such as the progressives, who will never be satisfied? Progressives will not be satisfied because their objective is open borders, amnesty, and free reign in America for all illegal aliens, regardless of their criminal posture.

I am not sure the critics can be satisfied ever because they are actually for the usurpation of American power by this foreign invasion. If you or I happen to lose our jobs so that they can feel good, well that's just some breakage they are willing to live with. Thank God America is a free country or I could not have even said that. Unless amnesty is granted, the guilt-ridden progressive hippies who are the ruling class today in America will not be satisfied with anything. They do not want the influx of illegal aliens to be stopped. They actually want it to continue at a faster pace and yet, because they are charmers at election time, we continue to elect them like as if they are not the cause of the problem.

We elected Harry Reid again, for example, knowing he is for unrestricted, undocumented immigration. But, many progressives were defeated and many more must be defeated in the next election. The good news for Americans is that we have elections at least every two years and we can rid America of all progressive leaders who have been delivering our country to the bad guys. This is the USA and not the old USSR, and we need to keep it this way.

Removal is the solution if occupation is the problem

With 30 to 50 million illegal foreign nationals on our soil and a good portion of Mexico's population on call to "come on down," we are occupied. There is no other term for it. The Southwestern states are in the worst shape, yet they are the ones who are OK with the situation. For the rest of us, we recognize fully that this is not a stray person here and there. We have been invaded, still are being invaded, and, when invaders settle into one of our neighborhoods, unimpeded, we are occupied.

The US immigration laws are seen to be so ineffective that those who want illegal foreign nationals free to be exploited by US businessmen are very concerned that any new law might hurt their business. Many businesses do not want enforcement that would cause an exodus to Mexico and further south for their illegal workers as it would make it hard for them to maintain their lofty incomes. Yes, in recent years, those lofty incomes have been coming right off the backs of exploited workers, who have taken the jobs of regular Americans.

Real American citizens want the illegal portion of the population to self deport and their jobs to be made available to the general American populace for fair wages. "So, what is wrong with that?" When the right thing is to do the right thing, there is no reason to go left. Unfortunately for the rest of us, Americans, who demand that our laws be enforced, face a powerful ruling class of has-been hippies, who are happy to give Mexico the upper hand. I think I have identified them many times in this book already. In simple terms, these are known as progressives.

Any law designed to restrict the "rights" of illegal foreign nationals will destroy the plans of progressives to give illegal foreign nationals full amnesty with an immediate green card and the promise of citizenship. And to punish you for being against their will and giving them a hard time, you will pay the freight for the illegals who live in America, to the tune of as much as a half trillion or more dollars per year. The notion of Americans paying for illegals is as absurd as the opponents of the Arizona law are absurd. Then again, the progressives are ruling America today and sanity has clearly been left behind.

The progressive pro-amnesty crowd and the biased US media have been so effective in damning the good intentions of Arizona and the US in general, to enforce its borders that they have caused protests in opposition to the Arizona law in over 70 U.S. cities. There have been boycotts and calls for boycotts of Arizona and Arizona products. Why anybody would take the side of a criminal over a US citizen is a puzzle indeed.

Many no-minds have joined the boycotts. Here is how dumb they are. Arizona Iced Tea, formerly the darling of the iPad and Twitter Crowds, was particularly singled out as a product to avoid. It contained that recently demonized word, *Arizona*. These non-thinking former tea fans vowed to switch to Lipton, Tetley, or even Snapple. Don't worry; they will not be invited to any TEA party any time soon. Some bright eyed tweets labeled Arizona Iced Tea as the drink of fascists. Hah! There was a little bit of a logic problem on the short-lived boycott since Arizona Iced Tea is actually brewed in New York. Dah!

On the lighter side, that reminds me of a W. C Fields movie in which he told a tale in which the settlers and the wagons were crossing a river and they were attacked by "Indians." WC

Fields in full character came out of the water with his Bowie Knife and he "cut a path through this world of human flesh, dragging his canoe behind him." A heckler in the audience said, "Bowie knives weren't invented then." Fields was ready for him. Without batting an eye, to keep the story going, Fields in full character, said, "I knew that but the Indians didn't."   Let's all have some nice TEA on that one.

~~Jim Dandy~~ Eric Holder to the rescue

The federal government, namely Attorney General Eric Holder, known to very few as a defender of the Constitution, representing the same government that is supposed to be protecting US from illegal invaders, chose instead to take Arizona to court. I kid you not. Eric Holder, still looking for the missing other-half of his brain, so he could have a matched set, went to court to challenge the Arizona law. Holder's argument is that the feds, and the feds alone, have the last say on immigration. It is exactly because of Holder's say, "come on down" that Arizona chose to defend itself against the illegal aggression and in many ways, the war that its people are facing.

By the end of July, 2010, Eric Holder's Justice Department had won part of its case. A federal judge blocked several parts of Arizona's new immigration law. U.S. District Judge Susan Bolton ruled that a number of provisions were unconstitutional including that law enforcement officers could not check the immigration status of offenders during stops for unrelated offenses. Some would suggest that Judge Bolton is a progressive, appointed by President Bill Clinton, and that she is a judicial activist. So, she got to make a new law contrary to US law. We must recall that the Arizona law is a subset of US law. By the way, here is the US law:

> Legal resident aliens are required to carry their registration card per United States Code: TITLE 8 > CHAPTER 12 > SUBCHAPTER II > Part VII > § 1304
>
> (e) Personal possession of registration or receipt card; penalties
> Every alien, eighteen years of age and over, shall at all times carry with him and have in his personal possession any certificate of alien registration or alien registration receipt card issued to him pursuant to subsection (d) of this section. Any alien who fails to comply with the provisions of this subsection shall be guilty of a misdemeanor and shall upon conviction for each offense be fined not to exceed $100 or be imprisoned not more than thirty days, or both.

Judge Susan Bolton however thinks law enforcement officers cannot be trusted with the checking of immigration status. Bolton ruled, "There is a substantial likelihood that officers will wrongfully arrest legal resident aliens under the new [law]. ... By enforcing this statute, Arizona would impose a 'distinct, unusual and extraordinary' burden on legal resident aliens that only the federal government has the authority to impose."

If this were really the ruling instead of this merely being a political delaying tactic so that progressives can get amnesty passed, AG Holder would send in some shadow federal reps to make sure the locals know how to do it right. But, it is about stopping anything that is not full amnesty. Holder, Napolitano and Obama make a great team of immigration law impeders.

So, the law faced tough scrutiny from Judge Susan Bolten and again in November from a federal appeals panel. The progressive liberal 9th U.S. Circuit Court of Appeals agreed with Judge Bolden and signaled its readiness to toss out the provision of Arizona's law that criminalizes the failure to carry immigration papers showing lawful residency in the United States.

In the hearing, U.S. Deputy Solicitor General Edwin Kneedler argued that the provisions in question violate laws making immigration enforcement the exclusive domain of the federal government. "If every state did this, we would have a patchwork of law," Kneedler said.

Arizona's legislature passed the law in frustration that the federal government hasn't done its job to stop the invasion at the nation's busiest illegal entry point. "All Arizona is saying is play by the rules," Arizona Counsel John Bouma said. "Arizona is bearing the brunt of the federal government's failure to enforce it."

After the November hearing, Jan Brewer, Arizona's Governor, clearly stated that Arizona would appeal any adverse ruling to the U.S. Supreme Court. She added that Illegal immigrants are overwhelming Arizona's health care systems, schools and prisons, and she noted that the Obama administration's lawsuit was misguided because the state law seeks only to address a growing problem in Arizona. Brewer made her point: "We are not the enemy — we are part of the United States," she said. "We need more help and support."

The *big trio*, Obama, Napolitano, and Holder will not be giving Arizona help any time soon.

Since the feds said it was their job to defend Arizona and at least for now, they won in court, Governor Brewer sued the feds. "Do your job then!" With good reason, Brewer's case said the Obama administration had failed to prevent illegal immigrants from crossing the border in huge numbers and had stuck the state with the cost of dealing with its failed policies. Brewer offered the reason:

> "Arizona did not ask for this fight with the federal government, but now that we are in it, Arizona will not rest until our border is secured and federal immigration laws are enforced."

Progressives are very resilient and very stubborn and from my vantage point, I would add, very anti-American. When AG Eric Holder, Homeland Security Chief Janet Napolitano, and President Barack Obama know full well that they can use all the help they can get in enforcing US immigration laws, and still they refuse the help, the only conclusion that is logical on this matter is that they have no interest in doing what is right for America. Thank you Janet Brewer!

After all, once amnesty comes their way, there will be 30 million to 50 million new progressives to continue to champion their cause. That's as many as 50 million new Democrats. If regular American citizens do not like what they are doing, too bad! Soon, the replacement citizens will be here and regular citizens will have their voices completely drowned out. And, the big trio will be smiling from ear to ear.

That seems to be the only logical reason for the big trio to be so anti US-citizen. The only way these progressive socialists can be defeated is for every regular American to vote them out of office. We get our chance every two years. Let's make the most of it each time we get the chance.

2011 Happenings

More and more states are looking at the Arizona bill and are creating laws that mirror Arizona. For example, In Indiana in the last week of February 2011, its Senate passed a bill similar Arizona's SB 1070. It passed quite handily with a vote of 31-18. So the bill is on its way to the House where it is expected to pass. Americans are fed up with the federal government and are looking for the states to help solve the illegal migration dilemma. The bill generally requires state and local law enforcement to ask for proof of legal residency from individuals the officer has lawfully stopped or detained if the officer has reasonable suspicion that the individual is in the country unlawfully. (*Id.*; SB 590) The bill also mandates that state agencies and state contractors to use E-verify and requires that only the English language be used in public meetings and public documents.

One state at a time is fine with me but let's make sure we get rid of the inept charlatans who claim to be securing our homeland next time around. They all work for the Executive Branch of our government and that of course is under the control right now of a man by the name of Barack Hussein Obama. Perhaps you have heard of him.

Chapter 32   Racial Profiling

Are we all racists?

One of the most innocuous definitions of racial profiling comes from the racetoeducate.com site. According to this group, "racial profiling is a form of over-policing, which involves the singling out of an individual for greater scrutiny or differential treatment by the police or security officials."

For years, police officers who worked the statistics, believed, wrongly or rightly, that black men were more prone to commit crimes than white men and so they would stop a higher proportion of blacks than whites while performing their duties of protecting the citizens. Understandably, this disturbed many law-abiding black people as they were being singled out solely because of the color of their skin in a matter that never, to the best of my knowledge, was affirmed as a proper rationale. In other words, I have never heard a confirmed public statement that one could use as a maxim that says that blacks or whites are more prone to be criminals.

The term racial profiling was affixed to this notion. Overall, most Americans can see that judging somebody by the mere color of their skin is intrinsically wrong and so racial profiling became quickly known as a bad, mostly hateful activity.
While the public does not have a clear affirmation or denial from the federal government or any government public policy group that certain "races" are involved in more crimes than others, it would be unfair of me to leave the reader with the notion that those on the front line, where the battles between lawmen and lawbreakers are fought do not "know" how it is. For them, they may be able to identify over twenty races, though there are, in reality, only three. They "know" how it is and they can taste it and if they ignore that while on the streets, they will become a casualty. It is that simple when political correctness must be removed from the scenario.

There just has not been a public policy statement on it saying it is so. Look up the crime statistics, however for Los Angeles, or any other major city you might name. The statistical reality is that blacks and Latinos are responsible for a far greater share of the city's crime than every other ethnic group combined. One might argue that this is because they are profiled and thus arrested more frequently than other "races." That may or may not be true.

There is so much pressure, however, by the ethnic interest groups that this notion cannot be affirmed. Yet, the truth does not lie. Lawmen whose lives depend on being right, know, and they must act accordingly while their superiors dodge the bullets from the civil rights groups and the media. One might suggest that only people like Bill Cosby have the real courage to do what is necessary to keep the streets of America safe. Other spokesmen are welcome to speak.

Today the term racial profiling has taken on far greater meaning than the past. Words certainly do have power. A companion term that goes right along with the forces that prevent any of the merits of racial profiling from reaching a point in which they can be honestly discussed is the word, *racist*. The word "racist" is thrown around an awful lot. In blogs that discuss the term, it appears that most people believe the term racist is "thrown around" by way too many people, not really knowing what it means.

Let's look at what it really means and then what it has become. Looking back at the word origin, the term was used as a belief that one's race was superior to another through biological differences. Whether one race is superior in any way to another is another notion that has no public answer. Science has determined that each race has its own hindrances and benefits. But, there is not one definable trait or traits that elevate one race as superior or push down another as inferior to another race from a biological perspective.

And, thus, the term in its colloquial use today is used to depict someone who doesn't like another race or another person simply because of their supposed race. That isn't racism, however, despite how the word is used. It is certainly hate or fear, but not racism. At least it is not racism yet, but words do evolve. There are lots of hates and lots of fears but most haters and most fearers are not racists.

The races in the race

Now, let's take a look at the word, race, the basis of both terms, racist and racial profiling as it has customarily been used and as it is understood by those who perhaps graduated from high school in the 1960's. The fact is that the notion of race (social, ethnic, etc) is a moving target but the characteristics that anthropologists used in the 1960's to classify humans have not changed. In high school, the sexagenarians of today learned that from an anthropological standpoint, there are three and only three races. The three races are as follows in alphabetical order:

- Caucasian
- Mongoloid
- Negroid

Caucasian is colloquially known as white. Mongoloid is colloquially known as yellow and also Asian, and Negroid is colloquially known as black and also Negro. There is nothing inherently good or bad about these classifications and they have been in place for many years. Over the years, they have been used by forensic anthropologists who examine long-dead human remains to aid in the identification of the body, including race. The fact is that the racial categories identified way back in the 19th century are in widespread use today among forensic anthropologists. Anthropological "race" has nothing to do with racial profiling, racists, or even illegal immigration. In their analysis, according to Wikipedia, scientists use this hierarchy to determine the race of human remains:

> "In many cases there is little doubt that an individual belonged to the Negro, Caucasian, or Mongoloid racial stock."

"Thus the forensic anthropologist uses the term race in the very broad sense to differentiate what are commonly known as white, black and yellow racial stocks."

"In estimating race forensically, we prefer to determine if the skeleton is Negroid, or Non-Negroid. If findings favor Non-Negroid, then further study is necessary to rule out Mongoloid."[

The bottom line is that there are only three races, no matter what popular thought has brought to the table. Hispanic and Latino, as two terms recently used to describe a race of people, are mere depicters of social, behavioral, or language characteristics. Hispanic is not a race. Latino is not a race. Hispanic is a very broad brushed term that we will describe in detail in this chapter. Whatever it may be, it is not a race.

Rightly or wrongly, anthropologists have dedicated copious amounts of research examining the relationship of the biological characteristics of living humans and their skeletons. This enables them to get a perspective about what a person was like when they were alive as at the time of their life a particular racial label would have been applied to them.

Hispanic or Latino?

Let me repeat. Hispanic is not a race. Latino is not a race. Like it or not, Hispanic and Latino mean the same thing to most people, who are not Hispanic or Latino. Ultimately, the determination of Hispanic or Latino is up to the person who potentially is classified using one or the other term. Unfortunately, there is no agreed upon universal definition, yet those who think they are Latino often argue that they are not Hispanic and they resent the notion with all the power of their being.

For the non-Hispanic and non-Latino, it is tough knowing sameness or differences when there is no strict definition of *Hispanic* or *Latino*. Let's take a look at a few definitions of Hispanic and Latino. Surely each of the organizations that put forth these sample definitions would like theirs to be universally adopted. From my research, I think the best we can expect if this ever happens is a combo pack.

> **Hispanic:** Spanish American: an American whose first language is Spanish related to a Spanish-speaking people or culture; "the Hispanic population of California is growing rapidly" Though part of the original Hispania, the Portuguese argue veraciously that they are not Hispanic.

> **Latino:** Latin American: a native of Latin America; an artificial language based on words common to the Romance languages; Hispanic: related to a Spanish-speaking people or culture; "the Hispanic population of California is growing rapidly"; Mexican American, Central American, South American, Cuban, Puerto Rican, Other Latino, Spanish origin, Hispanic; latinos - People who speak Spanish and originally come from Mexico and Central-America.

You tell me—but don't blame me if I get it wrong!

So, if you are either Hispanic or Latino, how would you identify yourself on official records? The College Board, the administrators of the Scholastic Aptitude Test, as an example, asks the student to self-identify. They are not interested in joining the conflict. The U.S. Census Bureau chooses to make no distinction between the two terms. It now defines Hispanics and Latinos as "persons who trace their origin or descent to Mexico, Puerto Rico, Cuba, Spanish-speaking Central and South America countries, and other Spanish cultures." However, an individual can opt out of the Census Bureau prescription. For example, if someone from Brazil says he's Hispanic, the census doesn't say, No, you're not.

The real question in terms of race is: Are Hispanics (1) Caucasian, (2) Mongoloid, or (3) Negroid. Theoretically, they may be any of the above, or a mix, just like most people today.

She invented the term Hispanic

Official Washingtonians and other US government officials credit Grace Flores-Hughes, a minor level bureaucrat, a wordsmith and a Mexican American "Hispanic" herself, with coining the term Hispanic circa 1970. She spent time working as an assistant in the old HEW Office (Department of Health, Education and Welfare). While there, Flores-Hughes coined the term and helped establish "Hispanic" as the government's word of choice for classifying people of Spanish origin. As a Mexican American, she was happy with her new word, but I can tell you my first cousin Frank, an American descendent of Spain is not quite as pleased as Grace. Frank says he is Spanish and considers his race to be "white." In 1980, Flores-Hughes' work made it into the official U.S. Census. I read an interview on her in a Web magazine. Feel free to look up Flores-Hughes for more information.

Flores-Hughes believes the word Hispanic represents the bulk of Hispanic Americans of the United States. Yes, I find it troubling that she used the term to describe the people to whom she was ascribing the term. She thought it best represents who the people are based on their Hispanic surnames. She is not in favor of the terms "Latino" (male) or "Latina" (female), in which one must know the gender in order to apply the label.

Flores-Hughes' problem with the terms, however is that she still feels those terms can also represent the people of the Mediterranean. With that, Portuguese and Italians would be included in the mix if you take it literally. In other words, Portuguese and Italians are not Hispanic, yet they are Latino or Latina.

She believes that this takes away from the Hispanic people of America that need to be counted in government surveys. Considering her work as a statistician of sorts, Flores-Hughes position was always to make counting of all categories easier. Hispanic as a checkbox accomplished this for her. That is what this is all about. Hispanic is a handy government checkbox, designed for Hispanics, by a Hispanic.

Flores-Hughes admits that it was not a rollover in HEW that caused Hispanic to be the adopted term. She asserted that the sides in choosing a term were very contentious. There were contingents in HEW who were pushing for the word "Latino." Flores-Hughes, however was steadfast in her belief that the term Hispanic captured the meaning she wished to present and gave the meaning therefore, the most justice. She really pushed for "Hispanic." She was the youngest one in the HEW group and so it was hard for her to get attention. Yet, her point of view prevailed since she demonstrated that the only way, in her opinion; to get an accurate count was by using the term "Hispanic." And, counting was Grace's mission.

For years Spanish people have not wanted to fill in forms in which they were to be classified as Latin American, when they were not Latin American. So they would not answer on the forms. Some would write in, "We're not Latin. We're Spanish." Over time the notion of "Hispanic" prevailed. Flores-Hughes admits that was a big part of her rationale for the term Hispanic in addition to it being one term versus "Latino and Latina." Could there have been another agenda in play?

Her group, in the US government, was really trying to open the doors for Mexican Americans to gain more government benefits. And in that respect, the term worked. Moreover, by having the word Hispanic carry over into the immigration debate, it adds to the arguments put forth by the amnesty team that Hispanics are disenfranchised and need American help. Of course, they prefer not to discuss the fact that the illegal Hispanics in the immigration debate have broken American laws and the help they receive is from American taxpayers who receive no such help.

In many ways, the use of the term, Hispanic, therefore was an affirmative action decision that helped those classified as Hispanic to get benefits for which non-Hispanic Americans were not entitled. It created the notion of Hispanic as a racial minority needing more care and feeding than other segments of American society. Yet, we know that many Hispanics, just like cousin Frank, are white by race.

Flores-Hughes sees the people in South Texas with whom she grew up as the Hispanics that best fit the classification she devised. Many of them were poor; others were disenfranchised. Flores Hughes' thinking was that they needed a classification so that those of this type of Spanish descent could argue for more federal funds or more federal help. By classifying as Hispanic instead of White or Yellow or Black, the only three available honest choices for race, they could know how many there were, able to request the funding necessary to support the needs of this large mass of people.

So, as a conclusion, we now know that Hispanic and Latino are not races. Bureaucrats coined these terms so they could be used as races had been used in the past to help place certain people into specific "racial" minority categories to help them gain government assistance before those in other "racial" categories. .

Though Flores-Hughes triumphed in the 1980 census and the term "Hispanic" won out over "Latino," today, the census combines three terms Spanish/ Hispanic/ Latino with slashes. According to Flores-Hughes this is good for government reporting as the numbers get higher and higher as more people are included, and that means more government benefits are provided for those who may choose to call themselves *Hispanic.*

Now that you know the differences between Hispanic and Latino / Latina, and you know that both terms, when used to classify races are contrivances and do not truly reflect race, don't you think it is a little burdensome on the rest of us? Suppose we are not Hispanic or Latino. Can we understand the subtle differences as well as the fact that personal preference plays a major role in whether an individual is classified by the government as Hispanic or Latino? Does it matter?

Some people get quite upset when they are called Hispanic v. Latino or Latina. "Latina" and "Latino" seem to have become more chic. "Hispanic" to many appears to be a much older term or a term for older people. Young people like to use the term "Latino." On the political scene, Democrats like to call themselves Latinos while Republicans call themselves Hispanics.

Even the media sees and acknowledges the battle of the dueling monikers. For example in an editorial or a printed piece, they'll use "Hispanic," and they'll use the word "Latina" later on just so they don't upset anybody. For those not engaged in the battle, it is confusing. However, under no circumstances should anyone think that Hispanic or Latino is a name for a race. There are still only three races.

Hispania

Historically, Hispanic can be seen as a cultural reference to Hispania, which originally referred to the whole Iberian Peninsula (Portugal, Spain and a few smaller countries as conquered by the Romans). The word "Hispania," which later became Esparia, refers to the people and culture of the Iberian Peninsula. It refers to Spain in particular. The term Hispanic evolved from the word Hispano and was used when referring to Spain and its subsequent New World - New Spain, its conquered territories, which cover most of what is referred to as Latin America.

Hispanic thus refers to people whose culture and heritage goes back to Spain and, as we look at second and third generation Hispanic-Americans, they may or may not speak Spanish, though this was once a differentiator. That is why in the Latino / Hispanic debate, today, as definitions are changing as we speak, beauty is in the eye of the beholder.

As simple as this may be to those who grew up with the terms, for most of us, it is confusing. Having words that mean different things depending on what geography they refer to is quite confusing.

On the site, http://www.angelfire.com/country/portugal/, a blogger known only as "*One of the Lusiads*," meaning he is Portuguese, does a nice job of differentiating Portugal within the Hispanic umbrella and in so doing he casts an illuminating light on the full meaning of the word Hispanic. If you have the opportunity to take a run out to angelfire, I think it would serve you well.

The big dictionaries in the US, as we have already demonstrated show "Hispanic" as being "of or related to Spain." The Websters' Dictionary, according to "*One of the Lusiads*," gets it right. They say, Hispanic means "relating to or derived from the speech or culture of Spain or of Spain and Portugal." In the US, however, the word "Hispanic" he admits has evolved into something different. It is used to describe all the Spanish-speaking immigrants and their descendants. Since the Portuguese do not speak Spanish, technically they are not Hispanic, and after fighting in so many wars against a dominating Spain, and surviving, they like it that way.

Oxford University Press, 1999, defines "new" words that have been developed in the 20th century. It asserts that the word "Hispanic" is a "new" word developed in the United States in the 1970s as meaning "*Someone Spanish-speaking. Applied especially to someone of Latin American descent living in the US.*" Perhaps they should meet Grace Flores-Hughes. Thus, again in making his case, "*One of the Lusiads,*" concludes that we are able to see that Portuguese people are thus NOT defined as Hispanic. That is, as a Portuguese person, he is not "related to or derived from the culture of Spain or of Spain and Portugal." He asserts that he is "related to or derived from the culture of Portugal alone — NOT of BOTH Spain and Portugal."

It is a simple phenomenon. Things that are confusing are confusing regardless of the attempts of complex people to make them appear to be simple. Hispanic is another word of many words in US culture that has both kept and lost its original meaning. How about the word: "Indian?" It no longer always means someone from India. However, we all know it eventually also became used to describe the natives of the Americas. And, there are many other such words.

In Flores-Hughes definition, the US government defines "Hispanic" as "*a person of Mexican, Puerto Rican, Cuban, Central or South American or other Spanish culture or origin, regardless of race.*" "*One of the Lusiads*" notes that even the Census Bureau has advised that those of Portuguese descent in America should not choose "Hispanic" in the census. Therefore, when filling out the census, the Portuguese should pick "not of Hispanic origin" in the ethnicity question just like all other non-Hispanics, and "white" in the race question.

Pedigree only matters to the eyes

Now we turn to the Irish, who thankfully are not in question in this book. Call us Micks; call us Harps; call us late for dinner because we quench our thirst at Happy Hour, but don't invent another term on the census to lump our national ethnicity along with any others to for a larger minority group. It seems that the term "white," is the term in which Irish are lumped today. To many Americans, Irish will still be lumped as white in thirty years or so.

Many Irish, such as myself are more pink than white. But for me, a full blooded Irishman (FBI) that is OK. I don't mind how I look. Likewise there is nothing wrong with the Mexican look; nor is there anything wrong with the Polish look, which my in-laws wear quite well. In fact, there is nothing wrong with the Italian look that my wine provider enshrines, or the German look that my buddy across the street exhibits.

All of this "look" stuff is meaningless in the US immigration battle, however, unless you live in Arizona or another border state. Facts are stubborn little things that are tough to avoid. The fact is the Irish, Polish, and Germans are not sending millions of settlers to America each year and the days of "squatters rights" are long gone. Another fact is that if the Irish were the culprits who were invading the US, other Americans of Irish descent, such as me would be working on the American side. Sorry cuz!

I see nothing racial in being able to identify somebody as "Black" or Mexican, Guatemalan, Brazilian, Haitian, Hispanic, Irish , Italian, or German. Our waiter on the Carnival Cruise that we took three or so years ago said he was from the Dominican Republic. I had no idea. Eventually after all the friendly banter, he confided that his nickname was "Sweet Chocolate." I think that is neat. And, I felt no need to suggest that vanilla or strawberry was a better flavor.

We are adults and life is life and good people are good people so we all would be better off without the idea that we cannot discuss the natural characteristics of the ethnic populations. They are very different and the differences are very attractive for those interested in how things look. If, somehow I could wake up and not have pink skin (shhhh!!!), I would still be OK. Yet, I am accustomed to how I am and how I look as are most people. So, pink skin is OK for me.

We are who we are

Most people do not want to change to something else because God has given us our definition when he stamped us out originally right before he had the stork deliver us to our new homes. I do know, however, that my pinkish whitish skin is about as bad as it gets for skin color, especially for somebody who likes the sun. When it tans it is dark red and it burns first. It never looks really tan and often is flaky (ughhhh!). So, why does that matter to me or anybody else? It sure doesn't matter to me!

In fact, if there is racial bigotry in the predominant public PC formula for OK-ness at all, it is the notion that all white people are merely white people. I do not think of myself as a white person. I think I am American of Irish descent. If color is important, most days, as noted previously, I look a bit pinkish and that's not too flattering but I am OK with it because that is how I look. I am a descendent of Irish immigrants who had one heck of a hard time making life OK in America after they were permitted to join the pack during the Ellis Island days--by the proper authorities. If I were Guatemalan or Mexican, I don't think I would want to be Hispanic—but I don't really know.

I don't think that being able to identify a Mexican person as Mexican is any more racial than being able to identify an Irish person as Irish. And, yes, when I get my mean face on, (very infrequently I hope) I don't look Irish at all. I look ---- hah, I am not going to say. See my point. You thought I was going to say French or German or Swedish. But I tricked you and I am not going to tell you.

Irish people may be taken for Scots or Brits or even Germans. Mexicans may be taken for Hondurans, Nicaraguans, Brazilians, and sometimes even Irish. I suspect very few Mexicans are taken for Irish but it happens and the converse is also true. Few Irish are taken to be Mexican. Genealogy is not perfect and so this surely happens. Who cares? Mostly nobody! And we have no reason to care unless we are looking for political advantage.

My point here is that there is also nothing racial and nothing nasty about supposing somebody is Irish. Asking somebody who merely looks Irish for ID would be OK if all Irish felt that it was OK. There is also nothing racial and nothing nasty about supposing somebody is Mexican. Asking somebody who merely looks Mexican for ID would be OK if all Mexicans felt that it was OK. If the Irish were invading the US in record numbers, as the Mexican people have clearly chosen to do in recent years, as an American, I would have to make a choice. Though I am Irish, I would have two choices -- America or Ireland for my allegiance. The choice would be clear for me. I am an American and it is only my blood line that is Irish.

Americans come from a melting pot

My spirit is American and I have been assimilated in the melting pot of the USA, and I am very thankful for that. I think it is fair to say that diversity of origin is great but either assimilate or get out. I see no reason to pretend that as an American, I should want to admit a person into my country, who does not want to assimilate as a full-fledged American. If you want to migrate but you don't want to be a real American, I would prefer that you go someplace else. Why come here otherwise?

One of my best friends of all time, to whom I recently mailed a campaign T-shirt, is an Osage Indian descendent. He is a great man. He was a manager of mine at IBM and I did not give him any extra credit or any less credit in my relationship because of his Osage background. Did I see some identifying characteristics in this Native American? No, not at first! Quite frankly I was not looking for any. It did not matter to me what he was. It was only after he told me his heritage that I could see how it could be so. Most of the time, most Americans are not into guessing ethnic lines. Now, if you are not speaking English—that is something I would notice.

My Syrian friends and Lebanese friends are both from the same general area of the world yet they think they are different. Can I tell them apart? Quite frankly, No! They are all good looking. By the way, I was unaware my old boss, the 1/2 Osage and 1/2 French person who I befriended about 30 years ago was either French or Indian. But, it did not take him too long to notice that I was Irish and I still am not upset with him for letting me know that. So what?

My point on racial profiling, racists, and race is that the battle is over. Everybody in America except the new people, legal and illegal know that Americans know they are part of the melting pot as a way of life.

The reason you have not been invited to stay, Mr. illegal foreign national is because you chose to disrespect all of us in America, who are proud to be American. If you like America so much as to want to live here, go back and sign up. Your time will come. In the meantime a brave person such as yourself should be able to help your own country evolve into a place where you can live peaceably. Think about it.

I'd like to wrap up this Chapter on Racial Profiling by presenting the candid opinion of Michael Kinsley from way back in September 30, 2001 from the Washington Post. Michael knows how to say what he is thinking and at least this time, he thinks like most Americans:

When Is Racial Profiling Okay?
By Michael Kinsley
Washington Post
Sunday, September 30, 2001; Page B07

"When thugs menace someone because he looks Arabic, that's racism. When airport security officials single out Arabic-looking men for a more intrusive inspection, that's something else. What is the difference? The difference is that the airport security folks have a rational reason for what they do. An Arab-looking man heading toward a plane is statistically more likely to be a terrorist. That likelihood is infinitesimal, but the whole airport rigmarole is based on infinitesimal chances. If trying to catch terrorists this way makes sense at all, then Willie-Sutton logic says you should pay more attention to people who look like Arabs than to people who don't. This is true even if you are free of all ethnic prejudices. It's not racism. "

Though this is not Fox New, it is a book by Brian Kelly; I would like this ending to this chapter on racial profiling to be fair and balanced. Within one day of this Kinsley article appearing, a gentleman by the name of Hizam Bitar offered a rebuttal. The title of his article is:

Race-Baiting at the Washington Post -- Refuting Michael Kinsley
By Hizam Bitar Oct 1, 2001--
http://www.counterpunch.org/bitar.html

Feel free to read Bitar's very one-sided analysis as he picked on many of the suppositions that Michael Kinsey used in the article, which I quoted from above. Beauty clearly is in the eye of the beholder. Bitar's piece was written because he is annoyed that anybody would suggest that trying to identify the bad guys by using the information that you have learned about their general or specific appearance should be permitted in a free society. It sounds like Mr. Bitar has a stake in the game and his arguments. As much as he picked on Kinsley's piece, Bitar's arguments were not so cogent.

When you look to see who Michael Kinsley really is, you can conclude that it must have pained him to logically conclude that there are times that certain things, such as the color of one's skin or their general aura can be effectively used to limit the suspects. One of those times is now in which a huge percentage of illegal aliens are Hispanic and they are flooding the American Southwest in a sea of illegal occupancy.

Michael Kinsley is a liberal progressive who should be against profiling Arabs and Hispanics, and even the Irish, but he is too smart to ignore the folly of checking nobody or everybody. Back in 1989, Kinsley took a position on CNN's *Crossfire*, along with conservative Pat Buchanan. Kinsley represented the liberal or left-wing position in the often heated debates. He was a foe with which to be reckoned and he rarely backed down. Instead, he used his dry wit, nerdy demeanor, and critical analytical skills to win the day against Buchanan and others. He is the last person to promote a conservative thought if he had not reasoned it to be correct. Let's look at a snapshot of Bitar's article in response to Kinsley's assertion that it might be OK to profile Arabs.

"...Before we start let's see if we can define who is an 'Arab-looking man.' Since there is no legal or scientific definition, Kinsley could be referring to common stereotypes such as a hooked nose, swarthy complexion, facial hair, and other physically unattractive attributes by Western standards. It's the images of Arabs most Americans have been conditioned by Hollywood to hate and to look out for. This stereotype excludes fair-looking Arabs from many Mediterranean regions as well as Black Arabs from African countries such as Sudan, Somal, and Mauritania. This exclusion leaves out a pretty sizable chunk of Arabs...."

There is more about Arabs in Bitar's piece but enough is enough. It is like the prose above. Kinsley must have really upset Bitar. From my perspective, Bitar does little here in trying to refute Kinsley than to beg the argument.

Even though most of us could probably identify an Arab with relative accuracy, admittedly, we would be wrong sometimes. The same goes for Irish and Mexican. So what if somebody's feelings get hurt if a planeload of people are saved and very, very few have to get groped or star in an x-rated TSA film to assure our safety. Even if we cannot identify in a non-callous way, the characteristics of an Arab, we do know for the most part what an Arab is not. That ought to help in critical identification.

For example, an Arab in this context is not a three year old or an 80 year old grandmother. Other hints that a person is non-Arab are a large or fat body, light straight hair, blue or green eyes, pug nose, fluent English or European language, not Arabic speaking, etc. etc. Of course Arabs may also have these characteristics but substantially less often than non-Arabs.

For a continuation discussion of racial profiling, with a different slant, please continue to Chapter 33 for a set of different perspectives.

Chapter 33   Racial Profiling: Another Perspective

Are brown-skinned people's feelings getting hurt?

© Copyright 2010, Russell D. Longcore. Permission to reprint in whole or in part is gladly granted, provided full credit is given.
http://dumpdc.wordpress.com/2010/05/07/arizona-immigration-and-racial-profiling-liberal-panties-are-in-a-wad/

Author's Note: Nobody ever says anything exactly the way you would say it or I would say it. So, I came across this piece on the Internet about racial profiling and though some of it, including the title as shown below is not exactly as I would have said it, this author's words in many instances are compelling. By demonizing the mere notion of profiling and labeling it all as racial profiling, supporters of too many other groups have prevented its legitimate use as the best tool in many instances -- such as terrorism and illegal immigration. This author gets to the heart of the matter with his quick wit and unique style. As adults all concerned about how to effectively control illegal immigration, this should be an enjoyable and informative read for us all.

"Arizona, Immigration and Racial Profiling: Liberal Panties are in a Wad –"
by Russell D. Longcore

OK, my friends. It's time for some truth about the law, truth about human nature and some desperately needed perspective.

The civil rights activists are not demonstrating to protect civil rights in Arizona. They are protesting to protect brown-skinned people from getting their feelings hurt.

Once again…I'm not a lawyer. There could exist lots of case law that rolls a grenade under the bed of my arguments. But this is a secession website. I look at EVERYTHING through the liberty-tinted glasses of state liberation from the tyranny of The United States of America. As such, I consider all case law and Federal law irrelevant to the new laws of a new nation.

First: stop listening to all the people telling you what this law says and read it yourself.

Arizona Immigration Law SB1070

All I seem to hear on the various media outlets is how the new Arizona immigration law COULD…not will…result in the dreaded practice of "racial profiling."

According to the redoubtable Wikipedia, Racial Profiling is "the inclusion of racial or ethnic characteristics in determining whether a person is considered likely to commit a particular type of crime or an illegal act or to behave in a "predictable" manner. The fact remains that racial profiling is also targeted against Europeans and others with similar ethnic features when abroad, as the practice has been common throughout the world for centuries."

Profiling refers to a GENERAL description of a particular type of offender as opposed to listing the physical characteristics or behavioral characteristics of a suspect or group of suspects…like cops do when on the lookout for a criminal (age 20-25, white, blue eyes, brown hair, clean shaven, wearing khaki pants and a red T-shirt).

Another less pejorative word for profiling is "generalize," which means "to infer trends from particular facts."

Human beings generalize every day because for the most part… generalization works.

Are farmers "profiling" beetles that eat his corn crop? He learns the particular appearance and behavior of the corn eaters. It ain't the Monarch butterflies munching on his crop.

You're on a dark street at night when five young black men approach you. If the young men are heavily tattooed with their pants hanging down, you'll probably react differently than if you are approached by five young white men in business suits all carrying Bibles. Are you profiling?

Parents see that the neighbor kids have spots all over their skin. Is it profiling to generalize that the kids may have measles or chicken pox? Is it wrong to keep your kids away from the neighbor kids because of what their appearance could mean for your family's health? Maybe you should keep your children away from ALL the other children, so the children with measles don't get their feelings hurt.

Consider this scenario: You are driving on a city street. A police car behind you turns on his blue lights, and you pull over. The officer comes to your car window and asks to see your driver's license, registration and proof of insurance. At this moment, you do not know why he stopped you. Before you ask why you were stopped, answer this question: Has the police officer violated your civil rights by stopping you and asking for your "papers?"

"No," you say? Why is this not a civil rights violation? Why is it not a civil rights violation for police to request to see your driver's license without FIRST giving their probable cause, yet it somehow violates a person's civil rights to ask a person to produce proof of legal residence other than a driver's license?

The driver's license serves as your proof of legal residence SOMEWHERE, even if you don't live in that state. So, unless the police officer suspected that your driver's license was a forgery, no further inquiry into your citizenship would likely occur.

Here's another example: You're a new employee in training at a bank. In training, they show you photos of past bank robbers, and give you a list of the common characteristics of people who rob banks. Is that profiling?

Another: Zimbabwe shares its southern border with South Africa. Let's posit that southern Zimbabwe has had a long history of criminal vandalism…toilet-papering houses. It is determined after analyzing arrest records that 99% of the crimes were committed by white Afrikaner men coming across the border from South Africa. You're a Zimbabwean border inspector. When you saw a white Afrikaner man with a backpack coming through the line, would you be profiling if you looked inside the backpack for Ultra Charmin?

Let's all agree for a moment that the US Constitution still has some relevance, since the majority of Americans still think that it is the highest law of the land. A discussion of constitutional authority is a topic for another day.

The Fourth Amendment says "The right of the People to be secure in their persons, houses, papers and effects, against UNNREASONABLE searches and seizures, shall not be violated, and no warrants shall issue, BUT UPON PROBABLE CAUSE, supported by Oath or affirmation, and particularly describing the place to be searched, and the persons or things to be seized." (Emphasis mine)

So please notice:

The Fourteenth Amendment, Section 1 says: All citizens BORN OR NATURALIZED in the United States and subject to the jurisdiction thereof are citizens of the United States and of the State wherein they reside. No State shall make or enforce any law which shall abridge the privileges or immunities of citizens of the United States; Nor shall any State deprive any person of life, liberty or property without due process of law; nor deny to ANY PERSON within its jurisdiction the equal protection of the laws. (Emphasis mine)

The Arizona immigration law does not abridge the privileges or immunities of citizens of the United States. It does not deprive any person of life, liberty or property without due process of law.

What the immigration law does is acknowledge that the predominance of illegal immigrants in Arizona are Latinos, and as such, empowers law enforcement personnel to use their common sense to investigate whether any individual Latino human being can proffer verifiable identification and proof of US citizenship. Said another way – if we know that nearly every illegal immigrant in Arizona has Latino physical characteristics, it is not an "unreasonable search" to require that they produce identification and proof of citizenship.

In my never-humble opinion, racial profiling for immigration violations is far superior to the DUI check-points that police like to set up on busy thoroughfares to check EVERY DRIVER for driving under the influence of alcohol. Perhaps civil rights activists would rather have those kinds of random checkpoints scattered throughout Arizona where EVERY DRIVER must produce an ID.

Then, Arizona officials would have embraced the very idiocy that we experience whenever we board a plane at any American airport. Is that what you want?

Speaking of airports and profiling, consider this: EVERY PERSON involved in the bombing of the World Trade Center in 1993, and EVERY PERSON involved in the attack on the World Trade Center on September 11, 2001 was a Middle Eastern male Islamist. No grandmas…no children…no blacks…no whites…no Latinos…no Asians…no active duty military personnel. Only Middle Eastern Islamists.

How about we go back to using common sense, and only inspect those people in line who APPEAR MOST LIKELY to pose a threat to public safety?

In conclusion: What is Arizona going to do WHEN…not IF…Washington decides to assert its superiority over Arizona in this immigration matter? Will Arizona kneel and obey? Arizona needs to secede from the Union. Once they secede, they will be free from the Federal idiocy under which they are burdened.

*** <u>End of Longcore essay</u> --→ >>   See, I told you that you would like this!

Chapter 34   Is the Enforcement of Immigration Laws Optional?

Illegal foreign nationals, progressive liberals & deportation

Let's start at the top. The Obama Administration believes that it is not a real crime to be an illegal foreign national in the US. Perhaps even worse, Obama does not believe it should be a crime. The Constitution and our un-repealed, still in-force, immigration laws, based on the Constitution say otherwise. On its own, the Obama Administration, which from 2009 to 2011 included a cult of radical czars along with the fully complicit 111th Congress, has decided the Constitution is imperfect on immigration and therefore, not worthy of enforcement. Where did they get that power? It is dangerous. Conservatives are hoping that the 112th Congress that is now in force, is not such a pushover on illegal immigration as the 111th.

Additionally, the czars have contrived that the President has more than enough executive power to do whatever he feels is the thing to do, without having to ask John Q Public, or his representative in Congress for permission.

When pressed about not defending the borders and not deporting illegal aliens, The Obamanites fire back that they are looking "just for criminals." That is why illegal foreign nationals now have safe haven all across America today. Whether the inflow rate is 10,000 or 10,000,000 per year, since nobody really knows for sure, there is apparently no reason for the Administration to want to know the real number.

Obama and his minions believe that through executive orders and regulations they have the power to trump US immigration law. Breaking into America, invading America, or jumping the border illegally, whatever you would like to call it has been a crime for centuries. The message the 112th Congress must deliver to the Obamanites is that these well seasoned immigration laws are still the laws of the land. Obama is not the dictator in charge.

Going back in time, the first time a specific law was passed on immigration was June 25, 1798. This represented the first federal law pertinent to immigration rather than naturalization. Provisions of the law included the following:

A. Authorized the President to arrest and/or deport any alien whom he deemed dangerous to the United States.

B. Required the captain of any vessel to report the arrival of aliens

At the time, immigrants came to the US from the sea. Over time, land and air were added to the immigration laws as a source of aliens.

Can president pick and choose laws to enforce?

So here we are centuries later and this President chooses not to enforce long-standing often modified legislation that spells out the enforcement of its precepts. This may be good for Obama but it is not good for America. Just because Obama and company choose not to enforce the law does not change the fact that the law is the law. Americans who still think the President has credibility are confused when they see the US chief executive picking and choosing the laws he enforces. All Americans who are paying attention wonder who gave him or any president that right? The answer is that President Obama has not such right to pick and choose the laws the Executive Branch enforces. He must, by his oath, enforce them all.

Yet in 2009 and 2010, the pansies in the 111th Congress were so tickled that our President was a Democrat, they chose to let him bully them into submission. They chose not to challenge his authority. Americans fed up with this love-Waltz between the branches of government showed a large number of House members the door in November, 2010, and they reduced the Democratic controlled Senate seats by six members.

The American people have begun to closely examine the actions of its government and in this endeavor; they quickly learned that the 111th Congress was simply not doing its job. One might ask that if Obama finds immigration law abhorrent to his very being and character. If so, what would his response be if he were the innocent victim of an errant parking violation? Would he outlaw parking laws?

The facts speak for themselves. Our highly touted and sometimes maligned President, Barack Hussein Obama has gone on record that he does not believe that "non-criminals" should be deported. Nobody thinks non-criminals should be deported. However, all illegal foreign nationals are criminals by the laws of the US. Once they hop the border unlawfully, an innocent bystander becomes a US criminal. They may be resident criminals but they are criminals nonetheless.

The President seems to be interested in a new brand of non-criminal that we would have to stretch the English language so we could call them *criminal non-criminals*. These are the folks who illegally crossed the border and invaded America. However, Americans see the border crossing as a criminal act, not merely a happening. So, it could be argued that the commission of another criminal act really makes the illegal foreign national in question a criminal criminal. None of us would ever expect Harvard-educated lawyer Barack Hussein Obama to agree to something so obvious.

Working it through the numbers, illegal foreign nationals begin their US careers as criminals when they break US laws by crossing the border and then by living in this country illegally. Obama says they are non-criminals because after breaking the law and living a crime, and maybe just a splash of ID-theft or SS# abuse here and there, they did not commit any other types of crimes.

My dear American citizens, try using that defense yourself in court. Would any of that malarkey work as an excuse if it were your American butt being accused of such crimes? But, Obama believes that these invaders simply are criminals under US immigration law, and thus, according to Obama, that does not make them real criminals. You and I and President Obama know he is wrong. He forgives himself because without a few good lies no politician ever gets elected. But, this matter is too serious for you and me to forgive him. Because this president finds little value in our laws, he has called off a good part of the illegal immigration work that had been underway in the Bush administration. How is that good for America? Answer: It is not.

Should criminal non-criminals be deported?

The bottom line for Obama is that these criminal "non-criminals" under Obamalaw should not be deported? Some suggest this is his doublespeak merely because he does not personally know the pain of being a real US taxpayer. So, it stands to reason that he would not know the repercussions of permitting illegal foreign nationals to live off the taxpayers' dime indefinitely. Yet, I have to admit, I don't think he cares an iota about the rest of us.

The good news apparently is that it is OK that criminal criminal-non-criminals be deported. However, these too historically have been spared or there would not be so many multiple offenders in the system. Obama apparently never heard of the no-spin zone as getting elected to office includes few lessons in the value of truth.

The President has his own reasons for apparently thinking that the US treasury has infinite depth? This President knowingly "pays" for every legislative bill with mythical dollars that are not yet in the treasury and they will never be in the treasury. You see, they exist in the treasury of President Hu Jintao of China. The US is broke. Some, who think explanations are necessary, say that Obama merely takes the money from his "stash." He takes over car companies and he would like to punish companies and individuals who use energy. In this foray, Obama believes he is lord of the immigrants.

Barack Obama – Dictator for life?

Many of us know that Woody Allen, either a great American role model or one-time-father-now-husband-of-his-daughter, depending on your sleaze aversion factor, thinks it would be a cool idea for President Barack Obama to be dictator for at least a few years. According to Allen, Obama then "could get things done without all the hassle of opposing views getting in the way."

Obama already runs America like he is a dictator. He takes whatever power he needs. He acts with no apparent countervailing power. The fifty states however, are at a tipping point on the President and his use of various powers over the states. Twenty-eight states at last count for example, are suing Obama on Obamacare. The last time in the courts, Obamacare was declared unconstitutional. A number of fine judges have risen up and have said: "hey, you can't do that." Since there are only 50 states, with 28 already joined in and others, such as New Jersey, applauding from the sidelines, that does mean that most of the country has big issues with the President on a number of issues. Arizona is not alone on immigration.

The President says illegal foreign nationals have done nothing wrong (other than violate US immigration laws) so he has basically ordered that they be free since he will not deport them by policy. Obama, who is a lawyer, thinks the law is not so good. So, he, as the big boss, feels he is not compelled to enforce laws that he does not like.

Of course this is not how the country is supposed to work, but Harry Reid and Nancy Pelosi and the 111th Congress were so corrupt, they gave Mr. Obama a blank check payable from the US Congress. For two years, President Obama found himself with no challenges on the immigration front. In essence his behavior mimicked that of a dictator.

So, has Obama become a dictator? Will Woody Allen become the regime's Impresario? Why did the 111th Congress permit the President to ignore the laws without a challenge? Will the 112th Congress stand up to this rogue President? How can it be that a constitutional scholar does not know that it is the role of Congress to make the laws and the role of the President is to enforce the laws?

Obama says our "guests" shall not be deported

In his own words, very clearly our President publicly said

"We are not going to ship back 12 million people; [Author's Note: there are more like 40 or 50 million people] we're not going to do it as a practical matter. We would have to take all our law enforcement that we have available and we would have to use it and put people on buses, and rip families apart, and that's not who we are, that's not what America is about."

But, Mr. President, it is the law and your job is not to amend the law on the fly in any way. Your job, Mr. President is to enforce the law. May I ask you a few questions, sir?

Thank you Mister Commander in Chief. Would you care to take that notion of the criminal non-criminals up to the Supreme Court to see if it flies? Have you forgotten that it is your sworn duty to deport illegal foreign nationals who come from any nation because their mere presence in the US means they have broken our laws? Moreover, you do realize, Mr. President that we do not know the intentions of the illegal foreign nationals once they are in our country? Since they owe their allegiance to a foreign power, in this age of terrorism, not knowing their allegiance should be viewed as very problematic. Crossing our borders without a passport is a crime. Identity theft is a crime. Mr. President, need we go on? Do you have plans to absolve real Americans and forgive all such crimes or is it just the foreigners who live illegally among us, who will be forgiven? Thank you for your time, Mr. President.

Are crimes of survival crimes?

All Americans, you and I and all of the other John Q's out there know that illegal aliens cannot exist in this country without committing many crimes, though those crimes are not necessarily rape, murder, assault or burglary. Barack Obama knows that also. Is he just kinder than we are? And, yes, a goodly share of illegals are in the clink for many heinous crimes, which they would not have been able to commit if bleeding hearts like Mr. Obama had not permitted them to extend their "visit."

The law says they should be deported when first touched. Besides hard crime, there are things that you and I would go to jail for that President Obama does not think are a crime if committed by illegal foreign nationals. It is unfair that for the same indiscretions, Americans go to the big house but those in illegal standing are ignored.

For example, you and I will go to jail for driving without a license. How about driving without insurance? The answer is jail time and a fine for you and I. How about Identity theft—the answer again is jail time and a fine for you and I. How about the use of another's social security number—the answer once again is jail time for you and I.

How about the ethics in entering a neighbor's home and taking from them? When illegal foreign nationals drink from the citizen's free cup in our country, they are stealing from Americans. Obama thinks these perpetrators who have misrepresented themselves to the US government should get away with it because he thinks it is small potatoes. When such perpetrators cause you and I to pay more taxes because the perpetrator gets free healthcare, while sending large sums back to friends in Mexico, that is a crime, and the potatoes are big. It is also unfair to those of us paying the bill. In fact, most crimes are crimes because they are unfair to the victim. We expect that bad things should happen to the perpetrators of the crimes. For those here illegally, deportation is the proper end to the problem.

When the illegal foreign national gets free education for his or her children that too is a crime. When the illegal foreign national takes from our treasury for any reason, it is a crime. It is theft and an honest conscience would see it that way. Yes, our laws at all levels foolishly permit these invaders to fleece the public of our treasures. These broken laws ought to make it a crime and the biased lawmakers that make these laws that permit illegals to run free should be arrested. This is not much different than the thieves in Bell California who paid themselves generously from the taxpayers' treasury.

Our legislators have been overly generous to unwelcome guests. They should take such largesse from their own pay packets. We the people have not authorized such foolish spending. America is broke and if we ever could have afforded the luxury of taking care of the world, merely because they break in and demand it, we can no longer do so. All of this is a shame and it is a crime, and we the people must continue to elect people who vow to change this. And when they break their vow just once, we should impeach them.

The illegal foreign national pays little taxes for their services and thus, they are stealing right out of the pockets of American citizens. It may be that the Obamanites would have us believe, it is all coming from Obama's stash? But his stash really is our empty treasury. You and I have no doubt that we would be in jail in Mexico if we merely stood in line for such services.

Besides the crimes, most people who come across our porous borders know they should have a passport. It is a charade for illegals to pretend that they do not need "documentation." These are not mistakes. Somebody does not show up in the US by mistake. Why doesn't Mexico just give them passports? The quick answer to that is that they do not want to be tracked and Mexico does not want them back. The exportation of the poor works better if there is no return path. A passport would mean just a quick visit and then an exit.

The norm for illegal foreign nationals travelling to the US is that almost all of them have found somebody (a coyote or a friend) to sneak them across the border. Since they know that they are sneaking around to avoid officials, you bet they know they are doing wrong. Just because Obama does not see it is a crime, it is a crime nonetheless, and it is a sin against God and the American people.

I've grown accustomed to your crimes

The illegal foreign nationals come from countries where crime, corruption, poverty, misery, anti-education, and even hate for Americans often have existed for decades or longer. It is no wonder they come here. They get a good deal from America but they do not reciprocate. Citizens of the US unfortunately are simply part of their notion of the "Ugly American." This is a great country but our illegal visitors are not in love with Americans or America. Over time, the disdain is becoming mutual.

Immigration law permits us to ask what these people have to offer America other than their comfort with crime, corruption, poverty, misery, anti-education, and even their subtle hate for the prosperity of Americans. The problem is they run the gate. They don't stop to be checked out. Nobody gets to ask them any questions. We all know this is wrong but Obama thinks we should just accept everybody who chooses to be like Eddie Murphy when they decide to come uninvited to America. But, Eddie had his own stash!

Regular Americans who want the homeland protected have no reason for guilt. Even if the President does not think so, as citizens with a Constitution to back us up, we know that we have a right to determine who comes across our country's borders. As harsh as it may sound to those in need, Americans should be able to limit access to our gifts. The US has far more liberal immigration policies than Mexico but that is no reason why we should be left with pot luck as the answer to who comes into the country and who does not. We should not have to accept any and all merely because the President chooses to not enforce valid US laws. The President is not doing his job and says he will not. So, perhaps the real solution is that the President, as he persists, should be relieved of duty.

I don't think you would find one American who would not agree to help Mexico in a war on poverty south of the border. But, invading our Southwestern states and forcing their way up to all of the continental 48 states and Alaska and Hawaii is not the way to engender love or sympathy for a cause. Why should Mexicans and others who crash our borders not be able to live in their own country with dignity? Is it fair that they merely change their venue and because they are not motivated to change anything else, they are destined to live with little respectability and in similar squalor from whence they came? Who does that help?

Cheap deportation—tell them to leave & mean it

President Obama will never mention this. However, by being here illegally, these foreign nationals, who owe their allegiance to other countries, are costing Americans the opportunity for prosperity in many ways. For one, they have stolen many American jobs and have made it almost impossible for an unskilled American to get a decent job.

If Obama simply ordered all illegal foreign nationals out of the country and he enforced it, after a length of time most would leave. Then, we would have to deport only those who dug in and refused the order. Regardless of the cost of deportation, and we go into this in some detail in other chapters of this book, the US would save lots of money on healthcare and other major costs paid by us. The taxes of US citizens would stop rising and could even drop. Sorry Mr. President but permitting 30 million, 40 million, and probably 50 million or more non-citizens to stay in the US indefinitely because they broke just one type of law is not a good remedy to the current immigration crisis. Nice try!

Designed for failure

The way we treat incarcerated criminals who are also illegal foreign nationals is just another reason why we have such a huge problem. Bureaucrats and the regulators in Washington have devised a system that is designed to fail. Can you imagine letting a criminal who is a definite flight risk out on his own recognizance until his next court date? That is what they do. By policy, the US trusts that illegal foreign nationals, convicted of crimes, will come back for their punishment on a set date. Sometimes you have to ask if this is the same intelligent country that first sent a man to the moon. Is there no intelligent life in government?

The scenario is laughable at best. Once an illegal alien is arrested, he or she is not eligible for deportation until any local charges against them are concluded. Then he or she can be deported. Now, we know why there are few deportations. In the meantime, of course, the taxpayer must pay for their food, medical needs and so forth. Now, let's say the illegal serves his or her full sentence. We are talking about somebody that would even be a criminal on Obama's standards—"the new rules." But, after their full local sentence is served, local officials must release them. If immigration officials are not at the door immediately upon the criminal's release, he or she is free to go. I kid you not. A sane person would not have designed such a system.

Perhaps if immigration officials were at the door to take them upon release, maybe deportation could begin at that time but that is hardly ever the case. And so criminals get to commit crimes again without deportation proceedings. In Florida, for example, illegal aliens are processed in Miami. Now, please do not laugh. They are then given appointment dates to return for deportation. Hah! I could not help it. I laughed.

They are then released pending their deportation date. They may come back to Martin County or wherever. Even the Sheriff of Martin County does not know what percentage actually return for deportation on the appointed dates. Sounds like the illegal foreign national criminals association (IFNCA) devised that system. Doesn't it? Are they a division of the A.C.L. U.?

Are these illegal foreign nationals really criminals? You tell me. What if you did what the most innocent of the illegal foreign nationals did in any other country and got caught? Would you be doing hard time? Of course! America is not supposed to be the sucker country of the world, but BOH does not mind us carrying that label.

Let's help Mexicans in Mexico. Let's help all countries as much as we can but let's not let Mexico, for example, take back the Southwestern states merely by invading them and populating them with illegal foreign nationals, regardless of whether the current president of the United States thinks it is OK!

Chapter 35   American Elites, Amnesty & Deportation

Can we afford to deport illegal foreign nationals?

Besides President Obama, who suggests erroneously that the cost to Americans to deport illegal aliens is unaffordable, there are many other progressives who feel exactly the same way. Surely, you are not surprised! Beware of who they are so you are not convinced by these super salesmen that Obama is the right voice on illegal immigration. He is far left of center on just about everything.

President Obama in many ways is a kind man but he is wrong-headed about too many things to be trusted with your well-being or mine. For example, he does not believe that Americans are more exceptional than people in other countries. He believes that the country that sent a man to the moon in the 1960's somehow cannot pull the resources together to deport illegal aliens.

If you are part of the regular people mix that works in union and non-union jobs, or you do not work at all, you are not part of the elitist former hippies, who are ardent Obama supporters. These guilt-ridden progressives often have huge fortunes, which separate them from the rest of mankind. The names I mention in this chapter shall we say, are the usual suspects, but there are lots more of them hiding behind the gates of their fenced-in communities. Like the illegal alien community, they need big separation from the regular people.

They all want control. That's why they don't always get along with each other. But they do get along in battles against their mortal enemies, such as you and I, and all things TEA and conservative. They are OK with poor liberals as long as they do not get too close. The only way to beat these people is to meet them head-on. When We *the People* rise up en masse in organizations such as the TEA Party, unaffiliated with government, unions, or corporations, we give the progressives great fear and they tremble at what we may do to undo their grip on power.

Us against them

There is no people's party per se but the people have taken notice to the excesses of the elite. Maybe it is not necessary to have a people's party. The closest thing is the TEA party. The TEA party really does invoke fear into the hearts of the liberal / progressive establishment -- the ruling class.

You have seen them on the evening news and elsewhere. You have seen Katie Couric, Brian Williams, and the gang mocking the TEA party as they have become their mortal enemy. An illicit media cannot exist with an aware public and the TEA party is the expression of the public. Besides the TEA party itself, they have made the truth as another of their mortal enemies. They have no use for the truth. Unless you are an elitist hippie from the 1960's, you are one of us. *We the People* now live and thrive in the TEA Party and we are being heard. Soon, no President will be able to ignore the laws of our country because we are watching, and every two years we get to vote.

There is no reason to be against rich people who use their own money for good things. There is a lot of reason to be against the nouveaux American elitist who wants to be rich or is rich and wants to use your tax money and my tax money instead of their own money to spend on progressive causes of their choice, many of which are not for the good of American citizens.

We should thank the real rich often, not in their role as part of the ruling class, but as the captains of industry who have assured America's prosperity for a long time. Prosperity does not come simply because poor people decide to spend more. Prosperity comes because people with money decide to invest in America. I have yet to find a poor person who was ever able to offer anybody a job. So, I respect the rich in their role of business executives and owners, and I thank them for weathering this storm caused by a severe anti-business climate in Washington. Those businesses who hire illegal foreign nationals, however, I have no use for at all.

Who are the bad guys?

So, who are the bad guys? They are becoming known as the "ruling class." The mainstream media would have you believe they are Republican businessmen. That is not true. Try to find a generous, people serving, kind bone in the body of George Soros. He is the major broker of progressive dribble and treachery in the Democratic Party. Soros and many like him are trying hard to include illegal aliens into the citizenry. Soros thinks it will help weaken America and he likes that. He is right. Illegal aliens are weakening America. Thanks, George, but no thanks! Go home, if you can find a country that will have you!

There is a very large coterie of progressives in the USA and they are very active. Many are Harvard graduates and there are also a lot of progressive wannabees, who are merely duped into following the next liberal cause. These people have decided that America should not be America anymore. They'd like to retest Marxian principles and create a destitute government-loving obedient and dependent working class. This is their ideal world. Illegal aliens by definition are very controllable and so they fit very well in their plans.

We cannot let them make it with their sicko, hippie, guilt-laden agenda. Because people like you and I have noticed their takeover tactics, we are diminishing their power by having sent many of their minions in Congress home for good in November and we have more planned for the next election.

A Republican led House took over in 2011from the worse Congress ever. Despite this success in November 2010, right now, the progressives still own the media even though. When dealing with the progressives who remain in the media and in the government, we need to hold our ground at all times. Watch what they say. Don't expect it to be the truth.

Remember that the lie is one of the greatest weapons in the progressives' arsenal. Don't believe a word they say. Remember one of the greatest propagandists of all time used these words to describe what the progressives do as a matter of policy: **"If you tell a lie big enough and keep repeating it, people will eventually come to believe it."** Beware.

Deportation ?

In huge numbers, the new progressives who were once called liberals think their voice should count more than yours on the deportation of illegal foreign nationals. Their numbers include American elitists as well as some rich stiffs from lands far away. Besides the President and your Congress, there are many other voices in this arena, which are against deportation. We sample just several in this chapter to give you the flavor of the debate and who is on which side.

These elitists and retro-guilt-ridden hippies all have an idea on what to do with illegal foreign nationals. Their ideas however are nothing like your ideas or my ideas. They think they are right and they have been trying to snooker Americans for years. But, they are wrong. First soundly delivered in November, 2010, they are getting our message. The messages will come again in 2012 and 2014. Can you imagine any of their names yet?

They pick illegal foreign nationals over Americans

It probably is no surprise for you to know that the all-important New York City Mayor, Michael R. **Rubens Bloomberg, a RINO, is one of the chieftains** behind this lunacy along with an Australian, who owns a good part of America. This progressive is billionaire Rupert Murdoch of News Corporation. Yes, my friends, this is the same Murdoch who owns Fox News.

Thankfully at least for now, Murdoch likes making money at FOX more than he cares about the issues of progressives. When and if the day comes that FOX is a little too fair and a little too balanced, you might very well be right in blaming its progressive owner. For now, thank God that he is more interested in capitalism than full-bore progressivism. Watch to see if George Soros doesn't begin to take a stake in Fox News.

By the way, word on the street is that Obama is so tickled with Bloomberg and his market minutes and also his public stance on the ground zero mosque that he has offered him the Secretary of Treasury position to replace Timothy Geithner. The word also says that besides not knowing economics, Geithner has no idea that Obama is getting rid of him. But that is another story.

Bloomberg and Murdoch both agree that the US cannot deport illegal foreign nationals. And, there are other big names who feel the same. Nobody offers proof that the US is too inept to get the job done. Besides Murdoch and Bloomberg, there are other progressives dwelling behind the closed gates of private communities away from the problems of the street. These joined forces with Bloomberg and Murdoch way back in June 2010 to hit the liberal progressive talk-show circuit. Their common theme was that they all support amnesty and full citizenship for all illegal foreign nationals. I wonder what they want to do with people who want to call themselves Americans.

Rather than label the foreign invaders as "illegal foreign nationals," or "illegal aliens," or "illegals," or something more descriptive of their sins, Bloomberg and company use the euphemistic term, "undocumented workers." Why do you think the name change is necessary? It is all public opinion. They want you to think these illegal foreign nationals are getting hosed in America simply because they lost a teeny slip of paper. Hah! But as Americans, you and I know that they never had that slip of paper in the first place. Nor do they care about ever getting it. Nor do they really want to assimilate to become Americans.

The US Labor Department chooses to officially refer to these invaders simply as illegal labor. They are in fact foreign nationals (owe their allegiance to a foreign country); they are aliens in this country, and they are in an illegal status. Only somebody wanting you to give your life savings for their support would label them otherwise.

So, who says we cannot deport illegal aliens?

We'll name a few by title but not by name today. They are the usual corporate suspects, namely, the CEOs from Hewlett-Packard, Boeing, and Disney, along with a ton of other big-city mayors before the big 2010 general election. Some of these are already gone from their once cushy jobs. Corporate moguls and politicians have joined this coalition of labor exploiters because they all have some skin in the game

You and I know the corporate supposed guilt-stricken moguls are simply looking for cheap labor. How about a minimum wage or a "no document wage," for a new crew of Disney workers who just happen to be illegal foreign nationals? Would the Disney executives like that? Will there be a big illegal labor deal for a new Mouse played by an illegal foreign national coming anytime soon?

How about those progressive big city mayors representing government? Can it be so small of them that they would bring people into the US against the wishes of their constituents merely to get re-elected? There has been no major outbreak of a political disease called altruism in politics or in corporate life of which I am aware. That disease could ruin their whole scheme.

Just like Martin Luther King, these supposed American leaders have a big dream. Unlike Martin Luther King's dream for a color blind world with equal rights for all, their dream is to enrich either their political careers or the coffers of their organization on the backs of a frightened group of people who have been lured to America by guilt-ridden hippies who think that by making more money they can be healed.

When we ask Genie the question, "Who thinks that we cannot deport the 12 million (more like 30 or 40 or 50 million) illegal foreign nationals, who live in American cities today," the answer comes up that it is Obama and the progressive clones of Michael Bloomberg. If we add most of the 111th Congress to the billionaires already mentioned, this is a very good representation of those who think we cannot deport illegal foreign nationals. It surely is not you and it is not me.

Whether you stop at Congress, the President, corporate America or the Union leaders in the US, the answer is the same. They do not want to solve this problem. If they wanted it solved, it would already be solved and we would not be talking about it. So, when Bloomberg and his clones speak about what you should do or what you should accept, reject them. Bloomberg is a progressive and their words are lies and their purpose is to make you weak and make them strong.

They do have a vested interest in keeping the wages of Americans depressed and they have the same preoccupation for increasing the number of people inclined to vote for the Democratic Party. Another objective in all this is to have all the people affected become dependent on the government instead of their God. Progressives have no god but government. Knowing this, it should be difficult now for any reader to believe anything they say.

Union leaders love illegal labor

But, you may ask, what about the faithful union workers? Their leaders have a deal cooking that they are not going to like. How will it benefit them if the union leaders support the call for amnesty and it is achieved? Will it be easier to have 50 million or so more new citizens in the union? Will today's American workers have jobs? Will union dues collections go way up while wages go way down? Should union workers have blind trust in their union leaders on the issue of amnesty?

The unholy hippie elitist progressives care more about themselves and their fortunes than they care about giving real grassroots Americans a break. They want all of the "undocumented immigrants," included, even if they have allegiance to Mexico and other countries, and even if they hate the US and its citizens. They want them all to be given a path to citizenship or better yet, a form of quasi-citizenship in which they are not fully free but are legal. But why do they want this? They hope to gain by continuing to exploit the illegal community, which will continue to grow years afterwards even if those before them are granted amnesty.

Bloomberg, the Mayor, the financier, the diplomat, the mosque defender, who has said an awful lot of dumb things lately, offers his own counsel on the deportation of illegal foreign nationals. He says it "is impossible and would devastate the economy." How does one devastate an already devastated economy, Mr. Mayor? Bloomberg also says that lawmakers who want to deport all illegal immigrants are "living in a fantasy world." Amazing! Bloomberg has a lot at stake.

You may recall that many thought John Kennedy was a loon for thinking we could actually get to the moon. Removing 12 to 40 to 50 million or more unwanted and uninvited guests sounds a lot easier than getting to the moon. Don't you think? Why would we let the heavy agenda-clad Bloomberg and his clones convince us otherwise? We do not have to do it all at once but we have to mean it.

Americans are great people who at this point in history have poor leadership. The 111th Congress is being nominated for worst Congress ever and the President is the most bumbling since James Buchanan. Still, if our leaders wanted to solve the problem of illegal foreign nationals destroying America all over the country, America would be able to solve this even now with perhaps 50,000,000 to deport. You and I know this is true. Suing Arizona is not on anybody's path to a solution. Our leaders have let us down, big time. The problem never should have gotten this big. In November, we got a chance to get a whole new House of Representatives and a 1/3 new Senate. We came pretty close and now there is hope to slow down the asininity in Congress and the administration.

In November, 2010 a few incumbents such as Harry Reid slipped in under the wire but we did not blow the chance to send a ton of these bad eggs packing. While we are at it, we know that our new 112th Congress can figure out a low-cost humanitarian way to get illegal foreign nationals back to their home country. While we are at it, let's use the D word [deport]. They can either self deport, or be deported.

Amen!

Chapter 36   Businesses Makes Huge Profits on Illegal Workers

Wholesale exploitation of illegal foreign labor

Whether you are in the thick of it or viewing it all from the sidelines, it is a wonder that so many illegal workers are employed in the US? You might also wonder about how they got a mortgage but that is too far into the issue to cover in this book. It sure seems that this could not have happened spontaneously or these millions of people would not have jobs and they surely would not have mortgages. This was planned by forces in business and government as a perpetration against the American people for purposes of labor arbitrage and votes. This was no accident.

If this is not part of a grand design, it would be quite remarkable. It seems like this "illegal" crisis happened overnight. How did all of the foreign nationals find jobs in America if our government did not really want them to find jobs? How are businesses able to employ illegal workers if it is really illegal?

Why do businesses hire illegal foreign nationals?

Businesses, for good reasons and for bad reasons think that survival is their most important responsibility. It is their most basic motivator and all else flows from that until that goal is accomplished. When survival is reasonably assured, profit takes over as the prime motivation for business operations. Illegal foreign nationals have been a means for many years for a number of businesses to assure their survival and while at it, "squeak out" a lot of additional profit.

The realists with a historical and business background understand how all-consuming profit must be in business. From an accounting perspective, just two-cents away from a profit are a loss. So, the lure of profit and the risk of a loss, spurs businesses in directions that sometimes seem unrelated to survival. The fact is that the more profit a firm realizes, the further it gets from the risk of a loss.
It is the risk of a loss and especially repeated losses that can bring back those survival instincts. As noted, illegal aliens in the American workforce are an answer for businesses to being able to produce with significantly higher profitability, and that is their raison d'etre—simple and pure.

Besides bringing illegal foreign nationals in to work in their organizations, these companies have been trying for years to make up for what they see as the hardships of doing business in the United States. Many of these companies went into Mexico under the North American Free Trade Agreement (NAFTA), hoping to outsource American jobs to Mexico. And they did. Such businesses are not really friends of the American worker. Clearly at all times, profit comes well ahead of what is good for America and Americans. It helps to keep that in mind. Businesses understand that when there is no profit, there is no business.

Unfortunately for Mexico and for the American businesses looking to make a killing with the help of substantially lower Mexican wages, shortly after NAFTA was the way to go, the corporate titans, found that the Mexicans actually wanted to live a little better than poverty line wages permit. So after the pushback, many of these same companies left Mexico and went off to the Far East without helping the Mexican people very much at all.

But, that was before Obama owned General Motors. While the American taxpayers are supporting both GM and the impoverished illegal workers in America during a period in which 9.6% of Americans are listed as unemployed, Government Motors (GM) invested $500 million of taxpayer dollars in Mexico. The plan is to produce a new vehicle as well as eight-cylinder engines in northeastern Mexico. This investment in GM's plant in Ramos Arispe, Coahuila state, is expected to create about 400 jobs. That's about 400 more jobs than Obama has been able to create in his GM plants in all of America. Viva la Mexico!

Though 400 jobs is a nice deal for Ramos Arispe, don't expect the illegal worker spigot to close between the US and Mexico. Lots more Mexicans still will be coming to the USA for work. American corporations, the same guys who want open borders, and who were once theoretically prepared to make Mexico the world's largest manufacturing country, could not sustain the pressures on the bottom line while their competitors were setting up shop in countries, in which the labor was cheaper than even Mexico. Ironically, only GM, with funding from US taxpayers could afford to prop up Mexican industry in Mexico.

If US corporations who made the trek, could have sustained their businesses and made them thrive, many Mexicans would have no need to be coming to the US and in fact, Americans may very well be traveling south for jobs. Corporations, unfortunately, have no heart. Though in the US, our laws can give corporations a form of citizenship, no law can give a corporation a heart. If a corporation were alive in any way, their physical image would be that of *The Tin Man*. For my money, I would take Oz's Tin Woodsman, however, over the corporation of today for at least he wanted a heart.

Corporate America, always looking for its true god, the highest bottom line possible, found even lower wages in other parts of the world than in Mexico and so they abandoned this hemisphere completely. China is now the largest manufacturer in the world, supported by American corporations and other selfish, uncaring corporations from all around the world.

If the Mexicans would only have accepted dirt poor wages in Mexico, maybe Mexico would be the king of manufacturing today. What does that say about the motivations of corporate CEOs and the politicians so ready to ship American jobs to Mexico? Now, they expect us to say they are right about not deporting Mexicans and other illegal foreign nationals living in America. The conclusion anybody with both halves of their brain working is that none of the above are on our side. Government and business have become allies on illegal immigration. Mexico is their friend and the American people are the only thing between them and a Mexican takeover of all American jobs. Profit is their only motive.

Why is there any work at all done in the USA?

There are jobs that must be done in the US. They simply cannot all be off-shored for practical reasons. In other words, there are industries in which the raw materials are created or grown in this country. Certain products such as those raised on a farm are perishable and meat harvested in a meat packing plant has a limited shelf life. Once preserved, the goods can be shipped anywhere. But, companies that manufacture such goods typically set up shop in the country in which they are grown or harvested.

So, farming and meat packing are two easy examples. There are other industries outside of food in which it is just impractical to do the whole job overseas. Try building an American home in China and then bringing it back and setting it up.

Try sending your home or a building to China to be painted or to have the plumbing repaired. You just cannot do it. So painting, home resurfacing, remodeling etc are chores that must be done in the USA for Americans but as you can see in every roofing job in America, the work is no longer done by Americans. At one time, this work was done only by Americans but the temptation to lower wages has resulted in more and more illegal foreign nationals doing non-farm work in the USA. Let's give a big thank-you to the do-gooder dimwit progressives willing to reduce the American worker to below-minimum wage jobs.

All jobs that require minimal skill are candidates for businesses to displace their American workers with illegal foreign nationals. Not only is the government not stopping this harmful act against Americans, they are in fact encouraging it to happen under a humanitarian guise. The influx of illegal foreign nationals is part of a sinister plan to offshore American jobs without having to move the fields or the factories overseas. I'd say they are right on the money with that notion. But it is surely not fair to Americans.

Bring the workers to the jobs

So, you have the saying, "If the mountain won't come to Muhammad, Muhammad must go to the mountain." This is the original statement and it applies to many situations. US corporations cannot ship farming and meatpacking and construction jobs overseas but they sure and heck can and do bring in foreign workers to work for as close to dirt cheap wages as they can get in those other countries. Our problem with illegal foreign nationals is all about profits for corporations and votes for politicians.

So, now we see that the same usual suspects -- corporations and government, and unfortunately unions, wanting to draw people from poor countries (illegal foreign nationals) to the US for a raw deal leading to a life of poverty, misery, squalor, and continued unhappiness. It is a raw deal for those lured into impoverishment and it is a raw deal for those of us who, in one way or another, actually have to pay for them to survive in the US. And, of course it is a raw deal for Americans whose jobs are targeted and swallowed up by the droves of illegal border jumpers trying to get what they see as their rightful piece of the American dream.

Where are the Unions?

What is the union role in all of this? Does it make sense that unions should want illegal workers taking the place of American workers? Do union dues have eyes? Union members want what is best for them but, just like the people in its relationship with the government, union workers are not represented well. Union leaders want more members and more union dues much more than what is right for their American membership.

Union members will fight hard against such accusations because the union bosses train them not to think. The union thinks for the union members. The union wants illegal foreign nationals to become members when they get amnesty and their green card. If they can slip this idea by their membership, once the new guys are members, they are protected too. Once in the union, no union member would go against a fellow union member. Union leaders, however are not very good representatives of the trust given them by their American membership? Union wages will go down but union dues are something that will keep going up even if the leaders do not serve Americans or their membership well.

Most American union workers do not see all the work that union leaders are doing to support amnesty and the legalization of this pool of new workers. After all, they already have American jobs. Meanwhile all three leaders, private sector corporate moguls, public sector captains of government, and union chieftains, all live safely behind the walls of their separate gated communities. The rest of America deals with the carnage all three create.

Getting good job statistics is good for government

Interestingly, with no uptick at all in business activity, by legalizing illegal foreign workers, the Obama administration would have the opportunity to play big games with the unemployment numbers and prove those nasty Republicans wrong.

Suppose all illegal workers become legal tomorrow. The pool of workers increases immediately as does the number of legal workers who have jobs -- perhaps even 1 to 1. In this way, the unemployment rate can theoretically get well below 9%. What happens is that most of the currently employed illegals (better than 8% of the US workers), become included in the count. It is simple since they already have jobs. So, without one new job being created merely by counting the new legal workers, they get added to the citizen and the legal labor statistics and the unemployment rate goes down. And, of course, President Obama takes full credit for it.

You see the worker pool denominator gets bigger while the numerator stays the same. So, the unemployed percentage is decreased by the formerly illegal workers thereby immediately giving the government better unemployment numbers -- without helping the economy at all. If Obama is not aware of this, please do not tell him.

This would be a double win for the Democrats who currently control the government, even without having 40 or 50 million more votes. Think of it, with real unemployment at 17%, this coalition of the selfish gets to feed the public a bunch of Gump to convince us that by bringing in even more illegals, we enhance the economy of the US by reducing the unemployment rate. How about that? But, for whom is this a good idea?

Come to America!

By having less restrictions placed on green cards, and a path to American citizenship for the estimated 12 million illegal immigrants (actually about 30 to 40 to 50 million) already here, the coalition of Bloomberg clones can encourage more illegals to come to work in America, decrease the average wage via labor arbitrage and at the same time, decrease the unemployment rate and increase union membership. Michael Savage would agree that for the Bloomberg clones, this would be "such a deal." if only the dummies like us would not see through it. Sometimes the rich do get richer by stiffing the poor. That is a fact but government is our biggest problem.

Chapter 37 Getting Displaced Americans Back to Work

Solve the corporate greed problem—using greed

I have a plan and a dream but it is not anywhere close to the spectacular one-of-a-kind thinking of Martin Luther King Jr., which I admire greatly. Let's start with jobs and jobs only and by solving the jobs problem if we choose, we will solve the illegal immigration problem. The plan for regaining American jobs that have been lost to illegal foreign nationals also helps to remove illegal foreign nationals from the US. Another side benefit is that the idea of deportation goes away as the illegal foreign nationals under this new methodology will more or less, self deport. The US will neither have to deport them or force American firms to hire Americans. It will all happen naturally.

The Kelly plan simply adds a per hour surcharge on each hour worked by each illegal worker. This would not be a tax that government could waste or a fee on the business. Instead, it would be a variable amount fine. For this to be most effective, this solution should be enacted at the state level as opposed to the federal government level for many reasons. The best reason is that the states really want the problem solved and the next best reason is that the feds will try to redistribute the savings back into the pockets of illegal aliens. Thus, each state would need to pass this legislation instead of sending money to the wild spenders in Washington.

Since it is not an immigration bill, per se, merely a variable rate state fine, it could be a temporary revenue generator for states until there are no more illegal foreign nationals working in America. There are many smart lawyers who ought to be able to figure out how to fashion such a law to make it Constitutional and to make sure the states and the feds are in synch.

To give this some real life, let me add some specifics. Any of the numbers used can be adjusted to assure that the primary purpose, self deportation, is achieved. I would suggest that a fair amount for the hourly fine would be about $10.00 per hour in 2010 dollars. I would suggest the fine be no lower than $5.00 per hour but the ten dollar fine would work a lot more quickly to solve the problem. That means that for each hour an illegal foreign national works in each state, his or her employer must pay a ten dollar fine to the state government.

Who would get these new dollars? I would recommend the state's unemployment compensation fund because the job displacement from illegal workers has presented a major drain on such funds. More than likely to gain the feds cooperation, sooner than later, there might have to be a small kickback to the federal government as a sweetener for its cooperation.

In essence this would be a variable fine administered as a surcharge using the same tax withholding system that is in place in states right now. The fine is for breaking the federal immigration laws by employing illegal immigrants in the workplace. With federal cooperation, the federal immigration law would remain the basis for the fine unless it becomes more appropriate for each state to use a federally fashioned, "Constitutional" state law for the purposes set forth. In this way, instead of fighting the states such as in Arizona and in the Obamacare battles, the feds could cooperate as the feds would also be gaining some funding by their cooperation.

The state in essence could advise businesses that they are going to be enforcing the federal immigration law (permitted under the statutes) regarding the employment of illegal foreign nationals and that any company that voluntarily complies and pays the fine will not have any other substantial state penalties assessed against them.

I realize that it would be tough to do this without it appearing as extortion but many laws that affect behavior, appear to be extortion. Not being a lawyer and not knowing how to write legislation have not stopped me from brainstorming how to come up with a simple plan to protect American jobs from being held by illegal foreign nationals. The beauty here is that self-deportation will come sooner than later as Americans will be able to take those jobs for far less than the cost of the hourly wage plus the ten dollar per hour fine.

Perhaps an additional rider to the legislation could be that the company pays the expenses of any worker and one or several family members who decide to emigrate back to their home country with the former illegal employee. The number of side ideas is limitless.

The fact that so many illegals are knowingly working in the US would mean that a number of the enforcement provisions of the federal law can be met. This simple idea can be fashioned by some great lawyers into a law that would be a major state revenue generator to help bolster unemployment compensation funds at a time when they are being depleted. As companies advertise for Americans and replace illegal workers with American workers, illegal workers will self-deport. Americans will take those jobs at some higher wage, and will no longer require unemployment compensation. The unemployment rate should be below 5% in no time.

The implicit side benefit, of course, is that would eventually result in illegal foreign nationals being released (fired) by companies who would then find American workers less expensive to hire. Illegals would have little choice but to self deport, after being replaced by bona fide Americans.

By the way, a number of companies use illegal aliens but do not pay them through payroll. They pay them through contractors so their books are not cluttered by illegal foreign nationals since they know this is against the law. Thus any method to collect the fine would have to include the contractors. It may matter to the lawyers that the contractors or the employers pay the fine. I would prefer the employers pay the same fine for all contracted illegal employees as they would for each illegal employee paid directly by the firm.

The moral of the story is that eventually companies paying ten dollars per hour more for using an illegal foreign national as a worker would hopefully find that it would be substantially less expensive to hire an American. That is really the objective. Their business could continue without disruption while they were in transition to American labor. They would have workers to produce their products until they were able to replace the illegal workers. There would be no public flogging for the social costs that the companies past actions had on US workers and US taxpayers. And the big bonus for management would be that as long as they complied, they would not be prosecuted. We're looking for a solution not a means of solving a vendetta.

To repeat the contractor deal, for companies that hire illegal foreign national subcontractors to supply labor, they get the same deal. For each hour a worker from an illegal Mexican contracting firm works in the business, the state unemployment compensation board gets ten dollars. For companies that choose to lie to avoid the law, prison sentences and / or treble or larger damages should be authorized to the tune of $30 per hour or more for each unreported hour.

A government looking for more revenue, albeit temporary, should like that idea, though companies accustomed to labor arbitrage working for their benefit will be dearly disappointed. This solution is so simple that it cannot fail when it is constructed into a Constitutional law. Government does know how to collect fines and taxes.

Admittedly this is hokey and the best way to solve the problem is to raid companies under the current law, fine them big-time for each illegal worker and then on the same day, send the workers back to their home countries, paid for by the company. We know that is the best way but are not doing it. By giving a dollar incentive for states to collect fines, the normal greed of politicians can contribute big time to solving the problem.

Straight forward ways to solve the problem

So, I admit the plan has elements of hokey-ness but it does not involve the federal government and so the states should be able to implement it with Obama's blessing. Every time that any of us look at any solution for illegal foreign nationals, it is more obvious that a country wanting to really solve the problem would just go ahead and solve it without having to use clever gimmicks such as this. The feds clearly do not want to solve this problem but the states, which are closer to the people, are more inclined to be for the people. Since I have not seen anybody tackling the real issues at the fed level other than to grant amnesty, or sue the states for trying, this end run plan has as much hope as any others. The people should insist on it.

Without trickery or gimmickry, as noted above, the way to solve the illegal invasion is to wage huge sanctions against employers who hire illegal immigrants. Everybody in government knows that and that is why it is not done. Enforcement should not cost the taxpayer a dime. Agents should code their time as a lawyer codes their time against each case, and when the case closes, in addition to the fine, the company pays all the costs of the process. If the company goes out of business, other companies who hire American workers will take their place. Too bad!

Not only is that fair—since the employers are also breaking the law—it would also curb the flow of illegal immigration. Some things are too sane to ever be adopted by our government.

That's why we should replace insane lawmakers from thirty years ago with anybody, even a person who appears to be a piece of guano. When guano is what you got, getting new guano is far better than rewarding the old guano just for being guano.

When word gets across the border that U.S. companies, large and small have stopped hiring illegal foreign nationals, if we can ever make that happen through the devices discussed in this chapter, the border jumpers will stay home. It will no longer be worth coming to Gringo-land. They say they come for jobs, after all, not to create issues in our cities.

Dick Morris is a pretty clever guy. For years, as their political advisor, he out-clintoned the Clintons, and they hate him for it. Morris is as astute as they come on immigration and other up-front American issues. His solution for illegal foreign nationals will work also

> "The real answer is not to round up Latinos in the streets of Phoenix and hope to catch illegals in the [same] net. Nor is it even to pretend that we can stop determined men and women from crossing the border by more guards, more troops and better equipment. The answer is to dry up the will to cross the border in the first place by stopping employers from offering jobs to undocumented workers. If there were felony penalties — jail time — for hiring illegals, they would not be hired. And, if there were no jobs, there would be no illegal immigration."

Dick Morris, like me, can probably write forever about this volatile topic. But he is not here now, so it is just me. The problem Americans have today is that neither the Congress nor the President has any interest in abiding by the wishes of American constituents. They want illegal foreign nationals to take American jobs for one reason or another—for the good of business for Republicans, or to line up a new voting Democrat.

In November 2010, the American people sent a lot of these Congressional buffoons packing and yet they are still trying to stuff amnesty down our throats. In 2012, make sure you do not help anybody who wants illegal foreign nationals instead of Americans to hold good jobs in American industries. We get our chance again every two years to have a Congress representing the people.

The Congressman Steve King plan

Congressman Steve King, who is highlighted in Chapter 1 of this book has another great idea to have companies hire Americans and have illegal workers self deport. His idea is very simple and in many ways has a similar effect as the Kelly plan. The more illegal workers earn, the more the company pays. The King plan would be done with Payroll in that every dollar earned each payroll by illegal workers would not be deductible. Thus, if the illegal payroll in a given week were $50,000, that amount would be added to the earnings and all taxes would be applied to it. Thus, the state and the federal government would gain revenue but the feds would get the larger share. Steve King is a great thinker and this plan would surely work.

Should there be employer sanctions?

Short of the $10.00 per hour illegal worker surcharge, as I offer in my notion of "it can be done," and yes, this is a form of a fine, the US solution for illegal immigration needs to be tough employer sanctions. Nobody says otherwise. Jail should not be off the table for companies that profit from the misery of others.

Guest workers?

After the illegal foreign nationals all go home, I can see an invitation-only guest worker program that is tightly controlled and completely paid for by the farmers. When companies can prove that Americans do not want particular jobs at recognized fair wages, there can be some but not substantial latitude to gain documented workers from other countries for short periods of time.

So, I have not ruled out bringing needed workers in legally, while paying them a living wage and then assure that they are on the bus at the end of the growing season when they are no longer needed. Because there is so much opportunity for corruption in guest workers trumping American workers, just as with the worker Visa programs, the legislation would have to be crafted to always favor American citizens and keep the penalties for abuse high enough to assure compliance.

If you are an illegal foreign national, on your way out of the country, on your own dime, or your prior employer's dime, you would be able to pick up a call back ticket and supply all your vitals so you can be contacted again in your home country when guests are invited back to fill any detected voids that cannot be filled by Americans.

Who Pays?

To pay for any border security, as well as unemployment compensation, as noted in prior sections of this chapter, the Kelly plan says it should not be free. It should add at least a $10.00 per hour fine for each hour worked by each illegal worker. In all cases, the fed gets some revenue and the state gets most revenue and the illegal worker is motivated to get out of town. The objective again is to have illegals self deport and so that it is always a better deal for companies to hire Americans.

If you are an invited-back guest worker, the taxpayer is not going to pay for regulating this program. There should be a fee for guest worker services also that might be as much as $1.00 to $2.00 or more per hour since the preferred worker in America is an American. The idea is that any guest worker program must pay for itself.

If we track illegal foreign nationals, then we know who they are, and we know where they are, and then we should know for sure that they are not taking American jobs (assured by the hourly wage surcharge / fine). Each of the 50 states suffers from the strain of supporting uninvited guests. Unfortunately, the federal government, which defends its right to defend our borders, is intentionally asleep. It does not seem to care about the influx of non-citizens plaguing the states.

Now, if we are really serious about keeping illegal foreign nationals out of the work mix, while American citizens are starving, this can all be made to work. Since the federal government has clearly shown its intentions to not permit anything involving America-first to work, the only real way to assure success is to have all immigration programs run by the states. If a state can find one illegal foreign national that the feds let in, then in my book, that state has a right to regulate its own "immigration." Now if only we could get all the lawyers to agree.

Some suggest that the USA, a country that may be in need of a younger set of workers to pay for our current and future retirees, might be able to achieve this by raising the allowed levels of immigration. I don't buy the argument. Bringing in a labor force of illegal foreign nationals already costs the states huge sums. The price of fruit may be 5 cents a pound lower, but the price of all other living, to support the freeloader part of the equation is staggering. Reduce taxes and raise the price of fruit. Let the market make it work, not the government.

I must admit that I have a problem with all this stuff (guest workers in the US) but if all the safeguards are in place, this may be an OK idea. If this is an OK idea, immigrants from all countries should be invited, however, not just workers from Mexico. I have a bigger problem with government bureaucrats making these decisions for an extended period of time as has happened recently while Americans are unemployed. State government is far more accountable than the federal government. All government is to answer to the people, not the other way around. The constitution permits throwing out a government that does not work for the people. We are at that point ladies and gentlemen with illegal immigration.

Chapter 38   Do American Workers Have the Right Stuff?

UFW Says Americans don't know how to work

Lots of people have an opinion on illegal immigration but the only opinions I care about are the opinions of regular American citizens. All of the others have an agenda or an ax to grind, and very few if any come forth and say their mission is for America and its people. So, that is how I would classify this somewhat recent trick by the United Farm Workers, who happen to have many illegal aliens in their ranks. In trying to embarrass American workers, they were not up to any good for America. I think that "shame on them," is the right thing to say to sum it up, but their agenda is way too big to accept a little shame along the way.

This past June 2010, the United Farm Workers AFL-CIO (UFW) began what they call the "Take Our Jobs" campaign. Though very clever, it is also a slap in the face to all able bodied American workers and the American unemployed. According to the UFW, the purpose of the campaign is to call attention to the importance of immigrant workers to the US food supply. Some might suggest they are saying to all US workers not engaged in farm work that if you guys can do it, go ahead, but we are betting you will fail. They are positioning themselves as the reason America eats well since Americans won't work even to provide themselves with food. This campaign is not very complimentary to American workers.

Additionally, it is supposedly to demonstrate the difficulties agricultural employers have in maintaining a stable, legal workforce. OK! Let's stop right there. In this case, logic suggests that the employers and the union are in cahoots so that the employers can employ illegal aliens instead of hiring Americans at a fair wage. How can a union be legally involved where the workers are illegal? Of course this is the era of Obama and all things are possible.

Poor foodless Americans

At the bottom of it all is the union's apparent belief that real Americans cannot do the work that illegal Mexican laborers provide because Americans are too prissy to work as hard as Mexicans. The UFW suggests that if it were left to Americans, US farms would not be sustained and America would soon be foodless. Americans have a right to be outraged. The UFW says basically that without illegal foreign nationals picking US crops, Americans would not do the work to even sustain themselves; the fruit would be left on the vine; and Americans would starve.

I find this tasteless and the utmost in bigotry. Isn't this racism according to progressive definitions? Are Americans being stereotyped as not being able to do the tough jobs? Can Americans, a motley mix to begin with, be the targets of some form of motley racism? If this were anywhere else than America and the target were anybody else but Americans, some group, someplace, perhaps the ACLU, would be complaining loud and hard. But because it is about regular Americans, nobody cares.

Not being a full student of unionism, I ask myself, "Is the UFW not itself an American union? Or is the UFW a labor group solely for illegal foreign nationals or for those on green cards?" What are they all about? Other than the research necessary to pen this chapter, prior to its outlandish claims, I had never had reason to know of the existence of the UFW.

Is the UFW made up of citizens of just certain ethnic descent? Is this not a valid question?" Is the UFW, an American Union for Americans?" If the UFW is for Americans, then why is it slamming Americans as worthless and lazy people while jacking up the status of Mexican workers as superior laborers compared to their "lazy" American counterparts. What is going on?

The UFW says that "We are a nation in denial about our food supply." I don't really get it. Why would the UFW not be fighting for better working conditions for their workers as in the days of Cesar Chavez, rather than taking pot shots at the "American" worker? Perhaps they are more interested in highlighting the need for a "legal" workforce of currently illegal foreign nationals than in being a union as we have come to understand the term.

Clearly, the notion of such a legal workforce can only be achieved through changes in US immigration policy. In fact, the UFW cautions that **without immigration policy changes, the domestic US agricultural industry could become crippled, and this, they caution, would lead to more "American" jobs moving off shore, leaving American crops rotting in the ground. I ask again, why people who represent illegal foreign nationals are being so hard on Americans. Americans should have those jobs. Perhaps the employers in concert with the unions are in violation of the many laws that are in place to protect American workers.**

Who should pick up the challenge?

Though this effort got underway in June 2010 with a letter to U.S. lawmakers, it was not until September, 2010, that the UFW boldly put its challenge out there in the big time media. Is it a ruse or are they asking ICE to send their whole ranks back to Mexico free of charge?

UFW says they have farm workers who are "ready to train [American] citizens and legal residents who wish to replace immigrants in the fields." They claim that this action is to encourage members of Congress to refer their constituents to vacant farm worker positions. But, this is nonsense like a lot of the stuff put forth by the pro-amnesty crowd against Americans. Reading between the lines, I regret to suggest that this is a veiled threat that the UFW has the power to shut down American agriculture if they do not get what they are asking for--"immigration reform," which we know is amnesty.

It takes a lot of chutzpah to look at the second leading manufacturing country in the world (second recently to China), clearly the most advanced civilization technologically in the world, with tough American-bred people who are descendents of the greatest generation, who fought wars for America's gains, and for better conditions throughout the world and to suggest that the United States is anything less than a great nation of exceptional individuals. This is an insult. Americans collectively and individually are the best. No apologies here. The UFW has no right to put our people down because as they say, "There are jobs Americans won't do." That's a lot of bunk and it takes a lot of chutzpah to deliver such balderdash.

We've heard the argument before -- even by former president George Bush, that "Americans" won't work on farms or clean houses or hotels, pack meat, put roofs on homes, or won't do the type of work illegal foreign nationals do routinely. This is a very myopic and ignorant viewpoint. It is poppycock ranting at its finest.

Let's say that there never were illegal foreign nationals in America. So, on the day that the last American was willing to work in any of the occupations now dominated by illegal foreign nationals, would American companies, engaged in these trades, have chosen to go out of business? No way! But nobody ever got to see what might have happened because cheap labor from across the border showed up and actually began to displace Americans in the workforce. These were Americans who were once gainfully employed, and only because of lower wages brought forth by illegal foreign workers were they eliminated. Their jobs were taken by illegal workers. . Businesses and Democrats were thrilled but American families had to get along with a lot less to survive. Who has been writing about that?

The present makeup of the workers in these industries does say something about normal Americans, but it does not say that Americans are lazy. It actually says Americans are smart. Americans are also too trusting. Americans believe deeply in the values of the system of the United States and its representative government and now are waking up to understand that their representatives in Congress are not representing them. Americans know the problem. So, the people, independently and in TEA parties across the US fired off their first round to reclaim their government. It was in the elections of November 2010. There will be lots more to come.

Government is the problem

The trust of US workers was violated by the government. Those who were displaced by illegal foreign nationals trusted that Washington would not permit this aberration for too long before it rose up on behalf of American citizens. With all the checks and balances placed into the structure of the US government by the Founders, American workers had reason for confidence that government would protect them. But Washington never rose to the occasion.

Washington chose not to solve the problems of illegal immigration and thus it did not solve the job loss caused by wholesale displacement of Americans in the workforce by illegal foreign nationals. Washington is too big or too unwilling to fix this problem. Probably both!

Yet, it certainly is a matter of state's rights and it is refreshing to see the states re-engaged in working to tame the overreaching authority of the federal government.

Among other things, the availability of Illegal foreign workers drives DOWN wages. Americans are smarter than to work for peanuts and have had many union uprisings over the years to prove that real Americans know how to receive a decent wage for their work. It is both a sham and a shame that American unions are not more aggressively taking the position of the American worker. Union leaders forget from whom the dues with which they lobby Congress come from. Why do unions fight to enable more, not less illegal workers? Follow the money and you will see the additional union dues at the end of the rainbow. Eventually as the country heads to Toiletville, union members will recognize their leaders as the captains of an immigration movement that is making America something a lot different than our parent's America.

With a combination of an unresponsive government, permitting a continual flow of workers across the US borders, and down-home industries clearly engaged in labor arbitrage, the US worker has little chance. Enter the higher availability of labor (especially the non-skilled) from foreign countries, illegal and legal as the case may be and the result is depressed wages in typically staple American jobs. One could easily conclude that it could never have happened if it were not well planned.

Small companies and large corporations, without seeing the faces in the windows, innately take advantage of the poor circumstances of illegal foreign nationals. They somehow think it is OK to employ them for slave wages, shutting out real Americans and their higher demands for wages from considering such "job opportunities." The UFW leaders know that and yet they feel right in suggesting that without illegal Mexican workers, nobody in America will eat well tonight.

The callous disregard for a living wage hurts Americans and it hurts immigrant labor from any source. The UFW membership should demand that the UFW do something about their conditions of employment. However, the leaders, not the workers, run the show. Union leaders are far more powerful than their memberships and through internal propaganda, they get their way. Unions don't readily discuss their distinct role in this tragedy of human existence.

If the cameras were permitted, I suspect that we would find UFW leaders salivating at the possibility of adding millions more members to their union rolls. Union leaders are ready to cash-in big time. The real stink here is that all of this is on the backs of people who have no choice. The illegal worker is caught with just one option. Americans, educated in America, know they still have a choice, though the situation is getting worse.

Along with the outright crimes that illegal foreign nationals commit in order to survive on this side of the border, there are even more crimes that they commit to be employed in the workplace. It is not just the illegal foreign national who is at fault in the workplace as we know well. US employers are part of this immense sea of illegality. For example, how much honesty is in the following?

- ✓ Ignoring US minimum wage laws and even minimum wage law exemptions
- ✓ Not worried about paying the 7.5% FICA tax (for only legal citizens)
- ✓ OSHA...Where are workers civil rights..benefits, and safety

Opportunity or threat?

So, if you are an American and you are out of work, and you see the UFW's entreaty to join the farm labor force, would you view that as an opportunity or a threat? Is there a real reason why Americans don't want to do those jobs? Can it be because employers get to use illegal foreign nationals as a bargaining chip against good wages for all Americans? Illegal foreign nationals gladly take the jobs in US farms. They have little choice. Like any human being, they would prefer not to be exploited but exploitation is a better condition than being exposed to the police.

Employers love the opportunity to make a killing off illegal workers. They pay a puny wage and then they do not have to worry at all about all those bothersome government requirements that hiring an American would entail?

Somehow, the progressives in America, who theoretically are for the disadvantaged and the impoverished, have a mindset that illegal immigration is OK. This makes the problem very difficult to solve. There is a stunning amount of ignorance that makes a decent solution next to impossible. The truth somehow never factors in. Nobody really wins in the illegal worker game.

Do carpets grow on farms?

Would the carpet factories of Georgia give us a different answer? Is life better there than on the UFW farms? Georgia's carpet factories are now well dominated by Mexican immigrant workers even though Georgia is not a border state. Would the UFW suggest that carpets are grown in Georgia on farms just like tobacco? But, wait a minute, carpets are manufactured from textiles. How did illegal foreign nationals get those jobs? Maybe Americans are getting ripped off in the carpet industry by illegal foreign national workers in much the same way as the construction industry or any manufacturing industry.

Soon, perhaps the manufacturing wages will again be so low that offshoring may not be a profitable enterprise for US firms. Will businesses bring jobs back to America because the wages have become affordable? Will Americans then take those jobs? Will Americans even be able to get those jobs?

Pay a decent wage

There is a point in the labor and pay continuum in which people will or will not perform certain work for certain wages. How pleasant or unpleasant the work may be, matters substantially to anybody looking for a job. Selling dresses in an air conditioned shop or being the desk clerk in a small motel might attract a lot of takers, even if wages were $7.00 per hour. On the other hand, digging ditches on the side of an asphalt highway when the summer temperature approaches 100 degrees is not something most rational people would find pleasant. So, for $7.00 an hour, these jobs may go unfilled. However, if the same job pays $17.00, most Americans will sign up as quickly as their pen can hit paper.

On the other hand, if you are not an American and you are scared to death from having fled Mexico, having been exploited by the "coyotes," cramped in the back of a closed truck for hours at a time in the searing desert heat, any job for any wages may sound like a good deal. And that has the effect of making wages depressed in any of the industries that attract the exploited. Moreover, it enables the exploitation of the uninvited to continue. Americans are tough but they are not stupid, and this bravado by the illegal foreign nationals who work the fields is not helping the UFW workers or the tolerance of Americans for illegal foreign nationals.

You don't have to be a math major to get the answer quickly. Take away illegal labor from certain industries and suddenly there could, in fact, be a labor shortage. That would mean wages would be forced to go up. It may also mean that food prices consumers would pay might also rise but even the experts suggest the amount of increase would be small. Food prices raise a lot more for example, when the price of oil goes up.

No company should be able to exploit any worker in any industry just so that a loaf of bread can be bought for 2 cents less. Likewise, nobody is asking GM to pay $7.00 per hour so cars can be cheaper. Paying slightly higher food prices is better than having depressed wages for certain farm-work. Wages must be fair or workers, in a real economy in which all workers are legitimate, will reject the jobs.

Americans will take any job in which the wage is right for the work. If illegal foreign nationals are the only workers who are taking jobs in a given company, that company is probably dealing in human trafficking and should be shut down. Since the feds choose not do this, the states must assert their Constitutional authority. Americans want to work. For that to happen, bad employers must reap what they have sown in a federal penitentiary --- the sooner the better.

And, by the way, UFW, Americans are waiting for your apology.

Chapter 39   Should Employers or Taxpayers Pay for Human Rights Violations?

We get the government we deserve

Every now and then on a local or even a national talk show somebody calls in and really gets it. America is truly in peril and there is a bumbledumber at the helm. So, more and more people, even people from other countries are praying for America to get out of its funk. Locally, in many communities, things are not going good. In my county in Pennsylvania, for example, one politician after another is now being taking down by the FBI. For all of the dirt kicked up by the small players trying to get lighter sentences, some of the big guys, like state senators and state representatives are just beginning to fall. Hopefully all the dirty will fall but for such a tall order that may have to wait for another day.

The reason we get bad government is simple. Americans have it so good, we often don't pay attention. After the politicians stole their "fair share" in the past there was typically something left. Those days are gone. The longer that a crooked politician is in office, the longer their reach, the more they grab, and the less attention they pay to you and me. They come to believe their terms of office are guaranteed and unlimited. That is a formula for bad government and we get it whenever we let the politicians tell us how things should be.

When we pay no attention to the bad guys and thieves that we elect into office, we always get bad government. We also get bribery, corruption, graft, and other vices and villainous acts. If you want a good government that cares more about American citizens than Guatemalan or Brazilian or Vancouver or Mexican citizens, you and I must stand up and be counted. We cannot let the mainstream press tell us that it does not matter who gets your vote as long as they are Democrats.

Likewise, don't let anybody tell you that the only organization that respectfully speaks for 70% of Americans, the TEA (Taxed Enough Already) party is bad. I can say that none of the government bad guys who went to jail because of the corruption in Pennsylvania were members of the TEA party. One hundred percent of them were Democrats, however.

Because there was no opposition in our City and county, the Democrata had full control. Republicans just don't get elected in Northeastern PA since their share of the voter block is less than 25%. Funny! I am a Democrat and I ran for Congress in the spring primary and I grabbed 17% of the vote, even without my party's support, and quite frankly a lot of just the opposite. The last thing bad government needs is new blood.

Dreams are not zero-sum!

The arguments of the redistributive progressive liberals is so strong, you might even think they believed in a good God instead of an all powerful government. They do not want you to give to charity to help illegal aliens because the government does not get its share when you give directly to help the needy. Government then has no say as to which cause to direct your contributions. No progressive politician can be there to take credit. Their convincing redistributive rhetoric is so powerful that one might begin to think that everybody should give up everything for the poor by giving it all to the government. It is part of their game. Then, who would help the new poor. Think about it!

Please don't let anybody make you feel so guilty that you even think that giving up your job and / or giving up your house is the sacrifice necessary so that illegal foreign nationals can have a better job and a better place to live. Ask those people, the progressive liberals, how much they donated to charity last year. You would be surprised at the paucity of their contributions, so hold your ground.

But, what if the illegal workers who took your job or are here to take your job are good people and they just need a better place to live. Should you hold your ground or give up your life savings or perhaps your home, as the ultimate charitable act so these folks can have a better life?

Don't even think about it! Dreams are not zero-sum. Goodness is not zero-sum. You can have your dream and they can have theirs. You worry about your dream and let these people go back home and cook up another dream that does not mess with your dream. Anything short of that let the progressives get their own wallets out and help. They have that right in a free country without taking from you.

Your job and your house are yours. Mine is mine. What we share is what we choose to share. It is our job to fight for ourselves against a government that is not on our side. The government wants to replace your freedom with regulations, and your wealth with a picture of an illegal family basking in the glory of your former home. OK, I am stretching a bit, but the message is keep your money and your belongings away from the control of the government. Keep all of your freedoms. Don't arm this government with any of the wealth that you may have. Dry them up so they have nothing to use against you. Help all the poor you can but not by giving government your treasures as they will surely squander them as they squander everything.

Problems from the beginning

Illegal workers begin their tour of duty in the US with major issues beginning with committing a crime just to get into America. Do not encourage them with your unconditional help. Let them get their own job in Mexico, the predominate state from which illegal workers originate. Let them get a job wherever they originate and let them live in their own house in their own country. Do not feel guilty because some greedy progressive wants to use your money instead of theirs to make them feel good

Your job and your house are yours, period. If the illegals can squeeze such amenities from Mexico without working, more power to them. If not, don't come here. We already had our revolution and that's why we celebrate the Fourth of July. We fought for our independence. Let them fight for theirs, and yes, we will help, but don't come here if you don't have the guts to face-off with your own government.

No American should be shamed by a redistributive progressive into giving their house or their job to anybody. Let the perpetrator in charge for the last several years, Barack Hussein Obama give up his fortune for the good of all indigent and suffering people in America— without government as an intermediary. Then, if you see him giving his, give some of yours if you wish. It is that simple. It is your choice. But, do not willingly donate to the government.

There are many victims of illegal migration

Can you really figure it out? The US is being invaded and Americans are being duped by the press and the progressives like as if it is happening to somebody else. Does everybody have to be affected for all of us to believe it is happening? Just because somebody jumps your fence, comes into your yard, and demands to be fed, does not mean that you should let them consume your breakfast. Chase them home. Don't bother calling the Border Patrol. They work for Obama.

Why is it politically incorrect to talk about the harm to both illegal foreign nationals and American citizens by a government that chooses to not enforce US immigration laws? I can answer that. It is because the progressives in charge of your government want you to acquiesce. They want to take advantage of your inherent goodness rather than provide for the goodness of all citizens of the United States. They do not deserve the right to even represent you. Do not feel guilty. The government is the "bad guys" in this scenario. Hold your ground. Replace them next time around.

Many Americans do not taste the problem

Despite Americans being the victims of progressivism, most American citizens have not been affected enough to be motivated to vote all of the bad guys out of office. If the illegal foreign nationals are granted citizenship according to the Obama plan, you can bet these new citizens will surely vote in every election to assure the thing that they just got (a good part of your measly wealth) does not go away any time soon. That is guaranteed. They know, from years on the outside, how important voting is in a democratic republic. They are counting on many Americans not knowing or not caring enough to know that you can protect yourself by voting.

Americans who have not suffered job displacement do not feel the pain and most want well enough alone. If some illegal aliens can benefit, then many feel God will reward them for their generosity. What about the 50 million illegal aliens? Whose country does this become when 50 million people living in the land are organized against individual Americans, who are not organized?

Sometimes doing what is right is hard. Of course dirty politicians know that most American citizens, who in many ways are still fat, dumb, and happy about the political and economic landscape, will not vote them out. They not only know it, they count on it. Your elected officials do not even want you to vote. That way, they can encourage only their select followers to go to the polls so these slime-balls can keep getting elected and thus, as hard as this may sound, we get the government we deserve.

The right to vote is precious

The fact is that over 50 percent of eligible voters have never ever voted in national elections. Higher percentages -- approaching 90% in some areas have only voted in local elections. The sick thing is that those Americans in these categories, who are motivated to vote though they know nothing of the issues, can be counted on to unknowingly help the dirtiest of the dirty politicians. The uninformed often listen to radio or TV media and they are affected by the major onslaughts of ads by those politicians whose coffers are full to the brim.

So, if this message reaches the ears of the otherwise uninformed, will it matter? The uninformed often are not paying attention to anything else. So, they don't get messages such as this but they hear loud and clear the voice of the incumbents and then they vote back the same senators and the same congressmen again and again and again and they have no idea that they are hurting their friends and themselves.

The TEA party and other organizations are hoping that they can get a force of American watchdogs out there. The people, as in *We the People* know that right now, the leaders in all branches of government in Washington are corrupt. Because they are corrupt, and because the stakes are so high, ordinary people who just go through the motions need to stop. No more motions. All people need to examine who we send to office and whether they are worthy of representing us.

There are many people who think Washington does not affect them. Yet, when the bean counter down the street tells them which doctor or doctors they are permitted to see, and their doctor is not on the list, perhaps that will be a wakeup call. If it happens too late, it will be a wakeup call to the death of America. Stay tuned or get involved. The death of America can be prevented.

Slavery revisited

Who knows what the long term solution should really be for all of the issues associated with the influx of illegal foreign nationals. Hijacking American labor and regulatory laws, such as OSHA, is not the way to do it. Enslaving illegal foreign nationals as a supposed solution to labor arbitrage or even a real labor shortage is a solution that is simply not right. Yet, employers victimize this illegal workforce every day, and each job an illegal foreign worker takes, some American, someplace suffers.

There are clever ways to solve the problem through fines and taxation. We discussed some of these in the last chapter and there are many other good ideas.

Employers who hire illegal foreign nationals, who will not give up the ghost, should not only be fined for hiring them, they should also pay to have them escorted back to their country of origin. Additionally, they should be responsible for them in Mexico or wherever they belong for another five years until they achieve success.

Don't you wish we had a positive remedy for the slaves who were brutalized in the 1800s so certain Americans could thrive? Some say, payback is a bitch! It is. The fat cats, living off the sweat labor of illegal foreign nationals need this come-uppance. Can you think of how historians will look upon this phase of American history 100 years from now? It is slavery revisited.

Are the illegal workers who are employed as slaves in American factories really slaves or do they have a choice? You figure it out. But, if we all figure that the employers are at fault, they should be treated like we all would have been happy to treat the slave-masters from several centuries ago. Don't blame the American people for not wanting illegal workers taking their jobs. Blame the businesses who depend on it and blame the Democrats for knowing about it but hoping when it ends, the will have a majority in both houses.

Should illegal aliens be deported?

Who says that brazen illegal foreign nationals, who break through our poorly protected borders to occupy our cities should not be deported? Check out Chapter 35 again for an answer. It is not you and it is not I, because the notion of not deporting a potential transgressor is folly in a sovereign nation. John Q Publics are everywhere and none of us are fools or we would not have "Public" as our last name.

Are illegal foreign nationals Americans? If not, then why does the President not think they should be deported to their countries of origin? I would suggest that whoever suggests that illegal foreign nationals should be given a free pass to stay in the US for whatever reason has something to gain that is not in the best interests of *We the People.*

Should employers have liability?

There are a number of apologists, who operate on behalf of employers. Some of them are paid by employers and so we know why they are who they are. They believe it is an undue burden on employers to assure that a person is American before they hire them. That is their argument but they also know it costs lots less to hire an illegal worker if you can get away with it. Americans have lots of opinions on this matter.

In a recent blog, for example, one particular business apologist writes this as an excuse:

> ..."many employers are not really trained in detecting whether someone is an illegal alien."

In the same blog, a reader responds:

> "HAHAHAHAHAHAHA! Thirty years in the construction biz and I can tell you that every home builder that I've ever worked for had no doubts about who was legal and who wasn't."

It's amazing that without the strong arm of the government, real people can know real things. Big government is a big impediment to what would be natural human acts.

Sheriff Joe

By the way, many of you have heard of Sheriff Joseph Arpaio. He is an elected Sheriff in Arizona and he has a low to no-cost prison that nobody really wants to be in. All the prisoners are dressed in pink. Joe believes that we can have all the prison space we want so our laws can be enforced. Go see Joe but not as a prisoner. He is most accommodating. Those employers who cannot pay the cost for illegal foreign nationals being caught within their premises should have their assets seized and then no matter what state they are from, they should be shipped to do some time in Sheriff Joe's prisons.

Arpaio and people like him have a lot of courage as true American patriots. He can give us the extra space we need in tents or outside without requiring huge building projects and political graft and payoffs. In this way, it absolutely would be a crime for illegal foreign nationals to give false documentation in employment applications. Put them in the clink just like you and I would be in the clink if we committed fraud. Because they are not Americans, they should be in the clink longer. Arpaio knows how to run the clinks real cheap. And, he is an American for Americans and for America!

The US has a pretty good system for verification of who's really who. With e-Verify, for example, it is so effective that the employer should also get jail time and face big fines to compensate the US unemployment fund and other sources for the human rights violations they committed. e-Verify is so good that progressive liberals no longer want it to be used.

If the employer has accepted the false documentation of an illegal foreign national without real proof of identification, through e-Verify, they should face time in the big house or the Arpaio tent-for-all. All legal expenses should be borne by the employer and not the taxpayer. They should also pay a share of the 20,000 ICE workers on the government payroll. Why should the people pay any of those tabs?

What does ICE do?

When you think about 20,000 ICE workers; what do they do? If, in addition to their other duties, they were expected to find one illegal foreign national within our borders each week, that would go a long way to correcting the problem as long as we sent them back. That would be roughly 50 deportations per person per year or 1,000,000 illegal foreign nationals getting their pink slips from the USA. per annum. Why do we not do that?

The Washington Post (WP) discovered a Feb. 22, 2010 memo that nets this out. The numbers of deportations and criminal removals are down from plan. In the memo, James M. Chaparro, head of ICE detention and removal operations, wrote that, despite what he called record deportations of criminals, the overall number of removals was down. I can't figure out how that can be. As a liberal progressive paper, did the WP print this because it was favorable for the illegal alien cause or because it was just good news? Too bad the press is not free in the USA.

While, from Chaparro's perspective, ICE was on pace to achieve "the Agency goal of 150,000 criminal alien removals," for the year ending Sept. 30, total deportations were set to barely top 310,000, "well under the Agency's goal of 400,000," and nearly 20 percent behind last year's total of 387,000," That averages out to 20 per ICE employee per year. As an aside, if citizens received a bounty for each turn in, it would save a lot of money. Of course each legal resident turned in should cost the citizen bounty hunter a small pay reduction as well.

Despite supposed increases in support for ICE, the government chooses not to get the job done. One million to three million enter each year and by design we put out under 400,000. Why? Who thinks that is a good number?

On August 27th, 2010, in what they said was a major policy shift, Immigration and Customs Enforcement (ICE) issued a new set of guidelines that sets their record straight. As shocking as it may sound to Americans who pay these people to keep out or to deport illegal foreign nationals, ICE is no longer expected to meet even the 400,000 number. The new guidelines clearly encourage illegals to stay in the US because it says the US is not going to deport them. The President feels more comfortable having them around.

Don't you want to know which law fostered that regulation? The federal government is derelict from the top down and now they are flaunting it to signal to the illegals that they may literally be home free. ICE and its Directors are acting against the will of the people and the will of the states, but probably well within the will of Barack Hussein Obama, who is always ready to snag a few more voters to his cause regardless of the American issue du jour. Without the feds involved, maybe there would be no illegal immigration issue at all as the states would be able to do a fine job protecting their people.

The new fed regulations go like this. If an arrested illegal foreign national is not already a convicted criminal or a terrorist threat, ICE will simply drop the case. Think of whether you trust government records to determine this status correctly even before you go through the asinine logic that such a policy should be OK for the US. In other words, the criminal alien will not be punished for identity theft, driving without a license, illegally accepting US services, or invading America without a passport. They may be prosecuted if caught for rape or murder or a big crime according to Obama. You can bet your butt, that if the illegal were you; your butt would be spending some time in the big house if you were caught.

ICE personnel are demoralized from this memo as you too would be. They know their job and they know Americans want them to do their jobs well and they are bewildered as to why Mexico or other nations sponsoring illegals in America have any say at all. Why would the President listen to Mexico about a real American problem? Don't we already know the solution?

To demonstrate just how relaxed the recent policy toward non-criminal illegal aliens actually is, an ICE news release from August 2010 trumpets the case of a particular arrested illegal alien. This individual had been deported from the U.S. on 8 separate occasions without being charged. Finally, he was charged with just one count of violating immigration laws after being found living back in the U.S. as an illegal foreign national for the 9th time.

Seems like an awful waste of time not charging these people as criminals. After all, they have broken American law. The fact is, as previously noted, the Obama administration believes that just being an illegal alien should not be a crime and so they are looking just for "criminals," according to a rulebook that does not mirror the US law. Don't forget that the Arpaio lockup has plenty of room.

Obama and the rest of Congress all know that illegal foreign nationals regularly take American jobs and good American jobs at that. If you think the H1N1 flu was pervasive, illegal foreign nationals in good American jobs have reached pandemic proportions. Relaxing enforcement is not the answer. Raiding American companies so that illegals will self deport is the only answer. If they do not self deport, then the company should pay big time for these human rights violations as well as the ticket home and the enforcement costs for these unfortunate souls caught in this web of business greed and deceit.

Bring back Elliott Ness

If you are from the Northeastern states especially, when have you seen illegal foreign nationals working farms? Not too often. Yet, there are 40 million to 50 million illegal foreign nationals in the US today, so how do these folks make a living? We don't have that many farm workers in America. If not on the farms, then, where are they?

For many, they are at your last place of employment, doing your old job--that's where. They are everywhere and our leaders do nothing. You've seen them waiting as day laborers and you've seen them at construction sites, painting sites, and roofing jobs, restaurants and hotels all over the Northeast. Our leaders know the invaders from south of the border are everywhere. Our leaders want to solve the problem by making them all legal. Try getting a job then. Perhaps dope dealers should be given airplanes and limousines to help them out. These people are criminals and they hurt America and everyday Americans, every day.

Do you remember Elliott Ness? He was the leader of the Untouchables. Even before prohibition was over, Ness put a big dent in illegal booze sales. What we have here is an illegal enterprise just as running and selling booze was in the 1920's. More and more illegal owned contracting firms are supplying labor to American companies so management can benefit from the lower cost of using the illegal labor. This is racketeering in the same way as running booze was in the 1920's and instead of ICE going soft on us, we need to toughen it up.

November 2 was the last opportunity to change to leadership who think of the American worker first and foremost. Most Americans got the message and sent back a new House in Congress to do the will of the people. Nonetheless, it was somewhat shocking at how many voters said they were OK with bringing the thief back into office by voting for long term inept or corrupt people from their districts. Nobody who advocates subrogating the will of the people should ever be invited back to office. If ICE wants to relax the rules, fire them all. If Congress wants to relax the rules, fire them all. And, if the President wants to keep playing games with American lives and American jobs, let's fire him too next chance we get.

Chapter 40   Crimes of Illegal Foreign Nationals

Selective Enforcement

The main focus of this book as you already know is the impact of illegal foreign nationals on jobs and the fact the government refuses to do its job of deporting illegal foreign nationals. This chapter takes a look at other crimes besides mere illegality of presence. These crimes, committed by these invaders from the south, occur often after the illegal perpetrator has gained a residence and a form of "illegal asylum" in the United States.

Whatever information the federal government statisticians and report writers have on illegal foreign nationals who commit crimes, they do not publish the information very often. After all, it would hurt their case for permitting illegal foreign nationals to wander free in the US on their own recognizance because. As you have learned, our know-it-all government chooses to concentrate on the "real criminals." This more than suggests that the simple border jumpers who live in America are welcomed by our government. This mere suggestion, in my humble opinion, means that the real criminals work for the US government and many are our elected representatives.

Like most news coming from the government these days, this notion of selecting the crimes to enforce is also a pack of lies. The Russians would properly call it propaganda aimed at convincing the people of the Unites States that all of the foreigners from south of the border seen on the streets in recent years are merely figments of our collective imaginations.

The propaganda would have you believe that even if there are some here, they do no harm. The perpetrators are all peace loving, law abiding people. The President himself suggests that just because they jumped our border, a crime in itself, does not make them criminals. Our government, despite our laws to the contrary has decided to take it soft on illegal foreign nationals at the border. Once they get here, Obama and his minions want to make life comfortable for them. Their votes may count one day. Our government should be ashamed of its performance and better than that it should have to defend its actions in a court of law. The Obama Administration is derelict in its duties to America and all those responsible should be fired post haste. Then, they should meet Sheriff Arpaio, and think pink! (See Chapter 39).

It can be argued without the slippery slope theory that President Obama is the epitome of a favorite lawyer joke, so let's go for it. "How can you tell a lawyer is lying?" "His lips are moving." The President has so many spokesmen out there, he can always say, "it wasn't me. I had pork and beans for dinner... that's one from soup!" Right! And ICE will deport only real criminals -- one strike and you are o-u-t. Whose lips were moving? It really does not matter as we know somebody in the administration was lying and continues to lie to the American people. They have gotten very good at it. We expect it and we forgive them too often for their lies.

If we were to go back to the last government study to get some facts, it would open some eyes about all of the institutionalized lying in government. I have a study that lists the statistics on the bad guys, (not working for government -- that would be another book) who jumped the border and the types of offenses they committed, and how many repeated the same crime. The most shocking part of the report is the section on repeat offenders: If we were already getting rid of the bad guys, as Obama suggests, we would theoretically have no repeat offenders. Nonetheless, the jails, which only speak the truth, are littered with them.

From the illegal foreign national's perspective, he or she should know that overall, they are treated quite well in the US -- at least outside the workplace. But, the burden to citizens to support their lifestyle is high and as noted many times in this book, it is not fair to ask everyday Americans, who are merely eking by, to finance the dreams of those who do not respect American sovereignty by living here illegally. In fact, the dreams of bona fide long-time American citizens are often cut short or fully crushed because illegal aliens dominate their trade and they can no longer find a job, or because they are a victim of a horrendous crime committed by somebody, who should never, have been permitted to stay in America.

It is argued often and it is true that most illegal foreign nationals' only crimes are border jumping and id theft. The latter of course would place any US citizen in the jail with no questions asked. What about real bad crimes? It is an inconvenient truth to the argument that all illegal foreign nationals are kind and benevolent that a disproportionately higher percentage of illegal aliens are criminals and their ranks include many sexual predators. That is a part of the dark side of illegal immigration. So, with Obama and company simply allowing the "good' in, we also get the "bad" along with them. There is no checking or none would get in. When we choose to let the "good" stay in the US, as in the unconstitutional Obama plan; the bad stay in the US right along with them.

Before we can even get into the notion of what is a real criminal, we have to ignore the fact that just being an illegal alien already makes one a criminal according to our laws. Also, according to our laws, criminals go to jail and illegal foreign nationals get deported. So, the question of how much really "bad" is acceptable regarding illegal aliens is a break we do not give our own citizens. Bad is bad. People everywhere who have compassionate hearts ask themselves: "what price are we willing to pay in terms of the collateral damage being inflicted by simply allowing all of them in?"

Back to government lies? When the Obama administration recently created press by admitting they only deport the bad guys, those of us tuned-in to the idea of "criminal" and "bad" and "degrees of badness." We asked ourselves, "so who gets deported?" Using the only really large study with clear facts that we have available, the GAO report from 2005, http://www.gao.gov/htext/d05646r.html, it is clear that bad for you and I is somehow not so bad for our government. And that, from my perspective is real bad. See what you think by taking the link above! We'll look at some specifics of the report below before we move to the next chapter.

The inconvenient truth is that illegal aliens with multiple offenses do not get deported. If Al Gore owns the copyright to the term 'inconvenient truth" let me know and I will conveniently cease and desist. Illegal aliens by the mere fact that they are illegal aliens are not even considered for deportation because Obama said so. Using a tinge of vulgarity to make my point, this leads me to the question, "Who the heck do we deport?"

The above URL points to the 2005 GAO report that also goes by GAO report number GAO-05-646R. Its title is "Information on Certain Illegal Aliens Arrested in the United States." The report was released during the Bush Administration on May 9, 2005. Make sure you have an airline bag handy. We are aware of no such report by the Obama Administration from which they can base any of their claims that illegals cause no harm.

Many of us are convinced that George Bush would have been as gracious to illegal foreign nationals as "Turn 'Em Loose Bruce" was fair to criminals. Former NY Supreme Court Justice Bruce M. Wright truly believed that White judges often did not treat Black defendants fairly so he created his own form of law and order. He denounced racism in the criminal justice system and he was known for his unique policy on bail, which prompted the Patrolmen's Benevolent Association (PBA) to call him "Turn 'Em Loose Bruce." If you were non-white, to make up for the work of the racists, Bruce would be sure to set you free. This was also the Bush philosophy. Is this fair?

The problem for Bush was that too many people were watching or he would have made them all legal at once and opened the borders permanently. That is why on the immigration issue; George Bush Jr. was not a favorite among conservatives -- Democrats or Republicans.

Most of the people of the nation served as Bush's PBA conscience and Bush cared about his approval -- but unfortunately for conservatives, not that much. If he had no constraints, let me say again that Bush would have let them all in and he would have kept them coming until we got rid of him. The people's issue with Obama is that he is doing what Bush wanted to do but did not do, without even having to pass any laws. Something about all that smells like an impeachable offense.

When at least we were trying to figure out how bad things were, before we issued forgiveness and / or complete amnesty notices to the thousands of criminals who made the report, it was a better world. This very readable document had to cost a zillion dollars for the Bush people to produce. For those who expect that government tries to do the right thing, the information in this report should give you a setback far greater than the extreme chill of a thousand neo-zombie movies. This report is in a simple word, scary.

Here is the letter of introduction for the report. In its briefness, it tells a lot with a frankness and casual tone. Notice again, a big friend of the American people on the issue of illegal invaders into the US is Congressman Steve King. Few people in Congress should gain any acclaim, but Steve King is one of the few who deserve the tag, *Honorable*.

May 9, 2005:

The Honorable John N. Hostettler:
Chairman, Subcommittee on Immigration, Border Security, and Claims:

Committee on the Judiciary:
House of Representatives:

The Honorable Steve King:
House of Representatives:

The Honorable Melissa Hart:
House of Representatives:

Subject: Information on Certain Illegal Aliens Arrested in the United
States:

The former Immigration and Naturalization Service estimated that as of January
2000 the total unauthorized immigrant population residing in the United States was
7 million.[Footnote 1] This total includes those who entered the United States
illegally and those who entered legally but overstayed their authorized period of stay.
A more recent study estimated that there were about 10 million illegal aliens living in
the United States as of March 2005.[Footnote 2] The study estimated that nearly
700,000 aliens entered the United States illegally or overstayed their authorized
period of stay each year between 2000 and 2004. Some illegal aliens in the United
States have been arrested and incarcerated in federal and state prisons and local jails,
adding to already overcrowded prisons and jails.

[The 700,000 aliens per year is an estimate. Other estimates show the number to be
as high as 3,000,000 per year and growing.]

On April 7, 2005, we issued a report on criminal aliens[Footnote 3] that were
incarcerated in federal and state prisons and local jails.[Footnote 4] Our report
contained information on the number of criminal aliens incarcerated, their country
of citizenship or country of birth, and the cost to incarcerate them. You also
requested that we provide information on the criminal history of aliens incarcerated
in federal and state prisons or local jails who had entered the country illegally. For a
population of aliens that entered the country illegally and were incarcerated in
federal or state prisons or local jails, this report addresses the following questions:

How many times have they been arrested?
How many and what type of criminal offenses have they been arrested for?
What states were they arrested in?

To obtain information to answer these objectives, we identified a population of
55,322 aliens that the U.S. Immigration and Customs Enforcement (ICE) in the
Department of Homeland Security determined, based upon information in its
immigration databases, had entered the country illegally and were still illegally in the
country at the time of their incarceration in federal or state prison or local jail during
fiscal year 2003. We then analyzed selected data contained in the criminal history
record, commonly referred to as the rap sheet, of these illegal aliens maintained
within the Federal Bureau of Investigation's (FBI) Integrated Automated
Fingerprint Identification System (IAFIS).[Footnote 5] To assess the reliability of
immigration databases used to make the determination about an alien's legal status,
we discussed internal control processes for ensuring data quality with responsible

ICE staff and found the data to be reliable for purposes of this report. To assess the reliability of IAFIS data, we discussed the data collection methods and internal control processes for ensuring data quality with responsible FBI staff and reviewed relevant policies and procedures. IAFIS may not contain all of the arrests for the illegal aliens in our study population since seven states report only their first arrest to the FBI. Subsequent arrest data is available only from the state's criminal history record system. While the magnitude of any undercount is unknown, we found that the data we used for our analyses were sufficiently reliable for the purposes of this report.

Several things should be noted regarding our analysis. First, an arrest does not necessarily result in a prosecution or a conviction. Second, our analysis is limited to the aliens that ICE determined to have entered the United States illegally. Third, since all arrests for an individual may not be recorded in IAFIS, our data represent the minimum number of arrests for these illegal aliens. Last, our analysis is not designed to infer conclusions about the arrest history of other illegal aliens not in our study population who entered the country illegally and have been arrested.

In April, we discussed with your offices the results of our work. This report conveys the information provided during those discussions (see encl. I).

We performed our work from October 2004 through May 2005 in accordance with generally accepted government auditing standards. Further details on our scope and methodology, including how we selected the illegal aliens in our study population, are discussed in enclosure II.

Results:

The briefing slides in enclosure I address each of our three questions. In summary, for our study population of 55,322 illegal aliens, we found that:

* They were arrested at least a total of 459,614 times, averaging about 8 arrests per illegal alien. Nearly all had more than 1 arrest. Thirty-eight percent (about 21,000) had between 2 and 5 arrests, 32 percent (about 18,000) had between 6 and 10 arrests, and 26 percent (about 15,000) had 11 or more arrests. Most of the arrests occurred after 1990.
* They were arrested for a total of about 700,000 criminal offenses, averaging about 13 offenses per illegal alien. One arrest incident may include multiple offenses, a fact that explains why there are nearly one and half times more offenses than arrests.[Footnote 6] Almost all of these illegal aliens were arrested for more than 1 offense. Slightly more than half of the 55,322 illegal aliens had between 2 and 10 offenses. About 45 percent of all offenses were drug or immigration offenses. About 15 percent were property-related offenses such as burglary, larceny-theft, motor vehicle theft, and property damage. About 12 percent were for violent offenses such as murder, robbery, assault, and sex-related crimes. The balance was for such other offenses as traffic violations, including driving under the influence; fraud--including forgery and counterfeiting; weapons violations; and obstruction of justice.

* Eighty percent of all arrests occurred in three states--California, Texas, and Arizona. Specifically, about 58 percent of all arrests occurred in California, 14 percent in Texas, and 8 percent in Arizona.

Agency Comments and Our Evaluation:

The Departments of Justice and Homeland Security reviewed a draft of this report and had technical comments, which we incorporated as appropriate.

We are sending copies to the Departments of Justice and Homeland Security and interested congressional committees, and we will make copies available to others who request them. In addition, the report will be available at no charge on GAO's Web site at http://www.gao.gov.

If you or your staff have any questions concerning this report, please contact me at (202) 512-8816 or by e-mail at Stanar@gao.gov or Michael Dino, Assistant Director, at (213) 830-1150 or Dinom@gao.gov. Key contributors to this report were Amy Bernstein, Ann H. Finley, Evan Gilman, Frederick Lyles, Jr., Jan Montgomery, Karen O'Conor, Jason Schwartz, and Laura Czohara.

Sincerely yours,

Signed by:

Richard M. Stana,
Director, Homeland Security and Justice Issues:

**** end of GAO report snapshot

Is your hair standing up yet? Yes, Virginia, this is the United States of which we speak.

So, is Obama or the government lying about this or do they just not know? We are not talking just about casual immigration violations such as ID theft and not paying taxes. As you can see, many, in this study of over 50,000 bad guys in US prisons, are career criminals. It is their shtick. Some die because of their shtick, but in all great things, there will be some breakage. Some of these "people" have been deported but like Jaws, that big nasty shark, they come back. When they come back, often they engage in heinous crimes right off the Arizona beachhead. Oh, think of things like indecency with a child, cop killing, and various other acts reserved mostly for wild animals and the scum of the earth.

Did somebody mention gangs? Many crimes are gang related. Gangs are a big threat to all Americans, whether they are home grown of comprised of illegal foreign national criminals. The well known and expanding Mara Salvatrucha (MS-13) gang, for example is notoriously brutal in carrying out its criminal activities.

Besides many fine essays on the Internet, one of the great works on the topic is Edwin Rubenstein's Criminal Alien Nation. Illegal aliens who commit other crimes while in the US are well recognized by law enforcement at the state and local level as a growing threat.

Some of Rubenstein's statistics include the following stuff. Again, data is hard to come by so a lot of this is not right up to 2010.

Back in 1980, for example, the total prison population of criminal aliens at the state and federal level was just under 9,000. Guess how far it grew by the end of 2003? Rubenstein accounts for approximately 267,000 illegal aliens incarcerated in U.S. correctional facilities. This is the breakdown:

- 46,000 in Federal prisons
- 74,000 in state prisons
- 147,000 in local jails

They cannot commit crimes if they are not permitted in the country. If they commit a crime to get here, they are more prone to commit a crime to stay here. No, that was not in any report. That's just common sense. Common sense is the once abundant sense that today is in short supply in Washington. It seems we have placed Common Sense in a lockbox that Al Gore refuses to open. Come on Al! Open it up to help us all while we are enjoying the great climate.

Rubenstein also did a bit of a cost analysis. For example he cites that in fiscal 2004, the federal government spent $1.4 billion to incarcerate criminal aliens. Just 25% of this tab is picked up by the feds and the remainder is borne by the states and local jurisdictions. All of these costs are borne by the taxpayer regardless of which pocket pays the tab.

Rubenstein agrees that the incarceration costs are not the only costs that need to be considered. There is a huge cost imposed on society for all illegal aliens and the costs are spiraling out of control. I have yet to see a cost analysis of jobs lost to illegal labor but major studies demonstrate that over 85% of new jobs at the entry level today are being gained by illegals and Americans are forced to sit on the sidelines. With proper border security and immigration enforcement, the costs would be lower, and the cost of crime would be lower, simply because there would be fewer illegal aliens.

These statistics clearly indict the federal government in administrations from Reagan onward as totally inept in immigration and border security. The US government in Washington has failed the people. In the Arizona lawsuit that was recently adjudicated, this joke of a justice department argued that it is their job to protect the borders. They are right, but according to immigration law, states are supposed to help. How can formalizing your approach be against the law? Kudos goes to Janet Brewer, for suing the feds to do their job. (Feb 2011)

Arizonans will have to pay the price for the arrogance and incompetence of the US government starting at the top and reaching at least as far as the Attorney General.

The thirty fold increase in crime by illegal foreign nationals from 1980 to 2003 as shown above is a great indicator that the failure of the federal government at the border permits more and more illegal aliens to violate the sovereignty of the United States and inflict real harm on its citizens. It is a poor report card for sure. Moreover, more and more of those who cross are criminals. In other words, the percentages of criminals to crossers are increasing.

Ironically, when the illegal aliens, who the feds admit is their job to keep out, commit crimes against citizens and then are arrested, the federal government has decided to pay less and less of the state and local costs of incarcerating them. Of course one could argue that they do this by paying less and less attention to the issue as more and more Americans are affected.

Though the cost of incarceration is notable, it is not the big cost. The cost to the public of keeping illegal aliens in the hoosegow is peanuts compared to the absolute carnage the criminals have imposed on their victims, *We the People*.

In total now, we are looking at well over 1 million crimes that would not have been committed. Today's biased media, who all but root that the illegal foreign national triumphs over those pesky and nasty American citizens, like to report that illegal immigration is a totally "victimless crime." Remember this saying, "they are only here to do the work Americans don't want to do?" With over 1,000,000 crimes, that makes over 1,000,000 victims, and that is a lot more than zero.

Add to that the illegal foreign nationals who get away with their crime because they are not caught and add in the new criminals crossing or re-crossing on a daily basis, committing more and more crimes every day while the bumbling federal government debates its role in the overall process.

Why should any of us feel safe?

Chapter 41   Offshoring -- Getting Work Done Cheaper

ITAA and Big Corporate Groups

This information put forth now in the front of this chapter is more or less a preface to the message of offshoring and legal onshoring with various visas. The ITAA is used as an example of the type of organization large corporations join to gain even more power over our legislators and against We the People.

The American way includes the belief that when problems arise, Americans create solutions. Americans, from obstacle one, have been great at solving problems throughout history. Today's problem is 50,000,000 illegal foreign nationals who reside in the country. From this group, a huge illegal labor pool has been made available to take American jobs. Regular Americans have seemingly been rendered powerless in this instance because of the unholy alliance of business, government, and unions. Each of these three choose to maximize their opportunities and there is only one paying customer left—the American taxpayer. The bottom line is that not all people, even those who are citizens, are good people. Thus their actions will typically not favor the people at large.

Let's start by taking a look at an innocuous sounding group, The Information Technology Association of America. As harmless and seemingly helpful as this group sounds to be, it is very powerful, and its focus is not on the American employee. It is for business success at all costs and worker considerations do not make the list. Because of that, they are very dangerous to the well being of American employees. It is OK with the ITAA, for example, if there are no American employees. I am familiar with the ITAA from my days as a Senior Systems Engineer with IBM.

Powerful groups such as the ITAA have been formed so that corporations have an especially powerful lobbying entity in Congress. Their mission is to represent the interests of corporations and only corporations. There is no similar group for technology employees, other than some unions. Though unions offer some countervailing power, overall in the technology industry most of the positions are non-union. In essence when the American worker goes up against groups like the ITAA, they are outgunned big-time. As hard as it may be to believe, our friendly Senators and Representatives line up with the big trade groups instead of the people.

Who is the ITAA?

The Information Technology Association of America (ITAA) is the leading U.S. trade association representing the computer software and services industry. Its more than 11,000 direct and affiliate member companies provide Internet access, on-line services, Internet software, Intranet development products, telecommunications services, business software,

software programming services, information systems integration services, and information processing services.

The TIAA actually no longer exists as a separate entity, but their principles remain within the group into which they merged. Therefore, we can consider the ITAA as part of an even larger and more dangerous industry group with powers equal to the size of a large country. Their mission statement does not include showing respect for American workers.

American Electronics Association (AeA), Government Electronics and Information Technology Association (GEIA), Cyber Security industry Alliance (CSIA), and Information Technology Association of America (ITAA) have merged to form TechAmerica. That is a lot of industry power. TechAmerica now is the largest and strongest voice and resource for technology businesses in the United States. The ITAA was huge as IBM was just one of its 11,000 members & affiliates. Can you imagine the size of TechAmerica?

Together, the merged company represents the industry's leading trade association, giving the tech sector a strong voice (lobbyists galore) and offering companies a broad array of exceptional programs and services. There are no programs for employees.

Feel free to research AeA, GEIA, and CSIA and TechAmerica. I would love to see a TEA party for workers to compete with this money rich organization. This group has to be more powerful and more rich (they cannot print money) than the US government itself. The ITAA was already bad enough.

It is all about lobbying Congress for special treatment against consumers and employees. Though in a Walgreens Perfect World, the government is supposed to represent the people, our experience shows that it most often fails in this responsibility. That's where the TEA party would come in. It is the only group today which actually has as its mantra to represent the people, not the special interests of America.

Being an IBM graduate and a professor of Business and Information Technology, I am quite comfortable with the topic of the ITAA and I know first-hand how anti IT-worker, the ITAA actually is. Many in my industry were offered jobs in India at the Indian prevailing wage because ITAA sponsored firms decided to no longer use American workers. I would expect some went to India, but those of which I am aware chose to stay in America working in less attractive scenarios than their former jobs, for substantially less pay.

The ITAA et al demonstrates to the world that corporations of all sizes have forgotten the people who made them successful. The charlatans who now run these huge corporations vote themselves excessive salaries while trying their hardest to get their workers' average salary as close to zero as possible. I think that explains it quite accurately. American corporations no longer care about American values. After all, like it or not, first and foremost, they claim to be "International Corporations."

Using this as a backdrop, let's now move to our offshoring case study, the story of the Furniture Store.

The Furniture Store case study

Long before offshoring as a business practice, companies learned to outsource. The furniture store, for example, found it difficult to have an integral manufacturing building creating their brand of furniture. The furniture manufacturer likewise found it cumbersome to own and operate a forest, a mill, and a lumber yard. The different types of laborers in these types of businesses were very expensive and the employees understood wood, and manufacturing, and not necessarily furniture sales. Eventually The Furniture Store concluded that there was too much vertical integration for it to continue its success.

Even more difficult to manage for a furniture store, was a forest and cutting trees into logs and logs into lumber. This was far too tedious for the furniture seller. Yet, how else could the company-owned and well pruned forest be cut and sent to the company owned mill to make the wood necessary for the onsite furniture manufacturing?

The Furniture Store also did its own financing and its own accounting and as computers became needed for handling transactions, it did its own systems and programming work. All of these unique business processes added to the difficulties in their wholly owned supply chain. It was actually too tough for The Furniture Store to continue in all of these different types of business at once when all they really wanted to do was sell furniture pieces.

So, eventually, this furniture store and many like it sold their other interests. They sold their forests and their mills and their manufacturing plants and they contracted with others to supply completed furniture to their stores. They contracted with banks and CPA firms for financing and accounting services. In order to focus on their core business, in essence they outsourced all of parts they could and they saved money in doing so.

America's top consultants at the time were recommending that companies end vertical integration and outsource all parts of the business that were not essential to the firm's identity. Companies who bucked the tide and subsequently failed had no excuse. So, most companies, guided like lemmings by the top consultants, went along to get along. Outsourcing, good or bad, became the norm.

Originally, however, American outsourcing was executed using only American trading partners. Then, the lure of exceedingly inexpensive options offshore began being touted by the major consultants. The lemmings again could not say "no." So, you could say that after outsourcing, offshoring was a natural progression. The work is still done by another company in another country. Offshoring therefore is outsourcing to a foreign company, rather than one in the home country.

The MFG Company offshores

The natural progression of the late 20th century would have found that the company to whom The Furniture Store sold its manufacturing plant, let's call them The MFG Company, would eventually have decided it too was going to outsource. Since manufacturing costs in third world companies were so much less expensive than the US, it was a natural. The MFG Company outsourced the manufacturing of most of its pieces offshore. Not having the mill or the forest attached to the business gave the MFG Company great flexibility.

The idea was to then bring the furniture pieces back to America and sell them to the same stores as prior to offshoring. Of course, The Furniture Store would be one of these. Unfortunately for the employees of the MFG Company, since the company found its best fit solution overseas, Americans were no longer part of the actual manufacturing process. In domestic outsourcing, many of the workers would have been acquired by the new company, but in offshoring, the former employees, who did not go overseas for the work at the new pay rate, became unemployed.

The MFG Company ultimately learned that China was the place for offshoring furniture manufacturing as they could build it and get it back for far less than it would take to make it in the US with US employees. So, The MFG Company offshored most of its core business, *manufacturing* to China. During the transition, certain specialized pieces continued to be made in the US but the number of US employees in manufacturing was reduced by 95%.

Instead of 95% of the products coming off the furniture line, this line was replaced by the loading dock with completed imported pieces from China arriving as regularly as the pieces once came off the line. A mostly unperceivable difference was that the products were really not manufactured in the USA. In just a few cases the wood was shipped overseas but in most cases, the wood was grown in China for even lower-cost manufacturing. The quality was not exactly the same but the cost savings were too good to pass up for The MFG Company. The name on the finished product was the same so American furniture stores that bought these goods could not easily tell the difference.

The plight of The Furniture Store and The MFG Company mirrors what has occurred in the US furniture manufacturing industry over the years. Though the product is typically quite heavy to ship back from offshore, labor costs are seen to be so much better that companies are able to ship the products back to the US and still make a substantial profit. The MFG Company's profits went through the roof. This story is like most offshoring stories. The company wins and the American employee loses.

Over the past twenty years, furniture manufacturing in the US has been substantially transformed by offshoring. Imports (when the products come back completed) have surged from $17.2 billion in 2000 to $30.3 billion in 2006, with virtually all of that increase in production coming from the lowest cost-producer, China. The furniture industry in the US meanwhile lost 21% of its jobs during the same timeframe. The worst is yet to come.

H-1B visas take the best American jobs

For those companies that could not offshore for one reason or another, corporations worked with your Congress in 1990 to give them another way to out-hustle American labor. The US has many visa types established to enable foreign workers to come to the United States to work in a number of different occupations. A writer could fashion a whole book on how poorly the US visa programs have treated American employees. Many US workers, who have seen their jobs go to H-1B visa holders are not as pleased as the 1,000,000 or more holders of various work visas, who are permitted into the US each year by plan or by chicanery.

The emphasis in this book is not offshoring or onshoring with visas. However, so many American jobs are lost knowingly by the government as it toys with foreign visa numbers; the Jobs Jobs Jobs picture is highly affected. For this discussion, rather than spend a whole book on visas, let's take a quick look at the H-1B visa, to which most Americans can relate.

If your son or daughter has just graduated from college and they can't get a job, you can probably thank the US government for permitting 65,000 H-1B visas to be granted this year. It won't be better next year because they won't be going home. Each of the H-1B visa holders can stay in the US up to six years. Then, their company typically lobbies for them to get a green card or when all else fails, they become an illegal alien without hopping the border. Few ever go back.

Before the economy actually tanked in 2008, your friendly lawmakers were being well entertained by organizations such as the ITAA and others to help them gain access to more quality foreign workers. They suggested there was a shortage of good US high tech professionals such as computer programmers and engineers. During this period the high tech companies in the US, such as IBM, Microsoft, and Apple were offshoring all the jobs they could and those they left behind could not get similar jobs in the US. The truth did not stop these corporate lobbyists from wining and dining our Senators. Despite record numbers of IT personnel out of work and record numbers of IT graduates unable to get their first job, the Senate was moved by the pleadings of ITAA and others to increase the visa caps. So, they did.

The Senate passed immigration bill 2611 on May 25, 2006. The bill was a real sweetheart deal for Sam Palmisano, Bill Gates, and Steve Jobs but it was not such a good deal for American hi-tech employees. The bill contained a number of increases in H-1B visas including the following:

- Raising the base quota from 65,000 to 115,000,
- Automatically increasing the base quota by 20% whenever it is reached with no provision for lowering it,
- Adding 6,800 visas for trade agreements separate from the base quota,
- Adding 20,000 visas for those with foreign graduate degrees,
- Raising from 20,000 to unlimited the number of visas for those with U.S. graduate degrees, and
- Making visas to non-profit organizations exempt from the quota.

Perhaps because the Senate is the House of Lords and the House is the House of Commons from old England, the Senate was easier to convince. After all, it was just common Americans who would be hurt and big shot executives would be able to make a lot more money for their companies. Cooler and smarter heads prevailed in the House, which refused to consider the measure. It died in conference and no H-1B increase was approved and Congress thus had little explaining to do at election time.

To backtrack a little, the H1B Visa is a United States nonimmigrant visa. It allows a U.S. company to employ a foreign individual for up to six years and, as a non-immigrant visa, it is not supposed to lead to a green card. But, Congress lied about that. It almost always leads to a Green Card. In other words, the 65,000 or 115,000 or whatever # that come in a given year, never go home.

The original intent was that no green card was to be given as these folks were temporarily filling gaps in the US workforce. It is a nonimmigrant visa. Today, businesses treat them as replacement players for US workers. It is amazing how the intention of Congress is modified in practice by the Executive Branch.

In a 2002 Computerworld article, Nobel Prize winning economist Milton Friedman was quoted as saying that the H-1B program is nothing more than a corporate subsidy. Many others hold this opinion and have testified before Congress. Congress has so far been unmoved and continues to lean against Americans and for lobbyists. Expert thought on the subject is that the statistics are all bogus. There has been no shortage of qualified American citizens to fill American computer-related jobs. In fact, studies show that in a number of years, the tally of foreign programmers and engineers imported outnumbered the tally of jobs created by the entire industry. In other words, before the first American can apply, all the jobs are taken. Thank you, Congress.

Another problem with the H-1B visa is that companies lie about the wages they pay. They use the H-1B visa program to help them in their labor arbitrage and this lowers the wage for all candidates for the positions that are available. Wage depression has been one of the major complaints about the H-1B program. Congress understands this but business has the upper hand always. Studies have shown that H-1B workers are paid significantly less than U.S. workers. In fact, displaced US workers claim that the program is primarily used as a source of cheap labor. There are only 545 individuals responsible for this pox on US employees. They include the following:

- ✓ 435 members of the House
- ✓ 100 members of the Senate
- ✓ 9 members of the Supreme Court
- ✓ 1 President.

You know the solution.

To recap, the H-1B visa type allows business professionals to work in the United States for a specific amount of time. The purpose supposedly is to give U.S. employers the opportunity to hire foreign professionals only if a U.S. citizen or resident is not available. Unfortunately, no program is perfect. From my observations, this is the first check mark to be ignored. Technically there are a lot of requirements but sharp placement firms can and do get around most of them. In essence this is the US government inviting 65,000 people a year from any other country than the US to take American jobs. And yes, 65,000 came in 2010 and they did not go back. And yes, another 65,000 are coming this year.

Technically, both the employer and employee must satisfy specific requirements.

Employer Requirements:

- The job offer must be in a specialty occupation such as architecture, engineering, mathematics, etc.
- There are criteria for wages offered and the actual job performed
- No U.S. citizen or resident must be available for the job
- The petition must be submitted by the company (not the employee)

Employee Requirements:

- A Bachelor degree
- Specialized skill
- Speak and read English

H-1B Visa restrictions and limits:

- 65,000 visas are issued every year
- Non-profit organizations are excluded from the annual cap
- Higher education institutions are excluded from the annual cap
- Over 130,000 applications were received during 2008-2009
- H-1B visas are issued for a maximum of 6 years

The H-1B program is criticized with good reason by Americans who are concerned about job loss. Even in this time of dire unemployment news, our all-knowing Congress chooses not to eliminate it. First of all, the wages are kept lower in certain H-1B related industries because foreigners accept a lower wage for the the same work. They are not supposed to. This gives them the opportunity to work in the United States. If they do not accept a lower wage, their American caretaking firm may choose to turn them in as a "not-good-employee," causing them to forfeit their visa and go home. So, nobody complains.

The reason American companies like these top of the line, low-cost pros is that foreigners cannot easily change jobs in comparison to a U.S. citizen or resident. This makes them much more attractive for many employers. The foreign employee is more or less a slave to the business. None of these H-1Bs are starving because they get paid very well. Though the pay may be sometimes half of what a high skilled American would be paid, it still is considered well in relation to all Americans. This fact is not missed on these super intelligent H-1B visa holders. They know better than to complain or join a union. They just do not get paid as well as an American would get paid with an equal level of skill. H-1B visas are in fact a way of corporations gaining top-level indentured servitude.

Universities do not serve American students well

Academia helps make matters worse for Americans. Universities care more about the university than they do the faculty or staff. The marketing people in universities joke among themselves that their mission is to get "meat in the seats." Marketing and Admissions work together. As crude as it sounds, the objective is meat in the seats. Among many other marketing contrivances, American Universities are incented by government visa programs to offer higher IT degrees to foreign nationals for the purpose of educating them to fulfill H-1B jobs in America. Who does this help? This is very discouraging to American citizens who might choose such degree programs. More importantly, it makes positions for those types of degrees just about unavailable for Americans.

Professional visas remove student opportunities

At the professional level, the H-1B visa and other such mechanisms are the professional moral equivalent of offshoring. Firms that require knowledge employees would prefer to have them located close to the corporate mother ship. H-1B permits this. In practice, however, the employees, though working in America, are not Americans. In fact, most of the companies are not American. Most are Indian. Indian companies have joked for years that the H-1B for them is an offshoring visa, as their employees come to America, get well trained as US employees and then go back to India to take American jobs. With H-1B, many get to stay behind. If our Congress were more concerned about American employees, they would have produced legislation that fosters American employees, not foreigners.

The offshoring story continues and there is news on a regular basis. The Federation for American Immigration Reform (FAIR have their collective ear to the ground on all matters immigration. They have done a fine job of explaining many notions so feel free to go for some of their gold at the FAIR web site.

FAIR Legislative Update January 24, 2011

For now, let's look at a few early 2011 updates on immigration from the Federation for American Immigration Reform (FAIR). This national, nonprofit, public-interest, membership organization of concerned citizens shares a common belief that our nation's immigration policies must be reformed to serve the national interest.

FAIR has a deep interest in all things immigration and those who abuse our visa programs are as much on FAIR's target list as are those who compromise our immigration policies and laws. As this book was going to press, FAIR sent me a legislative update about what is happening right now regarding the impact of the H-1B visa. Since I am a member of FAIR, I am providing this update for you below. When you have an opportunity, feel free to visit the folks at FAIR at http://www.fairus.org.

GAO: H-1B Program Falling Short

In a report released last week, the Government Accountability Office (GAO) concluded that the H-1B guest worker program – which proponents claim is for "high-skilled" workers – may not be serving its purpose and, in fact, "may be detrimental in some cases." (H-1B Visa Program: Reforms are Needed to Minimize the Risks and Costs of Current Program,GAO-11-26, January 2011) The GAO called on Congress to reform the current H-1B Visa program to help protect American workers and close loopholes.

The H-1B Visa program, which was authorized by Congress in 1990, allows U.S. employers to hire foreign workers for "specialty occupations." (Immigration and Nationality Act, §
101(a)(15)(H)) Originally, federal law capped the number of H-1B visas at 65,000 per year. (GAO-11-26 at 1) However, the cap has changed throughout the years in response to legislation passed by Congress.

It reached a high of 195,000 in the years 2001-2003; in 2004, the cap was returned to 65,000, and the following year an additional 20,000 visas were reserved for individuals with advanced degrees from U.S. universities. (GAO-11-26 at 13) Today the cap remains at 65,000 visas per year, with additional 20,000 H-1B visas available for individuals with advanced degrees from U.S. universities. In addition, universities, research institutions, and K-12 public schools seeking to hire foreign workers are not subject to the cap. Exemptions play a large role in expanding the H-1B Visa program.

In Fiscal Year 2009, for example, a total of 214,271 H-1B applications were approved. (United States Citizenship and Immigration Services, April 15, 2010)

In its report, the GAO found that changes to the H-1B visa program over time have diluted protections for American workers. For example, before 1990, H-1B guest workers were not allowed to apply for green cards. However, now H-1B holders are allowed to apply for green cards and are allowed to remain in the U.S. for an unlimited period of time while their application is pending. This has increased the number of H-1B guest workers in the U.S. significantly beyond what was originally intended, though DHS cannot say with any precision how many H-1B workers are currently in the U.S. (GAO-11-26 at 30)

The GAO also noted that Congress had lowered the skill level required in order to receive an H-1B visa. Before 1990, an H-1B applicant had to be "of distinguished merit and ability," coming to the U.S. to "perform temporary service of an exceptional nature requiring such merit and ability." Now, H-1B applicants need only be coming to the U.S. to perform services in a "specialty occupation" and have obtained a bachelor's degree in the specific specialty.

This change has expanded the pool of applicants significantly and reduced their overall skill level. In fact, despite the fact that businesses generally refer to the H-1B visa as a visa for high-skilled or "high-tech" workers, the GAO reported that 40 percent of H-1B guest workers only had a bachelor's degree and over half are receiving entry level wages. (See also United States Citizenship and Immigration Services, September 2008)

GAO also found that restricted agency oversight and statutory changes had weakened protections for American workers. For, example, although there are requirements and guidelines for H-1B programs in place, the Department of Labor only does a cursory review of applications.

In fact, Homeland Security recently found that 21 percent of the H-1B petitions they examined involved fraud or technical violations. (See also United States Citizenship and Immigration Services, September 2008) In addition, GAO found that while the bulk of complaints regarding abuse of the H-1B program are with respect to staffing companies – which apply for a disproportionate share of H-1B visas in order to place those workers in other companies – the government engaged in poor oversight of such firms. (GAO-11-26)

Regarding whether the H-1B program hurts the wages of U.S. workers, the GAO's findings were inconclusive, though it did find a "significant difference" between the earnings of several groups of H-1B and U.S. workers, evidence that H-1B workers may be having a negative impact on the prevailing wage in those occupations. (GAO-11-26 at 42) The GAO's survey of wages of H-1B workers and U.S. workers did not find significant differences. However, the GAO itself noted that because the government does not keep adequate data on the program, it "could not account for all factors that might affect salary levels." For example, the GAO explained that comparing the salaries of certain professions alone could not account for differences in age or skill level, which are key factors in wage levels. (GAO-11-26 at 41)

Among its many conclusions, the GAO specifically recommended that Congress reconsider the qualifications required for H-1B visas, exemptions from the cap, the appropriateness of allowing staffing companies to hire H-1B workers, the level of the cap, and allowing H-1B guest workers to apply for green cards.

Thank you to FAIR for this legislative update. FAIR also sent the following update as a Valentine's day (Feb 14) gift:

Senators Graham and Schumer Reunite to Push Amnesty

Recent news reports from Capitol Hill reveal that long-time amnesty supporters, Senators Lindsey Graham (R-SC) and Chuck Schumer (D-NY), are reuniting to push "comprehensive" immigration reform in the Senate. (Politico, Feb 7 2011) So far the pair has reached out to several organizations in the open-borders lobby including the U.S. Chamber of Commerce, the AFL-CIO, the Service Employees International Union (SEIU), Conservatives for Comprehensive Immigration Reform, and numerous evangelical groups. (*Id.*) Sen. Lisa Murkowski, who was one of three Republicans voting in favor of the DREAM Act last session, also confirmed that aides in Sen. Schumer's office contacted her staff to discuss the issue. (*See Senate Roll Call Vote 278 of 111th*)

*S*enators Graham and Schumer have indicated that the talks are merely in its opening round and that reigniting their coalition may take some effort in the new Congress. "It's in the infant stage," Sen. Graham told *Politico, Feb 7, 2011:* "I don't know what the political appetite is to do something." (*Id.*) Schumer shares Graham's sentiment, "What we're doing is beginning these preliminary talks, particularly with outside groups, to try and regain the consensus that was pretty nicely formed last year." (*Id.*) "And who knows, we might surprise everyone and get something done. We realize it is a tough thing to do, but it is very important, and it's worth a shot." he said. (*Id.*)

Graham and Schumer may be hoping to capitalize on the fact that five Senators have already announced they will not seek re-election in 2012—the same number of votes by which the DREAM Act failed in December—and are no longer accountable to their constituents—from (Politico, Feb. 7, 2011) For example, at a news conference announcing that he would not seek re-election next cycle, Sen. Jon Kyl (R-AZ) called immigration reform "one of the top items on the agenda" and said there may be an opportunity in the next two years "to tackle that in a productive way." (Arizona Republic—Feb. 11, 2011).

Yet, in a subsequent interview Sen. Kyl backtracked, saying that he was not referring to "comprehensive" immigration reform and that going down such a road again would be a "dead-end." Other Senators not seeking re-election in 2012 include Kay Bailey Hutchinson (R-TX), Kent Conrad (D-ND), Jim Webb (D-VA), and Joe Lieberman (I-CT).

Senator Graham and Schumer's efforts come on the heels of President Obama's State of the Union Address where he urged members of Congress to "address the millions of undocumented workers who are now living in the shadows." (NPR, Jan. 25, 2011); *See also(FAIR Update in this chapter.* Jan. 31, 2011) But, even with the support of the White House and the Senate, it is doubtful that an amnesty bill by Graham and Schumer would survive in the House this legislative session. Such a bill would likely have to make it out of the House Judiciary Committee, chaired by Rep. Lamar Smith (R-TX), an ardent supporter of immigration enforcement

Chapter 42   The Job Displacement Phenomenon

Illegal labor is cheap labor

Though we have discussed it often in this book, we have not, until now concentrated on the phenomenon of *job displacement*. It is one of the overlooked ways in which illegal immigration harms the American workforce. When native-born Americans lose their jobs to recent illegal immigrants, who will work for substandard wages, they become victims of job displacement.

As difficult as it is to believe, the US government, in this time of a Jobs Jobs Jobs shortage does not even want to look at job displacement as an issue. Government does not want to hear that the beginning of the solution is to deport 40 to 50 million foreigners who are illegally working in the US. Yet, that is the start of what some believe is the only solution that is fair to the displaced workers who are contributing American citizens.

Would you believe me, if I told you that sometimes an employer intentionally replaces native-born Americans? What if I said the replacements are illegal foreign nationals and the purpose is to gain a cheaper, more easily exploited workforce? Would you believe me? What if I said the displacement often comes through an intermediary? In these cases, work may be delegated out to subcontractors. The firms that want to use illegal workers and who want to pay them low wages gain again when contractors and subcontractors bid and underbid each other. Ultimately, the business that is not using Americans wins the work by being able to offer the lowest price.

In some cases, the ultimate employer, if they are already using contractors, may not even be aware that native workers have been displaced. But, I have a hard time believing this is true most of the time. Regardless, the effects on real Americans are all too real.

The furniture story -- continued

The furniture case study from Chapter 41 is not completely over yet. Over the last several years, the furniture manufacturing company, The MFG Company noticed many others in its business bringing manufacturing back home and still beating its price. They learned that it was achieved by using illegal foreign workers, which happen to be very available in most states, especially California. For business, these workers have a very special attribute: they work cheap -- dirt cheap.

The official sounding term for this is not illegal immigration. It is job displacement. It is a big problem for US workers in all industries. We might define job displacement then as the phenomenon of Americans losing their jobs to recent illegal foreign nationals, who will accept almost any wage for a job.

The US Immigration and Naturalization Service (INS), which is now called the US Citizenship and Immigration Services (USCIS) under the Department of Homeland Security says it this way:

> "The critical potential negative impacts of immigrants are displacement of incumbent worker groups from their jobs and wage depression for those who remain in the affected sectors."

One would conclude that since USCIS knows about the effects of illegal foreign nationals on native-born workers, or at least should, its cousin in Homeland Security, Immigration and Customs Enforcement (ICE) should be trying to shut down those who are making it tough for Americans in the workplace. Why is there no enforcement while Americans are taking it on the chin?

My answer to that is it is partly a result of government incompetence but also a result of progressive liberals in Congress and a President who chooses not to enforce the laws. Progressive liberals exist on both sides of the political spectrum. They have convinced themselves that illegal immigration is either good for America or good for them or both. We know it is not good for America. Yet it goes on, no matter which party is in office. *Money talks.*

It doesn't take a Rocket Science degree to know that it is a lot easier to run manufacturing in the US than it is by offshoring the whole plant to another country. Let's call the reasonably new phenomenon of using illegal foreign labor inside the US as *onshore outsourcing* or simply *onshoring.* Originally, companies outsourced to other domestic companies and this was thus called *domestic outsourcing.* Now, since illegal labor is very cheap domestically, we are seeing some of these companies coming back to the US to find a new supply of workers -- illegal foreign nationals.

When companies use an illegal workforce domestically to accomplish their business mission, we have come full circle in the offshoring cycle and so the newest labor game is *onshore outsourcing.* It is similar to plain outsourcing but it is different in that for the most part it is merely the labor component that is outsourced. Whether the company chooses to hire illegal workers via contractors or hire them directly, the result is the same. The company has onshored its labor supply.

Offshoring coming back home

Let's say a company formerly offshored its business overseas. If the company's US plant still exists and is available, and the company wants to try a return to the US plant, things can happen quickly if the plant can be reactivated. If not, another plant can be built so that manufacturing can return to the US perhaps within a year or so of the decision.

Executives who have offshored know that there is a new worker supply in the form of illegal aliens in the US. Their companies can go right to onshoring from offshoring. So, ccompanies that bring their work back to the US can gain substantial savings and in most cases, make operations easier. They can choose between direct labor or contract labor and both options are good for the bottom line. Whether the company chooses to hire illegal workers via contractors or hire them directly, the result is the same. The company will have changed from offshoring to onshoring.

Companies who may have been considering offshoring now have a new option—onshoring. This is lots easier thatn offshoring. Unfortunately for America, the next step after getting the illegal workers ready to go is to fire the domestic American labor force. Thus, onshoring is simply the outsourcing of jobs to illegal workers in America. American workers get fired nonetheless. The only good news is that the jobs, though held by illegal foreign nationals, are still in America. And that is better than the jobs being in the far east.

Though easier, there are still complex interactions required among factory openings and closings, choice of production methods, ethnic networking in hiring, and labor subcontracting. Together, however, all of these intricacies cost a lot less than offshoring. To play in this game, more and more businesses have gone illegal, and most of the US lawmen know who they are and they are letting them get away with it.

NAFTA today, India and China tomorrow

Some say what goes around comes around. For example, many North American Free Trade Agreement (NAFTA) jobs that went to Mexico for cheap labor were relocated to India and then China because corporations are obsessed with seeking the absolute lowest wage. Mexico has cheap labor, but not cheap enough. It is a dog eat dog world in the legal offshore labor market. For businesses, it is a lot easier pretending that onshoring is a legal enterprise. As long as the cops think it is OK, it is OK!

The Americans affected by onshoring actions are typically the lowest skilled, at least right now. Moreover, they typically do not fight back in any way. They really do not know what has hit them when they find themselves out on the street.

Illegals also battle illegals for the lowest wages

Though some companies do pay minimum wage or greater, many do not. When they pay outside contractors, the dollars go out through Accounts Payable rather than Payroll and are difficult to audit as onshoring operations. Thus, unless somebody is talking, the authorities are less likely to know. Some of the older stories about how tough contractors are in assuring the lowest wage for the company are still out there. Do you remember when the minimum wage was $4.00 per hour? Here is a story that goes back to that time.

A few older cases were easier to document before Americans became outraged at losing so many jobs. Now, it is not as easy to get people to tell the stories. There are cases, for example, in which legal workers in an onshore farming operation, who had been working for

4.00 per hour (minimum US wage at the time of the story), lost their jobs to a company offering better priced labor. So, even $4.00 was still not low enough to keep their jobs. The growers found other illegal aliens who would work for $3.35 per hour. The legal workers who had been doing OK at $4.00 per hour would not lower their wages and eventually none were ever hired to work that farm again.

The Federation for American Immigration Reform (FAIR) tells a great story about how one batch of illegal immigrants will get replaced by another batch of illegal immigrants willing to work for less: Here are some of FAIR's reports:

> "Sometimes, recent immigrants themselves are the victims of [job] displacement. In the raisin grape industry of California, Mestizos (the Spanish-speaking population of Mexico) were laid off and replaced with lower cost Mixtecs (the indigenous people of Mexico). According to a study of the industry, the Mixtecs "have driven the Mestizos out of the market."

> "In the furniture industry, [as in Chapter 41's example,] competition from immigrant-laden plants in Southern California closed all the unionized plants in the San Francisco area and removed natives from the workforce in favor of underpaid aliens."

> "Unions fall before the weight of imported labor. In the Mission Foods tortilla factory strike, management lowered wages by 40 percent, and when the native labor went on strike, the Mexican managers intentionally brought in newly immigrated strikebreakers to replace them. Some of the natives returned to work at the reduced wages but most left"

> "Similar phenomena have swept over the hotel industry as well, with immigrant workers displacing native black workers en masse. In Los Angeles, unionized black janitors had been earning $12 an hour, with benefits. But with the advent of subcontractors who compose roaming crews of Mexican and El Salvadoran laborers, the pay dropped to the then minimum wage of $3.35 an hour. Within two years, the unionized crews had all been displaced by the foreign ones, and without any other skills, most of the native workforce did not find new work."

FAIR has documented, through Andrew Sum, director of the Center for Labor Market Studies at Northeastern University in Boston, that a whopping 56 percent of the rise in U.S. employment from 2000 to 2005 was attributable to illegal foreign nationals.

The organization notes that nobody questions that Americans deserve decent jobs at decent wages. However what we have is unfair competition from imported foreign workers. As we discuss in many areas of this book, only the businesses win. The illegal foreign nationals are exploited to the point of indentured servitude and the native-born American with low skills loses his or her opportunity for any employment, ever. Often there is such a concentration of Spanish speakers in a location that an American who will work for the wage cannot be hired because he or she does not know the language.

We need to find lawmakers who are willing to get out of their comfort zone to stop the massive influx of foreign workers from harming the living standard of American citizens.

Some say they cannot be found. The illegal worker trade is too corrupt to ever end it on its own. Americans need to end it at the ballot box with strong American candidates!

Bringing illegal foreign nationals into the US to work for slave wages not only seems un-American, it is un-American. Yet it has become the norm. Still, many Americans, who remain seemingly unaffected, are not aware that it is so prevalent. Maybe that is why President Obama thinks Americans are not exceptional. Slaves and slave wages are not too exceptional in the 21st century.

The Offshoring / Onshoring scenario

In the prior section, we introduced the notion of job displacement as a result of offshoring and onshoring. Offshoring is about companies taking their core business products and moving their manufacturing to another country. Onshoring is when the company uses illegal workers in the US. It is also about companies making the big return to the US. In this case, the company must set up its plants or businesses again and then it must find illegal workers to "stock" the plants.

No, the comeback is not easy; nor is offshoring to begin with, but the prize of greater profits is alluring. Lots of people in lots of businesses along the way make lots of money helping companies do this. Companies that you would never expect engage in this labor arbitrage and enable others to do so.

IBM, for one, is a company that makes a ton of money from the misery of its employees and those of other firms. IBM benefits itself from lower costs but the company has gotten so good that it serves as a conduit, doing the dirty work for other companies. It is like laundering money but it is really the laundering of the perception. The idea is that the company that hires IBM looks like it is hiring American but then IBM offshores the work. The contracting company may choose to lie and it won't seem like a lie. IBM is the face of their offshoring.

Lightweight products like clothing were always ideal for offshoring and textiles were soon to follow. In order to sell in the US, with offshoring, the goods had to be shipped back so the lighter the product, the better.

Eventually, anything that was not literally nailed down could be theoretically offshored. IT, engineering, design, accounting, everything but the CEO's office and many other aspects of the corporation became available to the lowest bidder. People in other countries work for less and the US income tax rates for corporations are obscene compared to the rest of the world.

There are plenty of "business" reasons for companies to pack up and go for the gold. And, they do exactly that. The love of a corporation for the corporation is far greater than the love of a corporation for any particular country or person.

Onshoring v Offshoring

With onshoring, the illegal worker replaces the American who once held the job. With offshoring, you move the work to the cheap labor. With onshoring, you move the cheap labor to the jobs. If there were no governmental issues and no wage and safety restrictions, onshoring could be done legally in the US. But, because of the above restrictions, businesses who want to dump their American labor force and hire illegal workers must do so illegally. And, they do!

Everybody, including President Obama knows this is happening, and that includes the law enforcement community. Everybody knows it is against the law. Yet, it is the most popular new way of reducing business costs. The superiors of law enforcement officers in government are mostly constrained by their superiors on up to the top. Thus they do not permit the police and others to take the necessary actions to stop what is clearly a crime. And, so it continues.

Offshoring has been going on far longer than the "illegal immigrant worker" phenomenon. The corporate objective, however, is the same with onshoring. It is to decrease labor costs and in so doing reduce the US worker's average wages. Whether by offshoring or by onshoring, clever but unscrupulous businessmen are happy to hire Americans or workers from other countries anywhere in the world for less than minimum wages. The notion is sweetened further because there is no OSHA or other US governmental safety protections with which to cope.

For some reason in both offshoring and onshoring, the President and the Congress of the US along with many other government officials are knowing-participants in the game. The non-participants are the people, regular people, who complain through groups like the TEA party and who are ready to take over the government in a ballot's notice.

Big companies beat government and the rest of us

To get back to offshoring for a moment, the mouthpiece for tech companies was once the ITAA as we discussed in Chapter 41. It is not an objective voice, however, because it is owned by 11000 companies that wish to reduce the average US wage. Regardless, it speaks as a corporate organizational structure. The ITAA is a corporation itself consisting of member corporations.

ITAA says that 77 percent of the companies it polled see a shortage of qualified IT talent in the United States. They are not beyond lying to get what they want or shall we say, spinning the truth.

I don't see what ITAA sees. I see people out of work in the IT industry and as an IT professor, I see students not getting the good jobs. If you are new to the game, the ITAA's conclusion is corporate speak for trying to persuade Congress to permit more foreign workers in on visas to take more of those "higher paying" American jobs. There is no such talent shortage. It is just the opposite, My consulting business, which was once bustling is now flat, and IT people simply cannot find jobs as in the past.

If the ITAA could convince engineers and computer scientists to cross the Rio Grande instead, they would be lobbying Congress for Ferry Boats. Even though there is a theoretical shortage of people to fill these jobs, if you are an American, somehow you will find no jobs. It is not because your job search skills are not honed. Try as you may; you won't find a single one of those theoretically available jobs? The ITAA rhetoric is simply untrue. American companies look last for American employees.

There is no shortage of workers willing to work for decent wages. There are shortages of people who will work for poverty wages, however. The ITAA knows that. The sad commentary of America today is that our Congress knows it also. Yet, it bows to the gifts of corporate sponsors and says "bring 'em in." So, many Americans are now just waking up to find they are losing their jobs and that is OK with their US representatives. Unemployed Americans make great activists. Thus, activists operating independently or in conjunction with the only people's movement, the TEA party, are ready to fire many of the supposed representatives, one election at a time.

H-1B visas: a few more tidbits

In IT, to solve the mythical shortage of trained professionals, the ITAA solution as discussed in Chapter 41, is to import more foreign labor. They want the US to open up its tech jobs to workers across the world, legally so that the new guys will work for less and replace the company's current American workplace. This does not help America and it does not help the Americans who lose their jobs. It does help profit-centered companies who care little about Americans.

As we discussed, Congress uses the notion of an H-1B Tech visa to permit 65,000 legal immigrants per year so that the new college graduates in America are scratching and clawing to get jobs. In the last chapter, we noted that despite the 65,000 cap per year on H-1B jobs, over 220,000 were able to come in under the H-1B umbrella in 2010 while the unemployment rate was 9.6% . That's a lot of lost / displaced American jobs. And, they are not going home.

The bottom line business motivation for illegal immigration and for offshoring is that corporations and even many smaller businesses love to get their hands on cheap labor to increase their profits. In recent years, it does not seem to matter whether the cheap labor comes from valid visas or through the underground labor trade.

The ITAA itself is like a union of corporations with massive funds. Just about every major tech company from AMD to Xerox is a member. Understandably, they support boosting the number of tech visas way over the current limit of 65,000 per fiscal year, and they are brazen enough to lobby our Congress to get that done. Carly Fiorina, who was a candidate for the Senate in California in 2010 was one time the head of HP. While at the helm, she led a delegation to Congress to request permission to hire more and more foreign workers. Back then there was the ITAA and no TEA party, and Carly was not a TEA drinker anyway.

American corporations are designed to care only about profits. So, they care only about profits. No surprise. They cannot help it. It is in their charter. They have no room to care about American citizens unless it affects their survival. Despite not reveling in the American way, corporations know how to leverage the "idea of America." For example, to help get the pick of the crop in foreign workers, they do use tricks in their recruiting stations overseas in which they advertise putting the immigrants on a faster track to U.S. citizenship. The secret: just volunteer to come on down. Too bad we citizens can't charge for that good will sold by corporations overseas. It might help.

The fact is that no American job today is safe and this must be solved by our representative government once it is again made representative. Accountants and financial analysts may believe that it is OK for IT and other jobs to go overseas because IT offshoring has been successful for businesses, and because it is typically done for financial reasons. But it is not OK!

These guys, the ones who help ship IT jobs overseas, make a ton of money toiling for Wall Street and other major firms. Most pull in at least $100,000 and many are in the millions in salary. They think they are immune. They think they are so needed on Wall Street that their jobs are secure and that what is happening to IT cannot happen to them. I would advise them to not be so confident.

My advice to accountants and financial analysts in these days of onshoring with illegals as well as offshoring is as follows: unless you have the secret formula or "pictures," in today's world, nobody, including the CFO is safe.

Even my job may be eliminated—hah!

The Wall Street Journal reported recently on a severe shortage of professors of accounting, finance, and management in the US. As I am writing this book, I have been teaching for seven years on the faculty of Marywood University. So, this caught my eye. I am a full member of the faculty and I receive half a salary for handling 1/2 of a normal course load. Ironically, while I was reviewing this chapter for the first time, my job was eliminated. I am not kidding. I have always gotten fine evaluations. Since I improved my teaching techniques in my Operational Management and IT courses, my evaluations are the best ever.

I was informed by my Department Chair that the University was eliminating all of the half-time positions in the Business Department. That means me! They say they will be bringing in full-time professors. I would expect that they will be bringing professors in who have H-1B or other visas. This book, hopefully will be published before I know for sure how this goes. I will let you know on the publisher's web site, www.letsgopublish.com, when I know for sure.

Having begun this book months and months and months ago, and with its focus on jobs, and how scarce they are today, now being personally affected by supposed cutbacks or reshuffling or reorganization in my own university, I have a heightened awareness of the problem. I find it very amusing. I now can write about myself as a victim of the economy and bad US jobs policy. My employer may even be one of those bad employers that have decided to replace American workers with foreigners. I have the opportunity for my very own experience to enforce my research for this book. Like Aretha, I will survive.

As I understand it, Marywood will do a national search to secure two full-timers to replace four half-timers. Their last national search for the person I replaced wound up being a bit International in scope. The result appeared that Marywood brought in a visa person instead of a native-born American. The person I replaced was a nice enough guy and he had the coveted Ph.D., which made him a prize worth. As long as the Business and IT students believed he was doing the job, it was his.

Unfortunately, my predecessor, being foreign born, had a few problems with students because he did not have a great command of the English language. Because of that, I would suspect that his student evaluations were not as good as they should have been. He was just whisked away and that was that. Nice guy. Ph.D. Smart! But he did have a tough time communicating. Now it's me! Interesting! Believe me I am trying to find out if there are any other reasons for my position's elimination. For example, I am a conservative Democrat and Marywood is a liberal liberal arts college.

In the Wall Street Journal (WSJ) article, they noted that this shortage of business professors may cause some schools to curtail course offerings. Again they cried, "Americans won't take those jobs!" Yet, here I am already employed in the Business Department and I was not intending to leave Marywood University—this year at least. Yet, they have decided that it should be a piece of cake replacing me and the three other professors.

Is there a shortage of professors or is there not? Will the new professors be chosen nationally or internationally? The latter of course would mean they could bring in two visa professors for substantially less cost. It will be interesting to see in the fall who they have hired.   Give them a call and ask them 570-348-6211. I am sure they would like to hear from you.

The WSJ sees it this way. Universities are lobbying Congress to permit more foreign professors to teach American business courses. Try to get a job in a University if you are an American. I have been teaching part time and half-time in various American universities since 1980 when I got my M.B.A. I have been Assistant Professor at Marywood University for what some say is seven years, and if it were convenient, my 40 years of business experience and 30 years of college teaching experience could easily be filled by a new 24 year-old Ph.D from the University of Blittinfoggerolf in Crapsnoot. And that likely will happen.

By the way, as noted previously, I had written and completed this chapter a few months ago. While I was editing it last, I decided to add these few paragraphs since my own status at the University has changed from ongoing to a termination contract. In the original version of this section, I was talking about my experience at Marywood and my research and observations of what is happening outside of my university. And now, I too am included in the puzzle. There is some humor there.

Now that my own future has been interrupted, I am ever so curious to see if it is because the Wall Street Journal got it right. I will be gone from Marywood in the next few months. Before I knew I was on the termination block, I wrote these next few sentences which now mean a lot more to me:

"Good luck if you want to teach in America and you are American. They'd rather you go someplace else. I know. All of this is a ruse to decrease American wages."

I'll write an article about what happens at Marywood as I see what materializes in my case.

When employers in any industry, including Academia, conspire about how to cut costs, you can bet they look at labor costs first. It is not that they cannot find candidates. It is that they cannot find candidates to fill jobs at the wages they wish to pay. So, for those jobs they cannot offshore, they seek foreign-born workers, legal or illegal to fill the slot onshore. Because it is not popular nowadays for businesses to tell the truth, the truth that they are unwilling to pay a living wage, they choose to blame it on the character of the American people. They claim that there is a fundamental unwillingness of Americans to work in certain industries or professions. I know that is a combination of bunk, baloney, and bananas, and of course, balderdash. Hopefully, in this book, we have proven to your satisfaction that their claim is simply a lie.

The job displacement phenomenon for me is no longer a phenomenon. I have been displaced. Hah!

Chapter 43   Americans: The Company's Worst Nightmare!

Illegal workers available for most domestic jobs!

American business sees Americans as the biggest problem to their success. The problem, according to businesses trying to extend their profits to the stratosphere, is that they have found that most of the people in the domestic occupations, in which illegal foreign nationals are prone to penetrate, are Americans. This hurts American corporations who are looking for labor arbitrage. Americans get American wages, not poverty, under the table wages, as paid to illegal workers.

Since Americans still fill most positions, businesses want more and more illegal workers to take their jobs. In other words, each American job is a job opportunity for an illegal foreign national. And, of course Democratic lawmakers believe that if Republican businessmen get their wishes—cheap, albeit illegal labor; it will benefit the Democrats also. Yes, the progressive liberals in the Democratic Party are more than happy to trade all American jobs for Democratic votes. When progressives gain, who cares who suffers?

Illegal foreign nationals come from many sources. The easiest way to become illegal is to merely overstay your visa but those who predominate have jumped far across the Rio Grande. The latter find the least attractive work imaginable—manual, back-breaking, seasonal, benefit-less farm labor. However as soon as they see they can do better, they are off the farm and into the meat plant or the painting pail or the construction trade. They are willing to fill just about any of what you might think of as traditional American jobs while our government sits by idly as if to invite them in. George Bush did say Americans would not do that work?

In a 2006 the Pew Hispanic Center study just 3% of the illegal workers were engaged in farm work. The research shows that 97% of what might be as many as 50 million illegal aliens are working in construction, hospitality, manufacturing, restaurant, administrative and service jobs. Shall we ask George Bush or Barack Obama or both of them if these are jobs that Americans will not do?
Back when this survey was done, the least conservative Senators in the nation, such as the late Senator Ted Kennedy, and big-time RINOs McCain, Specter, Brownback, DeWine, Martinez, Hagel and Graham did all but indict American workers for being lazy and unmotivated to do a day's work.

Strangely, none could explain who did those jobs before profiteering employers opted to ignore the law by hiring a ginormous number of illegal aliens for pennies on the dollar. By the way, who does those jobs even today in states where decent, honorable employers are still hiring Americans, paying living wages, healthcare benefits and workers' insurance?

Not only do our Senators and Representatives mock Americans as being lazy, they seem to think they are the only living beings who have compassion for the 6 billion people living outside the industrialized world. Unfortunately, our representatives seem to care more about all of these others than they do Americans. They would love to see all 6 billion enjoying a better life in America, legally or illegally, on our dimes. That's why they want no restrictions on immigration.

These Senators and others in government also place their sympathies with the shady, yet influential employers that have a stake in keeping the illegal foreign nationals in the US so they can continue working for them. And, to prove that, consider the vaunted U.S. Chamber of Commerce that objects to granting Guest Worker status ONLY to those who have never--(not one time), violated US immigration laws. How many businesses who are Chamber members find continued increased profits from the backs of illegal labor?

Whatever we do, let us not, as these Senators chose to do, blame the American worker. Corporations and government and unions should stand guilty as charged. The American people built this country with a work ethic second to none. This has not changed. The failure here isn't in the work ethic of Americans. The problem is with the louses and louts who run American companies—the CEOs, business owners, university and hospital administrators, university presidents, and of course we must include the corrupt government officials who either knowingly look the other way or accept a little graft in the hand.

Some might even blame the consumer as we all benefit from cheap labor, but I do not buy that argument. Companies simply choose not to offer the wages and benefits necessary to attract sufficient numbers of legal workers at wages that provide fair return for the value of the work. If you think about it, it has been said that is why they call the labor market a market. But corporations think of it as a game, not a market. Since corporations run the game, they have made it an illegal game, and American citizens are the big losers.

Fortunately, there is an election in the US every two years and after each of these Novembers, Americans have reason to expect that more attention will be paid to the will of the people. It is time to stop protecting American corporations, union leaders willing to eat their own, university executives who do not care what is best for students, and corrupt public officials. It is time for the people to retake America and protect fellow Americans from the abuse the government has been sponsoring.

Admittedly, most illegal workers in the US are not accountants or programmers or financial analysts, simply because corporations cannot find enough of them. So, it is mostly Mexicans who mow the lawns, clean the motel rooms, kill and process the hogs, pick the blueberries, and otherwise do the jobs that George W. Bush wrongly said, "Americans won't do." And they most often are paid less than the acceptable wage, if not less than the minimum wage, because that is the corporate way. The game is fixed, but since Americans still own the playing field, we have a right to expect our government to straighten this out. So far, they have let us all down. But, in America, every few years, we do get to change the government.

There is plenty of proof that Bush and Obama are wrong about Americans and the type of work we are willing to do. You might call this good news. Of 465 occupations that were studied in the latest Immigrations Studies report, only four of them had a majority of illegal foreign nationals dominating the industries. It seems that Americans are already doing a lot of work "that Americans won't do." You'd be surprised which industries topped the list:

1. Plasterers and stucco masons
2. Agricultural graders and sorters
3. Personal appliance workers
4. Tailors and dressmakers.

Though you might not believe it with all of the jobs seemingly taken, in just about every other low-level occupation, including janitors, maids, groundskeepers, etc. the large majority of worker positions are still filled by native-born Americans. But, who knows how long that will continue? The report concluded: "The often-made argument that immigrants only take jobs Americans don't want is simply wrong."

You knew that when Bush said it. It was crap then. Now that Obama acts it out, you know it is still crap. Rather than trying to put it in your face like George Bush, Obama lets his thoughts out by telling the ICE patrol to let the illegal foreign nationals alone—the non-criminals. His directive is for ICE to let the illegal foreigners keep their jobs while Americans are forced to sit by idly watching the illegal Mexicans and others gain the work opportunities.

To give you all an idea on how many jobs are taken by illegals, the Center for Immigration Studies released the following statistics. As noted, many job categories often thought to be overwhelmingly held by illegal foreign nationals are in fact mostly held by American Citizens. But, look at the large percentage of people who are clearly illegal who hold jobs in all industries. Each job held by an illegal is a job that should be held by an American. Think of it that way.

How can we count them and not know where they are located? If we can count them, shouldn't ICE know where each illegal foreign national is located? shouldn't ICE be deporting them out of here so Americans can regain their jobs. Many Americans still work in these industries. If business and our politicians have their way, judging from their track record, all of these jobs will be given to illegal foreign nationals now that Obama has proclaimed that he wants them left alone and not to be bothered.

With a government like this as a friend of Americans who needs enemies? When will the illegal foreign nationals take all the jobs and deliver low wages and deplorable living conditions to all people living in America? Check out these statistics:

✓ Maids and housekeepers: 55 percent native-born
✓ Taxi drivers and chauffeurs: 58 percent native-born
✓ Butchers and meat processors: 63 percent native-born
✓ Grounds maintenance workers: 65 percent native-born
✓ Construction laborers: 65 percent native-born
✓ Porters, bellhops, and concierges: 71 percent native-born
✓ Janitors: 75 percent native-born

Though it is not exactly in synch with other surveys, according to a new survey by the Pew Hispanic Center, these numbers are about right.

Knowing that Americans will take just about any job and in fact do just about any work, it is merely an inconvenient truth for the propaganda mongers in government and business, who try to suck Americans into being submissive while foreigners take their wages. The facts for supporting illegal immigration do not include "Americans not willing to work." The facts are the same in the US as everywhere else.

Many employed Americans whose jobs have yet to be affected by the rush to hire illegal replacement workers, seem to be OK standing by watching other people lose their jobs. Surprisingly there is no major uproar. This is not good. They may be OK now. However, slowly, but surely illegal worker disease is coming their way—probably sooner than later.

With the additional people who will come from a government backed amnesty, US citizens may have to take jobs as guest workers in Mexico to get some work. Then, and perhaps only then, will all Americans understand that we have been attacked, not just by illegal foreign nationals, but by our own government, who continually play with the dark side at our expense.

Let me say it again. Companies want cheap, disposable labor and there is plenty available and more coming in every day. At the same time, politicians and the union bosses want to secure more and more votes.

Slowly but surely, unless you stop them, you too will be unemployed. It is that plain and that simple. Illegal foreign nationals are complicit in their plight but those who will burn in hell for delivering squalor, instead of their promised reward are the people who brought them in by act or by policy or by illegal employment.

Chapter 44   Should Americans Bother to Apply?

Illegal workers tell "white racists" to go home

As time goes by the answer to this question for America's entry level and other unskilled jobs is coming into clear focus. The answer is "No! Americans are better off staying at home as their efforts at being employed will go for naught. It's been pretty bad for American workers now for at least twenty years. Look at this excerpt from a May 8, 2006 article in the Washington Times, "Immigrants and wages," which reports:

> "Examining more closely the pattern within the 2000-2005 period provides compelling evidence illegal immigrants have been used deliberately to force down wages. In most industries that use illegal immigrants heavily, inflation-adjusted wages rose modestly during the first years of the current decade. Yet soon after, they dropped significantly. Obviously, the nation's restaurateurs, hoteliers, contractors and cleaners decided paying workers $12 per hour and often less, with few or no benefits, was outrageous. In response, they stepped up efforts to bring Mexican and Central American labor markets and standards into the United States.

> "The wage trends in illegal immigrant-heavy industries make it clear these sectors are not facing shortages of native-born workers. They're facing shortages of native-born workers who will accept poverty-level pay. If the president and Congress have any interest in ensuring American immigration policy helps raise and not depress living standards, they'll tell these employers to stop the special-interest pleading and do what their predecessors throughout U.S. history have done: Raise pay high enough to attract the U.S. workers you need, and if your business models aren't good enough to accommodate living wages, invest in developing new labor-saving technologies.

> "Denying pauper-wage industries the crutch of a wage-depressing flood of illegal immigrants is essential for keeping the United States a high-wage, First World economy. It is also essential for offering real economic opportunity to legal immigrants and native-born low-income Americans. The wage trends in illegal immigrant-heavy industries make it clear these sectors are not facing shortages of native-born workers. They're facing shortages of native-born workers who will accept poverty-level pay."

By the way, most of the available data showing the statistics of immigration is from before 2006. Ironically as the problem of illegal workers gets more severe, those commissioned with protecting our borders and enforcing our laws have been MIA in delivering truthful information to the public. Despite the lack of current statistics, it is self-evident that this problem has gotten much worse over the last five years.

A Bears Stearns 2005 white paper on illegal immigration noted that the company had analyzed several other very credible studies indicating that the number of illegal entries has crept up to 3 million per year. This is more than triple the government's figure. Thus, my contention that the number of illegal aliens in America is between 40 and 50 million holds much credibility.

It is agreed by experts that without jobs, the illegal workers would simply go home and so, 3 million extra per year migrating to the US illegally has quickly brought the unemployment rate from 4.6 in 2007 to 9.8 in 2010. As the recession worsens, Americans have even less opportunity to work as companies are emboldened by past practices that they no longer see the need to hire Americans. When the President signals that there will be no enforcement of immigration law per se, there is no risk to unethical businesses, which practice labor arbitrage using illegal foreign nationals.

The National Academy of Science reported in *Dropping Out - Immigrant Entry and Native Exit from the Labor Market, 2000-2005* that from 1980 to 1995 the labor market saw a 44% decline in the real wages of high school dropouts as a direct result of illegal immigration.

Who cares? Unfortunately, this affects the poorest of America's poor citizens but the malaise also drifts into middle class jobs such as meat packing and construction. Since Black and Hispanics Americans lead the statistics in dropping out of high school, this means that illegal aliens affect these two groups the greatest and is a great contributor to the high unemployment rate in this segment of the population.

Americans should not feel guilty at all that we see it as a major imposition that uninvited people have broken into our country and are taking it over with the help of a bunch of incompetent boobs in Congress. The following excerpt comes from this web site:

http://thelastgringo.com/wordpress/2010/07/21/job-openings-americans-need-not-apply/

It is from The Last Gringo and it is titled, Job Openings – Americans Need not apply. ? I decided to write this book with this title long before I discovered this piece but I was duly impressed.

> "American workers are losing their jobs and the future doesn't look good either. Nothing personal. It's just that they get paid "too much" and U.S. corporations can't compete with the slave shops in Asia and other hell holes of the world. So they have a policy of replacing Americans with third worlders."

Figure 44-1 Picture from the Last Gringo Site

Since cheap labor is an essential part of globalization, a growing number of American transnational corporations don't consider American citizens as potential employees. Think about that. American citizens are being shut out from earning a living by American corporations and our elected representatives, who do not shut down the borders and then vote to raise the limits on work visas. This policy has been actively pursued for several decades. It is permanent but because the progressives are about to be put out, it can be reversed.

The Mexican invaders in the photo in Figure 44-1 happen to be standing on American soil. They are most likely working for an American company. Yet, they have become so emboldened in their right to be in America, without having earned that right, since they don't belong here, that they are willing to take the whole US on to show how tough they are. We are racists because we noticed their invasion. Hmmmm!!

They really do not want to be Americans, and that's why Americans are annoyed. They want to have a right to be in America as tough foreign nationals but not as Americans. Signs like these and frequent violence against Americans are common in parts of the Southwest. And many places give these criminals sanctuary.

The latest American company to flee the US

I regret to inform you all that even Whirlpool closed the doors of its Indiana plant and moved its operations to Mexico. If the economy starts to recover, there will be few jobs for

Americans when you have a cheap work force next door. It started with Bush. Now Obama is working with the same game plan. In the near future the words "middle class" is more than likely to be obsolete.

Figure 44-2 The GM Plant in Mexico

On July 3, 2010, Whirlpool's plant in Evansville, Indiana, closed its doors. For over a half century, the company was producing goods there for its worldwide marketplace. Where did the 1100 jobs go?

They went to Mexico!

Evansville Indiana and America lost 1100 jobs to Mexico, where the wages are much lower and often don't include benefits. Despite being unionized, the unions could do nothing for the Whirlpool employees but they did refund thirty years worth of union dues. Well, not exactly. If they had not invested it in the Obama campaign, they may have been able to give something back, but, then again, thee was the Kerry campaign, and the Clinton campaign… well, you know. Besides, many would suggest that it was the union wage that helped drive Whirlpool to Mexico. Meanwhile the unions want illegal aliens to achieve amnesty, knowing it will drive down American wages. Why union members accept that is a big puzzle.

What if I told you that GM also went to Mexico? Actually, GM has been building vehicles at their modern plants south of the border for some time, because they too like the cheap wage. See Figure 44-2 above. FYI, the top pay for auto workers in Mexico back in 2008, was just $3.50 per hour. Ford and Chrysler have built plants in Mexico also. Even illegal aliens would balk at $3.50 per hour for work in America. Of course, the US minimum wage does not permit legal employees to work for slave labor. But, then again there is no illegal minimum wage in the US.

Just as GM and Ford, when Whirlpool literally went south, they said the relocation was necessary to streamline operations. That is code for the offshoring crowd to mean cheap labor.

Not that it helped matters at all, but there was a commissioned study regarding Whirlpool which found that there was a major ripple effect caused by the loss of the 1100 jobs that could mean more than 1,500 additional jobs would be lost in Indiana. For those checking the dollars, that would be about $138 million in income plus a reduction in tax revenues of another $17.7 million. The tax revenues would come from property, sales and income taxes.

Since no job displacements happen to American workers without a period of unemployment compensation kicking-in, it is estimated that the compensation benefits for the displaced employees would cost yet another $4.15 million to the taxpayers. So, Indiana gets whacked for $21.8 million while Whirlpool makes a nice profit and leaves major wreckage in its wake. At a minimum, Americans ought to be able to make such situations cost-free.

Stories of American plants closing and setting up shop overseas are all over the place as the business race to leave America continues. If Whirlpool had contracted for illegal labor rather than moving to where the illegal labor price is achieved without the labor being illegal, and with no safety issues and no concern for employee benefits, there would be no such story. That would not be a good story either. Perhaps it is the selective opinionated journalism of the "free press" to ignore the loss of jobs from illegal workers in the US that is the real problem here.

The American "free" press is on the other side!

The press wants the scenario for illegal workers to be clean and un-messy and so they would not want to present a story that made corporations that hire illegal workers look bad. The press, you see, along with the government, along with the unions, want illegal workers to have nice jobs in America and then one day be declared citizens through a great Harry Reid or Nancy Pelosi orchestrated amnesty program, such as Harry Reid's big D.R.E.A.M.

Consequently, there would be no commissioned study and there would be no negative press for Whirlpool if only it could have figured out how to fire 1100 workers without anybody noticing. Then Whirlpool could have whisked in about 1100 illegals, and hired them quickly to replace the Americans.

Corporations across America along with small businesses have been doing just that quietly and quickly for thirty years and the only complainants are the displaced workers. But the press ignores them because they are on the side of the illegal foreign nationals. The same charred wreckage occurs as if the company offshored the work instead. Yet, it goes unreported.

Regular Americans might infer that the CEO of Whirlpool or GM or Ford, woman or man, would or perhaps should have some love of America and some regrets for such labor actions. Don't look there as you will find nothing and you will just be disappointed. Corporations have no loyalty to their country. They are glued in loyalty in terms of obligations to their corporations. They have great loyalty to their corporations and employees, wherever they may be located globally. But, the corporation always comes well before the employees as the employees are merely a means to an end. The end is corporate profits. Employees have value only when they are in the corporate plan.

Yes, when it benefits them, corporations do partner with governments but even then employees get left behind. Because of offshoring and more recently onshoring, many American workers have become unwelcome as part of their own country's workforce. They have no opportunities because profits rule and thus in many cases, Americans have little future. That is why *We the People* must eliminate this unholy alliance of government, unions, the press, and corporations and regain control of the government to give all Americans back their opportunities. These "potential good fortunes" have been paid for by American blood dating back to the Revolution

Many of the people that are worshipped by American Business Students are the very ones who would be happy no American graduates get hired anywhere.

Bill Gates, for example, the richest man in the world, does not care about Americans. "A policy that limits too many smart people (Indians) coming to the United States is questionable." Bill Gates, CEO Microsoft, April 28, 2005. In other words, US graduates are so dumb, imports are needed.

Bob Galvin, descendent of the founders of Motorola, who serves as the company's current CEO, does not care about Americans either: "It's no contest. We're in the business to make a buck. American labor can't compete." Bob, what is it that you are looking for?

Mexican H-2B workers do not care about American workers:

> "Companies don't want to pay high salaries to American workers, so they recruit Hispanics who will work hard for less pay. The wages though, are still much greater than in Mexico."

So, because you guys sneak into the US and work for pin money, Americans should be OK with that?

The H2B working visa is like H-1B as it is a nonimmigrant visa. It allows foreign nationals to enter into the U.S. temporarily and engage in nonagricultural employment, which is seasonal, intermittent, a peak load need, or a one-time occurrence. Your Congress permits these Mexicans to come in legally and take "Jobs that American's won't do." Of course in these Obamatimes, with many Americans out of work, I have not seen many jobs that Americans won't do. By the way, do you think these H-2B visa people ever go back?

In today's massive recession, Business leaders are crying out as if they are the wounded ones saying that they want a clear government policy on energy and taxes before they will decide to add one more worker. One thing is for sure. Nobody has ever been hired by a poor person.

I do not believe the rich should be whacked with increased taxes. They will just take their money and play offshore. I would like to see the rich work with the American people to help assure that at some point in the future there are real Americans, not just illegals, in the US workforce. Government is mostly incompetent so trusting them with anything is pure folly. I would trust the greedy corporations before the incompetent government. Most corporations are not dishonest. They are predictably greedy.

No company ever wants to hire more workers. Increasing the workforce is only a good strategy when there are opportunities. The US government itself with its business restricting policies is limiting the opportunities of businesses and so supposedly American businesses choose to not invest their capital in America. They choose to get by with what they have unless they see an opportunity.

In many ways, government policy and exceedingly high taxes in the US make the US one of the last places in which many businesses want to set up shop. Evansville Indiana is happening across the whole USA. Add to that the employment trauma caused by lax H-1B and H-2B visa oversight, other legal visas, and of course illegal workers and the scenario says that getting a job is almost impossible for American workers. Unfortunately, because they think there will be more burdens by choosing Americans, when American corporations choose to hire more workers, they intentionally don't want to pick Americans. There are many financial incentives to pick somebody else. We can change this.

Americans really need not apply

Companies like Whirlpool and many others will use cheap foreign labor simply by moving their operations to places (offshoring) where a cheap and friendly work force will work for pennies per hour, up to 100 hours a week with no benefits. If they could get away with that in the US without moving the plant, they would opt to onshore. Either way, Americans are left at the gate with no opportunity to even gain an interview.

Why do you think we have so many unemployed people? Why do you think American business has no plans to rehire Americans? Besides the ease to offshore to avoid American bureaucracy, companies can just hire illegal workers. It is that simple.

To increase profits, companies will do just that. Sending their factories out of the country is more expensive than dirt cheap labor from Mexico and elsewhere.
Companies have other options as noted, such as importing legal foreign workers with various visa types for temporary employment contracts.

No industry is immune to the requirement for increased business profits. Ironically, our government works with industry to make sure everybody but the American voter has a job. Meanwhile most American voters, who can change government every two years if they choose, often stay home on Election Day. This is beginning to change and it needs to change big-time for the picture to get better.

The industries affected more or less include all industries—farm labor, manufacturing, meat packing and construction jobs. These go to Mexicans and hi-tech jobs go to Asians, in particular India. The H-1B visa as we have discussed is another jobs killer as it replaces the new college graduate or MBA from American universities with a foreigner for pennies on the dollar.

Billionaire Bill Gates says he wants all the H-1B visas he can get from Congress so he can continue replacing Americans with Indians and other "smart" workers. Congress has been most accommodating. Microsoft also has shipped many of its jobs offshore so perhaps Mr. Gates should clarify his message to all Americans so we know whether Microsoft products are still worth our time.

The biggest irony on the jobs scene is that the green jobs, the progressive's favorite jobs, are also being sent overseas. Though many were funded originally with American taxpayer money, there is no loyalty where greed is concerned. No, it is not fair. But, it's what you get when government meddles too much in business affairs. Do you really trust government to do anything?

Do governments answer to a higher power?

There are no plans to make it better but there is a lot of rhetoric. Our rich industrialists and our rich government leaders will surely make what is a bad situation today, even worse. Check out this excerpt from the notes of the Council on Foreign Relations (CFR), an elite group of the most important people in the world. This group would like to completely open the borders between Canada, Mexico, and the US.

> "To make companies based in North America as competitive as possible in the global economy, Canada and the United States should consider eliminating all remaining barriers to the ability of their citizens to LIVE and WORK in the other country. This free flow of people would offer an important advantage to employers in both countries by enabling them to move quickly to where their skills are needed."

Cynics on the Internet, when reading this excerpt have asked, "Would the workers still be picked up at the Home Depot parking lot?"

The CFR report continues:

> "In the long term, the two countries should work to extend this policy to Mexico as well, though doing so will not be practical until wage differentials between Mexico and its two North American neighbors have diminished considerably."

See the Council on Foreign Relations (CFR) plan, pp. 26, 27. It is an eye opener against all Americans. Bringing down the American wage is one easy way to help remove the wage differential between the US and Mexico.

All of the work of the CFR and other elite organizations is to make the worker think that there are other disadvantaged who need to have somebody else's wealth distributed to them. It is your wealth they are talking about, however, not the wealth of the elites. All three nations in North America would like the wages of all North American workers to be more uniform and much lower. This would permit North American corporations to compete against the world and succeed, and for these corporations to win, so what if some small people, such as you and I, have to sacrifice by earning a few dollars less. The American worker has been nominated to be the "someone to carry that burden" and the process is well underway. The new mantra is: "work for slave wages or don't work at all."

For a sample of the nightmare scenario rolling toward the rest of America, consider this:

In Los Angeles, since at least 2008, half of the workforce is immigrant and most of those are illegal. Many think this is a USA trend and LA is merely at the bleeding edge. The rest of the story suggests that this will get only worse from here. As the baby boomers retire, more and more cities will emerge with the same pattern. LA demographers predict that by 2025, most of the growth in the workforce in the US will be from immigrants, illegal or otherwise. It is safe to conclude that this is because all of the bleeding heart progressives believe that the citizens of America will stand idly by and let this happen to us.

Executives in foundations that pay attention to demographics believe that places in the Southwest, such as Los Angeles, are at a crossroads. These cities have a big question to answer: Will they choose to be a 21st century city with shared prosperity, or will they be a Third World city in which there is an elite group on top, but the majority are at poverty or near poverty wages. So far most contend that the verdict is that LA is irreversibly headed toward becoming a Third World city. When there are visible pockets of the Third World in America, perhaps then Americans will choose not to work in those pockets, but until then, Americans want to work and all forces seem to be against the American worker.

The Obama Apology Tour

Much has been written about the Obama Apology tour of 2009. When President Obama completed his whirlwind 2009 Apology tour unscathed, he may not have hurt his personal reputation in the rest of the world, but he did stir up the ire of those Americans wondering why the US should be apologizing for anything. Obama, fostering the notion of the *Ugly American*, took this way too far. After all, the President is also an American.

It seems like Americans are being set up across the world as scapegoats for everybody else's sins. The Presidential apology tour played right into that. So, Americans looking for jobs outside and inside America are the last considered. "Looking for a job?" The fact is that if you are an American, you are perceived to be an "arrogant American," thanks to President Obama and his coterie. It would be better for you to search elsewhere for a job. But, where is elsewhere?

Some companies operating in America would say to Americans, "try any company but our company." An information technology staffing firm based in Rolling Meadows, Ill. for example, posted an ad for a tech writer that had an ominous message for Americans. The ad cautioned that an "arrogant American" would not flourish in the position. Yes, Illinois is in America. Because the company took some heat for the ad, they removed it but they noted in so doing that their Chinese client wanted somebody respectful of Chinese culture and they felt an arrogant American would be exactly what they did not need.

Isn't that just great?

Chapter 45   The War on the American Worker

No bullets yet Americans are getting hurt

Have U.S. international corporations and other American businesses declared war on America and the notion of American employees. There are many more ways today for an American to be denied a job or to lose a job than there are ways to gain one. The focus of this book is illegal foreign nationals taking American jobs. However, Americans, just as in a major battle in any war, were first softened up by major artillery fire before the ground troops of the Mexican invasion began to take over American lands and American jobs. For your information, one of the best sources on the web for information about the job losses of Americans to illegal workers is the following:

http://www.usillegalaliens.com/impacts_of_illegal_immigration_jobs.html

The bottom line is that Americans have been losing good jobs at a staggering rate for some time and the assault is continuing. The influx of illegal workers from the second half of the 20th century was record breaking for sure but while the invaders were slowly making inroads, American companies were figuring out a thousand ways to separate American workers from their jobs in US plants.

The public outcry to offshoring provided massive cover for companies stepping up their acceptance of illegal aliens into the workplace. The loss of manufacturing jobs in America has already reached epidemic proportions, and this disease, instead of slowing, is actually spreading. A look at some simple statistics is very revealing.

Since 2001, for example, companies in the US have closed over 42,000 factories, each with 500 or more workers. And, yes, there have been many smaller companies who hopped on the offshoring or illegal worker bandwagon making the assault even more severe for American workers. Which evil is worse one might ask. Is it better to have no plant or to have foreign workers holding all the jobs in the plant. Whichever, Americans need not apply.

The situation today is so bad, even the politicians find cover by paying lip service about the reindustrialization of America. To be re-industrialized, of course America must first have been de-industrialized and that mission is well on its way to completion. The fact is our domestic manufacturing sector has been decimated, and those companies that are left, look to foreign workers, cheap labor from legal and illegal workers, to help sustain their profits.

Other than what must absolutely stay in America, manufacturing is just about gone. From trinkets to electronics to clothing to oil, and even now to food products, the company locations have disappeared from the American landscape. Now that manufacturing is basically gone, what is next you may ask? The lure of greater and greater profits achieved by offshored manufacturing now has major corporations salivating at the thought of destroying the US service sector.

More and more innovative practices are being used to bring service jobs overseas. Internet technology and high speed communications are now easily deployable to theoretically reduce the distance between the consumer and the overseas company representatives. International businesses are trying to prove that it does not matter where their workers are located so they can operate with the lowest cost possible for labor.

Companies hope to bring more and more service jobs to overseas nations with the lure being substantially lower labor costs. Even this trend is not new but since offshored manufacturing was so successful, companies are investing heavily to assure they can gain similar benefits from offshoring the service sector. Admittedly, it is not as easily done as manufacturing. However, as firms gain the expertise and the consulting companies begin to sell offshoring service packages that are guaranteed to work, more and more American service jobs will be lost. It is in the cards, so to speak.

My brother Ed, who recently passed to the Lord, found out firsthand how well the service industry is doing overseas. Companies such as Dell and Microsoft and a lot of consumer IT firms have shipped many manufacturing and service jobs overseas. When my brother called for service on his new Dell PC, he did not find it so bad that Peggy was speaking to him with a rough highly accented man's voice, but he was quickly disappointed.

He had a difficult time understanding ole Peggy on the other end of the line and his PC was not repaired at the end of the call. It was still broken. Worse than that, a means of getting it fixed had not been established. Ed learned by reaching his wits end on the phone that if he got frustrated, he could ask for an American. After that, his calls were much less eventful and more productive by using this little trick. One would expect this costs companies big time and this door will be one of the first closed for consumers when Americans are softened even more so to accept poor service.

Many of us have had similar situations when we have problems with our computers, printers or other types of devices. When you call the toll free number, you go through the usual menus and questions until you finally get through to a service representative like the one my brother found, and your time investment begins. You can tell it is a male or female and you can tell it is someone talking to you from Ireland, India, Indonesia or a host of other countries a zillion miles away. Next time this happens, think that this is someone who is taking an American's job.

Americans have some power in all of this but we are not organized to cause enough issues for the companies so that they choose to rethink this approach. All of these companies need the American people to continue to buy their products, yet they do not want to give American's jobs. My prediction is that as the TEA party blossoms, more advocacy segments will appear that give Americans advice on which companies to work with and which to stay clear from. Corporations are big hypocrites, but as long as they get our money, they do not care. When Americans organize against this in the near future, life will be better for all of us but it may not be so good for "Peggy."

By the way, the all-time spoof on just how bad the foreign call center experiences are is summed up well by the humorous yet realistic "Peggy" ads. "Peggy" is the ultimate spoof on poor overseas call center service. "She" is a bearded, clueless and very male credit-card customer-service representative. The thickly accented Peggy works for "USA Prime Credit" in a snowbound shack in the middle of nowhere. His inability to answer simple consumer questions -- beyond giving his phone-bank name and responding to most other queries with a less-than-convincing "yes" -- is the primary shtick in Discover Financials latest ads from Interpublic Group's, The Martin Agency. The Ad is so effective because it immediately creates the sense of emotion that most of us feel when we get sandbagged to endure our poor support from someone such as "Peggy!"

Bravo to the Martin Agency for bringing this home so we can see it as it is. The goal, according to the shop and client, is reaching consumers who have endured such service trials and, naturally portray Discover's offering as superior. It is effective and the good news for Americans is that companies are still at least paying lip service to the notion of customer service, and thus all jobs cannot yet be offshored. However, as enforcement of illegal workers becomes more and more lax, we may find the same Peggy, whose alias might then be Poncho, working in the heartland on a bogus SS#, taking client calls from Americans looking for support.

Corporations will not ever fully give up on America and concentrate all efforts in overseas regions of growth. They still make too much money in the US to do that. But, as noted, they may very well try to take even more advantage of onshoring, the phenomenon of hiring illegal workers in America for dirt cheap wages to replace Americans.

Will offshored jobs ever come back?

Without any changes in legislative policy and tax policy, and without a change in the attitudes of Americans to being slapped around and not slapping back, there are a number of things that may slow and perhaps even reverse offshoring in the coming years. But, don't hold your breath waiting for any of them to happen.

One of these is the cost of energy. As the US energy policy becomes more anti-domestic in terms of drilling and mining, the cost of-oil may very well hit unprecedented levels. The instability in early 2010 in the Middle East and the impact on oil prices may make this happen lots sooner than anybody would have predicted.

This would impair the ability of international corporations to take advantage of the world's slave labor markets to manufacture products and ship them thousands of miles back to America. It may very well become cost-prohibitive and many corporations will see their profits plummet. They may be forced to use American employees regardless of the labor cost, and if they cannot re-adapt to the change, they will not survive.

In the meantime, China has become the world's largest producer. At the same time, with the influx of capital in China, the Chinese are looking for safe investments. They continue to loan or some might say invest mega-billions of dollars in America because of the size of our consumer-driven economy. If China cannot ship to America so readily and find willing consumers, perhaps it will come to believe it no longer needs to invest in America. This may have major repercussions on US solvency. To get a good grip on this potentiality, there are many sources of information from books to articles as freely available material on the Internet. So far, it looks like China and the US are latched together for awhile.

The point in this chapter is that the current situation, in which huge corporations continue to hardheartedly pillage America and its workers, cannot be sustained or America cannot be sustained. No country can survive when all of its citizens are out of work. Continued contempt by corporations for American labor will bleed this nation and our consumer-driven economy dry. Radical change must come to America and I believe that it will come but it does not have to be driven by radicals. We will not experience a monumental economic collapse but we surely will be playing brinkmanship in order to avoid irreversible damage.

The 800 pound gorilla in all of this is that right now Americans need not apply for jobs for many reasons and corporations and other businesses are benefitting from the backs of Americans as well as illegal workers. From offshoring to legal visas, to poor government policy, clearly all of these contribute to the plight of the beleaguered and long-unemployed American employee. None of these situations are good. But, the one that gets right under the skin of Americans the most is the one they see all the time -- illegal foreign nationals, speaking in foreign languages while taking American jobs and claiming that Americans do not know how to work hard.

It is a shame that the main stream media still believes that there are jobs Americans won't do. And, for the press, they seem tickled pink that illegal Mexicans and others from south of the border and around the world are able to work for peanut sized wages. Why is this?

Maybe it doesn't matter but the press is way wrong that this is the fault of Americans. It is the companies who declared the war; the illegal workers are their allies along with the press. It is the native-born Americans who are the victims here, no matter what race they may be. Perhaps the main stream media cannot understand that native-born Americans are not all white as they seem to want this to be a racist thing.

Even with the depressed wages, caused by illegal aliens working for just enough pay to barely survive, it appears that there are still a lot of Americans willing to do the jobs the press says only illegal immigrants will do.

There was a Wall Street Journal Article on January 17, 2007 titled, "*An immigration raid aids Blacks for a time*. The main stream press must have missed this one:

> "STILLMORE, Ga. -- After a wave of raids by federal immigration agents on Labor Day weekend, a local chicken-processing company called Crider Inc. lost 75 percent of its mostly Hispanic 900-member work force. The crackdown threatened to cripple the economic anchor of this fading rural town.

> "But for local African-Americans, the dramatic appearance of federal agents presented an unexpected opportunity. Crider suddenly raised pay at the plant. An advertisement in the weekly Forest-Blade newspaper blared "Increased Wages" at Crider, starting at $7 to $9 an hour -- more than a dollar above what the company

had paid many immigrant workers. The company began offering free transportation from nearby towns and free rooms in a company-owned dormitory near to the plant. For the first time in years, local officials say, Crider aggressively sought workers from the area's state-funded employment office -- a key avenue for low-skilled workers to find jobs. Of 400 candidates sent to Crider—most of them black—the plant hired about 200.

"... For the first time since significant numbers of Latinos began arriving in Stillmore in the late 1990s, the plant's processing lines were made up predominantly of African-Americans."

"The sudden reversal of economic fortunes in Stillmore underscores some of the most complex aspects of the pitched debate over immigration: Do illegal immigrants take jobs from low-skilled American workers?"

The answer in this plant in Stillmore says it is clearly a "yes." Illegal immigrants do take low-skilled American worker's jobs. Considering that meatpacking jobs in the 1980's paid as high as $19.00 an hour, the greed of the meat packers is almost sickening.

The USAILLEGALALIENS.COM site notes that this plant once had predominantly black workers. When it realized it could lower wages by replacing the black workers with illegal alien Hispanic workers, the company took up the challenge and increased its profits. When this rare immigration raid occurred and illegal aliens were removed from the plant, the company went out of its way to raise the pay scale and accommodate legal American workers. The black workers got their jobs back. The company stayed in business. Who noticed?

Even so, these are not the $19.00 per hour wages once given in the 1980's. So, the plant had problems keeping its new workers satisfied at such low wages. One might conclude that this is an argument for needing workers that will "do the work Americans won't do" but this is not the case. Instead, this demonstrates that the free market equilibrium of supply and demand is still not functioning in the plant. The "indentured servant" status of illegal workers forces them to accept wages that nobody in their right mind would accept. Their fear is being shipped back to their home countries or put in jail. Such fear creates plenty of willingness to compromise that would not be seen in a free market.

The lure of high profits from labor arbitrage still prohibited the owners of the plant from paying a decent age to get good workers. The old mindset is still prevalent to pay the lowest wage possible. Meatpacking is an unsafe and dirty job and the smaller pay means that consumers might pay ten cents less for a pound for chicken. Yet, everybody loses in this situation.

Not only is it grossly unfair, plant managers using cheap labor are less inclined to perform needed modernization, automation, and mechanization where productivity would go up. This would result in even more skilled and higher priced employees producing a more pure product, a better packaged chicken for sure than what the lower priced employees could do for the same total labor costs. Unfortunately, until all the illegal aliens working in all the other chicken processing plants have been removed the free market will still be distorted. And, the chicken processing industry is merely one of many in which the predominant workforce is illegal.

It is worth remembering an article by Robert Engler from 2004 titled,

"Illegal Immigration and Black America."

It has been cited by many people who have written about the effects of illegal immigration on the job prospects of all Americans. Engler's piece dealt mostly with the impact on black Americans. I might suggest that those who champion the notion of illegal foreign nationals to satisfy their progressive agenda should pay attention to this. The minority community in general is more than likely in one way or another also on the progressive agenda. So, the problem outlined by Engler and felt by Americans of all races is surely a result of the law of unintended consequences. Here are some sections from Engler's work, as published on hiphoprepublican.com.

> "The fact of the matter is, illegal immigration, especially illegal immigration from Mexico, is hurting Black Americans. If Democratic candidates ever getting around to speaking the truth, they will have to tell Black voters that illegal immigration is taking jobs away from Black Americans, cutting into resources available for welfare, and restructuring public schools and many urban areas. In short, the votes of Latinos are bought by the Democrats at the expense of Black America.

> "Tony Brown, author of *What Mama Taught Me,* knows all too well how Black Americans are injured by illegal immigration. He writes, '"The U. S. Census Bureau reported in the *New York Times*... the poor Black and Latino communities lose the most income of any group of Americans, including all Americans who did not finish high school and all Americans who are paying higher taxes to subsidize welfare benefits for illegal immigrants and businesses that hire them. Illegal immigrants overuse welfare benefits and services and underpay income taxes for a net loss to local, state and federal taxpayers.

> "The Federation for American Immigration Reform (FAIR) http://www.fairus.org, has also documented the detrimental impact of illegal immigration on Black Americans. In California, Blacks are being forced out from communities like South Central, Los Angeles, where they have long lived. "This once predominantly Black neighborhood is becoming largely Hispanic. South Central is being transformed. Here we talk about 'Black flight.' People are leaving neighborhoods where they have lived for years because they don't feel like they belong any more reports Terry Anderson in the *San Francisco Examiner,* (Feb. 3, 1999.)"

> "The Federation for American Immigration Reform continues in its report that, 'Other statistics are also sobering: a GAO study found that a decade of heavy immigration to Los Angeles had changed the janitorial industry from a mostly native Black, unionized workforce to one of non-unionized Latinos, many of whom were illegal aliens. According to the Census, the employment of Black Americans as hotel workers in California dropped 30 percent in the 1980s, while the number of immigrants with such jobs rose 166 percent. A similar story can be told of the garment industry, the restaurant business, hospital work, and public service jobs."

One can expect Blacks in Illinois to suffer the same declines as illegal immigration from Mexico continues.'

"Immigration researcher and commentator Roy Beck noted in his 1996 book, *The Case Against Immigration* that: "To review the Black side of our nation's immigration tradition is to observe African Americans periodically trying to climb the mainstream economic ladder, only to be shoved aside each time. It is to see one immigrant wave after another climb onto and up that ladder while planting their feet on the backs of Black Americans ... The most racist policy in this country for the past 25 years has been our immigration policy, because it has been the worst thing that has happened to Blacks from the federal government since slavery.'

"The Harvest Institute also documents the impact of illegal immigration on Black Americans. "Dr. Claud Anderson, president of The Harvest Institute, a Black research and education organization, announced that The Harvest Institute does not support President Bush's recently proposed amnesty for illegal immigrant aliens and has released an Information Alert (available at www.harvestinstitute.org). Dr. Anderson said, "Despite the stance of many civil rights groups, immigration's impact on native Blacks and their communities is disproportionate, direct and devastating. Blacks are losing faith because the government continues a pattern of bestowing the rights that should first go to native Blacks to immigrants from foreign countries. Native Blacks are ignored and patronized with symbolic and ceremonial actions by both political parties. The issue of immigration is roiling within Black communities and has become ... divisive.'

"As the Democrat's 'multicultural' candidate, Barack Obama has little to say about this multicultural issue. You can read his position papers and look at his website and find no recognition that illegal immigration from Mexico is hurting Black Americans. One has to wonder what kind of immigration policy Obama will vote for if he ever becomes a U. S. Senator. One has to wonder even more why Black Americans continue to vote Democratic, when the Democrats are not looking out for their interests.

"This article is referenced not to slam Obama or the Democrats, because the collateral damage from illegal aliens is affecting all Americans of all political parties, but to illustrate that the Democrats know it disproportionately impacts their primary voting block the greatest but still are doing nothing about it illustrating it doesn't make any difference what political party the inept politicians belong to."

I have yet to hear Jesse Jackson or Al Sharpton or any of the supposed "black leaders" offer a caveat to Democrats to begin to do what is good for all Americans, including Black Americans. Robert Klein Engler would make a good leader for black Americans for sure as his caring seems to be non-agenda oriented and clearly for the benefits of an underrepresented minority.

Mr. Engler *lives in Chicago. He is a graduate of the University of Chicago Divinity School. His book, A Winter of Words, about the turmoil at Daley College, is available from amazon.com. Thank you, Mr. Engler for speaking up.*

Because I came to like Engler from my reading of his work on various sites, I would like to share with you another quote. Engler is very upset with the notion of liberalism and the misuse of the term civil rights to include illegal aliens at the expense of the suffering blacks who fought for their rights. Nancy Pelosi and Barack Obama could get a great lesson from Robert Klein Engler, a truly self-made man:

> "Let's hope ordinary people like those who run the hardware store in my old South Loop neighborhood understand political metaphors better than liberal intellectuals. This hardware store is located near a subway entrance. The owners have grown weary of people coming in all the time and looking to change bills for coins to ride the train.

> To discourage this behavior, they put a big sign on the door that reads, NO CHANGE! Each time I go there to shop, I compliment them on their anti-Obama campaign sign. Not all metaphors are dead."

Amen!

US tax policy makes corporations offshore jobs

In other chapters of this book as you have seen and will continue to see, we explore how America's offshored jobs can come back through a major change in US tax policy. American corporations are taxed higher in America than by any other country. The American government is responsible for American corporations taking defensive action against large taxes by moving offshore.

In a sense, the war against American workers by corporations was started by the government initiating a war of taxes against all corporations. Clearly the government and the American public are losing by this policy and I would expect that one day, as a business friendly administration steps inside the Capital and the White House, this will reverse and America can become strong again. Then, American workers will no longer be looked upon as the enemy.

Soon again by policy or by the action of our civilians working together, Americans will win this war just as we win all wars, which we choose to win. Then we will all be able to apply for all jobs, and we will be hired again. It may not be exactly as Frank Capra's "It's a Wonderful Life," but if the right forces fight the negative side of business, and government (Anybody for some TEA?), Americans will do all right. After all, a business with no consumers is not a business at all.

Chapter 46   Businesses Bleed Illegal Workers of Humanity and Dignity

Are illegal foreign nationals America's new slaves?

The promise of the American dream followed by living conditions and the absolute destitution of thirty people living in a three bedroom house creates just one of the major disappointments that await the dream-chasing illegal worker. The businessmen who make those promises are the lowest people on the humanity chain. Collectively, they have kept millions of human beings captive and effectively powerless. Yes, it is because of their illegal status, but many companies, more than you would like to hear about, lure illegals from Mexico for just one reason:
P-R-O-F-I-T. They exploit these workers both politically & economically and they drain them spiritually.

The large number of illegal foreign laborers today is a symptom of a very severe economical & political collapse in the US. The moral collapse in all of this is even more profound. In many ways, the illegal foreign national faces a plight in the US similar in some sense to the slaves of Africa who were stolen from their homelands.

The slaves were promised nothing and they knew, once captured that their new prisons might very well resemble hell on earth, and they did. Clearly their captors were the most evil of all sinners. For years slaves lived away from their families, without freedom, at the bottom of life's subsistence chain providing only for their masters. This was as bad as it could get for humankind as the oppressed had done no wrong, and the oppressors' greed and malevolence trumped all rationalization.

Though not at the same level as indentured servitude and all of the evil of the slave trade, today's masters of the illegal worker also know better. Yet they persist in their evil deeds by a sense that they are engaged only in simply a labor arbitrage, not the dehumanizing prostitution of modern day bondservants. Some don't see it so kindly.

The analogy of serfdom is appropriate though the businessmen and politicians in their gated communities do not want to see it that way. How could they enjoy their fig pudding at the holidays in the comforts of their homes surrounded by loving family, knowing they have placed such a burden on humankind? So, they rationalize their role. They are disingenuous. They are evil. They are takers.

To be OK with their own lives, they lie to themselves so that they seem like better people than they really are, and they use their power of propaganda of all kinds so that those who do not see their huge financial or political gain, will believe that they are in fact humanitarians, and not the villains, which they really are. The biggest sin perhaps is that they dupe themselves into thinking they even belong in humankind. For the truth is: they do not. They proclaim and defend the rights of illegal foreign nationals knowing the destitution their motives will bring on these unsuspecting future serfs.

Serfdom for all?

To refresh your memory, and to point out the similarities between serfs and illegal foreign workers, consider that serfdom has always been a socio-economic status of bound peasants. It began in the days of feudalism. It is a condition of bondage in which an un-free human being is forced to labor on the fields of landowners. For what purpose?

In return for labor, they received protection and the right to work in certain activities, which benefited the landowner or master. It is not a far stretch to suggest that illegal workers are un-free and are chained to their jobs while operating outside the light of day. It is also not a far stretch to draw parallels to those involved in their subjugation—the politicians who permit open borders; and the businessmen who gain from their labor, and the union leaders who greedily await their ability to sign up and pay dues.

While businessmen and politicians bleed illegal workers of their humanity and their dignity, the American people on the other hand have deep sympathy for the circumstances laid upon this new illegal class of people living among us. Despite that sympathy, US citizens want the practice ended as Americans are being exploited right along with the illegal foreign nationals.

And so, after many years of putting up with something they felt they could not control, today, the people have had enough and they desire to maintain an America for Americans. Americans do not want to give a share of America to Mexico or Mexicans. The lands and opportunities the citizens have won through hard work and many wars, including the Mexican-American wars are not something US citizens are about to give up easily, and right now, we are at a tipping point.

Chapter 47   Screw You Americano—We're Taking Your Jobs!

Businesses and illegal workers share the blame

Debbie Schlussel on the Web has a picture that she shows that is not captioned (Figure 47-1). More and more Americans see this picture as the real picture of what illegal foreign nationals, mostly from Mexico think of America.

Figure 47-1

The picture above easily speaks the words that many feel is the illegal foreign nationals' response to all the good given to them. "Screw you Americano, we're taking your jobs like it or not," screams loudly from this picture. Admittedly, they could not get those jobs if businesses in American did not invite them in. So, it is a shared blame for sure. Regardless, illegal workers from all over the world, are taking American jobs, and in the strangest places.

In addition to this picture, Debbie offers lots of poignant commentary. In September 2010, for example, she posted information about the BP Oil spill efforts going on in the Gulf. Her post was to point out the difference the public eye brings to different circumstances. You see, there was another oil spill this same summer.

The spill of which she spoke was in mid-Michigan. It was small potatoes compared to the Gulf, but big for Michigan and it needed its own cleanup effort, not tied to the Gulf. The spill was 820,000 gallons of oil, which found its way into a tributary of the Kalamazoo River. http://www.debbieschlussel.com/26636/labor-day-obama-used-illegal-aliens-to-clean-the-other-oil-spill/

While, for months in the summer of 2010, Americans had all been hearing about the huge BP oil spill in the Gulf of Mexico, most of us had not heard much about this "little one" that happened in July. What you would find interesting–no, *outrageous*!–is that while Michigan is at about a 15% unemployment rate, the jobs for cleaning up the spill, a tragedy that sent 820,000 gallons into a Kalamazoo River tributary, were not given to Michigan workers. Instead somebody figured out how to do it on the cheap and the job was given to illegal foreign nationals.

You heard me right.

Among all of the many jobs, which we note in this book, that cannot be off-shored because of location (US), but could be given to illegal foreign nationals who work for cheap wages, nobody would have thought that a city tragedy would evoke a call for illegal workers from outside that city. That's like pouring salt on a fresh wound.

But it did, nonetheless, because the City supposedly did not know how to pay for the tragedy. Not many would expect that cleaning up an oil spill would be on the mythical list of jobs Americans won't do. Somebody in Michigan did not get that message. Despite the many hungry, desperate, and able-bodied Michigan men and women, who would have gained tremendously by working on cleaning up the river spill, they were not hired. Who got the job? You guessed it: illegal foreign nationals. One would think they were from Canada and had crossed our Northern border. No, they were from Mexico and they had crossed our southern border.

There was a guy named Phillip Hallmark who was chief instigator in the Michigan snafu. His company, Hallmark Industrial chose not to hire Americans though it was an American river. Hallmark chose to increase his take on the job by hiring illegal foreign nationals. Hallmark chose not to have a Hallmark moment [this guy is nothing like the wonderful greeting card company or maybe he is -- see story below].

He successfully got illegal foreign nationals to work on the cheap. Not only was the spill a bad situation but Phillip Hallmark created another bad situation. Yet, the work was approved by President Obama's Environmental Protection Agency (EPA), which oversaw the whole spill clean-up. Maybe it is part of a plan, not just an aberration. The Obama team sees little difference between illegal workers and American workers.

Does that not make you sick? Americans, especially the citizens of Michigan got nailed twice on that one—once for the spill and the other for the cleanup. They were victims pure and simple of a disaster and then greed. Considering that the illegal foreign nationals were already living off of the backs of Michigan citizens regarding their benefits and services funded by those who are here legally, Hallmark declared that Americans were too expensive to get the cleanup jobs.

It is ironic that business is a predator in this regard, and the government is an accomplice. But what does that say when major labor union leaders in America side with the illegals. Yes, union leaders protect and support this kind of job predation by illegals, hoping one day to have these people (illegal though they may be now) among their voting ranks.

With the government wanting to fashion labor laws to protect illegal workers, where does the American voter go today looking for protection from abuse sponsored by our own government? The only answer is to go to the ballot box each November and vote out all of the incumbents who gave us this upside down world in which we live. Your vote against all office holders, regardless of their names and whether they have ever kissed your babies' butts, is the only medicine for a better economy and a better America.

Let's take the argument ad absurdum for effect. If a few drug dealers, bank robbers, burglars, prostitutes, etc. know the police either cannot or will not arrest them, soon they tell all their friends that it is open season on the American public. It is! So, what happens -- more drug dealers, more bank robbers, more burglars, and more prostitutes? You don't even have to be good at math to know the stats. Those crimes will be going up if there is no countervailing power.

So, now, how about a child molester? If he knows he won't be stopped, he preys on more victims with impunity. You know where this is going. If an embezzler thinks he won't get caught and does not get caught, he stays at it and continues living quite well on his victim's financial loss. So, why is it OK for an illegal foreign national to prey on Americans with federal help?

Hallmark, card company outsourcing work to China

When I wrote the piece about Phillip Hallmark, I was all set to contrast him with the good Hallmark, the card company. They also have the highly spiritual cable TV channel that shows "good triumphs over evil" type shows, especially during the Christmas season. This little trick of Hallmark's changes lots. They took their card manufacturing to China and it cost hundreds of Missourians their jobs.

A subcontractor of theirs, the Carrolton Specialty Products, Company was forced to close two American plants after they lost the card assembly work they performed for Hallmark. Hallmark was looking for a few extra bucks that they could not extract from their American workers. So, they offshored the business to China.

Figure 47-2 -- Carrolton Plant Once Made Cards for Hallmark

If we can't trust Hallmark or the Hallmark Company to do the right thing for American workers, who can we trust? Please do not say the government

The pain of carrying documentation - Hah!

It is no secret for anybody living in North America that it is a crime for US Citizens to travel into Mexico or Canada without documentation Likewise, it is a crime for Mexicans or Canadians to travel to the respective other two countries. Drivers' licenses and birth certificates won't do. To enter the US, for example, from land, air, or sea, you need a passport -- even if you are a returning American.

In 2007 the laws were made tougher than they had been. Like it or not, it is a crime to trespass into the United States without a passport. So, even if you are a US citizen, traveling to Mexico or Canada, as previously noted, you need a passport to get back into the US. You can be arrested, since you have committed a crime.

Yes, Virginia, it is a crime for illegal foreign nationals to cross our borders. It is a crime just like when robbers and the burglars commit their crimes. When millions of illegal foreign nationals pour into our country, it is actually more than a crime. It is an invasion.

We've spent a lot of time talking about the types of jobs illegal aliens take when they jump the border. How is it they get those jobs? Let's name some names. The blame lies with greedy business managers such as the CEOs of big companies like Hormel, Tyson Chicken, and Wal-Mart for starters. Go to a big city restaurant and check it out. All those foreign speaking people, while working, are more than likely—illegal foreign nationals. Get out of town? If you already know that, are you happy with it? What do you plan to do about it?

What about fast food restaurants? Is your happy meal or your big moose whopper served with an English brogue or no words at all? These companies love to hire illegal workers because it helps their bottom line. There are more than 30 and probably more like 40 or 50 million illegal foreign nationals in this country who will work for pocket change. Will you?

And there are just as many greedy companies who will hire them. And as you can see by the picture at the top of this chapter, the illegal workers are not thankful one bit to Americans for being able to work here.

As we have discussed, there are a lot of others (large and small businesses) who make life worse for themselves and other Americans by adding illegal foreign nationals to the list of those who they employ. There are even cities in the US called *sanctuaries* in which technically the illegal foreign national can commit crimes and not have to worry about any repercussions.

Though you may find it difficult to believe, even American city governments regularly hire illegal foreign nationals to save money. They do this while their taxpaying citizens are on unemployment. Local contractors pick up illegal workers, like those in the picture above, to help with painting, dry wall, building and housing construction, pool cleaning, landscaping, and of course dish washing, motel cleaning, car washing and any job that cannot be offshored. This is the new underground economy. Even regular citizens hire illegal workers for gardening, house work and roofing, and if you are George Bush or Meg Whitman, you might have even hired an illegal nanny or housekeeper.

But, who is complaining? In my humble opinion, not enough Americans are complaining, though they feel something is wrong. The idea of fighting back is about keeping America as America. Mexico, the closest source of illegal foreign nationals to America has not done so well in keeping Mexico a country in which it is desirous to live. The proof is how quickly its citizens are willing to come here even if they are not invited.

Americans should be in the streets complaining because the jobs are disappearing one at a time while the media tells US everything is all right. It is not all right and your job is next. The media is so pro-illegal and pro-amnesty that it is unpopular for even big burly union guys to complain openly about the Mexican invasion. Why is that?

The majority of Americans, who unfortunately are fed their thoughts by the anti-citizen Marxist-leaning mainstream press take it on the chin and do not complain about a bad situation, heading to terrible. Not only do most Americans say nothing. They do nothing. Things are changing somewhat as more and more Americans are inclined to join a TEA party today and clearly the TEA parties address this well.

The message to Americans is that it is time to end the siesta. Americans must stand up for themselves and be counted! Remember the picture at the top of this chapter. Your replacement worker from a foreign country often has great disdain for you and for your America. You will like yourself a lot more and you will preserve the last bastion of pure freedom the world has ever known if you speak up and if you vote each November for only the candidates who are pro-American.

God Bless America!

Chapter 48   Is Illegal Immigration Bad for America's Health?

Border hoppers don't stop for physical exams

So, now that we have examined the impact of illegal workers and criminal aliens on the American landscape, can anything be more revealing? What if illegal foreign nationals actually made Americans sick?

Dr. Manny Alvarez wrote a short but reasonably complete article about this very subject. Dr. Manny as he is called is the managing editor of health news at Foxnews.com. He is a dedicated medical professional and pioneer of innovative advances in medical technology. As a doctor and as a university professor, he is a very accomplished medical professional. He is also one of the most popular contributors to the FOX News Channel

So, let's repeat the question, "Is Illegal Immigration Bad for America's Health?" Dr. Manny says that the simple answer is: "Yes." For his conclusion Dr. Manny cites the typical precautions that are used by countries to prevent disease from entering the country. There are always a set of checks and balances. You may have been to various countries in your travel and on your return flight, you were always asked a series of health questions as well as to whether or not you were bringing any plants or living organisms into the country.

The purpose for many of the checks in the process of screening legal immigrants and returning citizens is the prevention of certain communicable diseases. Let's say you are foreign born and you want to come to the US on a visa to be a resident for a time. There is a set list of tests performed in the physical exam that must be A-OK before your application can be approved. These are required by the U.S. Department of Homeland Security's Citizenship and Immigration Services (USCIS).

When you look at the list, you will be glad that those with such diseases are kept out until they can get well. Here is the list according to Dr. Manny:

- ✓ Tuberculosis
- ✓ Syphilis (for applicants 15 years or older)
- ✓ HIV (blood test)
- ✓ Gonorrhea
- ✓ Narcotic drug addiction

- ✓ Physical or mental disorders with associated harmful behavior
- ✓ Chancroid
- ✓ Lymphogranuloma venerum
- ✓ Granuloma inguinal

There is no such checklist for illegal immigrants because they are presumed to be OK! Can I be wrong on that? The real truth is that they are presumed to be staying in their home country. Yeah, that's it! So, when they run the border, they bring all they have with them, including any major communicable diseases.

I know what some of the diseases in the above list are, but there are a few of which I am not quite sure. I just would not want to ever get one of those guys. The legislators who crafted our immigration laws actually did a good job in many ways. One of these is that any immigrant, permanent or even temporary must be checked out before infecting the whole population.

As noted throughout this book, you will see that the government officials in charge of immigration and border security as well as the President, people who are supposed to assure the safety of Americans, have not done well in this regard.

Thankfully for legal immigrants, they do an OK job on that enforcement front. In addition to all of the preventative tests, the law says that a foreign national applying for residency or even requesting residency while already in the US, again, according to Dr. Manny is required to receive vaccinations to prevent the following diseases:

- ✓ Mumps Measles-Rubella
- ✓ Polio
- ✓ Tetanus and Diphtheria Toxoids
- ✓ Pertussis
- ✓ Haemophilus influenzae type B
- ✓ Hepatitis B
- ✓ Any other vaccine-preventable diseases recommended by the Advisory Committee for Immunization Practices

This list is not just an American standard. The same list or similar lists exist in most developed countries around the world. Dr. Manny says that "without a system of checks and balances, we run the risk of having diseases that have otherwise been eradicated in this country coming back in a big way. When people travel here illegally, they could have the potential to spread certain diseases that could be very devastating to the general population."

Of course if they asked to be checked first to spare us from any disease they might carry, their frightened little butts would be sent back to wherever they came from if the Obama team is on duty that day. And, what is wrong with that?

There are big issues out there. For example, active tuberculosis is a very dangerous communicable disease that is easily spread if someone is an active carrier. There are now many strains of TB very resistant to the standard medical treatments so permitting infected foreign nationals in the country, legally or illegally is unwise.

In addition to TB, other diseases are making a comeback in less developed countries. Malaria and Chagas disease, a parasitic infection in the blood stream – are being seen more frequently in areas of the country where some of these diseases were not present in the recent past. There are many dangers with having a forgiving nature towards infectious persons. For example, if infected blood is given to a patient with a compromised immune system, the results can be deadly.

Dr. Manny is thankful for his own American dream as he is of Hispanic origin. He is also thankful for the goodness that is his families. He is a good man and not an advocate in the political battle of the immigration issue for those who are Hispanic and those who are not. It does not matter. Dr Manny sees a point of no-compromise "that the health of the American people be protected, because if we do not protect the health of our citizens, the long-term effects could be dangerous."

So, besides the usual reasons that Americans, concerned about the rapid influx of foreign nationals see as problematic, in this chapter, we now know that the inability to stop communicable diseases at the border is a major concern on the side of what is right. So, let's assure that our government does what is right! What other choice do we have?

Chapter 49   Federal Government Is AWOL on Illegal Immigration

The protector has become the problem

So, where is the Federal government? They protect us from exploitation and poor working conditions, right? Yet, especially recently under Barack Hussein Obama, the feds are pretty quiet on illegal foreign nationals. The feds know that the people of America, the citizens of the great USA, want an America for Americans, not an America for Mexicans and other non-citizens. Since Obama has not given the feds this mission, they are AWOL on illegal migration.

The unions are missing from the battle also but their leaders are quiet publicly only so that their membership does not know that they are advocating for foreigners before Americans. Union leaders hope to bring in foreign workers to compete with American workers to automatically drive their current members' wages down and bring union dues collections way up.

For its reasons, mostly because of a progressive / Marxist ideology at the top, the federal government has decided not to enforce immigration laws or OSHA laws or other labor safety laws in the country's largest meat packing plants and other venues. You don't think that the Political Action Committees (PACs) representing meat manufacturing's corporate interests have been making significant contributions to members of Congress for nothing. Is there a quid pro quo going on in the workplace? Is Congress on the take? If not, why has a blind eye been placed on this intolerable situation?

Are the representatives of the people of the US so easily touched and so obviously callous to the plight of these illegal foreign workers? You would have to tell me. In many ways the 111th Congress literally stunk up Washington with their corruption and disregard for the people. If these representatives looked look like thieves and most of them did, perhaps they were thieves. They only wear the sheep's clothing at election time. Finding a corrupt, dishonest, thieving politician in the 111th Congress was no problem. The 112th Congress seems different but the temptations for representatives are severe so let's all hope for the best.

As you know, illegal foreign nationals do not take American jobs just in meatpacking, farming, roofing, and construction. We've been through the lists. It's anything they can get away with. And, to add to the pain of Americans, it is not just huge corporations who exploit their workers for bigger profits. It is small businessmen too. Anything for the almighty dollar!

Residential painting contractor

Consider a residential painting contractor in North Carolina who at one time had six American employees. To get the business for which he competed, this contractor bid the lowest price he thought he could sustain. His bids had to be priced low or he would not be considered. However, by law, he was required to pay overtime, even if employees would be willing to forego the time and a half. He had to also pay at least the minimum wage for each hour worked. Moreover, he was burdened with government regulations -- OSHA and EPA standards. It was tough satisfying everybody and still seeing the business survive.

During the last twenty years, this business owner found the company was losing work to its competition on a more frequent basis. Even old reliable business sources seemed to dry up and his competitors were getting the bids. His quotes somehow were coming in high for about the same number of hours per job. It did not take the businessman long to realize that his competition was not playing fairly. They were using illegal foreign nationals rather than Americans to keep the costs down. Rather than beat them and turn them in, which he should have done, this businessman like many others decided to join them in their loathsome practice.

So, the owner realized that he would have to cut his labor costs. Short of paying starvation wages and doing business in an illegal fashion, the only available way to get back on track in his business was to begin to use cheap illegal labor. Otherwise, he would not be able to keep his business operating and would have to close down operations. This story is repeated across the nation and yet our federal government and the unions are as quiet as church-mice about it. You know the result. Six Americans lost good paying jobs and they will never get them back. Soon, they will lose their homes.

Because the contractor did not want to run into trouble with the feds, he always complied with labor regulations, OSHA, EPA, and anything that was requested. He ran a good business and was a fair person. Hiring illegal foreign nationals to replace Americans is illegal. He knew it was illegal. If he wanted to be illegal, he could have kept the six Americans and asked them to keep quiet about his new practices, but skimping on wages, overtime, records, safety, and environmental laws could cause him jail time if he were discovered. And, his American workers might not understand his plight and might be more likely to turn him in than would illegal foreign nationals, whose very shadow existence depends on contractors running their businesses in an illegal fashion. So how did this contractor solve his dilemma when he is not interested in breaking the law?

Subcontract for illegal workers

Lawyers and loopholes saved the day for the contractor. But the six native-born American citizens were not part of the solution. The painting contractor decided to go from six employees to zero and so the risk of being discovered was virtually eliminated. But how? He found many different Mexican firms with whom he could contract and they would supply him with all the labor he needed. There was no paperwork on employees required. He paid one amount to the labor contractor and did not have to account for employees, hours, minimum wages, overtime, or safety. The Mexican contractor was a non-entity to the US government, since the company was run by an illegal Mexican and it used illegal foreign nationals as contract laborers.

So, the painting firm was able to hire illegal labor. By using subcontractors who have no allegiance to the US, he was able to avoid an illegal act. It is funny there are no government agencies trying to enforce this abuse. Maybe there are no laws broken. Apparently, it is not wrong to contract for labor or anything else from a foreign firm.

You and I know it is a sham at best and in many ways illegal racketeering and human trafficking. Instead of like dope or like booze during prohibition, the product is illegal workers. Try to find these back alley contractors even if the government cared. There are no records. So the American painting contractor stays in business with no American labor with six jobs lost. And, as for Elliott Ness, well, he probably would not get hired today by the Obama administration.

Let's go over the problem one more time. The American painting contractor has no employees any more. Yet, to get painting contracts he needs labor. To get cheap labor so he can win the contracts, rather than hire illegal foreign nationals directly, and be subject to US laws, he subcontracts with a wholly owned Mexican labor company that has workers who can paint. The company itself is run by an illegal Mexican foreign national who does not pay his people very well. Technically this too is against the law but it is far more difficult to prosecute the owner.

The foreman for this Mexican firm is not concerned about how well he or she treats employees. So, the Mexican supervisor has no qualms about paying workers under the table, ignoring OSHA safety rules, overtime labor laws, minimum wage laws etc. Try to catch this illegal Mexican employer by looking at the paperwork he files. He files none. He is clean. The illegal Mexican company files nothing and reports nothing so it remains in the shadow economy undiscovered.

There are no taxes or social security taken out so nothing is traceable. The illegal laborers are not required by their Mexican national employer to file tax returns and thus, they are unable to complain. Only the bottom side of the table knows for sure what has happened. Since there is no systematic means to locate or track workers or contractors in this scenario, you can see that these are the reasons illegal Mexicans will always be cheaper to hire than Americans. I suppose we won't wake up and fix this until it starts hurting all Americans--not just one industry at a time.

Perhaps when school districts begin to hire Mexican teaching contractors, our teachers will complain, and perhaps when TV stations in the liberal media begin to hire illegal announcers and camera personnel, perhaps TV employees will complain. But, maybe there will be no complaints, even then.

Government creates an uphill battle for all Americans

ICE officials know very well what motivates employers to take the risk. They get a cheap, compliant workforce that allows them a major competitive advantage over people who comply with the law.

In a poll conducted by Angie's list contractors, 47 percent of the businesses complained that they suffered because their competition had no problem using illegal foreign nationals as workers. By paying their employees less than required, they were able to undercut the prices of the contractors who used American only employees.

So, Legal American contractors are complaining openly that they cannot afford to remain legal and compete. Some said they would be going out of business after many years or they would have to fire their American workers to compete. It is real and it is now and if it does not stop, why would anybody hire an American?

Some contractors have tried to solve the problem themselves by confronting other contractors who do business in their area, suspecting underground employees are being used. To whom do the good contractors report the bad contractors? ICE would only laugh at them. The word on the street is that the illegal workers are being paid about $8.00 to $10.00 per hour under the table while legitimate contractors, such as painting forms have to pay at least $17 an hour. Additionally, legitimate contractors must carry liability and workers' compensation premiums for each employee.

American employers who want to stay above board have no place to take their problems to. The feds do not care. The big problem for Janet Napolitano is dealing with all the advocacy groups who support the illegal workers and so she has relaxed enforcement to a standstill. If you are American, you are on your own.

Napolitano claims she is stopped by groups throwing down the race card suggesting that anything resembling enforcement has something to do with racial profiling. I think it is more than that. Barack Hussein Obama does not want illegal migration enforced in any way and Napolitano works for Obama. ICE works for Napolitano.

We have several chapters on racial profiling in this book. In many ways in practice it is a myth. It is easy to find the illegal foreign nationals on any jobs site. They are the ones who look like they came from south of the border. How do you know they are illegal? Ten years ago, there were no people from south of the border in those trades.

If you don't get them on the job site, then in the past, before Napolitano, the Police would get them when they committed small crimes in the neighborhoods. Police encounter illegal aliens overwhelmingly because they have done something stupid. Like the rest of us, illegals foreign nationals get caught speeding or urinating in public, or drunk in public, not because they belong to a particular racial group. There is no racial component there.

What if the police determine that the person is in the country illegally during the encounter over the small crime? Janet Napolitano now wants officers to go slow on that and perhaps ignore this because the alien only committed a minor infraction? Let's say the police officer is actually trained to enforce immigration law. Should the officers ignore that Mexican nationals illegally residing in a locale perfectly fit the profile of, say, a Mexican?

Immigrant rights groups want the bar set so high that a Mexican would have to scream out in English, "I am an illegal alien," multiple times before there would be probable cause. Even then, they would argue that the perpetrator was only kidding. They simply do not want any police officer to question anybody about their immigration status and so the bar they set can never be reached. Janet Napolitano has gone along with them because the bad guys, not the American people, are the only ones to whom she listens. Since she took over in 2009, she changed many policies to be contrary to our national interests. She does not think she must please Americans. Both she and the new policy make a mockery of the law.

Don't you think that if you had a posse of government workers under your management, you would be able to solve this problem? So, why are the feds AWOL on the problem? You have heard this again and again in this book. The US has bad leadership. From the President to the Congress, to the Head of Homeland Security, to the state and local officials, progressive liberals do not want to solve the problem. Thankfully, every two years, you are able to fire most of them. Try to assure that nobody in office gets to ever sit in that seat again. Check their records. If they are not for the American people, remove them from office.

It's time!

Chapter 50   Meat Packing – A One Time Great Job for Americans

Killing live animals is not such a great job

Whether it is on a farm, on a hot rooftop, or in a meat packing plant, Mexicans are doing work that Americans will do, as bad as the work may be. Americans are a rare breed filled with moxie from about four hundred years of working for, and achieving better lives. Hard work pays off in America and real Americans know it.

Will Americans work in a hog processing plant? The answer is found in this statement: "The arrival of illegal foreign nationals was not coincidental with the first pig being slaughtered for food consumption in the US." Illegal Mexican workers often give themselves a little too much credit when they prop themselves up as indispensable to the American way of life.

Now that we have made that statement, it is a fact that those who know say that one of the worst places to earn a living is a hog processing plant. I would add that any plant that has live animals arriving as input on the receiving dock and dead, dismembered animals served as raw meat as output from the shipping dock has got to be a "down" place to work. But there are lots more to the difficulties and dangers in these plants.

When I was a kid, there was a slaughterhouse down around Breslau, PA where I grew up. It smelled to high heaven. Native-born American citizens worked there. You could sense the blood and guts inside and that had to make the plant a nasty place to work. Strange as it may seem, when I rode my bike around there, it was eerie. I am not superstitious, but you could almost feel the spirits of the slaughtered cattle in the air.

To borrow from Star Wars, there was some kind of disturbance in the force. I could see from just this childhood experience and the thought of what goes on in a slaughterhouse, that in these businesses, such as hog processing plants anywhere in the country, if given a choice, nobody would want to work there. It would be tough and unpleasant work. Companies would have trouble finding workers. Add low wages to these impediments, and the job of finding an American to do such work would be very difficult.

Illegal foreign nationals did not always dominate the meat packing industry. It wasn't always this way and there are many stories about how the large corporations in meat-packing plants turned their managers' attention to illegal labor to fill the jobs that "no one else wanted." Because the jobs were lousy to begin with, as killing animals all day is not fun for anybody, the average hourly earnings of workers in this industry before the influx of foreign workers were not bad at all. In fact, they were about 20 percent above the overall manufacturing rate of the 1980's. Union wages in meatpacking plants back then were as high as $19.00 per hour. At 19.00 per hour it was not difficult at all for these plants to find competent labor. Lines of people showed up for these very high paying jobs in meatpacking, despite the unpleasantness of the workplace. That was thirty year ago.

With good wages, Americans will take any job wherever it is offered. Americans are not babies. Americans have no problem working hard for a fair wage and these jobs originally paid very well. As unethical managers sought to increase profits, they moved the plants to locations outside of the union-influence, began to hire illegal workers, and wages plummeted faster than anyone would have imagined. Over time, one plant after another moved from the big city to the heartland to get out of the influence of the union (fair) wage. As the exodus progressed, the union workers, Black and White, but mostly Black, stayed in the big cities, without jobs. The new plant managers began to have it all their way.

In the beginning of this era of illegal workers, back in the early 1980's, wages were still fairly high in the meat industry even for the few illegal foreign nationals who had gotten through the net. Very soon after, however, the populations of whole towns became predominantly Mexican as the plant managers shamelessly hired anybody who would work for lower wages and then even lower wages. The downward push on wages known as labor arbitrage was on, and it continues to this day.

Illegal workers have few options. They are not Americans and businesses take advantage of them for sure. It has nothing do with the moxie of Americans to do hard work. It has everything to do with greedy businesses engaging in offshoring practices right here onshore in America. These businessmen ought to be put in jail for a long time for the misery they cause to Americans who lose their living and to Mexicans and other Hispanics or Latinos who take on this work for little more than slave wages.

The good wages ended when plant managers discovered they could offer lower wages and still attract a large number of illegal workers, and still not be arrested by the feds. Even at the federally mandated minimum wage, the average illegal Mexican worker does lots better in a meatpacking plant than in Mexico -- lots better. Wages, which peaked at $19.00 per hour thirty years ago in 1980, now are down to less than $8.00 per hour and they are not moving upwards despite continuing inflation.

Benefits are nil yet somehow the companies are also able to get away with very poor working conditions—conditions that a real union shop would not permit. Somehow progressive politicians have been able to help their friends in meatpacking management by taking the sting of government labor inspections / raids off their backs. In these plants, illegal foreign nationals toil all day, as much as 12 hours per day and more, with no overtime. They perform demanding tasks in a very hazardous environment. Even at $8.00, for this level of work, they receive relatively low wages. But, these jobs help them survive and so they take them gladly.

Long shifts of punishing production line work are tough on the body and the soul. In some Omaha plants, for example, it is reported that the workers cannot leave the line even for bathroom breaks. As a result, it is not unusual at the end of a shift for a number of employees to show the signs of having urinated in their pants while working on the line. Yes, these workers are exploited -- because they are illegal.

How could any person do this to another? The one word answer is greed. There are a lot of greedy people who put their needs for self actualization above the needs of others for mere sustenance. Lots of bad things happen to good people, even in America.

Consider an incentive plan in which plant managers and their foremen on the line receive a good part of their compensation from bonuses tied to production and performance. As labor costs drop, management bonuses increase. Foremen and lower level supervisors, those in better positions in the plant, are paid by those who live behind gated communities, to exploit their fellow human beings to drive the labor cost down. They get away with it because the workers are illegal and they will not squeal because they cannot exist without the jobs. American workers do not have such constraints. Americans, especially Americans with union protection, will squeal like pigs until the abuses are corrected.

To make things even more efficient, the top managers, tucked safely behind their gated communities eventually found that their Spanish-speaking supervisors and managers were able to communicate better to the illegal workforce than their former American floor leaders. By understanding the language they were able to force a bigger pile of sand each day from each worker. Illegal Mexicans were thus used as first line supervisors. They worked cheap and to be blunt, they were very harsh taskmasters on their illegal Mexican brothers and sisters, who they supervised.

How do the meatpackers get away with it?

Before meatpackers had to worry about the feds, they first had to deal with the unions. They used coldhearted, cutthroat tactics throughout the eighties and nineties to free the plants from union control. One of the most well-known tactics employed by one of the largest meat-packing companies in the country was simply to close down a plant. They would pull this trick when its workers voted in a union or began to get too "grabby." They had one objective: to control the wages whether the shop was union or non-union. But they had no patience with union tactics. They would have no qualms about opening another plant in another city with nonunion workers, thereby giving them full control. Sometimes, after closing a plant, they would have it sit idle for awhile, and then, they would magically reopen the same plant with newly recruited, often illegal workers.

There were so many illegal aliens working in these plants that management had to be concerned about protecting themselves so they would not be charged with a felony if caught -- under US immigration law. Fat chance of that happening today with little enforcement but it still causes some managers to worry.

One would think that if anybody working in a plant accepts such low wages, it should be cause enough for ICE to raid the facilities as proof that illegals work there—to support the US immigration laws. But, as we point out continually in this book, government officials are not always trying to enforce the laws so having this, another reason to do so, is moot.

Some plant managers have been clever enough to figure out a solution to the risk of incarceration for violating immigration and OSHA laws since they have a lot to lose. As the supervisors and foremen extract more work from illegal employees, upper management must be concerned that their poor labor tactics become so obvious that they get noticed. If they don't get reported by people overhearing illegal foreign nationals discussing the topic outside the plant then they can be reported by Americans who want a chance to work at the plant.

Under the law anybody can fill out an immigration complaint that might cause ICE to act. A displaced American worker for example could complain theoretically prompting ICE to take action. This is a standard issue at meatpacking plants. Companies have had to figure out ways to make what they are doing appear to be legal so that at least they have a defense if raided. Versions of the painting subcontractor technique discussed in Chapter 49 are often used but in large meatpacking plants, the techniques are much cleverer than how it would be done by the small painting contractor.

Chickens are no easier to deal with than Hogs. They call chicken farming "factory-farming" Using versions of the contractor methodology, all of the legal hoops are done to benefit the company owner and not the contractor. Thus, factory-farming is inherently unfair. Tyson, for example awards contracts, and the contractor must sustain the cost of building, repairs, improvements (even company-mandated ones), wages, and poultry losses due to disease or weather. In exchange, Tyson provides the chicks, feed, veterinary services, medication and technical advice, and sets the price it will pay for each bird. If a contractor, or grower, doesn't like the terms, or falls into disfavor by demanding more support or better pricing, Tyson simply cancels the contract, leaving the grower holding the financial bag.

So, in many ways, just like the painting contractor in the last chapter, for Tyson, the "legal" solution involves sub-contracting the work. The illegal laborers work for the contractor and the contractor is responsible in many cases, for everything. All of the unskilled labor that is needed to get the job done is employed by the contractor. The illegal employees work for the contractor and not the firm, so the firm does not have illegal workers on its payroll. This does not fully exempt the ultimate plant beneficiary, Tyson, in this case from the law but it makes it lots more difficult to see anything clearly.

So, subcontracting continues to accomplish the desired end and American companies continue to engage labor contracting companies that can be owned and operated by Americans or even illegal Mexicans. All of this seems like it would be prohibited by the RICO act instead of the immigration laws but we'll see how this plays out over time. Will the 112th Congress choose to force the President's hand to get some real enforcement in this and other objectionable industries?

It is a lousy job, plain and simple

You might never eat meat again if you got a look or you got a whiff of a hog-processing plant or a chicken factory. Working conditions are equally appalling. Poultry plant workers suffer just as Hog processors. They have twice as many injuries and illnesses as any other manufacturing sector. The same cutting and twisting motions are used in highly manual, dangerous operations thousands of times a day. Think of the high-speed saws, and huge, sharp knives. Yes, lacerations and even amputations are common. Work areas are not pristine and are often so crowded it is a lucky day when nobody gets cut. Employees walk and stand on floors with s slurry, slick with blood and trimmings.

In many cases, more than half of the workers in chicken factories are Latino and/or female, and their language skills make the work even more dangerous. Additionally, they lack familiarity with US law so many of the violations and / or the injuries that occur are not reported in a timely manner to claim compensation. Then again, there is always the threat of being deported for asking for too much.

Implied in the above discussion is that sanitary conditions are not so good. Think about this fact. If you have unsanitary conditions in a plant, then it's generally not too safe a place for workers, and it's generally not good for producing safe food to eat. There is a story that at one Tyson's facility, workers would bring in their own drinking water because the plant's system had gotten too contaminated from use. Employees who put up with these conditions for a long time do get paid for their work, but they also can catch debilitating diseases that are not easily curable when found in humans. For example, workers at a hog-processing facility reported contracting a disease called brucellosis. This is a bacterial infection leading to fever and chills. Other than those working for years in hog processing plants; this disease was usually limited to livestock. It is hard to treat in humans.

As you would expect, subcontracting to Mexican illegals makes working conditions even worse and it cuts wages even further. It is funny in a twisted sort of way that American meat packing corporations claim they have no illegal workers yet, mostly all of them, if not all, had to shut down on Primero de Mayo a few years ago for the annual Mexican national holiday parade. This is the Mexican equivalent to the U.S. Labor Day. They had to stop operations because they had no workers. What does that say?

This holiday is not to be confused with the more popular fifth of May, which is observed in Mexico and Mexican-American communities in the United States to commemorate the Mexican victory over the French in the Battle of Puebla in 1862. There is a misunderstanding that this is Mexican Independence Day, which is celebrated on September 16. As an aside, 2010 was the Bicentennial celebration of Mexican independence.

If you are a Mexican, these holidays are very important and they are a cause to celebrate. If you are an American, more than likely you are not celebrating Mexico's big holidays, and vice versa.

Why not just solve the problem?

It would be lots easier to solve the illegal worker crisis in America if we could only find some leaders in Congress and a President who are Americans first. I would like to see patriotic individuals who are America-first in all aspects of government. Let the churches and the charities fight for the rights of foreigners in our country. Our Constitution provides enough protection for all, including visitors. Our laws however make it a crime to invade America. Our lawmakers and the President don't get it. If they are good Americans, then I cannot think of a place to go to find bad Americans. Our leaders are the bottom of the barrel in terms of their care for America and Americans.

George Bush took a big poke at his fellow Americans when he blamed the work ethic of Americans on the illegal worker problem. I have brought this up numerous times in this book because it is a contagion. It is an untruth that makes it seem ok to perpetuate the fraud that illegal foreign national workers are necessary for America. I am not interested in class warfare but George Bush grew up filthy rich. What can he know about the American work ethic?

Obama simply has no idea. His five formative years in Indonesia gave him a poor start in understanding Americans and then his adolescence in Hawaii and not on the mainland did not really make up for it. Born of a Muslim father and then later raised by a Muslim stepfather during the formative years, Barack Obama is not the typical American. For example, he moved back to Hawaii when he was not much more than ten years old. Where in Hawaii is there a bad neighbourhood? The best I can say about him is that he just doesn't know better, but I am really not sure of that.

Obama acts like the US is a big board game and he is in control of the game, the money, the houses and the hotels. He has the deeds to everything and he likes taking things from one party and giving them to a more deserving party. He does not seem to care about whether somebody is American or non-American. Everybody is the same. He is the ultimate boss. That may be good for the elites in his One-World game, but it doesn't work for the regular Americans in the United States.

Obama might make a good president for the National Redistribution Corporation but he is not a good president for hard working Americans and don't expect him to become one any time soon. He does talk a good game and he is so good at the talk that he is tough not to believe. He sounds like he is telling the whole truth. Don't be fooled. Obama does not understand real life, nor does he seem to care about the plight of real Americans. He surely does not care about all of the Americans who are in poor shape because 50,000,000 illegal foreign nationals get favoured treatment from his regime.

Welfare state has many issues

Despite how many times it is refuted, I still see the progressive pro-amnesty crowd using the old clichéd argument that Americans won't do certain jobs. That phrase is more than annoying. It is pure claptrap. Native-born Americans have no problem doing those things— if they're paid decent wages, and given safe working conditions. Americans can and do perform all jobs.

Now, why might some bleeding heart progressive see it that way? The US, has unfortunately, to many observers, become a welfare state and many people have lost spirit and have taken the bait. These people, who have removed themselves from the workforce, are not going to work on a farm, a meatpacking plant, or even as the caretaker of a CEOs office. They live on the couch and watch TV and it is the nation's laws and the people's generosity as Americans that created people such as this.

Benefits of the welfare state are bad for the spirit of Americans. Yet, Americans get sucked in. It is easy to get sucked into the welfare state. It is a Rod Serling experience but unfortunately, it is all too real. Though Americans lose their spirit in the welfare state, the benefits that prostrate them are not supposed to be available to foreigners at all. Illegal foreign nationals by law cannot participate in the American welfare boondoggle. So, there are potential workers, shall we say lower-skilled Americans who simply take themselves out of the job market. They cannot say no to the welfare opportunities and the do-nothing life.

Lower Class Economics 101 (LCE101)

Everybody has become an expert in lower class economics 101 (LCE101). If you pay a man or a woman, for example, $800 per month for *not* working, that person is not going to be interested in a job paying $1000.00 a month. They'd be working 175 or so hours to get a $200.00 a month increase. And, that's before taxes. LCE101 says don't take the job because the take-home pay is less than not working.

That's a big, but different problem from the notion that Americans won't take certain jobs. Because of the welfare state, these guys won't take any jobs. When you see the progressive liberals pushing for blanket amnesty and the progressive liberals pushing for the welfare state, you notice it is the same people pushing. Two wrongs do not make a right. With amnesty, you get the same result as welfare—an intolerable situation for working Americans caused by do-gooders, guilt ridden hippies from the 1960s who are way too smart to understand the lessons of LCE101.

Today's problem is not the American workingman and it has never been the American workingman. The welfare state provides a perverse incentive to not work. The extremely low wages accepted by illegal foreign nationals is a reason why Americans choose to go from unemployment compensation to welfare. It is LCE101 and a new member of the lower class is created every minute by the poor economy, the welfare state, and illegal workers in sub minimum wage jobs.

This phenomenon does not just exist in hog processing plants. Many jobs in poultry plants across the South that had previously been held by American Blacks are now dominated by illegal workers. Even textile plants are run largely on the backs of illegal Hispanic workers. Now, more and more we see this even in mines, such as the Kentucky coal fields. Mining companies are looking for miners from different countries, such as the Ukraine to save money on both wages and safety. They say that there are no unions in the Ukraine and the new miners would not be caring as much about safety. Whether you are Mexican, Ukrainian, or Irish; it doesn't matter. If you are an illegal foreign national, somebody is ready to exploit you and some would say that it is time to get out while the getting is good.

We began this chapter with meatpacking so let's finish it with some more interesting information. Why is meatpacking dominated by illegal workers? Is it that killing and dismembering of the pigs, sheep, and cattle of America that is so unpleasant? Is it just so nasty a business? Are there too many risks to one's survival working in the plants? Is it that Americans really will not do these jobs?

We can dismiss the latter since long before the illegals were here doing any work, anywhere, in the 1960's America was not a country of vegetarians. American businesses that employ illegal aliens try to gain public opinion by saying that these are jobs Americans won't do. Their objective is to create just enough doubt that all of America is not joining hands picketing these dirty un-American SOBs.

It is pure silliness to suggest that native-born Americans will not work in meatpacking. It takes little skill. Meanwhile less and less Americans are finishing high school these days so we do have the workers available. Who would not want a $19.00 per hour job? In the 1970's the unions assured safety and the high paying American-born meatpackers made a ton of money and they would not give those jobs up for "nothing."

Armour, Swift, Wilson, and Oudahy got out of the slaughterhouse business at the same time Americans stopped getting the jobs. Is there a real connection there? Why not ask these four corporations why they exited the business? By the 1990's meatpacking had become the most dangerous industry in America, manned principally by illegal foreign nationals. The industry itself needs a cleanup and along with it a change to American labour.

Americans would do those jobs, if they were offered a fair wage. There is no such thing as a labor shortage. Businesses of all kinds in meatpacking and elsewhere have no willingness to pay sufficient wages to induce legal people, citizens of the USA, to work for them. It's time to find Elliott Ness once again and this problem too can be solved.

Chapter 51   Illegal Foreign Nationals & Their God-Given Right to American Jobs!

Americans are accustomed to long, hard hours

The United States is a nation of hard workers. Compared with many other developed countries, the U.S. boasts high rates of labor-force participation and productivity and has traditionally had a very low unemployment rate. (Until a certain President took office) Information freely available on the Internet shows that Americans work longer hours than Europeans—over 1,800 hours per worker for the United States, compared to over 1400 in Germany and over 1,500 in France, according to the OECD.

Americans are hard workers who expect a return on their labor investment. America has a middle class that expects to continue to exist and to grow. Labor arbitrage with illegal foreign nationals is a ploy to eliminate the middle class. Americans will not let that happen.

> FYI -- The Organization for Economic Cooperation and Development -- provides a setting in which governments compare policy experiences, seek answers to common problems, identify good practices and coordinate domestic and international policies. – Some of the information in this chapter is from their reports. Permit me to take a little diversion here in the beginning of this chapter.

> The Social Security system, enacted under Roosevelt in 1935, was designed as a safety net for American employees to have a dignified retirement. The idea was that through contributions and investments, all Americans who contributed would receive retirement benefits.
> Unfortunately politicians looked at the huge surplus in Social Security for many years with a jealous eye. Politicians unfortunately were entrusted to assure it remained solvent. But, they are politicians first and money managers second. Lyndon Johnson could not say no and so the fund has been raided and pillaged by Congress from the Vietnam War to the present day, Americans therefore do not have benefits as good as the Europeans perhaps because European politicians are more trustworthy.

> American politicians are not as good at caretaking the assets of the people as they are at protecting their own assets. The American Congress has not been a good caretaker of the funds in the social system and in fact they have raided the contributions of Americans. Though, from the inception of Social Security and Medicare, Americans have dutifully contributed each payroll, the Congress's reckless

pilfering has placed both funds on the verge of collapse. Yes, Congress should be put in jail for that.

Americans must work to 65 to collect Medicare and to about 67 to collect social security. So, In September, 2010 many American workers were surprised to learn that the French mandatory retirement age is 60 years old. The US has no mandatory retirement age but 65 and 67 are big numbers for those waiting to retire. The French were picketing and demonstrating and almost rioting because their government was raising the age of collection to 62.

French unions went nuts. They put on a nationwide strike because in late 2010, as their government prepared to increase the mandatory retirement (pension collecting age) from 60 years old to 62. Meanwhile there is an anonymous contribution in italics below. If you do not like attempts at being cute, feel free to skip to the end of the italics.

In the US, "Fozi Bear" and "Miss Pigy" and a team of other misspelled furless Mupets, including the two old farts in the balcony, all reported living well in Alexandria Virginia. These almost-Muppets, have been in control of Social Security (SS) for years. Thus, the poor state of the social security trust fund has been openly described as a product of "utter mismanagement by government."

[Hint, if the politicians were little fur-balls such as the Muppets, they would not even measure up to Mupet standards. They have done such a poor job; it would have had to have been intentional.]

The "Mupets" have less positive things to say. Our dearly beloved progressives in Congress (they still do run the country you know), are secretly preparing another of their potent solutions. Besides ingredients such as "eye of nute," which is back in everything nowadays, the secret dirty plan is to lift the SS retirement age to 70. Hey maybe we can sneak into France! Would we be welcomed with open arms if we crossed their borders with no documentation? I guess we'd have to check their border policy to see how well we would do as undocumented "citizens."

Let's go back now to being serious and on-point. The warmup—c'est fini!.

Our government cannot seem to get anything right. They can't do anything right, and they can't even see how messed up that have made this country. They have already messed up SS and Medicare and they can be expected to use those same skills to protect American citizens from the invasion of illegal foreign nationals, who swallow up American jobs upon arrival into the country. Do you trust them?

I cannot get over the current street talk, as reported by the unabashed US media. In this media, it is increasingly common to hear politicians, CEOs, and immigration activists impugn American workers as a bunch of shiftless gadflies who spend their days drinking beer and wondering from where the next handout is coming. Somebody better update their statistics. Even those on welfare in the US don't have it that good anymore. But, the folklore is there any way to give excuses to look to the illegal foreign nationals to solve non-existent labor shortages.

Good jobs are not beneath any American's dignity. But as we have discussed ad nauseam so far, the CEOs, safely tucked behind their gated community walls say, that is why their companies must turn to foreign nationals—some of them legal, many of them illegal.

To hear CEOs tell it, you would believe they'd much rather hire English-speaking, tax-paying U.S. citizens. You'd think they'd rather have people who won't disrupt operations by getting rounded up in Homeland Security sweeps. But they lie. They say they can't find any Americans willing to do their jobs. They lie again. President Bush himself once said, the US needs a temporary guest-worker program that would "match willing foreign workers with willing American employers to fill jobs that Americans will not do." This of course is pure bull, and not the kind of "bull" found in meat packing plants. American businesses feel cheated when they must hire Americans instead of cheap labor.

President Bush, who has always represented the business interests over the people's interests, was OK with businesses driving the American wage down. It was good for business. The former President had his big day during his second term when he chose to disparage American workers in favor of Mexicans. Now, President Obama thinks the same and he is not even a Republican. Maybe it is an oval-office bacterial infection. Bush wanted cheap labor and Obama wants more Democratic votes. We all know that. Their politics and greed are ruining our country.

Do you think either President really believes that Americans won't do farm work, meatpacking, painting, construction, and many other jobs, if the wages are fair?. Obama has yet to fully assign blame that the jobs issue in this country has arisen because Americans are just too lazy to do the work that hard working Mexicans do without complaint? But, he makes so many errors in judgment, you know one day he will slip and say it.

Knowing how valuable Mexican human resources are in America, in a September 2010 TV commercial, President Obama's Labor Secretary Hilda Solis is shown; telling illegal workers that she will help them get paid a "fair" wage. Solis insists that it doesn't matter if a worker is documented or undocumented; they still deserve to be paid "fairly." Does it not make sense that if Hilda can find these people to make their lives better by bringing in the power of the government to assure them higher wages, then she should just as easily be able to give them their three month notice to get the hell out of the country or else.

Moreover, if Hilda knows who the bad employers are, why not just shut them down, rather than attempt to legalize illegal entry into the US using the back door. Considering that traveling Americans to Canada and Mexico for the last several years cannot get back into the US without passport, how is it that Mexicans are immune?

At eyeblast.tv, an astute blogger noted:

> "Sure you can't legally earn a wage but golly if you manage to break our laws and gain unlawful employment we will make sure that you get paid a 'fair' wage."

Hoffman Plastics

Everybody who has a horse in the race knows the story of Hoffman Plastics. The illegal foreign nationals who invade America in search of their own dream do know that they are violating the border that separates our countries. Yet, they believe they have a sort of intrinsic right to do so. Way back in the famous Hoffman Plastics case, however, the Supreme Court ruled that illegal workers are not entitled to American benefits; Hilda did not get that message.

Because this case is so compelling, let me tell you the story. An illegal foreign national without a passport or proof of legal entry into the US was working at a Hoffman Plastics factory. He decided not to let well enough alone and so he decided to help a union that wanted to organize the factory. He and the union theoretically wanted a union so "everybody could do better." There was only one problem; he was not an American citizen.

All Americans have an implicit right to organize a plant without the risk of being fired. The key word there is "Americans." If he were an American, his employer would have violated the National Labor Relations Act (NLRA) by firing him for helping to organize a union. And that they did. One might call an illegal organizing against his or her employer ungrateful or brave or whatever but since all acts of an illegal in the US are technically illegal, this person was bold indeed to sue his employer.

Why the employee was not carted away by ICE before the trial began is a puzzle though, Isn't it? Ironically, he was supported by the company union and they argued with the Supreme Court that he should have the same rights as an American. For union workers reading this, I bet your leaders don't really tell you folks what they are doing with your union dues.

For those of you with law degrees, the question the Supreme Court had to decide was whether the worker could receive the usual remedy of "back-pay," for the time he was not working. According to the union, he, just like an American in similar circumstance, had been illegally fired.

We all know what back-pay is. It is the money that an employer is required to pay a worker to make up for wages the worker would have earned if she or he had not been illegally fired. The court's decision was to decide whether the worker could or could not be awarded back-pay because he was an illegal foreign national. He got nothing in the end. He was an illegal.

Part of the rationale in the Hoffman case for the denial of back-pay was that the worker had used fake ID and had fraudulently gotten the job. Though Hoffman has stood for some time as case law, there are many who think that illegal people should be able to take American jobs and benefits and have the same rights as any other "American" in the workplace. OK, take some time now to find your airline bag.

One case at a time, but the fact is that bleeding heart judges, living in gated communities, never tasting the aura of real neighborhoods, will continue to make it easier for illegals to operate their shadow underground in the un-gated communities of America. A federal judge in early 2009 for example ignored Hoffman and ruled that workers who've entered this country illegally have the same right to sue for overtime pay as any other workers. No wonder many Americans question our legal system. Too bad we could not get Moses back to put the robes on in all courtrooms.

Amazingly, progressive, former hippie, bleeding heart judges, who have never had to work a real day in their lives think that illegals and Americans are equal. They are equal under God surely, but not under the Constitution. Why should anything distinguish the legal worker from the illegal if all men are created equal?

There is so much corporate money backing the illegal worker community that this fight is far from over. The bottom line for most American citizens is that these illegal foreign invaders have their own country in which they are supposed to live and work. Let's tell them to let our country alone and please if you have come here illegally, get out now!

Bleeding heart progressives argue that if the illegal foreign nationals are not made citizens, the companies would continue to be able to take advantage of illegal workers, knowing that the illegal foreign nationals have no recourse in the workplace. OK, that may be true and that is not good, but rewarding all the bad actors in this scenario is the worst solution of all. It's time to punish those who hire them and remove the lawmakers who see things through progressive lenses.

Judges are not rocket scientists and there are lawyers from the bottom of the class as well as the top. Some judges passed the BAR the first time; others took years. These people are part of the elite throwback hippie culture that wants to take everybody else's money to right some wrong they might have done when they were smoking dope in the 1960's. That's baloney! If life is so good in these circumstances, your honor, come out of your gated community and get a better taste and smell of the squalor your rulings sustain.

These judges don't give a damn about the multitude of American citizens, *We the People*. They already have their opinions. The law and law-abiding American citizens be damned. In Hoffman, however, the Supreme Court at 5 to 4 was clearly saying that the government can't force employers to pay wages that couldn't have been legally earned in the first place.

The real conundrum for guys like me, who think about this stuff perhaps too much, is: How could four Supreme Court of the United States (SCOTUS) justices have voted against it. I can only conclude that the Marijuana campfire from the hills of Woodstock is still sending smoke signals to their brains. These Hippies ruined their own lives and because of their parents' social and economic status, they all made lame partial recoveries and now, empowered only by their age, and status in the ruling class, and the fact that somehow they are now judges, they try to ruin the lives of other Americans in the guise of compassion for all.

The Obama Department of Labor (DOL) is a bit too kind to lawbreakers for my money or yours. It makes me wonder if Obama's DOL is going to make sure that drug dealers are paid a "fair" wage by the gangs that employ them. I mean is that not the same situation? Is this not an employer, which knowingly and illegally employs someone and exploits them? Will the Obama DOL make sure *all* people illegally employed are paid a "fair" wage or just the ones whose political cause they support? And even if they do try to help all people employed illegally does that make it any better?

How can anybody justify any of this as a good idea? Shouldn't the government be trying to stop people from finding illegal employment rather than helping them keep their ill-gotten job and gain higher wages once they've obtained it?

Doesn't anybody care that foreign citizens, with full allegiance to their country of origin and choice, residing illegally in the USA, are taking American jobs?

Chapter 52   The End of Entry Level Jobs for Americans?

Where have all the good jobs gone?

Should American citizens really care that illegal foreign nationals take our lowest paying jobs? After all, nobody makes a lot of money in any of those jobs. The answer is an abrupt, "Yes we should!"

But, here is the real question: "Should American citizens really care that illegal foreign nationals, change what would otherwise be good paying jobs into low paying jobs?" Again, "yes" we should care very much, but we need also realize that this question has repercussions far more sinister than the fact that American companies are now engaging in out and out labor arbitrage. The lowest wage wins in the US and laws be damned. .

So called "American" companies, who were not able to make a windfall by offshoring are now finding that they can use illegals in the "onshoring exploitation of illegal labor." The business profits are quite lucrative. Thankfully for American workers, most of the companies that did not offshore could not offshore. For one reason or another, their businesses were tied to US production and they could not move them overseas easily enough—for economic reasons.

There may be no immorality or unethical behavior involved here. But, then again, maybe there is. American corporations have citizenship of their own in the USA and do not have to care at all about the American citizens who have the real beating hearts. These passion-less, semi-robotic entities (corporations) are equipped with a drive for profits and profits alone and they are not built to care that they may leave the charred bodies of American workers in their wake.

It is not an accident that illegal foreign nationals drive down wages. It is part of the same plan that caused whole companies to move their manufacturing plants offshore—the lure of the lower wage—pure labor arbitrage. And, yes, a caring Congress should be addressing this. However, the 110th and 111th Congresses have been occupied conveniently as ostriches on this issue since 2007. Perhaps, with the changes that occurred this past November 2010, one can hope that in 2012, the people will fully clean the House, the Senate, and remove the rats from PA Avenue, and whip a brew of Ostrich stew. No rats needed for the stew.

It would be nice for Americans to change the Thanksgiving bird from the Ostrich back to the Turkey in 2012, while Americans purify the government further by voting every November from now on.

Illegal foreign nationals are actually hurting the young citizens of America from being productive in the future as they have taken over a very important part of the education chain—on the job training. It is gone for young Americans since they cannot get entry level jobs and the future looks even bleaker.

No entry, no nothing

One of the most disturbing aspects of the notion of as many as 50,000,000 mostly Mexican invaders, whose intentions are not really known, living on American soil is the denial of entry-level jobs for Americans. Though more and more students seem to be going to college, only about 23% of the American workforce is college educated. That means that despite what it seems, 77% do not graduate from college and are at some point out there looking for their first job. So, what jobs can they get when they don't graduate from college? The answer at the college level of course is they get the jobs that the government has not given away to legal foreigners on various visa schemes. But, unfortunately, because of the foreigners, even for these jobs, as we have covered in this book, the wages will not be very high.

I am not suggesting not attending college. Indeed register and attend and graduate and your chances of success blossom. But facts are as they are. For the recent high school grad, who does not even want college, things are worse than ever.

Will you get your first job?

The sane and rational thing to do, which most baby boomers had to do when dad finally said "get a job," just one week out of high school, was to look for an entry level job (perhaps a laborer) in a trade if possible. Those jobs were always hard to find but they were good to get. Today it is virtually impossible for an American to get one of these jobs in most cities in America. Americans simply need not apply as we are the last considered. Let's talk about why.

In the 1950's through the 1980's, when a trade job was impossible for many reasons, the job of gas station attendant or hotel night clerk, or ash hauler, soda truck delivery man, or part-time cabbie was almost always possible. Sure the non-collegiate often had a goal of starting his or her own business but this did not typically come about until the new American employee was in his or her late teens or early twenties. The first job gave them a little cabbage and a little drive and a little experience in one or several jobs. It built their confidence that they could succeed. This set them up for the rest of the jobs they would have in the rest of their lives.

Where have all the flowers gone? The hippies of the 1960's, today's ruling class in America ate them all, and with the flowers, they ate all the jobs. Once these "leaders" got their birthright positions, they began to worry about the world and mother earth and other esoteric things. After all, "we are the world." They could not have fouled the world up any more than if they had actually been trying. They are idiots. Look what these former hippies, zealot progressives have done to America.

Ask your non-college children to go find any job that is not in the trades or government that is something for which today an employer might consider hiring an American. You would be surprised. Though not impossible, the chances are probably about the percentage of the impurity in ivory soap. Remember Ivory is 99 44/100 % pure. That does not give your teenage children and my children many chances for employment in this new shared world—shared with unwelcome illegal-job-takers visitors, mostly from Mexico.

Employers have many choices today for unskilled positions. Applicants, American and otherwise are everywhere. People line up in double and triple digits for the opportunity to get a meaningless job if it is advertised. We are in a big recession. Then, in the midst of this almost hopelessness with 35 and 40 year-olds hanging around their parents' homes all day, because that is where they live, salt comes pouring in on wounds. Who is doing this?

Can you believe it is our own Department of Labor? Yes, we find the US Department of Labor (DOL) pouring salt on the wounds of real Americans. Our own DOL has decided that it should help illegal foreign nationals in the workplace. Not only does our government not bother arresting illegal foreign nationals in the workplace, they now want to help them get better wages and better conditions from their employers. As I said previously, DOL should turn them in to be deported and then DOL should turn themselves in to be fired. .

The saddest part of this is that it is a clear signal that jobs will not be available for entry level Americans any time soon. The government, our government, thinks it is OK that foreigners hold the jobs instead of Americans. In fact our government mocks Americans like as if only the foreigners have what it takes to hold these lousy entry level positions.

It does not look good for American youth or for any American wanting to restart their job life. Why would any American think they would ever be able to gain or hold a job again, especially those types of jobs that have traditionally been entry level positions? Any American in the past, who was responsible and wanted to move forward, would excel at such positions and would be hired immediately. But, today those jobs are reserved for illegal foreign nationals simply because they work dirt cheap and they do not hold the rights of a real American. I am not OK with that and no American should be OK with that.

So, unfortunately, a substantial portion of the entry-level jobs and unskilled jobs are now being held by Illegal Mexican laborers. You and I know that. Our children are coming home to live until they are thirty-five and maybe even older nowadays because Mexicans are doing exactly what their American counterparts did in the past before they moved on to better jobs. Instead of our children, the illegal foreign nationals get the job training and then it is the illegal foreign nationals who start their own businesses using the entry level training knowledge from the same type of training that was once given to young Americans, without college degrees, who were just starting out. Too bad Americans have no leadership.

Somewhere in all of this, there is the notion of the American Dream. Remarkably, the press seems to revel in the work ethic of these illegal workers while totally ignoring the effect on Americans. A whole generation of taxpaying American businesses is being replaced by businesses owned and operated by illegal Mexican foreign nationals with allegiance to Mexico and Janet Napolitano thinks it is OK as long as they know how to say please and thank-you.

See for yourself is this is not true -- but who would you ask? These new businesses, the new order Mexican entrepreneurs, thrive while they leave carnage and many individual American carcasses behind. They intentionally provide an on-shore shield for businesses in much the same way as offshoring shields US firms from the pain of seeing the effects of the low-wages, which they demand in other countries of the world.

I am not suggesting that the illegal foreign national contractors are sophisticated in any way at this early stage of evolution. However, I can see a day when Mexican labor cartels become a force to reckon with in the US heartland. Today it is the choice of greedy US businessmen but tomorrow, they may be forced to pay high wages—but not to US workers, instead to a cartel of Mexican foreign national businessmen who control the US labor force. Can this really happen? Ask yourself if what you now see could have happened looking at it from about ten years ago?

These labor supply companies may choose to incorporate in the US and gain many protections from our government, yet they will not be from America. Meanwhile these "human traffickers," so to speak will deliver bodies to worksites, caring less than even the greedy business person who hires them, for the well-being of the worker. A new Robber Baron culture mentality is emerging.

In this world, do you think any of these companies dominated by illegal foreign nationals from Mexico will really care about withholding federal, state, local and social security taxes? Do you think these companies would be at the top of the statistics list for entities that adhere to U.S. Labor laws? Do you think they will make life better for their countrymen or ours?

This next quote from broowaha demonstrates this point even further. It is telling.

http://www.broowaha.com/articles/1572/the-disturbing-side-of-illegal-immigrant-workers

> "The message is really simple: Illegal Mexican workers are taking jobs and opportunities away from Americans. It is elitist and arrogant to assume otherwise. The illegals aren't trying to write for the Washington Post or be the next ABC news anchor, but they are taking jobs that many Americans want. Further, the illegals are interfering with the upward mobility of American workers by limiting the American worker's ability to enter the workforce. And it is disingenuous to assume business leaders aren't driving this process."

Touche'

Chapter 53   Illegal Workforce – Cheap Labor Adds to the Bottom Line

Who needs foreign labor?

Does the US really need foreign labor or should illegal foreign nationals be deported? I am not a business magnate of a large corporation. I run a very small one-person consulting business and I have been a partner in a few other very small enterprises. So, I have no alternative motivations when I ask this question. I am not hoping that by spending small amounts of capital for an illegal workforce, I can save in labor costs and gain a significant advantage in dominating the world business of my choice. I am not in any such business so for me, the notion is moot. I do ask this question, however, like you would, as a regular human being, and as a lifelong, US native-born citizen. Do we really need foreign labor, especially illegal labor, or should those who have illegally entered our country be deported?

This question is often not a point of discussion in the arguments for or against permitting illegal foreign nationals to operate as citizens, or as workers in the big hiring plants. Let's talk about it. Has the influx of illegal workers into the US made the United States indebted to our neighbors from the south and around the world? Surely, these countries have supplied needed inexpensive labor that some might argue has permitted US citizens to relax, play more golf, and pretend to be fat cats?

Can the United States no longer perform its own work because its people have free time and don't want to give any time up for the mundane things in life such as work? I sure hope this has not happened to US. Gains from sloth and laziness are short lived indeed. If the gift of inexpensive labor is now so important to the well-being of the US, one must critically ask how this work was ever done in the past when, for example, Mexico was Mexico and the US was the US and each did its own work.

In other words, who do we think did those lousy jobs before we were flooded with illegal foreign workers who depended on them to survive in the shadows? Were the jobs never needed before? We Americans are not fooled by the rhetoric of the progressive liberals that we are no longer relevant as the muscle behind our business engine.

As the progressives attempt to minimize the role of real Americans in everyday life, the more it is up to real Americans to stand fast and true. Americans did these jobs and for the most part still do the jobs that are credited to our illegal visitors. American businesses have succumbed in many ways to methods such as labor arbitrage with illegal workers. Suggesting the American worker is to blame for this distortion is one of the charades businesses invoke to cast off the blame from their own shoulders.

America was built by strong hearted and rugged individuals. Their subsequent generations carried on the tradition and brought America from a break-away republic to the world's foremost super-power. When Americans were the first in line for American jobs it was because they were the best workers, not a mere second best.

Americans were paid a fair wage and in industries in which the wage was not fair, unions came and championed the cause of the workers. When productivity increases were not as sharp, perhaps because of a lack of investment on the part of the firm, unscrupulous businessmen noticed an opportunity to drive wages down by hiring illegal workers, who would work for far less money than Americans. This has created a poverty class in the US similar to the Robber Baron days at the turn of the century. This is not good for America.

American workers eventually negotiated fair wages and they received proper benefits so they could live modest lives. As time went by, the government got in the act and insisted that all plants employing US workers in America had to comply with government safety regulations. Nobody, including illegal workers really wants to go to work to do a difficult, lousy, job, especially if they are not paid appropriately to do the work. For its own reasons, however, the US government no longer checks all of the health and safety regulations if Americans do not work there. Why? Maybe it is because Congress and the President find little value in American workers. Then again, maybe it is because it gives illegal workers an advantage. What do you think?

Once the US was flooded with illegal foreign nationals, formerly poor Americans were displaced from their meager jobs and they were replaced by foreign workers who were below the radar of the government watchdogs. These Americans became destitute with no choice as they saw their wages plummet if they were fortunate enough to be invited in to take a job working alongside an illegal non-citizen. Americans were forced onto unemployment and then welfare.

One would suggest to the doubter of this modern day phenomenon that they travel to places in the heartland that have yet to be flooded with non-Americans taking American jobs, and then they travel a bit further, not much further to see the plants in which few if any are citizens. American business and American government together have created this pox on the people of the United States.

When you step outside of the illegal worker comfort zone, you will more than likely see Americans doing the very jobs that the UFW (United Farm Workers) or others claim Americans will not do. Without competing with a force of millions who will work for destitute wages, Americans have no problem working in places where there are actually real jobs that pay the prevailing wage. So, how is it that where the notion of illegal foreign nationals is not accepted as part of the US landscape, America still survives? You already know the answer. Government is the problem.

The fear for businesses of course is that Americans will continue to have jobs with decent wages. That means they will have to pay them. That will keep profits down. A bigger fear is that if companies are forced to use Americans, the incentive for a foreign national to jump the border to take a job decreases. Once an American business uses illegal workers and does not go to jail, the propensity for that company to choose to expand their proportions of illegal workers to American workers increases substantially. For that business risk, they expect big gains on the bottom line. Businesses are accustomed to taking risks but now, their risks include breaking the law simply because they can and nobody in law enforcement seems to care. Ask Janet Napolitano, Big Sis, the big boss.

Americans are not hired when companies are looking to save a buck while planning to exploit illegal foreign nationals. So, if we can put an end to illegal migration, Americans will indeed, once again, be permitted to gain employment in these jobs. To keep sleazy employers from hiring illegal foreign nationals, many think that relying on ID systems such as E-Verify as the law of the land will do the trick. It is easy to notice that in 2010 as the economy worsened, about two-years after Obama claimed the depression was over, Americans were in fact picking crops. Unfortunately again, they were picking at a wage that was substantially lower than if they did not have to compete with an illegal work force that among other injustices, pays little to no taxes.

What country would permit those outside its borders to invade and take the good wages once earned by its citizens and give them to a set of invading marauders of Illegal foreign nationals. These people are in America for its bounty. They care nothing about America or Americans. Additionally, they do not care that their mere presence decreases America's opportunity to provide that bounty to anybody, illegal or legal.

As noted previously, the incessant flood of immigrants continues to drive wages and living conditions in US cities toward those of the Third World. A look westward in the US would show that this notion has already claimed California and Californians as its dead victims. As beautiful as the state of California is and how wonderful it is as a sight-seeing place for all Americans, regular Americans are not happy that California thinks it can become a magnet for the invasion and then be bailed out financially by the rest of America. America has spoken – no more bailouts – even if one day California becomes Mexifornia.

Puppet masters prevail when people become puppets

There are lots of bad things this invasion engenders; among those are a tidal wave of imposed sprawl, gridlock, pollution, and environmental damage on the metropolitan areas of this nation, and yes, even in the homes of the less capable.

Nobody gains when the illegal foreign nationals and their puppet masters have their way on the population of the US.

Chapter 54   Shipping Illegal Workers Back Home— a Choice?

Please appease, please?

Most Americans are very sensitive about calling anybody names, even if they deserve it. The idea of political correctness has gone so far that Americans are sickened by it to the point of inaction. If Vladimir Putin, for example, for example, one day decided he did not want America to defend itself because it was an insult to the Russians, one would almost expect the progressive PC crowd in charge of the government to ask if we might consider handing him over a few states and maybe full control of the oceans and space so that his ire would calm down. Eventually, however, you run out of land and you run out of sea and the invader wants what you have in your pocket. It would be nice to find a brave politician or diplomat in the US today who would consider America first.

Politicians will save the day! Hah!

Have you ever met a dishonest politician? Our dishonest politicians keep telling us that US Immigration laws are broken and we need a sort of a "comprehensive" solution to make all of us well again. But, the astute among us know that these are code words for amnesty. The facts suggest that it is actually our politicians that are broken, not our immigration laws, and we need a comprehensive cleanup to make that all OK again. Some fumigants in their former offices would also help. Some new chairs may also be needed. If you will kindly pardon my French, my first cousin, Jimmy Brady, could say it better than any politically correct politician. Jimmy was a wise one for sure. He always reminded me that you cannot bull-s a bull-s-er. Yet, despite that indisputable fact, our government feeds us one untruth after another, hoping we will all shut-up and play nice. Thank God we are Americans and the game is not over.

The fact is that our immigration laws are not broken. The US Government has merely chosen that they do not wish to enforce them. So, Obama and company have not enforced them by design. It is not an accident. It was deliberate. Throwing the bums out is the only plan to fix this problem. The election of November 2010 began a process that cannot end until the rot is fully removed from Congress.

Ala Carte Justice: Prez picks and choose the laws he defends / enforces

On February 23, 2011, President Barack Obama ordered his administration to stop defending the constitutionality of a federal law, the Defense of Marriage Act, which bans recognition of gay marriage. This law was signed by Bill Clinton and it represented the best that we could all get at the time. Obama doesn't like it so using something called the rule of man, rather than the rule of law (the Constitution), as dictator in chief; he has decided that law just doesn't count.

Obama has done this before. For example, he decided not to prosecute a number of voting rights violations and in fact Eric Holder, the AG has clearly stated that violation of voting rights by a minority group will not be prosecuted! Who is this man who can invoke the rule of man instead of the rule of law. Obama has said not to arrest illegal aliens who have not committed other crimes, yet this to is a violation of the rule of law in favor of the rule of man.

First, it was voting rights and then, border enforcement. The latest unconstitutional act by the Obama administration is the announced betrayal of the Defense of Marriage Act. By choosing to not defend the law of the land, Eric Holder consistently waves the lawlessness of the Obama Administration in the face of Americans. What law will the dictator in chief choose not to enforce next? It is time to openly discuss impeachment as his reward for the utter disregard for law. The ultimate impeachment comes in 2012, when Obama goes back to live with the Emanuel's in Old Chicago House.

Obama creates the broken pieces

Americans who can still think know that the broken piece of the puzzle is the American political system and the federal government's control of immigration. Why do Americans have to put up with a group of bureaucrats who feel it is OK to publicly state that it is OK that they not do their jobs, among which is border enforcement and shipping the invaders home. It is not OK.

Is it not an atrocity when God-fearing Americans elect corrupt / pandering/ lawless politicians who put party, lobbyist, & self-interest ahead of the Constitution of our USA and the rule of law! It may be easy to accept this in good times, but these times are really tough. With the politicians in charge, you can bet things are not going to get any better any time soon.

Suppose the US Congress were able to ram through an amnesty bill to "solve the ills of the country." The proposed immigration amnesty would more than likely benefit the 12 to 50 or more million illegal foreign nationals (illegal aliens) who are currently living in the United States. An amnesty for illegal aliens program forgives their acts of illegal aggression and implicitly forgives other related illegal acts such as illegal driving and working with false documents. It also tells others back home in Mexico and other nations to come on down! The result of an amnesty is that large numbers of foreign nationals, who illegally gain entry into the United States, are rewarded with legal status, green card, or the grand prize,

American citizenship for breaking the line while breaking US immigration laws. It is not fair and it is not right.

President Barack Obama said "we are not going to ship back 12 million people." Note that the President uses the number 12 million though he knows it is more like 50 million. You can't bull-s a bull-s-er. Obama said; "we're not going to do it as a practical matter. We would have to take all our law enforcement that we have available and we would have to use it and put people on buses, and rip families apart, and that's not who we are, that's not what America is about." What a bunch of hooey! I suspect it could rightfully be categorized as bull-s.

What would it cost to deport illegal aliens?

Is the President correct that we cannot afford to ship people back? Has the President been right on many matters over the last few years? Is President Obama suggesting that this poor hapless country called the United States that fought countless wars to keep its freedoms, now cannot protect its own borders from potential aggressors? This country somehow was able to put the first man on the moon and through its exceptionalism has become the most powerful nation on earth. But, the President believes we don't have it in us to remove the perpetrators that occupy our lands illegally. I think the president is wrong again. In many ways, deportation is our least costly option. Why would we permit Mexico and others to export their poor in such a way that we Americans may barely survive?

Before the end of the 1960's while other countries were still trying to accomplish more simple endeavors, such as perfecting moonshine, the US was on to one-of-a-kind major accomplishments. The Southern US had already perfected moonshine. Let's not forget that President Kennedy, a person, who loved America and Americans, toasted heartily the work of Neil Armstrong after his moon walk in June 1969, months ahead of schedule. Can it be that Obama was kidding about America not having the will or the capability to deport 50,000,000 aliens?

Since these aggressors have now chosen to live on American soil, and they do not appear willing to leave on their own, what are we to make of the current President's posture? Does he think that this poor, once mighty, but now apparently helpless country of ours will ever again be able to muster the resources to protect its citizens by locating and deporting the perpetrators that have snuck in through our porous borders? While we are at it, the US has what it takes to fix the borders also.

Does President Obama like US?

President Obama is coming very close to becoming the worst president in history or at a minimum, the worst in my lifetime. His record on immigration is worst than George Bush, and that my friends is B-A-D. He may be America's best orator ever but he lost some credence in 2010 when he substituted the former best orator, Bill Clinton into a press conference about the tax hikes for the rich. Maybe Obama is # 2 and Mr. Clinton is again # 1? Either way, he is a fine speaker.

However, the content of his speeches is not as good as the delivery. With his constant apologies and his attacks on the spirit and the capabilities and the exceptionalism of Americans, it makes you wonder if he is for US or against US. Obama does not seem to like the type of America in which he finds himself. Most Americans have become who they are because their families have been dipped into the melting pot in North America known as the US of A. At the risk of sounding like a birther, perhaps the Prez has not had enough of a dipping to like who he says he is.

Why does the President seem to find solace in marginalizing the American people and praising others? His words are at once demoralizing and stimulating because they make me angry. They also make other hard working Americans angry and that stimulates many of us to fight this asininity and to prove the President wrong on the will of America. I know I do not have to convince our countrymen that America can do anything it well pleases. Americans as a whole always choose to do well, and the spirit of a huge melting pot provides the ingredients to ensure exceptionalism.

If Obama and Congress won't do it for us, it is time for all good Americans to show them the door. Good leadership is a lot easier to find than a few hundred million good people. Americans are good people. You are good; we are good. We are in fact, exceptional and capable of many good and truly amazing things. Can we send 50,000,000 invaders back to their home countries? We can do that in a heartbeat with the right leadership and we can figure out how to do it without it costing a dime of taxpayer money.

When Charles E. Weller was looking for a good typing drill, he chose the sentence, "Now is the time for all good men to come to the aid of the party" His phrase was picked up by many typing books. However, over time, the phrase was improved to the variant "Now is the time for all good men to come to the aid of their country." This happens to exactly fill out a 70-space line if you put a period at the end so it is perfect for typing school. I would like to suggest that if we use the older use of "men" to mean "a human regardless of sex or age," the term is also perfect to describe what all citizens of the United States must now do to protect our country from being overwhelmed by illegal foreign nationals. Let's repeat this one more time and type it if we must to remember it well in this, the second decade of the new millennium: "Now is the time for all good men to come to the aid of their country." Thank you. Are you ready?

Can we afford deportation?

Mac Johnson has done a lot of work trying to figure out whether we could really afford deporting illegal aliens if we chose to do so. Of course the President has America pegged as the country that "can't," so we won't refer to Obama any more in this chapter on whether we can or can't. I like to say that "if you think you can't, you're right," so let's leave the doubting Obama at the door as we figure out what we can do. He thinks we can't. He's wrong!

Mac wrote a piece on the Web titled, "What Would it Cost to Deport Illegal Aliens?" Maybe one day he can write another piece that discusses reasons why it is OK and not politically incorrect for all of us to talk about deporting illegal aliens. Of whom should we be afraid?

Talking about it is the first step to getting it done. That's why subtly the notion of deporting illegal foreign nationals is on the media politically incorrect list. Too bad! Talk, talk and talk some more about ridding our country of these foreign invaders and soon we will be able to do so. That is a much better alternative than merely accepting that they will always be among us. I am not suggesting again that they are bad people. The bad guys are the businesses that made their lives miserable while they made millions, the unions who encourage politicians, and the dirty politicians who let it happen. If it were up to me, I would deport them all, the unwelcome visitor, person who lured them into America with the promise of a job. And the dirt bags that want their votes once they are registered.

Deportation has been a US prerogative for centuries and now the pro-amnesty crowd thinks it should be unacceptable in practice and even in open speech. From having read the other parts of this book, you know that the government and union leaders, and corporations, and even smaller businesses do their best to convince American citizens that they should accept illegal foreign nationals as part of the landscape and stop complaining. They do not tell you that the only group not to gain in this scenario is you. You represent a part of what can be called, "current American citizens." Over 70% of the citizen population thinks as we do about illegal immigration.

We'll have none of it. We the normal everyday citizens of the country have been sold out by all of the important people in the above groups in America who comprise the ruling class. These groups all gain from illegal aliens being permitted to do as they please in our country. *We the people* do not gain. We lose. It's time to put a big thumb to your nose to these people who gain at your expense. Tell them to find another back to break to have their dirty little secret mission fulfilled. This is our country. Let them try Russia to find good, cheap employees. Get out of America!

It is so asinine that it defies logic but the stakes are so high that there is institutionalized lying by the establishment to get Americans prepared and fully buffaloed. Our leaders want us to get ready for a country in which we must cohabitate with people who care nothing about the ideals of America, which helped found our great nation. We shall overcome. They were good words when used in the Civil Rights Movement and they are good words now again in this the Citizens' Rights Movement, which some have called the TEA Party Movement.

On August 1, 2005, Mac Johnson, a columnist for Human Events Online **http://www.humanevents.com/article.php?id=8387** wrote about the cost of deportation. "

> "Imagine that you came home tomorrow and found a stranger living in your home. Would you pay $148 to have him removed, or would you instead just legally adopt him and give him the run of the place to save the $148? The *Center for American Progress*, a liberal think tank headed by liberal John Podesta and funded by billionaire

interventionist George Soros, based in Washington, D.C., thinks the *practical* thing to do would be adopt the *undocumented family member* that broke into your home."

Are these tough questions? I don't think so. Can you imagine that they said, that in one way or another, we should choose to live with the illegals among us, rather than tell them to go home? This progressive group put forth the notion that it is better to take an occupier into your home (far better) than trying to deport illegal foreign nationals. Their argument for you having another mouth to feed is that it will cost more to tell him to leave (deport him.) Their conclusion therefore is that the US should give amnesty to all 50 million illegal aliens in the country because; after all they had a tough time getting here. They smuggled themselves into our homeland and they have already been living with us all these years so, so what's the big deal? Hah?

Johnson continued in his article:

> "According to the study, which was dutifully reported by the Washington Post, and others interested, it would cost the Federal Government $41 billion per year over a five year period to take what they call the "draconian" step of actually enforcing our immigration laws.

> "Let's pretend, for just a moment that the ghost of the bloody Greek King Dracon is not laughing hysterically at the idea that being deported home in an air-conditioned bus is now considered "draconian." And while we're in fantasyland, let us also pretend that the $41 billion per year figure is even remotely accurate. The Federal Government has an annual budget of $2.34 trillion per year. [2005 figure] Our Gross Domestic Product is a staggering $12 trillion per year [2005 figure]. $41 billion would be just 1.7% of the Federal budget, and a miniscule 0.34% of our GDP.

> "Yet the *Center for American Progress [far left group]* would have us believe that this sum is so far beyond us that we should instead surrender our country to whomever shows up in whatever numbers, rather than pay it. To put it in perspective, 0.34% would be $148 for someone earning $43,527 per year, the median family income in America. This is probably no more than what you paid for the locksets in your home."

Dollars per citizen for deportation

The spin on the trauma caused to illegal foreign nationals by sending them back home for free is worthy of a big laugh.

Let's look again in 2010 terms about that $41 billion per year figure. The feds' budget is so huge that in 2010 it was too big for the Congress and President to even create a budget. There was no budget on into 2011 but there was a big fight in 1Q 2011 (March) as the progressives thought they can dump the irascible results of their wild 2010 spending spree on the backs of Republicans in the House.

Thus, theoretically, 2010 can be looked on as the year of limitless Democratic spending as Pleosi and Reid and Obama controlled it all and though they were supposed to turn in a budget, they had all the power and decided to not go through the work so voters would not see how bad it was at election time. Even if I had not told you, you would agree that it sure seems that they saw a checking account with no bottom, and they used it and used it and used it. So, to suggest there was no money for deportation is quite disingenuous.

Any shiny little item in the store has already been purchased by the Obama Administration, paid for by the grandchildren of the people of the United States, and made available to anybody who has an affinity for the Muslim religion. At any rate, I am sure you agree that "limitless" is lots more than $41 billion per year.

Despite having no money in 2010, Obama and the 111th Congress spent IOU's the whole time they were in control, and then they keep on spending. In September 2010, you may recall, after the teacher and union bailout, the Administration pushed for another small stimulus for unions of a mere $50 billion. Independent thinkers saw this as a payoff so that no union member was forced to suffer any pain whatsoever from the recession. The wrapper on this legislation has a big bow on it that said, "Thanks for your vote." And, yes, Virginia, the taxpayers footed the bill for a $50 billion Obama campaign promise to unions.

What a slap in the face for those of us who actually work for a living, who have to pay for this nonsense! When there is a gift to unions from Obama, $50 billion is considered chump change. However, when it might take just $41 billion a year to give all illegal's tickets to get home, that is a huge expenditure from a poor and destitute country and it is thus deemed unaffordable by the dictator in chief. Somebody is lying and lying repeatedly and his administration begins with the letter O.

What might the next lie be? Besides the typical every election day scare for seniors that the "ghost of George Bush is going to take away social security," how about this for a little thicker prevarication. None of this is close to being true so do not let these fear mongers get to you. The next lie may be that "if all of the illegal aliens are not granted amnesty post haste, social security will go broke in three days and Medicare will be taken over by the Kevorkian Institute of Happy Deaths." Yes, on the last note, I am definitely kidding.

Even though that is intended to be in jest, it is still chilling. I can see some goof in the US Health Department making a proposal to that effect some time soon. Perhaps Cass Sunstein, Obama's all-everything regulation czar, will weigh in on that one. Do you trust the government to do what is right for you and your country? Do you trust the government to fill in a pot hole with cold patch correctly? How have they been doing lately?

Russia once was the propaganda leader

If Communist Russia had as fine a Propaganda Minister as the three mainstream TV networks in America, plus the federal government itself, the USSR would still be the name of a place to live. It would still be alive. Eventually the lies catch up to you. Mr. Gorbachev turned out to be a good man at a good time and so Russia is now merely Russia, and Poland is Poland. The brutal USSR is dead while Obama is trying to reincarnate all of the ills of the USSR right in our own backyard.

Americans know in their hearts that their politicians have and continue to deliver to them the proverbial "sh--ty end of the stick." My apologies for that. But it is one lie after another. Sometimes the proverbs are left behind, metaphorically speaking.

I would not be the first to suggest that the $41 Billion deportation cost would pay for itself and be a big bargain for taxpayers even if it were an accurate number and we know it is way too high.

Cost of deportation in numbers

Suppose all illegal foreign nationals were gone tomorrow. How much would that save the US per year as a rough estimate?

- Direct Cost to the Federal Government: $12 Billion
- California -- amount to provide services to illegals $10 Billion
- Other states -- amount to provide services to illegals $25 Billion
- Total per year -- $47 Billion minus Deportation Cost $41 Billion = $6 Billion

These cost numbers are low. So, at the very least, there would be a net gain of $6 billion. Sounds like a good deal already. Looks like we can afford to deport all illegals and have it over in 5 years and make some money on it. We can actually make some more money.

What about property seizure like they do in drug actions? Can we do this? It is done all the time for drug related crimes so the answer is yes we can. Since it can be readily presumed that every employed illegal foreign national earns money. Therefore they own something and they probably have some small savings. So, there are theoretical sources of assets to seize.

To prove this amount, it is well known that Illegal immigrants send as much as $20 billion per year to their home countries. Some say this amount approaches $100 billion but let's stick with $20 billion. These are recorded in the process of making the wire transfers from America to Mexico. All of this is contraband earned by illegal means, and so it can legally be confiscated. But, admittedly, one interrupted wire transfer and that would be the end of getting the dollars that way. Let's say we can get a one-time amount of $20 Billion through this cash source. Over a five year period, this would be $4 Billion per year.

Is there anything else? Most people, including illegal aliens have at least a clunker of a car and small amounts of personal property. Suppose this all amounts to about $4,000 in total for each illegal foreign national in residence. That would mean that each of the 30 to 50 million illegal foreign nationals in this country have $120 billion worth of assets in total subject to seizure. If you say there are not 30 million illegal foreign nationals, I would argue that point. My personal estimate is 50 million. I'll chop off 10 million to make it more realistic for the doubters. So, we start the numbers at 40 million.

But let's even cut this in half to save the arguing and we now 20 billion aliens at $4,000 each or $80 billion worth of assets to seize. If we take this over a five year period, the time the *Center for American Progress* thinks it would take to deport all illegal aliens, this would mean that deporting illegal aliens would earn the United States a profit upwards of $16 billion per year in seizures. Let's now redo our numbers:

- Direct Cost to the Federal Government: $12 Billion
- California -- amount to provide services to illegals $10 Billion
- Other states -- amount to provide services to illegals $25 Billion
- Cash -- $4 Billion
- Assets -- $16 Billion
- Total per year -- $67 Billion minus Deportation Cost $41 Billion = $26Billion

So, the net gain for the country would be $26 Billion per year. Let Timothy Geithner tell me why we have any financial reason why we cannot deport illegal foreign nationals. These are people who have invaded our country and who are demanding in many cases that we fund their daily lives ad infinitum along with the lives of their children.

I know that Americans do not want to take anything from poor people. Clearly illegal foreign nationals who are not employed in the drug trade or in criminal activity are poor people. If an illegal alien broke into your home and stole $4,000 would you want it back? If you let them keep it, even if caught, would they not go after $4,000 from somebody else next time they needed something.

Illegal foreign nationals have broken into our country and they use up government services paid for by taxpayers. The toll they exact on America needs to be paid back or just like any thief (sorry I have to use that term), they will be back. If they did not use US services and they paid their own way, it would be a different story. Then, it would be merely their presence in the US (50 million uninvited people) that would be a problem, but they have taken from us, and we have a right to take it back.

However, even if our hearts will not permit us to seize their meager amounts of cash and their clunker cars etc., looking at the numbers only, by sending them back home, the US would still save $6 Billion per year minimum using the conservative estimates above.

Even these estimates are off by a long shot, however. They are very, very conservative. In other words, the savings would be substantially more. In July, 2010, Ed Barnes of FOX news wrote an article about a study that had just been completed to get some real numbers for the cost part of the equation. I do not mean the $41Billion to send them back home; I mean what it costs us to not send them home. The numbers are actually astonishing:

> "The cost of harboring illegal immigrants in the United States is a staggering $113 billion a year -- an average of $1,117 for every "native-headed" household in America -- according to a study conducted by the Federation for American Immigration Reform (FAIR)."

So, this makes it an even more financially compelling notion to send them home right away. Many Americans are taking more notice to the flurry of illegal foreign nationals living among us with impunity. Americans not only see jobs being taken, they see direct withdrawals from the local, state, and national treasuries, mostly from services taken and not paid for. There is also a decrease in the quality of life along with an increased level of fear of being harmed by some of the not-so-nice illegal foreign nationals who are in the 50 million.

Most citizens cannot believe our government has permitted it to get this bad. If citizens have not been paying attention for the last 30 years, they may be surprised, but most are now well aware of what has been happening, and very few are happy about it.

Lou Barletta of Hazleton PA is a hometown hero who was just elected to Congress to see what he can do about the mess the country is in. He was interviewed by the Reading Eagle in Reading, Bucks County, PA in October, 2007. Barletta has a number of specifics about what was affecting the "quality of life" in Hazleton, and it is captured in this quote from the Eagle:

> "Barletta said he actually is just the mayor of a small, financially strapped Luzerne County city who is trying to improve the quality of life for legal residents with laws penalizing landlords and businesses that exploit illegal immigrants.

> "Thirty percent of the drug arrests we made in the last two years were illegal immigrants," said Barletta, who has made headlines nationwide with his stand. "Thirty percent of the gang members are illegal immigrants.

> "It's estimated that 10 percent of our entire population is illegal.

> "We were watching the quality of life being destroyed. How could I sit back and do nothing?"

The people just cannot figure out when government decided it was in charge, instead of the people. The dictator in chief is only dictator is we let him. Why do immigration laws mean nothing while city property tax ordinances are powerful enough for you to lose your home after no payments for just a few years? How patient must taxpayers be with a government that demands but does not deliver?

Our representatives passed these laws. Perhaps they were easily influenced by the guilt-ridden hippies from the 1960's or they are one and the same. The people wonder why government is no longer working for real Americans and it no longer has the fiduciary responsibility for assuring that our treasury is either saved or spent for the causes advocated by real Americans.

The Federal Government saw a major musical chair movement, one of the biggest of all time on November 2, 2010. There was a two-month lame duck session to give the bad guys time to pack. Unfortunately, this Congress with many members who had just been kicked out decided to try to inflict some additional damage before they were fully packed. Among other things, they tried a de-facto amnesty bill that was defeated. Who do they think they represent?

Is it not an untenable situation that we have these foreign nationals living among us in the shadows and the darkness? Of course it is. Worse than that, in many cases, honest, hard-working Americans are paying their way. How did that happen and why has deportation been taken off the table by Obama when each day illegal foreign nationals come to collect their free services? Did President Obama not take an oath to uphold the laws of the US and the Constitution? Was he kidding? Does he think he is dictator in chief?

Consider the following:

What if we just informed illegal foreign nationals that they had a month or more to get out for good? We should not have to round them up and deport them at $41 Billion per year. That is way high. Instead, how about getting them to leave on their own? Start by telling them to leave and making sure we mean it. I found a plan on the Internet that looks pretty good for Americans. Here is that plan in a nutshell:

If you cannot prove you are here legally, then the following should happen to you:

- ✓ You will not be allowed to work here.
- ✓ You will not be allowed any kind of social services, except life threatening emergencies.
- ✓ Your children will not be allowed in our school systems
- ✓ Your babies will only be US Citizens if both parents were here legally at the time.

Soon the travel bookings out of the US would be at all time highs.

Here is another list of notions that I found on the Internet as additional reasons for deportation. These would theoretically be the ones Obama would enforce, though unfortunately, I don't really think we can count on him. Do you?

How about deporting the illegals that:

- Get arrested for anything.
- Drive without a license and insurance.
- Use someone else's social security.
- Live in buildings higher than the safe occupancy rate

Illegal foreign nationals should do time in prison and earn their own money to be escorted to their own country. There should be no free rides to Mexico so they would not be encouraged to pay the cost to come back.

Somehow we citizens of the US are numbed by the progressive / Marxist / liberal media to not believe even the obvious: People who sneak into our country are forgiven even though they are breaking the law! The male illegal foreign national who chooses to father children with another illegal foreign national knows the child will be an American. How dumb is that for a country trying to dissuade perpetrators from crossing its borders. If you were looking for more illegal foreign nationals, you would have a policy that made the children of the violators, citizens? Maybe that is what the government is doing.

Oh, and then our laws (who made those laws?) force our states to pay medical care for illegal foreign nationals. Sometimes the law says states must pay housing and education. And, there needs to be no reimbursement back to the citizens ever, and the person getting the service can stay in the country with impunity.

Why should Americans make it easy for those who have abrogated our sovereignty by their very presence in our country? Why do we permit them to keep taking advantage of our American systems? Who made such silly laws? The answer to most of the problems in the US today can be given in one word: Congress. But there are a lot of state legislatures who share the blame. We as citizens must replace our Congress and these errant legislatures as many times as need be to get a set of representatives that thinks first for America.

Employers that hire illegal foreign nationals serve as the magnets that attract them like mayflies. Employers of illegal workers, whether the worker comes as an employee or from a contractor should not only be fined for paying them for their work, the big perpetrators should have their businesses compromised by special taxes. Of course the executives can agree to imprisonment and that would be OK for me. Employers should pay to have all of those hurt by the new deportation plan, escorted back to their country in style.

Does the US need foreign labor?

I know I have asked this question in this book before. It is the consummate question. Does the US need foreign labor? No way… no how. It is a ruse to get Americans to accept others doing their jobs on the cheap. Recently it has been a ruse to get Americans to accept others taking their jobs.

The end comment is that we can and should deport illegal foreign workers. We can afford it and we probably would make money on it by not spending as much to support these folks.

Alan Keyes

I can talk about Alan Keyes forever as he is one of my favorite statesmen. He is a great American who makes me proud to be an American. We have a great man living among us today, Ambassador Alan Keyes. He is a great thinker. You may know that he ran for president several times and the US would be a better country for sure if Alan Keyes were ever to get a shot at running the country. We can only pray.

Keyes has a few succinct bullets on borders and immigration, and let me come close to a close of this chapter with bullets to link you to what Keyes writes and writes and writes. He is one of the best. The bullets below are not just bullets on his Web site, they are the titles of essays he has written on the subject of illegal immigration. As you can see, Keyes has been writing on the topic for quite awhile. You would enjoy any of these essays so go read them when you have a chance. Feel free to plug an essay title into Google or your favorite search engine and have a good read. Keyes' bullets include:

- Vigilant maintenance of our sovereign territory and borders. (Aug 2008)
- Enforce existing laws against illegal immigration. (Oct 2007)
- Sovereignty is betrayed when our borders are not defended. (Oct 2007)
- Immigration, yes; colonization, no: oppose guest workers. (Oct 2007)
- Control border first, or no other laws mater. (Sep 2007)
- Blacks are hurt first by cheap immigrant labor. (Sep 2007)
- Excessive multiculturalism weakens American culture. (Sep 2007)
- Rescind Bush's order allowing Mexican trucks on US roads. (Sep 2007)
- Oppose amnesty & guest workers until unemployment under 5%. (Sep 2007)
- Extending privileges to non-citizens invites lawbreaking. (Sep 2004)
- Expand legal immigration; curtail illegal immigration. (Jul 1996)

Thank you Alan Keyes,

Thank you for understanding American exceptionalism.

No amount of illegal labor can remove the American people of its spirit and its desire to keep America strong. The use of illegal foreign nationals as workers in that process is not only unacceptable, it is unnecessary.

Chapter 55   Bear Stearns Report: Underground Labor Force Rising To the Surface

Prologue by Brian Kelly

The Wall Street investment firm Bear Stearns published a report, The Underground Labor Force is Rising to the Surface, in January 2005. Their report claims that the illegal alien population is double the official government estimates and was closer to 20 million, at that time. In this book, we use 40 million to 50 million as what appears to be a more appropriate number. Bear Sterns made this report available for free in many venues on the Internet and so, because this is a landmark work on the real problem of illegal immigration and jobs, we present it here in its entirety. You don't see truth like this very often anymore.

Many readers know that Bear Sterns was one of the first casualties of the subprime mortgage crisis. If you think you have heard of Bear Sterns, you are probably right. With all of the clandestine activity shielding the government's and business's collusion to protect the illegal workforce, perhaps it was no accident that there is no longer a Bear Sterns. They will never be able to write another scathing commentary, laden with facts, about the business aspects of illegal immigration in the US. Bear Sterns is gone for good.

Could the fate of the Bear Stearns Company in the United States have been sealed so that when the subprime mortgage crisis hit, the company was viewed as not worthy enough to save. After all, it was not Goldman Sachs. Bear Sterns trip to oblivion did however spark a great deal of public comment and concern but nobody tied anything back to this report on illegal immigration. Perhaps there is no link. Perhaps there is.
You may recall that in just one month, Bear Sterns stock value fell from almost $100.00 to $2.00. Bear Sterns was headed for bankruptcy. However, before bankruptcy took place, the company was quickly acquired by JPMorgan Chase on March 16, 2008. That this could happen so quickly gave great concern that the American economy was in serious trouble. You know the rest of the story.

Sit back now and enjoy this expose from some of the smartest people in the world, the folks at Bear Sterns. Unfortunately, perhaps in its key business, Bear Sterns was a little too smart for its own good.

Enjoy!
Robert Justich and Betty Ng, CFA
January 3, 2005

Illegal immigrants constitute a large and growing force in the political, economic, and investment spheres in The United States. The size of this extra-legal segment of the population is significantly understated because the official U.S.Census does not capture the total number of illegal immigrants. In turn, the growth of the underground work force is increasingly concealing the economic impact of this below-market labor supply. Our research has identified significant evidence that the census estimates of undocumented immigrants may be capturing as little as half of the total undocumented population. This gross undercounting is a serious accounting issue, which could ultimately lead to government policy errors in the future.

Though we cannot conduct an independent census of the United States population, as investors, we need not accept the accuracy of the official census immigration statistics, which are widely recognized as incomplete. There are many ancillary sources of data that provide evidence that the rate of growth in the immigrant population is much greater than the Census Bureau statistics. School enrollments, foreign remittances, border crossings, and housing permits are some of the statistics that point to a far greater rate of change in the immigrant population than the census numbers. At the risk of appearing dogmatic or taking a leap of faith, we have applied the rate of growth from these other areas and have drawn several conclusions about the current immigration population:

1. The number of illegal immigrants in the United States may be as high as 20 million people, more than double the official 9 million people estimated by the Census Bureau.

2. The total number of legalized immigrants entering The United States since 1990 has averaged 962,000 per year. Several credible studies indicate that the number of illegal entries has recently crept up to 3 million per year, triple the authorized figure.

3. Undocumented immigrants are gaining a larger share of the job market, and hold approximately 12 to 15 million jobs in the United States (8% of the employed)

4. Four to six million jobs have shifted to the underground market, as small businesses take advantage of the vulnerability of illegal residents.

5. In addition to circumventing the Immigration Reform and Control Act of 1986, many employers of illegal workers have taken to using unrecorded revenue receipts. Employer enforcement has succumbed to political pressure.

6. Cell phones, internet and low-cost travel have allowed immigrants easier illegal access to the United States and increased their ability to find employment and circumvent immigration laws.

We believe that immigration is becoming one of the most significant economic themes of this decade. The investment implications for 2005 and 2006 will hinge on the forthcoming government policy decisions in amnesty, employer enforcement, and monitoring systems, as well as the effective enforcement of the laws. Over the coming year, we intend to monitor and analyze the benefits and costs of assimilating a demographic group the size of New York State into the financial and legal mainstream. Though this challenge is not quite the magnitude of, say, German reunification, we believe most investors are underestimating the magnitude and significance of this theme.

The growing extralegal system in the United States has distorted economic statistics and government budget projections. The stealth labor force has enhanced many of the economic releases that investors follow closely. Payroll numbers understate true job growth and inflation has been artificially dampened by this seemingly endless supply of low-wage workers. The large infusion of the imported labor supply has reduced average annual earnings by approximately 4 to 6 percent. Real estate prices have been boosted by the foreign population infusion. The productivity miracle may be exaggerated because the government is incorporating the output of millions of illegal immigrants but not counting their full labor input. Long-term budget projections are probably overstating the potential growth of the U.S. economy because productivity is inflated. Or, stated differently, are long-term growth projections dependent on a steady flow of illegal immigration that no one is taking into account?

As census procedures improve and the immigration numbers are revised closer to reality, many of these questions will be answered, and public perceptions will change. Many government forecasts, policies and procedures will be modified to compensate for the undercounting. The public sector will incur significant costs in assimilating a reclassified population. An abrupt increase in employer enforcement could have a negative impact on GDP. In the short-term, an adjustment to immigration policies could squeeze small business profits and increase the budget deficits. Longer-term, we believe the effects will be more balanced as this invisible work force provides aid to the demographic problems of social security. Increased enforcement of legal employment procedures should also boost tax revenues.

The implications of these massive inflows of workers are enormous. Although there are economic benefits to cheap, illegal labor, there are significant costs associated with circumventing the labor laws. The social expenses of health care, retirement funding, education and law enforcement are potentially accruing at $30 billion per year. Many of these costs lag and will not be realized until the next economic downturn and beyond as new immigrants require a safety net.

On the revenue side, the United States may be foregoing $35 billion a year in income tax collections because of the number of jobs that are now off the books. Illegal aliens offer below market labor costs and many employers circumvent regulations to take advantage of the laissez faire government enforcement process. We estimate that approximately 5 million illegal workers are collecting wages on a cash basis and are avoiding income taxes.

The United States is simply hooked on cheap, illegal workers and deferring the costs of providing public services to these quasi-Americans. Illegal immigration has been America's way of competing with the low-wage forces of Asia and Latin America, and deserves more credit for the steroid-enhanced effect it has had on productivity, low inflation, housing starts, and retail sales.

From a personal standpoint, our research does not take sides with any of the emotional arguments of the *Crossfire* mindset. We are grateful to have had the opportunity to speak with immigrants, local business owners, realtors, and police officers. This project afforded us the opportunity to see into the past and look into the future of the United States.

Problems with the Census: The missing half

The Census Bureau estimates that 8.7 million people are illegally residing in the United States, while the Urban Institute estimates a total of 9.3 million people. The Current Population Survey (CPS), a joint project of the Bureau of Labor Statistics and the Census Bureau, puts the number at 9.2 million. In a recent report released in November 2004, the Center for Immigration Studies (CIS) stated that the CPS could have missed as many as 10% of illegal aliens, suggesting a total illegal population of 10 million as of March 2004. We believe that these estimates fall short. The Census Bureau's counting process for the migrant population has some shortcomings. According to our discussions with illegal immigrants, they avoid responding to census questionnaires. For this reason, the official estimates do not fully capture this group. The CPS, the Census Bureau, the Urban Institute, and the former INS (now part of the Department of Homeland Security) all use similar processes to determine the total number of immigrants, and which immigrants should be categorized as legal and illegal. In essence, this has created a circular equation that relies on a singular source of inaccurate statistics that gives the impression of independent, multiple verifications.

According to a recent study by the Migration Research Unit, University College London, a wide range of methods have been used to measure immigration flows, which by definition eludes registration and statistical coverage. "Estimating the numbers of illegal resident persons in a country is a task made extremely difficult by the unrecorded nature of the phenomenon, by the problems of the data that are recorded and the different definitions, data sources, collection methods and legislative differences between countries. The dynamism and fluctuation in the size of the illegal population is as much related to the intricacies of the immigration law as to the movements of the migrants themselves." Studies of methods used to calculate the illegal population have concluded that no existing method "provides a well-founded or rigorous method by which to measure the illegal population."

The Congressional Budget Office acknowledges "deriving estimates of the number of unauthorized, or illegal, immigrants is difficult because the government lacks administrative records of their arrival and departure, and because they tend to be undercounted in the census and other surveys of the population. Unauthorized immigrants generally fall into one of two categories: those who entered the United States illegally and without inspection and those who were admitted legally as visitors or temporary residents but overstayed their visa."

According to Maxine Margolis, author of *An Invisible Minority: Brazilians in New YorkCity*, the discrepancies started well over a decade ago. The 1990 census, for example, recorded only 9,200 Brazilians in New York City, while the local Brazilian consulate estimated 100,000 Brazilians at that time. The Brazilian foreign office placed the number at 230,000; Dr. Margolis also noted that comparisons of the Boston Archdiocese and Brazilian consulate records with U.S. census records show a startling 10 to 1 difference.

The latest census taken in 2000 significantly revised the number of illegal immigrants upward versus 1990 projections. The INS also increased their estimates. Upward revisions to such projections have been a consistent trend.

The Implications of Illegal Labor

Regardless of the politics of immigration, getting an accurate read on the size of the current wave is important. Tax collections, budget projections and school capacity planning are a few of the public sectors functions that rely on accurate head counts. Eventually, the official statistics will catch up with the new reality that global migration is exploding. When population and labor force statistics are properly synchronized, we will see an impact on financial markets, economic statistics and social policy.

These revisions will bring some difficult decisions to the surface, as it seems that we have been living in a state of denial for almost a decade. If indeed, the number of illegal immigrants is 20 million people, approximately the equivalent of New York State, any amnesty or legalization and assimilation process will require significant public sector resources.

Illegal immigrants work very hard to conceal their identities and successfully avoid being counted. Even apprehended illegal migrants will hide important personal data on their status to avoid removal. Census officials and academics underestimate the ingenuity and the efficiency of the communications network among immigrants. Understandably, illegal immigrants go to great lengths to maintain a low profile and conceal their identities, not only for census purposes, but for tax purposes as well. The risk–reward trade of dodging census inquiries is severely skewed. Migrants that pay large portions of future earnings to gain entry into the United States make the sacrifice of leaving their families behind, or have trekked through physical obstacles and thousands of miles; accordingly, they have no downside risk in discarding census surveys.

Employers also have incentive to hire undocumented workers off the books, taking advantages of inefficient immigration enforcement. The competitive winds of deflation from overseas labor markets have forced U.S. employers to find extra-legal, innovative ways to capitalize on sources of cheaper labor to stay competitive. These employers have, in turn, placed pressure on the government to ignore the flood of cheap labor. INS enforcement of employer violations has decreased dramatically over the last five years. This trend is counter intuitive, given the substantial rise in illegal immigration during a new era of national security.

Evidence Beyond Anecdotal

The strongest evidence supporting our theory that the actual illegal population is double the consensus estimates lies within several micro trends at the community level. We see very dramatic increases in services required in communities that have become gateways for immigration. States with high populations of undocumented immigrants have experienced extra demand for public services. The top nine states, California, Texas, Florida, New York, Illinois , New Jersey, Arizona, Georgia and North Carolina account for approximately 50% of the undocumented population. Although the federal government has the sole authority to govern immigration flows, the responsibility for providing support to legal and illegal immigrants rests with the state and local governments

The de facto administration at the state and local level reinforces our premise that we must look at local statistics to extrapolate the most reliable headcount of immigrants. **The increases in services, including public school enrollment, language proficiency programs, and building permits all point to a rate of change far greater than the census numbers would imply for the demand for these local services.** The growth in these areas indicates that more people are moving into these communities than the official estimates.

Chart 1. INS (now USCIS) Enforcements

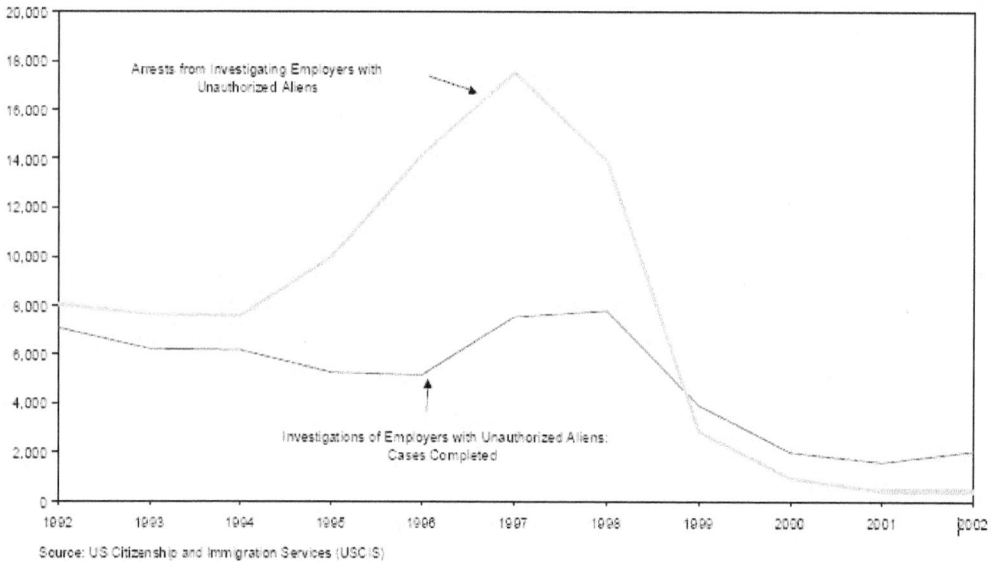

Source: US Citizenship and Immigration Services (USCIS)

Based on several criteria, we believe that immigration is growing significantly faster than the consensus estimates:

1. Remittances
2. Housing permits in gateway communities
3. School enrollment
4. Cross border flows

Remittances

Many immigrants, particularly those with immediate families in their native country, provide financial support to those left behind. Remittances are surging because many immigrants send home on average $1,400 to $1,500 per year through money transfers. In 2002, people sent $133 billion worldwide, according to the World Bank. Developing countries accounted for $88 billion of the total, up 33% from $60 billion in 2000.

Countries that are experiencing migration outflows are having very large increases in remittances. Remittances from the United States to Mexico have tripled to $13 billion between 1995 and 2003. For Mexico, this is an important source of funds that has surpassed foreign direct investments and tourism receipts in 2003, and is second only to petroleum export revenues.

Most importantly, this explosion in remittances is not consistent with the estimates of legal and illegal immigrants from Mexico. The rate of increase in remittances far exceeds the increases in Mexicans residing in the U.S. and their wage growth. Between 1995 and 2003, the official tally of Mexicans has climbed 56%, and median weekly wage has increased by 10%. Yet total remittances jumped 199% over the same period. Even considering the declining costs of money transfers, the growth of remittances remains astounding.

The rapid addition of bank accounts by Mexicans living in the U.S. is also revealing. According to the Pew Hispanic Center, 39% of surveyed Latino immigrants cited legal status as a concern for opening bank accounts. This motivates many immigrants to remit cash through private money centers such as Western Union and Money Gram, which charge very high fees. Since late 2001, however, many major banks including Citibank, Bank of America, and Wells Fargo Bank began accepting *matriculas*, photographed identity cards for Mexicans living in the U.S. These cards show the local addresses of the holders, and any legal or illegal Mexican can obtain it at one of the 45 Mexican consulates across the country. The removal of legal status as a concern for opening and using bank accounts has led to a boom in retail business for some banks. Wells Fargo opens an average of 700 new accounts everyday based on this identification, representing the fastest growing segment for the bank. To date, around 2.5 million *matriculas* have been issued, and the number is growing.

Housing permits

In major immigrant gateway cities, the influx of immigrants has led to overcrowded dwellings and a housing boom unexplained by official population growth. Many illegal immigrants, especially those who just arrive, reside in congested dwellings in cities, with the hope of finding jobs and upgrading to better living conditions later. These congested dwellings often house far more tenants than they are built for, and their landlords have no qualms about cramming in additional renters for a surcharge. Even so, new housing demand in these illegal immigrant enclaves outstrips those in other areas.

Chart 2. Mexican Remittances from the US, 1995-2003

Index

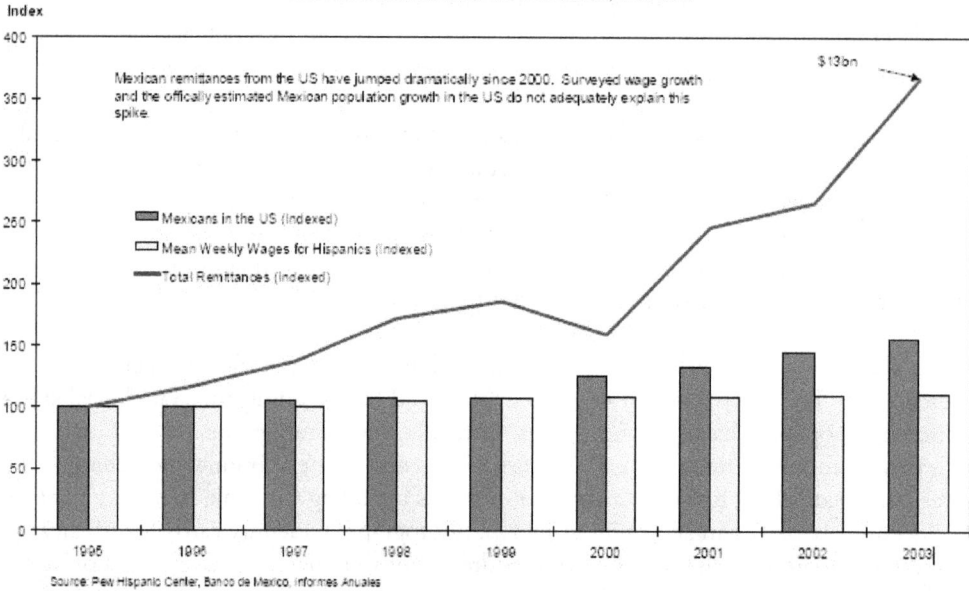

Mexican remittances from the US have jumped dramatically since 2000. Surveyed wage growth and the officially estimated Mexican population growth in the US do not adequately explain this spike.

$13bn

- Mexicans in the US (Indexed)
- Mean Weekly Wages for Hispanics (Indexed)
- Total Remittances (Indexed)

Source: Pew Hispanic Center, Banco de Mexico, Informes Anuales

In New Jersey, the three gateway towns of New Brunswick, Elizabeth, and Newark exemplify this trend. According to the census, the combined population in these three towns between 1990 and 2003 grew only 5.6%, less than the 9% reported in the rest of the three corresponding counties. Yet housing permits in these three towns shot up over six-fold, while the rest of the three counties only saw a three-fold increase. More importantly, 80% of these permits were designated for multiple dwellings, so the corresponding increase in people accommodated are even greater. Official statistics state that illegal immigrants in New Jersey have jumped 110% during the same period – an estimate that is inconsistent with the housing statistics, our discussions with local realtors and the changes that we have visually observed in the demographic landscape.

School Enrollment

The major immigration gateways have experienced school enrollments much higher than projections. The decrease in the number of births in the past decade had led education administrators to expect decreasing school enrollments as a post echo boom trend. A higher immigration rate, however, has offset the impact of declining births. The enrollment statistics for a sample of school districts that included Queens, New York, Elizabeth, Newark and New Brunswick, New Jersey and Wake County in North Carolina revealed explosive growth in immigrant students, far beyond numbers consistent with legal migration limits.

Chart 3. Housing Permits in New Jersey Immigrant Gateways: New Brunswick, Elizabeth, and Newark

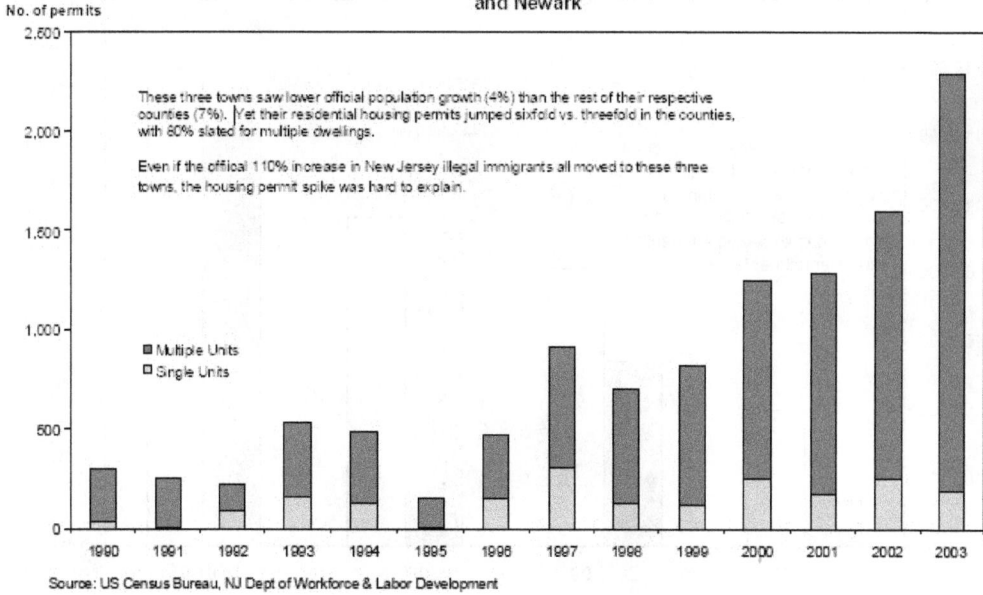

No. of permits

These three towns saw lower official population growth (4%) than the rest of their respective counties (7%). Yet their residential housing permits jumped sixfold vs. threefold in the counties, with 60% slated for multiple dwellings.

Even if the official 110% increase in New Jersey illegal immigrants all moved to these three towns, the housing permit spike was hard to explain.

◪ Multiple Units
◻ Single Units

Source: US Census Bureau, NJ Dept of Workforce & Labor Development

According to the Urban Institute, children under 18 comprise approximately 17% of the undocumented population, with only half attending school, making the sharp increases in school enrollment more telling. We can extrapolate that for every undocumented immigrant child in the public school system, there are potentially 8 to 9 additional undocumented men, women and children living in the United States.

In New York City, nearly one-quarter of the general population is under the age of 18. Approximately 55% of these children were enrolled in grades pre-K-12 in the 2001-2002 school year. It appears that the ratio of illegal immigrant school children to adults is much lower than the general population, and understandably so. Historically, the transition of illegal immigrants is lead by single males, followed by single females, who establish a presence, a job and home before starting a family or relocating other family members from their native countries.

Chart 4. Student Enrollments in Wake County, North Carolina

No. of Students

%

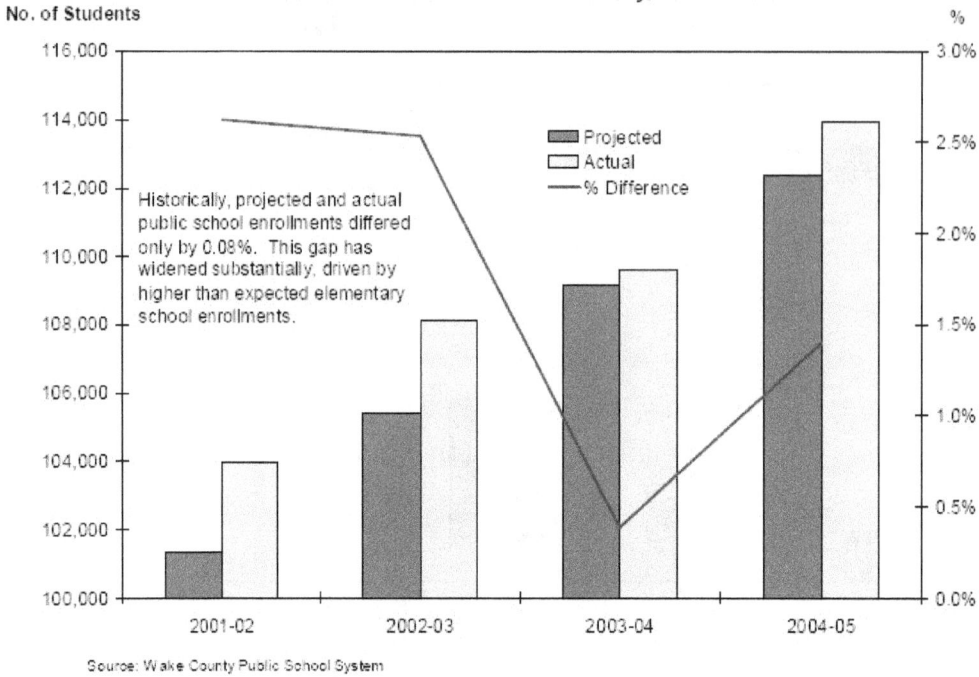

Source: Wake County Public School System

With a total enrollment of 1.1 million students, the NYC public school system is the largest in the nation. Immigrant student enrollment for the 1998-2001 period was 103,000, with Queens accounting for the largest share, 37,000. Between 1990 and 2001, more than half of New York City's school districts increased their enrollments 10% or more, driven by a high number of immigrant students.

Demographic and enrollment trends according to the New York City Public Schools system state:

• "To a significant degree, high rates of immigration offset the effect of a declining number of births on school enrollment." Administrators have been surprised that school population growth significantly exceeded earlier projections, thus creating overcrowding in many school districts.

• "In the three-year period from 1999 to 2001, 102,867 immigrant students registered for grades pre-K-12 in New York City Public Schools, with many predominant countries of origin, other than Mexico, including the Dominican Republic, China, Jamaica, Mexico, Pakistan, Ecuador, Colombia and Haiti."

Chart 5. Declining Births and Increasing School Enrollments in New York City

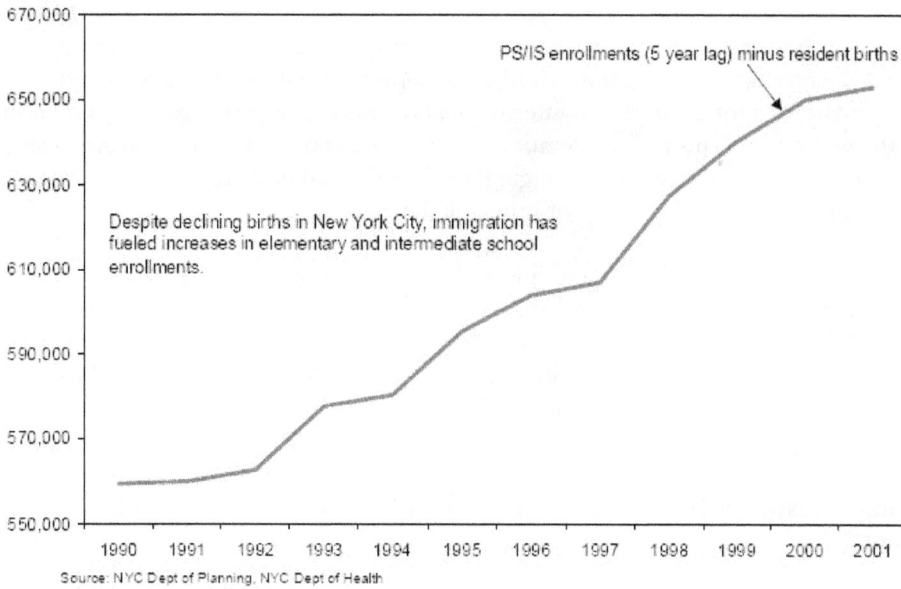

Source: NYC Dept of Planning, NYC Dept of Health

Cross Border Flows

Pulitzer Prize reporters Donald L. Barlett and James B. Steele recently reported for *TIME* magazine that "the number of illegal aliens flooding into the United States this year will total 3 million. It will be the largest wave since 2001 and roughly triple the number of immigrants that will come to the U.S. by legal means." The *TIME* investigation, according to Mr. Barlett, relied not only on figures projected by the U.S. Border Patrol, but also on the reporter's extensive investigations along the Mexican border at factories, local communities, and the district offices of the U.S. Border Patrol.

Though more resources have been designated to patrolling the Mexican border, *TIME* argues that "the government doesn't want to fix it, and the politicians, as usual, are dodging the issue, even though public opinion polls show that Americans overwhelmingly favor a crackdown on illegal immigration." It can be strongly argued that enforcement at the work place is a much more efficient way of controlling illegal flows because the primary incentive for sneaking into the United States is money and jobs. A telephone verification system was designed under the auspices of the Immigration Reform and Control Act of 1986 for employers to confirm the legal status of potential employees. As of today, this system is still not running.

Migration is a Global Macro Trend

The world is undergoing the largest migration wave since the late 1800's. Over 175 million people are in motion. The dramatic increase in human mobility has left the public sector and policy makers behind. The specific and general understanding of migration flows has not kept pace with the growth, complexity and implications of this phenomenon. The economic implications of demographics have increased tremendously over the last 20 years. In no other time period during the last century have demographics undergone such a subcutaneous change in the United States.

The human race is on the move – human mobility is increasing drastically, according to the International Organization for Migration (IOM), the Population Division of the United Nations. It estimates the total number of international migrants is approximately 175 million or 2.9% of the world population. The migration wave has two components – transnational and rural to urban, and these waves are changing the dynamics of government, economics and lifestyles more than any other driver of human behavior.

Governments are seriously behind in recording and comprehending the current phenomenon, and more importantly, governments are making economic and social policy decisions based on flawed information. Like corrupt corporate accounting practices or poor national security information, the United States is struggling with its immigration policies because of false assumptions and unreliable data.

Far Reaching Investment Implications Hinging on Government Policy and Enforcement

The importance, rightfully or wrongfully, that markets place on economic data can be demonstrated in the bond market reactions to employment releases. Employment releases are like earnings releases in that investors count on the information to be accurate, within a reasonable margin of error, so that good analysis can lead to prudent evaluations of risk and reward.

In the case of household employment numbers, there is a 90% confidence interval for monthly changes in employment, which equates to a margin of error of approximately plus or minus 350,000. A 350,000 margin of error on a labor force of 135 million people is acceptable, but the current migration wave is distorting total employment by the millions, we believe. This presents serious statistical problems that can lead to faulty investment decisions. Unless the government and investors get the numbers on immigration correct, the market will fail to grasp the extent of the required policy changes. The consequent adjustments could be drastic and disruptive to the bond market.

To a large extent, U.S. immigration policy is adhoc, according to Robert Shiller, Stanley B. Resor Professor of Economics, Yale University:

The system that developed countries currently use to keep people from less developed countries out is inefficient. The United States has strict immigration policies but lax enforcement; so many people manage to slip illegally over the border. Once here, the illegal immigrants pay dearly in terms of quality of life. Then, periodically, the United States considers granting amnesty to illegal immigrants. This is a crazy system, and we could imagine a better one that could someday handle immigration.

Belated policy responses no doubt complicate efforts to assess the number of illegal migrants. However, the focus on the migration issue is growing. The profile of the immigration topic is rising in the media, the legislature, and in grass root movements. Many documentary and feature films are exploring the immigration themes. State and local governments and medical institutions in the gateway states are being financially impacted by the increased demand generated by these new American residents. Arizona's Proposition 200 may represent a new trend to address the state and local strains associated with this unanticipated and underestimated population growth. We expect that the coverage, the tangential issues and the political emotions will be magnified in 2005. In this paper, we have merely outlined what we see as the magnitude of the current migration wave. We have barely touched on the economic and investment implications. In the coming months, we will explore further the specific relationship between public policy, enforcement and the more specific implications for the economy and the bond markets.

References—not well organized—sorry!

Fernando Lozano Ascencio, 2004. "Tendencias recientes de las remesas de los migrantes mexicanos enEstados Unidos." Centro Regional de Investigaciones Multidisciplinaries de la UNAM.
Donald L. Barlett and James B. Steele, September 20, 2004. "Who Left the Door Open?" TIME magazine.
Steven A. Camarota, October 2004. "A Jobless Recovery? Immigrant Gains and Native Losses." Center for Immigration Studies.
Steven A. Camarota, November 2004. "Economy Slowed, But Immigration Didn't. The Foreign-Born Population, 2000-2004." Center for Immigration Studies
Joel Dreyfuss, Scott Silvestri and Thomas Back, March 2004. "Western Union. Margins Shrinking. Send Customers." Bloomberg Markets.
Kevin L. Kliesen and Howard J. Wall, April 2004. "A Jobless Recovery with More People Working?" The Federal Reserve Bank of St. Louis.
Maxine L. Margolis, 1998. "An Invisible Minority. Brazilians in New York City." Allyn & Bacon
Kevin O'Neil, June 1, 2003. "Remittances from the United States in Context." Migration Policy Institute.
Jeffrey Passel, May 22, 2002. "New Estimates of the Undocumented Population." Migration Policy
Institute.
Charles Pinkerton, Gail McLaughlan, John Salt, 2004 "Sizing the illegally resident population in the UK." Migration Research Unit, University College, London
Ray Stone, January 21, 2004. "Payrolls – Illegal Immigrant Workers, the Missing Link?"
Dilip Ratha, October 1, 2004. "Understanding the Importance of Remittances." Migration Policy Institute.
Edwin S. Rubenstein, 2004. "Illegal Immigration – Unmentionable Answer to Household vs. Payroll Survey Controversy." ESR Research Economic Consulta
Roberto Suro, et al, 2002. "Billions in Motion: Latino Immigrants Remittances and Banking." Pew Hispanic Center Report and the Multilateral Investment Fund of the Inter-American Development Bank. "World Migration, 2003." The International Organization for Migration. Mexican Embassy, Washington D.C.
The New Jersey Department of Education New Jersey Department of Labor and Workforce Development.
The New York State Department of Education
US Census Bureau
US Department of Homeland Security, Office of Immigration Statistics.
US Border Patrol, telephone interview.
Wake Country Public School System, North Carolina
Wells Fargo Bank, October 2004, interview.
World Bank.

Chapter 56 Two Liberals with a Great Idea— Solving Illegal Migration!

Will anybody listen?

Sometimes we can't just ram our own great thoughts through the mesh and claim victory. When people disagree with us, they have their 7,000 valid reasons, which surely are offset by what we see as our own 700,000 valid reasons. However, if the number of all of our reasons trumps reality, then no matter whether a winner is declared, nobody really wins.

Giving up one's personal fabric to embrace another is not a sustainable approach either. So, the best we could expect is for people, who are not compelled to accept the asinine ramblings of the opposition, to occasionally sample what opinions the opposition might have about important matters. We all can learn a lot by knowing why an opponent feels as they do about our ideas and vice versa. This does not mean that we may ever move from our entrenched positions, but we may learn enough to make our positions better, more effective, and more defendable than they otherwise would be. At a minimum, we learn why the opposition is as good or as bad as we thought. I had the pleasure just recently, as part of this research to review the work of several liberals on the matter of immigration. I was tempted not to read the material but I am now very glad I did.

Richard D. Lamm and Lawrence Harrison are two writers worth hearing. On October 15, 2010 they were published from their roots in Denver and Vineyard Haven, Mass. They penned what they call "A bold plan to solve America's illegal immigration problem." Type that phrase into Google or Yahoo to get the full Web experience. If you know these people are liberal and progressive and you are conservative, you may just write them off. Likewise, if you know that these people are conservative and you are liberal and progressive, then you may write them off just as quickly.

Now, I might say to not label anybody just right yet but then again, look at the title of this chapter and you already know where I am coming from. Knowing these two writers are Obama supporters would certainly endear them to the left and just the same would repel them from the right. Since Obama's position is already well known, they are giving him some lip about it in this piece. Obama wants all illegal foreign nationals free to do as they please as if they already were citizens. The President is very progressive and would be happy to create 50,000,000 new Democrats tomorrow if not today. Having these two liberal guys telling their man, Obama that they have an idea different from his is an awful tempting proposition to which to listen. So, I listened.

They have something to say and I will offer a brief commentary after I let you hear their prose immediately below:

"We can end the political stalemate if we summon the courage to end illegal immigration, provide amnesty at a price, and be more selective about who we welcome into the country.

As the debate on immigration policy intensifies, Americans are caught in a false choice between tougher border protection and amnesty for illegals. A compromise solution that both parties can rally behind is possible—but only if we have a revolution in the way we discuss our national identity and values.

At bottom, we must:

- ✓ Substantially reduce levels of legal immigration and end illegal immigration, while providing amnesty—at a price—to most pre-existing illegal immigrants.

- ✓ Be selective about future immigrants' country of origin, and terminate multiculturalism as a national value.

Not a right-wing concern

Concerns about immigration are not confined to the right end of the political spectrum or to "xenophobes" and "nativists." Both of us, we hasten to add, are avid supporters of President Obama.

The consequences of unchecked immigration affect all Americans. The US population in 1900 was about 76 million; today, it is about 310 million, of which about 47 million are Latinos. Richard Lamm observes:

'In my twelve years as governor of Colorado, high levels of immigration, predominantly from Mexico, made virtually every major problem more difficult to solve. At least 50 percent of immigrants today come from Latin America, and they are acculturating much more slowly than prior immigration waves.

Additionally:

- ✓ A substantial proportion of the patients at the Denver Public Hospital are illegal immigrants, virtually all poor and poorly educated.

- ✓ The percentage of Hispanic students in Denver public schools has risen quickly, to 54 percent.

- ✓ Public housing in Denver is filled with both legal and illegal immigrants.

- ✓ Nationwide, 20 percent of our prison space is occupied by foreign-born inmates, disproportionately Latinos.

Fifteen years ago, when these problems were less severe, Democratic Congresswoman Barbara Jordan, chair of the bipartisan US Commission on Immigration Reform, called for an end to illegal immigration and a calibration of legal immigration levels to the demonstrated needs of the economy. She understood then what is even more true today: High levels of legal and illegal immigration hurt all Americans, but they especially hurt US citizens, disproportionately black and Latino citizens.

With so many of our citizens unable to find jobs, we must be willing to lay aside our biases and work toward a solution that works for everyone.

Solving the amnesty issue

The first crucial step is to tackle the so-called amnesty issue.

We believe that amnesty for illegal immigrants is a bad idea, proven to encourage subsequent illegal immigration by the experience of the 1986 amnesty. But we also believe that the US government shares the blame because of its failure to enforce immigration laws. We consequently propose the following sketch of a compromise.

First, a bipartisan, commission must certify (1) that our borders are under control, and (2) that an effective system of employment verification is in place. Then, all illegal immigrants who can prove that they have been working or at school in the United States for at least five years are eligible for amnesty.

Each illegal immigrant who applies for amnesty must pay a fine of $10,000 per person, over a five-year period if necessary, before becoming eligible for amnesty. Family eligibility will be limited to the nuclear family: spouses and children who have lived in the United States for five years, or since their marriage/birth.

Some may argue that the $10,000 per person fine is excessive. But look at the numbers. In 2008, remittances from Latino immigrants in the United States, mostly to families in their homelands, totaled about $60 billion – $25 billion alone went to Mexico. That shows that Latinos in America are capable of generating serious income. With five years to pay, the $10,000 fine should be manageable.

This approach could generate as much as $100 billion in new federal revenues.

End multiculturalism

The second crucial step is to end multiculturalism as a national value and be much more selective about who we welcome into our country. Immigration isn't just about quantity. It's about quality. Since immigration should serve the national interest, it's fair to ask:

- ✓ What does America's work force need?
- ✓ What choices leave our children the best, most sustainable America?
- ✓ Aren't there significant differences in the speed and completeness of assimilation among different immigrant groups?
- ✓ Doesn't it make a difference whether we take 1,000 Chinese, Japanese, or Koreans as opposed to 1,000 people from south of our border?

Just look at the astonishing Asian success rates, and the failure of so many Latinos to graduate even from high school—and the divisive evolution of Spanish to become, de facto, our second national language.

With an unemployment rate near 10 percent, why are we importing close to a million people a year? America has experienced zero job growth since 2000, yet we have added 10 million legal immigrants plus millions more illegally. By the Jordan Commission standards, we are importing too many immigrants, particularly too many unskilled immigrants.

America in 2050

In 2000, the US population totaled 281 million, of which 36 million, or nearly 13 percent, were Latinos. By 2050, the Census Bureau projects our population will reach 420 million, of which 103 million, or 24 percent, will be Hispanic. That's nearly a tripling of the Hispanic population in a half-century. Indeed, it means 1 in 4 Americans will be Hispanic. How might that change America and American values?

The late Mexican-American columnist Richard Estrada captured the essence of the problem in a letter he wrote in 1991:

"The problem in which the current immigration is suffused is, at heart, one of numbers; for when the numbers begin to favor not only the maintenance and replenishment of the immigrants' source culture, but also its overall growth, and in particular growth so large that the numbers not only impede assimilation but go beyond to pose a challenge to the traditional culture of the American nation, then there is a great deal about which to be concerned."

His point is underscored by the recent reports that more than half of the children born in California, Texas, and New Mexico were born to Latino mothers.

Action steps

The policy implications are clear:

1. We must end illegal immigration by enforcing the laws on employment and strengthening our control of our southern border.
2. We should calibrate legal immigration annually to (1) the needs of the economy, and (2) past performance of immigrant groups with respect to acculturation and contribution to our society.
3. We should declare our national language to be English and discourage the proliferation of Spanish language media.
4. We should end birthright citizenship, limiting citizenship by birth to children with at last one parent who is a citizen.
5. We should provide immigrants with easy-to-access educational services that facilitate acculturation, including English language, citizenship, and culture.

In his controversial final book, "Who Are We? The Challenges to America's National Identity," the late Harvard scholar Samuel Huntington got it right – as he usually did—when he identified growing Latino immigration and avoidance of the melting pot as the principal threat to our unity and progress as a nation.

If we can begin to speak honestly about who we are and where we'd like to go as a nation, we can meet this threat.

FYI, Richard Lamm was the governor of Colorado from 1975 to 1987. He is currently the codirector of the Institute for Public Policy Studies at the University of Denver, where he is also a university professor. Lawrence Harrison directs the Cultural Change Institute at the Fletcher School, Tufts University. He is the author, most recently, of "The Central Liberal Truth: How Politics Can Change a Culture and Save It from Itself." Both Gov. Lamm and Mr. Harrison are members of the advisory board of the Federation for American Immigration Reform (FAIR); however, the views expressed above do not reflect FAIR's position on amnesty.

**** End of Lamm / Harrison Article

Brief Analysis of Article

I think I might trust Lamm and Harrison if they signed up to be the implementers of their policy. They are sincere and they are going against the "mainstream" thought of the progressive liberal agenda, of which they have hitherto subscribed.

However, I am not confident that this progressive government of ours can be trusted to assure that any commission will ever be able to certify honestly that our borders are under control, and that employment verification is in place. I would need somebody to certify that the certification would be valid. Then, I might be convinced that this is a good start but clearly we've got a long way to go, and ideology will be a major impediment.

With the TEA Party and conservatives who have not even joined the TEA party on full alert, I think there would be revolt if the progressives declared the border secure with a false certification. Yet, since I do not trust the government and whatever faith I have in the good of government is waning, I can see these scoundrels trying to use a good Obama speech to mask the deceit. I know that is not a good starting point but it is how I feel. Can we trust the government of the US to get this right? If you think we can, then why have they failed us so miserably, so far?

All of this makes me love the TEA party even more. Those without the political will for the people's business no longer should get invited back to Washington by the people. The TEA party, as long as it does not become a political party can be trusted to certify that the border is secure and that real employment verification is in place. But, would the ingrained politicians in government ever let that happen?

No reward for crime

I am against any reward for illegal immigrants, especially if they can prove that they have been working or at school in the United States for at least five years. These are the people who have been costing the US over $100 billion per year. I think the path to citizenship or a path to a green card needs to be through the home country, not through the back door in America. Unions and corporations should have no say. So, in order to get in line to come back, illegal foreign nationals in my scenario, would have to go to their home country to register. On the way out, they could pick up a priority certification that would acknowledge their act of good faith in self-deporting. Then, they would have to wait until they were called.

I have a huge problem changing the culture of our country by admitting 50 million people over five years, who are all of the same or similar culture. By design, we know this culture would prefer to dominate rather than assimilate. We've seen their protests with allegiance shown to the foreign nation. It would be a far different America if this were the solution for those who are here illegally. I have a problem with the composition of ethnicity in America in the wake of such a generous policy to one "race" of people.

I do think this Lamm / Harrison proposal is worth sitting down at the table and discussing. It is a good start, especially being offered from the other side where the progressives typically live.

Whether the $10,000 per person fine as the amount, over a five-year period is enough needs some work but again it is a good idea as a start. I would prefer an $8,000 fine with the first two thousand of the ten thousand used to self-deport and reregister for a comeback. There needs to be some appropriate cost born by those who in many ways have been freeloading and taking American jobs in America. Self-deportation is the first cost.

Some stiff fine is surely necessary. I would like this fine or perhaps a larger fine, plus a battery of tests, including health checkups, oaths of allegiance, and many other stipulations before becoming eligible for any citizenship opportunities. I would also offer an extra percentage or two in Income tax, forever as a make-up for past services used, and no participation in Social Security or Medicare without a huge buy-in amount or a higher percentage of contribution. The transgression of crossing over illegally should in no way ever be an advantage to those who have placed us in the untenable position of trying to figure out what to do with them in America.

Fifty million new citizens or new green cards are simply unacceptable. We need to come up with the right number of people from the 50 million that we will permit back each year. How many of those in the former illegal category are we willing to accept as legal immigrants in a given year? Then, we can work from there. There should be no real reward for line jumping but those who do self deport, go back, and formally say they are sorry, can receive a good-faith priority.

Once the number of amnesty re-migrations per year is established, all other factors can be considered. For example, if 50 million illegal foreign nationals are in our country today, and there may very well be, I would not be OK with 10 million new citizens a year of Irish descent. I would not want 10 million new Germans, Italians, or any ethnic culture. But, I especially would not want a culture that considers itself a different race than the three that are pre-established by anthropologists, and which insists its language should be co-equal to the de-facto national language. There are lots of things to work out.

This type of change would redraw the whole political and cultural landscape of the country too fast. I would like to see the US set up some help stations in exporting countries like Mexico so that those who go back can receive some type of assistance, funded by Mexico and other originating countries, so that their return can be easier. I do not want Irish living in America long term. I want Americans. I want melters. This is not a five year solution.

Helping the migrant in their own country is something that we may be able to afford. Foreign aid to Mexico or Honduras or Nicaragua, or any Southern country should be directed to helping their people prepare for a life like that in America. With the Internet, all kinds of standardized citizenship courses can be taken from the home countries in much the same way as CLE courses are taken. Additionally we can study why people come to America and help their countries fashion make their countries like the things they like about America.

Then, perhaps Americans will be trying to migrate to those countries or vacation there if the notions are universally popular.

Some who want to protect American jobs at all costs might not agree with me on this. To remove foreigners from the US jobs marketplace, I would like the US to incent certain industries, such as perhaps meat packing to move some plants to Mexico or elsewhere south to help these folks have non US jobs that pay as well as US jobs. Let US jobs be held by Americans. Why not? If business could trust government instead of having to pay them off, maybe these things can be possible?

How many new citizens per year can the US absorb?

Perhaps the US can accommodate as many as 250,000 new citizens a year. The Kelly plan would have a lottery for the citizens who wish to come back after self-deporting. No others would be eligible. Those who want to be eligible would engage in a lottery conducted in Mexico and several other southern countries. Once a re-*migrater* goes through whatever the hoops need be to become a candidate for citizenship, they can enter the lottery. There is no guarantee. The only guarantee is that the US will help their country fashion itself in such a way that the US is not so important that they must come here permanently.

The notion of a lottery was found to be a fair way for the Selective Service to determine which young men would be selected to serve their country during the 1970 time when the Draft was in effect. We know it is an effective method and it is implicitly fair. No credit should be given for time in this country while self-deporting foreign nationals were in an illegal status and were costing this nation since they were using US services.

Family visitation

I might agree to family visitation for as much as three months per year but past amnesty offenses regarding family reunification have been so egregious, much care needs to be taken. You may recall that some new citizens after the Reagan amnesty brought in as many as 100 "relatives." Each visitor, of course would have to be vouched for and citizenship for this batch of illegal aliens could be revoked for a long period of perhaps up to up to 50 years into the future if there is any chicanery.

There should be no immediate nuclear family reunification. That is too easy for abuse. I can see a priority being set and any reunification on humanitarian grounds would count in the 250,000 or whatever the appropriate immigration counts for that year happens to be. We must remember that there are Africans, Ethiopians, Cantonese, and even some Irish wishing to preserve their spots in America. I also like the idea of the pledge of allegiance if we can sneak that by the current Congress and the Obama regulators. How about a pledge of allegiance contest with a few winners each year gaining the right to a lottery selection?

I agree with the authors that late Harvard scholar Samuel Huntington got it very right. Many Americans are concerned that the Irish Bartenders in NY are going to take over the country. Being Irish, I am not as concerned because at an early age I learned to mix drinks. But Huntington's identification of growing Latino immigration and the Hispanic / Latino avoidance of the melting pot as the principal threat to our unity and progress as a nation is right on the mark. Nobody wants somebody in this country who does not really, really, want to be an American. Say the pledge of allegiance everywhere in the US.

Unfortunately, the underground illegal alien community seems to have no particular interest today in pledging allegiance to the flag. They don't seem to like regular Americans as we walk by, and the gangs that have come with them are a fear unto themselves. I would need to see more evidence of something good before I gave anything more away to these people. But, as evidence by my reading an article by Obama supporters, I am ready if you are ready.

If we can begin to speak honestly about whom we are and where we'd like to go as a nation, I agree that we can meet this threat. But, it will not be through demagoguery and liberal progressivism.

In the meantime, the default should not be "let them stay." It should be to follow our laws and deport them quickly. I think anybody who volunteers to leave the country should get a quick return ticket and be one of the first let back in when this is ultimately resolved. I just don't see granting citizenship to somebody who is illegally in the country. If they really want US citizenship, work for it. Get your return ticket, go back home and get in line. This would indicate that a person really wants to be a citizen, and does not merely want to gain benefits that they have not earned.

What happened to the melting pot?

A majority of citizens appreciate the diverse and pluralistic people in the society of America. This includes the notion of E Pluribus Unum (out of many, one). Few are interested in a philosophy of diversity as practiced by the nouveau progressives—E Pluribus Pluribus (out of many, many). This progressive notion is the antithesis of the melting pot in which, among other things, the new residents choose to no longer melt.

Instead recent migrants to American are not even interested enough in covering their charade to learn how to speak the language. Surely, well spoken English would not be a dead give-away to immigration status. The new migrants thus refuse even to learn the English language as they would prefer to maintain their separate national identity and their allegiance to a foreign power. They don't want to melt. They do not want to be American.

Because they no longer find enough value in America to adapt to our customs and ways, many Americans find little value in these new illegal residents and see them as undesirable to the American way of life.

We feel that if offered a helping hand, they would spit on our hands. Who was taking thi picture on the next page that would engender such outrage from the "models?" Was it just an American getting a look at those illegal foreign nationals who disrespect our country so much?

Figure 56-1 A reminder that all illegal aliens are not nice!

Many long time Americans are concerned that today's illegal aliens, often Mexicans, as an example, even when they have an opportunity to become citizens, would choose not to assimilate into the general culture and they would stay Mexicans and not become Americans. The "finger to America" says an awful lot about their love of America. Mexican protests of the past many years have emblazoned this picture or another like it in the minds of US citizens. Mexican flags and nasty comments about Americans fill the minds of Americans observing the arrogance of these illegal "visitors." If this is all they have to offer, send them back Donald Trump, please, and do not wait a minute longer.

This is unlike earlier US immigrants, including immigrants from Mexico. So, the majority of Americans do not like this. We have big concerns that with so many Mexicans now living in America, without concern for America or Americans that these people just want to take from us and give nothing back. Consequently as time goes by, Americans who had been indifferent on the issue of illegal immigration are stepping to the plate. They want the illegal entry and the illegal inhabitance stopped right now, immediately.

With the porous borders and the corrupt business and economic culture inviting more to come every day, there is concern about whether anything much is really melting in the melting pot. If it is, what is it, if anything? Americans are not interested in a two-pot, or multi-pot system to accommodate diversity. E Pluribus Unum. There always was a large diversity of ingredients in the pot, and that was the good part because the American melting pot was the pathway to an assimilated culture and citizenship. When everybody melted together, the result was one nation, one people under God. There were no Latinos and Hispanics and Italians, and Polish and Irish. From the pot came true Americans.

Today it seems that the new residents want to sponsor a foreign culture in the pot, perhaps dominated by Mexican people who really do not want to be Americans. Just like the Italians did not want the Irish to dominate America and vice versa, nobody is looking for a culture dominated by Mexicans. Melt if you want, but if you choose to stay separate and un-melted, you will never be allowed to be an American. Worse than that, the more separatists there are, the weaker will be this nation. So, Americans must say no to those who do not want to be real Americans. Feel free to go home.

Multiculturalism is multiple pots

Some might suggest that the notion of multiculturalism is the idea of having multiple pots in which to melt. It is a great analogy. Europe is suffering from the ills of multiculturalism so much so that they have begun to speak about it in public. We call it diversity here in the US and even here it has gotten out of hand—all caught up in the PC world. Why bother melting if you have to choose pots? Why not make your own pot and just claim victory? Somebody would cover your story! What happens when there are lots of pots and they sign up to antagonize what was once the only American melting pot? Multiple pots are not a good idea for cultural stabilization and a gaining the cherished moniker, "American."

The idea of illegal immigrants and American melting pot assimilation may not have anything to do with the alarm about Islamic militants who have made Britain one of Europe's most active bases for terrorist plots. But maybe the ideas are very similar. Prime Minister David Cameron has recently been slammed because he has mounted an attack on the country's decades-old policy of "multiculturalism," saying it has encouraged "segregated communities." Thus, in those segregated communities, Islamic extremism can thrive.

Cameron condemned the former "hands-off tolerance" in Britain and other European nations that had encouraged Muslims and other immigrant groups "to live separate lives, apart from each other and the mainstream." To net it out, Cameron thinks that these folks care nothing about Britain and they live in a bottle that has begun to pour acid upon the rest of Great Britain. It is strange in today's world to find people actually speaking the truth. Obama, of course has not yet caught "truth disease" so he is still silent on the problems with diversity and multiculturalism.

There is clearly a parallel here to our own foreign nationals, legal and illegal, living separately in America, and working mostly against the American people. They do have the blessings right now of the government, unions, corporations, and greedy small businesses, but the American people are taking back control. E Pluribus Pluribus is now not even a good idea in England. In America, soon if you are eligible to melt and you choose not to melt, you will no longer be popular, even in your own neighborhood. And you will not be permitted in the pot.

Real Americans have a right to protect their identity.

To many, it seems that the new immigrant, legal and illegal continues to be Mexican (Hispanic) in language and culture. Many see the toll of the illegal foreign national on schools, hospitals, and the welfare system, and they have concern that the potentially dominating culture of the future, those who arise from a second pot if you will, are ones who want all the benefits of the American way of life, paid for by American citizens in what once was the one pot, without having to give the loyalty to the country that assimilated citizens have always provided.

LETS GO PUBLISH! Books by Brian Kelly:
(sold at www.bookhawkers.com; Amazon.com, and Kindle.).

LETS GO PUBLISH! is proud to announce that more AS/400 and Power i books are becoming available to help you inexpensively address your AS/400 and Power i education and training needs: Our general titles precede specific AS/400 and other technology books. Check out these great patriotic books which precede the tech books in the list.

The Trump Plan Solves the Student Debt Crisis
Solution for new student debt and the existing $1.3 Trillion debt accumulation

101 Secrets How to be a High Information Voter
You do not have to be a low-information voter.

Why Trump?
You Already Know... But, this book will tell you anyway

Saving America The Trump Way!
A book that tells you how President Donald Trump will help Merica dn Americans wind up on top

The US Immigration Fix
It's all in here. You won't want to put it down

I had a Dream IBM Could be #1 Again
The title is self-explanatory

Whatever Happened to the IBM AS/400?
The question is answered in this nee book.

Great Moments in Penn State Football Check out the particulars of this great book at bookhawkers.com.

Great Moments in Notre Dame Football Check out the particulars of this great book at bookhawkers.com or www.notredamebooks.com

WineDiets.Com Presents The Wine Diet Learn how to lose weight while having fun. Four specific diets and some great anecdotes fill this book with fun and the opportunity to lose weight in the process.

Wilkes-Barre, PA; Return to Glory Wilkes-Barre City's return to glory begins with dreams and ideas. Along with plans and actions, this equals leadership.

The Lifetime Guest Plan. This is a plan which if deployed today would immediately solve the problem of 60 million illegal aliens in the United States.

Geoffrey Parsons' Epoch... The Land of Fair Play Better than the original. The greatest re-mastering of the greatest book ever written on American Civics. It was built for all Americans as the best govt. design in the history of the world.

The Bill of Rights 4 Dummmies! This is the best book to learn about your rights. Be the first, to have a "Rights Fest" on your block. You will win for sure!

Sol Bloom's Epoch ...Story of the Constitution This work by Sol Bloom was written to commemorate the Sesquicentennial celebration of the Constitution. It has been remastered by Lets Go Publish! – An excellent read!

The Constitution 4 Dummmies! This is the best book to learn about the Constitution. Learn all about the fundamental laws of America.

America for Dummmies!
All Americans should read to learn about this great country.

Just Say No to Chris Christie for President two editions – I & II
Discusses the reasons why Chris Christie is a poor choice for US President

The Federalist Papers by Hamilton, Jay, Madison w/ intro by Brian Kelly
Complete unabridged, easier to read version of the original Federalist Papers

Companion to Federalist Papers by Hamilton, Jay, Madison w/ intro by Brian Kelly
This small, inexpensive book will help you navigate the Federalist Papers

Kill the Republican Party! (2013 edition and edition #2)
Demonstrates why the Republican Party must be abandoned by conservatives

Bring On the American Party!
Demonstrates how conservatives can be free from the party of wimps by starting its own national party called the American Party.

No Amnesty! No Way!
In addition to describing the issue in detail, this book also offers a real solution.

Saving America
This how-to book is about saving our country using strong mercantilist principles. These same principles that helped the country from its founding.

RRR:
A unique plan for economic recovery and job creation

Kill the EPA
The EPA seems to hate mankind and love nature. They are also making it tough for asthmatics to breathe and for those with malaria to live. It's time they go.

Obama's Seven Deadly Sins.
In the Obama Presidency, there are many concerns about the long-term prospects and sustainability of the country. We examine each of the President's seven deadliest sins in detail, offering warnings and a number of solutions. Be careful. Book may nudge you to move to Canada or Europe.

Taxation Without Representation Second Edition
At the time of the Boston Tea Party, there was no representation. Now, there is no representation again but there are "representatives."

Healthcare Accountability
Who should pay for your healthcare? Whose healthcare should you pay for? Is it a lifetime free ride on others or should those once in need of help have to pay it back when their lives improve?

Jobs! Jobs! Jobs!
Where have all the American Jobs gone and how can we get them back?

Other IBM I Technical Books

The All Everything Operating System:
Story about IBM's finest operating system; its facilities; how it came to be.

The All-Everything Machine
Story about IBM's finest computer server.

Chip Wars
The story of ongoing wars between Intel and AMD and upcoming wars between Intel and IBM. Book may cause you to buy / sell somebody's stock.

Can the AS/400 Survive IBM?
Exciting book about the AS/400 in a System i5 World.

The IBM i Pocket SQL Guide.
Complete Pocket Guide to SQL as implemented on System i5. A must have for SQL developers new to System i5. It is very compact yet very comprehensive and it is example driven. Written in a part tutorial and part reference style, Tons of SQL coding samples, from the simple to the sublime.

The IBM i Pocket Query Guide.
If you have been spending money for years educating your Query users, and you find you are still spending, or you've given up, this book is right for you. This one QuikCourse covers all Query options.

The IBM I Pocket RPG & RPG IV Guide.
Comprehensive RPG & RPGIV Textbook -- Over 900 pages. This is the one RPG book to have if you are not having more than one. All areas of the language covered smartly in a convenient sized book Annotated PowerPoint's available for self-study (extra fee for self-study package)

The IBM I RPG Tutorial and Lab Guide – Recently Revised.
Your guide to a hands-on Lab experience. Contains CD with Lab exercises and PowerPoint's. Great companion to the above textbook or can be used as a standalone for student Labs or tutorial purposes

The IBM i Pocket Developers' Guide.
Comprehensive Pocket Guide to all of the AS/400 and System i5 development tools - DFU, SDA, etc. You'll also get a big bonus with chapters on Architecture, Work Management, and Subfile Coding.

The IBM i Pocket Database Guide.
Complete Pocket Guide to System i5 integrated relational database (DB2/400) – physical and logical files and DB operations - Union, Projection, Join, etc. Written in a part tutorial and part reference style. Tons of DDS coding samples.

Getting Started with The WebSphere Development Studio Client for System i5 (WDSc).
Focus is on client server and the Web. Includes CODE/400, VisualAge RPG, CGI, WebFacing, and WebSphere Studio. Case study continues from the Interactive Book.

The System i5 Pocket WebFacing Primer.
This book gets you started immediately with WebFacing. A sample case study is used as the basis for a conversion to WebFacing. Interactive 5250 application is WebFaced in a case study form before your eyes.

Getting Started with WebSphere Express Server for IBM i Step-by-Step Guide for Setting up Express Servers
A comprehensive guide to setting up and using WebSphere Express. It is filled with examples, and structured in a tutorial fashion for easy learning.

The WebFacing Application Design & Development Guide:
Step by Step Guide to designing green screen IBM i apps for the Web. Both a systems design guide and a developers guide. Book helps you understand how to design and develop Web applications using regular RPG or COBOL programs.

The System i5 Express Web Implementer's Guide. Your one stop guide to ordering, installing, fixing, configuring, and using WebSphere Express, Apache, WebFacing, System i5 Access for Web, and HATS/LE.

Joomla! Technical Books

Best Damn Joomla Tutorial Ever
Learn Joomla! By example.

Best Damn Joomla Intranet Tutorial Ever
This book is the only book that shows you how to use Joomla on a corporate intranet.

Best Damn Joomla Template Tutorial Ever
This book teaches you step-by step how to work with templates in Joomla!

Best Damn Joomla Installation Guide Ever
Teaches you how to install Joomla! On all major platforms besides IBM i.

Best Damn Blueprint for Building Your Own Corporate Intranet.
This excellent timeless book helps you design a corporate intranet for any platform while using Joomla as its basis.
4
IBM i PHP & MySQL Installation & Operations Guide
How to install and operate Joomla! on the IBM i Platform

IBM i PHP & MySQL Programmers Guide
How to write SQL programs for IBM i

www.ingramcontent.com/pod-product-compliance
Lightning Source LLC
Chambersburg PA
CBHW080323270326
41927CB00014B/3084